Can you provide the energy the world needs today and preserve the earth for the generations to come?

Mankind needs energy to fuel the processes that create light, heat, shelter, transportation and goods - the basis of our modern civilization. Yet as the world's population grows, so does the demand for improved quality of life. Energy consumption increases daily, and with it the threat to clean air, pure water and fertile soil. These natural resources are not inexhaustible.

It is not too late. Man's creative ingenuity can solve the problems he has caused. ABB provides some of the answers. As a global leader in electrical engineering we have the technical expertise to generate, transmit and distribute energy with great efficiency. Our leading environmental control technology reduces environmental strain. Our industrial systems improve productivity, reducing the amount of raw materials and energy required. And our advanced train and mass transit systems help to conserve energy, too.

ABB is committed to the principle of sustainable development. The balance between mankind's needs and the conservation of the natural resources of our planet depends on clean and efficient technology in the fields of electrical engineering, industry and transportation. That's where we come in.

Yes, you can.

ABB
ASEA BROWN BOVERI

ABB Asea Brown Boveri Ltd., Reader Services Center, P.O. Box 822, CH-8021 Zürich, Switzerland

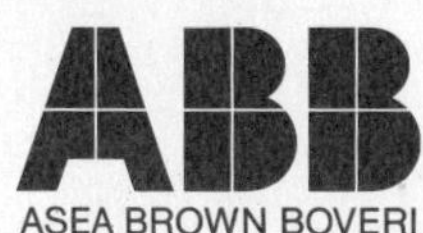

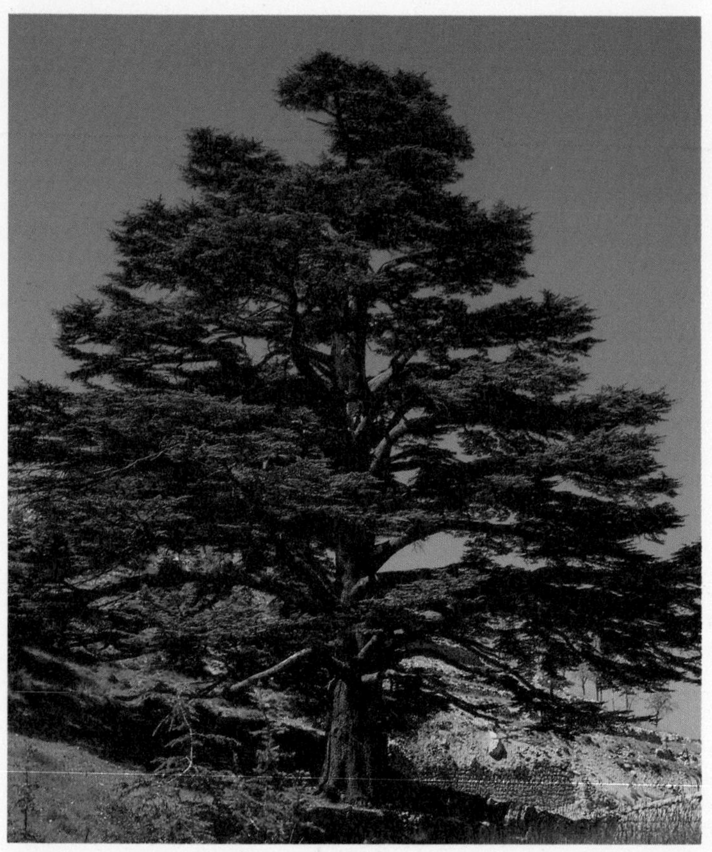

The cedar tree – symbol of Lebanon and of MEA, the national airline – has a long and wonderful history. In ancient times it generously yielded its timber for Egyptian pharaohs' palaces and funerary boats, and panelling for many ancient temples. The great forests of Lebanon have become less prolific over the centuries but the cedar endures.

Lebanon is endowed with many natural blessings; a small country moderately populated with abundant natural water springs, rainfalls, forests, sunlight and bordered by beautiful sandy beaches and snow-capped mountains. Also enjoying clean air, moderate temperatures and four full seasons. These in addition to its rich heritage of many civilisations and its entrepreneurial and hospitable people, placed Lebanon as one of the top touristic attractions of the world.

The Lebanese, conscious of the value of Lebanon's natural resources, water, land and air, had always made the necessary plans to keep it a pollution-free country. These plans, however, were "frozen" as the result of the war, which additionally aggravated the ecological problems.

Consequently, and as soon as tranquillity prevailed, the Lebanese Government introduced a portfolio for Environment and Ecology.

The first task after the war was to ensure that the newly activated factories did not render smog-laden air. Thus, the installation of filters on all factories and smoke-producing operations is now imposed.

Additionally, legislation was introduced to control the industrial process as a whole to ensure that chemicals and waste are not dumped into the Mediterranean sea.

The preservation of forests and land has always been a top priority to the Lebanese. During the war, vast areas of woods and forests were burnt. Some precious trees like the **CEDARS OF LEBANON** were neglected and severely infested with destructive parasites. A committee of concerned citizens attended to this matter promptly by ensuring that the trees were treated and protected. Simultaneously, they made plans for the replanting of the burnt areas.

Middle East Airlines Airliban, the only Lebanese passenger carrier, and the roving ambassador of Lebanon, is both deeply concerned and actively involved in facilitating all efforts to bring Lebanon back to its status of being one of the healthiest places in the world to work in and to visit.

MEA 263

Earth Summit 1992

Published by
The Regency Press Corporation,
Gordon House,
6 Lissenden Gardens,
London NW5 1LX.
Tel: 071-284 4858
Fax: 071-267 5505

Editor
Joyce Quarrie
Project Controller
Jane Gee
Marketing Consultant
Brian Parrish
Marketing Executives
Robert Hodgson
Clive Hunter-Dunne
Brian Rollason
Sonia Seymour-Williams
Richard Verden
Michael Walsh
Distribution Manager
Bill Newnham
Publisher
Richard Kyle
Design
Esterson Lackersteen
Cover
Brian Cronin
Pictures
Mark Edwards/Still Pictures,
199 Shooters Hill Road,
London SE3 8UL.
Tel: 081-858 8307
Fax: 081-858 2049
Since 1972 Mark Edwards has specialised in photographing environment and Third World development issues. His reputation as one of the world's foremost photographers in this area has been recognised by the United Nations; in 1990 he became the first photographer to be named to the prestigious Global 500 Award listing. He founded Still Pictures in 1987 which now holds the work of 20 top international specialist photographers and is one of the few agencies in the world which is able to illustrate all the issues relevant to Agenda 21.

Satellite images
pages 46 & 217 DRA/Still Pictures
Colour Reproduction
Precise Litho
Printed by
Severn Valley Press
Publisher's Note
Printed on Sylvancoat mattcoated recycled paper which is made from 90 per cent recycled paper comprising de-inked waste and clean white waste. No chlorine based bleaches are used. Sylvancoat is produced in the UK for Paperback Ltd. Premier Holland B.V. inks used in the printing process are water insoluble and use harmless pigments which are bonded with resins based on vegetable sources. The cover is laminated with Clarifoil cellulose diacetate film manufactured primarily from wood pulp sourced only from managed forestry. When used with suitable adhesives it assists recycling by helping to de-ink the board without the need for chemical treatments.

ISBN 0-9520469-0-3

Acknowledgements
America Economia, James Capel, Dun & Bradstreet International, Europa Publications Ltd, Richard Sandbrook and Koy Thomson of the IIED, Jiffy Packaging Co. Ltd., Longman Group Ltd., The Municipal Journal Ltd., The Morrison Environmental Directory, North Aegean Petroleum, Walden Publishing.

The publishers would like to express their thanks to all the sponsors of this publication. With special thanks to:
Arab Bank plc,
Banco Crefisul SA,
Banque Nationale de Paris,
Caribbean Development Bank, Caribbean Cement Company Ltd,
Cemex, Cimpor, Companhia Vale de Rio Doce,
Dansk Energy Management,
Dead Sea Works, ESKOM,
Ferruzzi/Montedison,
Haldor Topsoe SA, ICI,
IMCO Recycling Inc.,
Investor AB, Ipocork, ISKI,
ITT Flygt, Jamaica Public Services Company Ltd,
Kuwait Airways,
Logica Space & Communications Ltd,
Methanex, Novo Nordisk,
Paperinkerays Oy, Qatar Petroleum Corporation,
Sulzer Brothers Ltd.

Contents

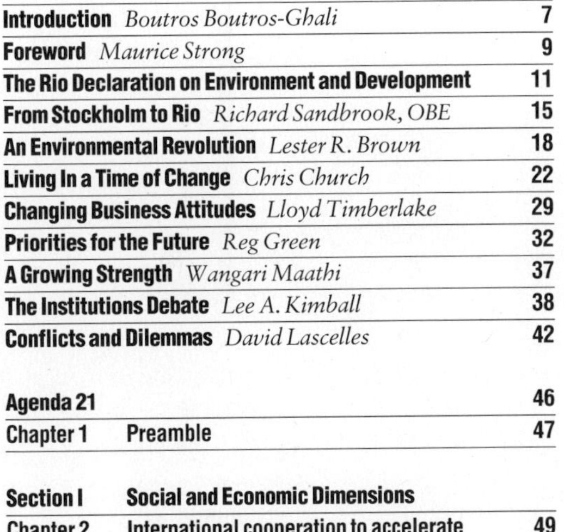

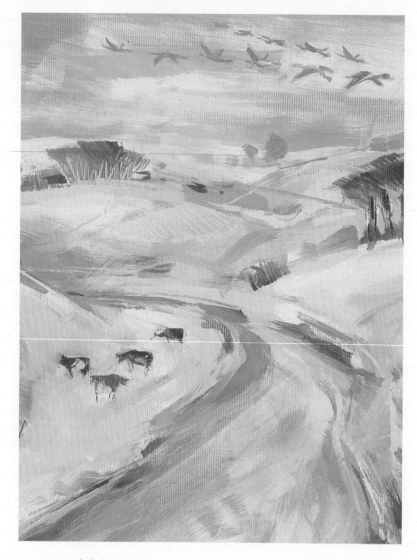

Introduction

Boutros Boutros-Ghali

In his opening address to the United Nations General Assembly in September 1992, Boutros Boutros-Ghali, UN Secretary-General, commented on the United Nations Conference on the Environment and Development held in Rio de Janeiro earlier this year.

The Earth Summit held in Rio de Janeiro in June marked an important milestone in awakening the world to the need for a development process that does not jeopardise future generations.

The Rio Conference achieved consensus in more than one area: first, it secured a set of agreements between governments which marks a significant advance in international cooperation on development and environment issues. Second, it marshalled political commitment to these arrangements at the highest level and placed the issue of sustainable development at the heart of the international agenda. Third, it opened new paths for communication and cooperation between official and non-official organisations working towards developmental and environmental goals. Fourth, it led to an enormous increase in public awareness of the issues that were tackled in the process – an awareness that ought to facilitate the adoption of policies and the allocation of additional resources to fulfil the task.

A comprehensive and far-reaching programme for sustainable development is Agenda 21 which constitutes the centrepiece of international cooperation and coordination activities within the United Nations system for many years to come. Its role in galvanising international cooperation will be crucial. Building on the spirit of Rio, the implementation of Agenda 21 must be seen as an investment in our future. I call on the donor community to ensure a flow of new resources which will serve the common interests of the whole world.

Foreword

Maurice Strong

Maurice Strong, who was appointed Secretary-General to the United Nations Conference on Environment and Development in 1989, is the leading voice in international environmental and developmental concerns. In 1972 he was active in the organisation of the Stockholm Conference on Human Environment, the predecessor to the Earth Summit.

The United Nations Conference on Environment and Development held in Rio de Janeiro early this year offered a unique opportunity to establish the basis for the major shift required to put this planet on the path towards a more secure and sustainable future.

At the core of this shift there is a need for fundamental change. Change to our economic life, a more careful and more caring use of the Earth's resources and greater cooperation and equity in sharing the benefits as well as the risks of our technological civilization. Of particular importance is the need to integrate the ecological dimension into education and culture as well as in economics.

I will mention some of the major Earth Summit achievements:

- Agenda 21 – a comprehensive blueprint for the global actions to affect the transition to sustainable development;
- The Rio Declaration on Environment and Development – a series of principles defining the rights and responsibilities of States in this area;
- A set of principles to support the sustainable management of forests worldwide;
- Two legally binding conventions – aiming to prevent global climate change and the eradication of biologically diverse species – that were signed by representatives of more than 150 countries.

Of course, satisfaction over some of the Earth Summit achievements must be conditioned by what has not yet been achieved. We cannot ignore the reality that some of our goals have been weakened, that we need much stronger commitments on finance, that targets and timetables must be set for conventions to be effective. But overall, Agenda 21 constitutes the most comprehensive and far-reaching programme of action ever approved by the world community.

And the fact that their approval was at the highest political level lends it special authority and importance. For the first time in international politics we have consensus that the future of the planet is at stake if we do not reverse the process of abusing it.

The real measure of success will be in what happens now, after Rio, when government leaders and citizens alike have returned to their countries, to their organizations, to their immediate preoccupations. It is up to all of us to build on the foundations laid by the Earth Summit to ensure that the decisions that have been taken at the global level be translated into national politics and practices at all levels.

A new world order, as we move into the 21st century, must unite us all in a global partnership – which always recognizes and respects the transcending sovereignty of nature, of our only one Earth. We have to make sure that the road from Rio is a fast track, if we are to realise our hope that the United Nations Earth Summit really was a quantum leap forward on that road to sustainable development.

The Rio Declaration on Environment and Development

The United Nations Conference on Environment and Development, having met at Rio de Janeiro from 3 to 14 June 1992, reaffirming the Declaration of the United Nations Conference on the Human Environment, adopted at Stockholm on 16 June 1972, and seeking to build upon it, with the goal of establishing a new and equitable global partnership through the creation of new levels of cooperation among States, key sectors of societies and people, working towards international agreements which respect the interests of all and protect the integrity of the global environmental and developmental system, recognizing the integral and interdependent nature of the Earth, our home, proclaims that:

Principle 1 Human beings are at the centre of concerns for sustainable development. They are entitled to a healthy and productive life in harmony with nature.

Principle 2 States have, in accordance with the Charter of the United Nations and the principles of international law, the sovereign right to exploit their own resources pursuant to their own environmental and developmental policies, and the responsibility to ensure that activities within their jurisdiction or control do not cause damage to the environment of other States or of areas beyond the limits of national jurisdiction.

Principle 3 The right to development must be fulfilled so as to equitably meet developmental and environmental needs of present and future generations.

Principle 4 In order to achieve sustainable development, environmental protection shall constitute an integral part of the development process and cannot be considered in isolation from it.

Principle 5 All States and all people shall cooperate in the essential task of eradicating poverty as an indispensable requirement for sustainable development, in order to decrease the disparities in standards of living and better meet the needs of the majority of the people of the world.

Principle 6 The special situation and needs of developing countries, particularly the least developed and those most environmentally vulnerable, shall be given special priority. International actions in the field of environment and development should also address the interests and needs of all countries.

Principle 7 States shall cooperate in a spirit of global partnership to conserve, protect and restore the health and integrity of the Earth's ecosystem. In view of the different contributions to global environmental degradation, States have common but differentiated responsibilities. The developed countries acknowledge the responsibility that they bear in the international pursuit of sustainable development in view of the pressures their societies place on the global environment and of the technologies and financial resources they command.

Principle 8 To achieve sustainable development and a higher quality of life for all people, States should reduce and eliminate unsustainable patterns of production and consumption and promote appropriate demographic policies.

Principle 9 States should cooperate to strengthen endogenous capacity-building for sustainable development by improving scientific understanding through exchanges of scientific and technological knowledge, and by enhancing the development, adaptation, diffusion and transfer of technologies, including new and innovative technologies.

Principle 10 Environmental issues are best handled with the participation of all concerned citizens, at the relevant level. At the national level, each individual shall have appropriate access to information concerning the environment that is held by public authorities, including information on hazardous materials and activities in their communities, and the opportunity to participate in decision-making processes. States shall facilitate and encourage public awareness and participation by making information widely available. Effective access to judicial and administrative proceedings, including redress and remedy, shall be provided.

"IIED has, more than any other organisation I know, helped to prepare the way for the 1992 Earth Summit in Rio de Janeiro and is well placed to play a key role in its follow-up and implementation".

Maurice Strong,
Secretary General, UNCED

Photo: Mark Edwards/Still Pictures

IIED is the largest environment and development think tank in Europe.

It is a leading non-governmental organisation engaged in the promotion of sustainable development through research, policy studies and information, and advises governments, UN bodies and aid agencies.

IIED works closely with local communities in the Third World and with decision-makers through its different Programmes covering sustainable agriculture, climate change, environmental economics, tropical forestry, human settlements, drylands management and institutional development.

Recognition of IIED's work has come from many quarters. Many of its books have won prizes, and members of staff are among the winners of the 'Global 500' award.

Most recently the Institute has been honoured with the prestigious Blue Planet Prize. Sponsored by the Asahi Glass Foundation of Japan, the Blue Planet Development and Implementation Award is given for:

> *"Outstanding achievement in executing environmental projects, establishing and implementing environmental policies, realising widely applicable research and development results, undertaking education and awareness programmes, and conducting environment related writing or media activities".*

IIED

International Institute for Environment and Development

3 Endsleigh Street, London WC1H 0DD, England
Tel: (44-71) 388.2117 Fax: (44-71) 388.2826
Telex: 261681 EASCAN G

Principle 11 States shall enact effective environmental legislation. Environmental standards, management objectives and priorities should reflect the environmental and developmental context to which they apply. Standards applied by some countries may be inappropriate and of unwarranted economic and social cost to other countries, in particular developing countries.

Principle 12 States should cooperate to promote a supportive and open international economic system that would lead to economic growth and sustainable development in all countries, to better address the problems of environmental degradation. Trade policy measures for environmental purposes should not constitute a means of arbitrary or unjustifiable discrimination or a disguised restriction on international trade. Unilateral actions to deal with environmental challenges outside the jurisdiction of the importing country should be avoided. Environmental measures addressing transboundary or global environmental problems should, as far as possible, be based on an international consensus.

Principle 13 States shall develop national law regarding liability and compensation for the victims of pollution and other environmental damage. States shall also cooperate in an expeditious and more determined manner to develop further international law regarding liability and compensation for adverse effects of environmental damage caused by activities within their jurisdiction or control to areas beyond their jurisdiction.

Principle 14 States should effectively cooperate to discourage or prevent the relocation and transfer to other States of any activities and substances that cause severe environmental degradation or are found to be harmful to human health.

Principle 15 In order to protect the environment, the precautionary approach shall be widely applied by States according to their capabilities. Where there are threats of serious or irreversible damage, lack of full scientific certainty shall not be used as a reason for postponing cost- effective measures to prevent environmental degradation.

Principle 16 National authorities should endeavour to promote the internalization of environmental costs and the use of economic instruments, taking into account the approach that the polluter should, in principle, bear the cost of pollution, with due regard to the public interest and without distorting international trade and investment.

Principle 17 Environmental impact assessment, as a national instrument, shall be undertaken for proposed activities that are likely to have a significant adverse impact on the environment and are subject to a decision of a competent national authority.

Principle 18 States shall immediately notify other States of any natural disasters or other emergencies that are likely to produce sudden harmful effects on the environment of those States. Every effort shall be made by the international community to help States so afflicted.

Principle 19 States shall provide prior and timely notification and relevant information to potentially affected States on activities that may have a significant adverse transboundary environmental effect and shall consult with those States at an early stage and in good faith.

Principle 20 Women have a vital role in environmental management and development. Their full participation is therefore essential to achieve sustainable development.

Principle 21 The creativity, ideals and courage of the youth of the world should be mobilized to forge a global partnership in order to achieve sustainable development and ensure a better future for all.

Principle 22 Indigenous people and their communities, and other local communities, have a vital role in environmental management and development because of their knowledge and traditional practices. States should recognize and duly support their identity, culture and interest and enable their effective participation in the achievement of sustainable development.

Principle 23 The environment and natural resources of people under oppression, domination and occupation shall be protected.

Principle 24 Warfare is inherently destructive of sustainable development. States shall therefore respect international law providing protection for the environment in times of armed conflict and cooperate in its further development, as necessary.

Principle 25 Peace, development and environmental protection are interdependent and indivisible.

Principle 26 States shall resolve all their environmental disputes peacefully and by appropriate means in accordance with the Charter of the United Nations.

Principle 27 States and people shall cooperate in good faith and in a spirit of partnership in the fulfilment of the principles embodied in this Declaration and in the further development of international law in the field of sustainable development.

From Stockholm to Rio

Richard Sandbrook, OBE

Richard Sandbrook is the executive director of the International Institute for Environment and Development. He has 21 years experience in development and conservation sciences, was a co-founder of Friends of the Earth UK and a participant in the 1972 Stockholm Conference. He has been continuously involved in the financial and personnel management of a wide range of practical environmental projects worldwide and has many years experience in the affairs of bilateral and multilateral donor agencies and their project procedures, as well as with the analysis of development objectives. He is a recipient of the Global 500 Award.

Twenty years ago the first environmental conference was held in Stockholm. Just some of its achievements include the adoption of the first global action plan for the environment and the creation of the UN Environment Programme as an international instrument to build environmental awareness and stewardship. Above all it placed environmental issues on the world's agenda.

The ideas in this book may seem to be remote from what we have come to know as the environment issue. This is due largely to the fact that the commentary to which we are most often exposed is via the media and influenced by people who push the environment as an important issue, but who often have a specific interest to promote; and these interests usually relate to rainforests, disappearing species and pollution.

What happened in Rio last June was not their event. The United Nations Conference for the Environment and Development concerned all nations who had priorities other than this narrow definition of environment. To put these priorities and the Rio conference into perspective, we need to turn back the pages to the last global environmental conference which took place twenty years ago. How did events which occurred there and those which have happened since help to shape the 1992 conference?

The United Nations Conference on Human Environment was held in Stockholm in June 1972. In many respects, it was a dialogue of the deaf between the rich and the poor. The rich world, particularly the USA, had to face up to the effluence of affluence. In those days, the rivers foamed with pollutants, we had shipwrecked tankers like the Torrey Canyon, and weeks of winter smog over our cities.

In order to clean up the world in which we were living, governments of the industrialised and wealthy world wanted all nations and industries to agree to act together. If only one or two began serious clean-up operations, those few would be at a disadvantage because their industry would have to carry an additional and unfair cost. So it was in the interest of both industry and government to go to Stockholm to create a level playing field where all would agree to clean up.

The poor Third World did not see Stockholm in that way. They wanted industry, even with its inherent pollution problems. For them the problem was, and still is, poverty. In order to tackle poverty, they were prepared to adopt western ways and accept the environmental problems as part of the package. Few in the northern sector of the globe took much notice of the problems of the south. It was in response to this indifference that Indhira Ghandi said: "Of all the pollutants we face, the worst is poverty. We want more development." She nor any other of the Third World countries got what they wanted.

Stockholm achieved success by making its mark. The western world began to see the error of its ways. Pushed by active pressure groups, much was done to improve matters.

There now exists a veritable library of rules and regulations to cover most western environmental ills. Rules that govern the air we breath, the water we drink, the habitat in which we live, the food we eat. Not a perfect system, but it would be a cynic indeed who said that advances had not been made in environmental issues since 1972.

However, what has changed dramatically over the last twenty years is the number of things which we now do that have an impact on the environment and the increasing rate at which that impact registers. In particular, what we push into the atmosphere by driving cars, destroying forests and burning coal. In the early 1970s around 5.5 billion metric tons per head of carbon dioxide was released into the atmosphere. Today that figure has increased to 7 billion and so too has our awareness that it causes climate change. Our knowledge of its global effect has increased. Now it is not only our own resources that are affected but those of others and the effect is registered on a global scale. The oceans are suffering and land belonging to nations who do not cause the pollution suffers too. The damage has been magnified and has been shown to cause the destruction of forests and contribute to the disappearance of species, as well as have effects on climate change. The industrial countries came to Rio to solve the issues of climate, forests and endangered species.

The South did not come to Rio for the same reasons. They still face appalling problems related to poverty. In 1892 the average Indian had an income approximately half that of the average European. By the 1940s the gap had grown to 40 to 1. It now stands at 70 to 1.

In the twenty years since the last environmental conference, the food output per head in Africa has declined and the number of people living below the poverty line has grown by over one billion. The major cause of childhood death is foul water.

At Rio the poor nations insisted that the agenda should include development as well as environment. This time they had a bargaining tool. If, in the interests of halting climate change, the North wanted the South to halt deforestation, to slow down the consumption of coal and oil, to reduce birthrates, then the North would have to pay.

Time and time again over the last twenty years, the poorer nations have argued that the price they receive for their goods in the market place is too low; that their debts are intolerable. If all the aid given by the North is subtracted from all the interest that is paid on the debt by the South, they end up paying us more than we give them. Trade and debt have always been, and still are, the issues. Unless these problems are addressed, the South does not see how problems such as the destruction of the environment and the growing birthrate, so closely linked to poverty, can be tackled.

Issues such as corruption, bad management and dictatorship contribute to the problems; it could be argued that the Third World is its own worst enemy. But many there would argue that the Northern management of trade and debt issues are the fundamental causes of their ills.

The Earth Summit in Rio was inspired and guided by a remarkable document published in 1982 by the Brundtland Commission which tried to balance the arguments concerning North/South responsibility and suggest ways forward. Intended as a progress report on achievements since the Stockholm conference ten years earlier, the impetus for the Brundtland report came from progressive nations and organisations. Many of them had been involved in the Stockholm conference and were concerned that the agreements and goals of the 1972 event were not being achieved. These governments, with some notable exceptions including the USA and the UK, set up an independent commission with a brief to investigate the links, or the lack of them, between environmental destruction and development worldwide.

An unusual departure from similar commissions in the past was the diverse and respected group appointed to report to the commission. An American industrialist, a European prime minister, a radical Third World feminist and the Secretary-General of the Commonwealth formed just part of the influential and knowledgeable group who were given the brief.

To the informed minority the findings of the commission were not surprising. They concluded that if we continue to use up natural resources as we do at present, if we ignore the plight of the poor, if we continue to pollute and waste, then we can expect a decline in the quality of life.

To describe the way of halting this decline the commission coined the term sustainable development. This is best described as economic progress which meets all of our needs without leaving future generations with fewer resources than those we enjoy. A way of living from nature's income rather than its capital account.

Sustainable development is not easy to achieve. It demands changes in lifestyle, particularly for the more wealthy nations who continue to draw on nature's capital, and it requires much more attention to the destructive and wasteful effects of poverty.

For wealthy nations, sustainable development means policies concerning issues such as recycling, energy efficiency, conservation, rehabilitation of damaged landscapes. For the poor nations it means policies for equity, fairness, respect of the law, redistribution of wealth and wealth creation.

Worthy thoughts concerned with worthy deeds which for once did not fall on stony ground. Two important factors helped bring the report in to the public domain. Firstly, Mrs Gro Harlem Brundtland, the chair of the commission, became the Prime Minister of Norway shortly after working on the report in 1987. She was thus in a position to promote the conclusions of the report at the highest possible level. And this she did. Ironically, she was joined by Mrs Margaret Thatcher, the UK prime minister who had originally opposed the commission. But, as a scientist, Mrs Thatcher had become deeply concerned about the discovery of the hole in the ozone layer. As a result she decided to promote the environment issue at the United Nations and was joined by Gorbachev, Mitterand and Gandhi.

Thus, the environmental beauty contest of world leaders was set in motion. By the end of 1988, some 50 national leaders had come out in strong support of the conclusions of the commission, with many calling for a major event to discuss and act upon the Brundtland report.

The resulting debate in the UN in 1989 saw resolution 44/228 passed. This stated that there should be a UN Conference on Environment and Development and determined the ground which the conference should cover. The mechanics of the United Nations demand that such a resolution be passed by a consensus process, a long and complex methodology in which all governments have input allowing them the means to introduce issues of particular importance and relevance to their own countries. This process might not be the most effective way of doing business, but contrary to popular belief, it does not always result in the lowest common denominator. Some of those involved fight hard for their ideas and wear down their opponents.

Eventually, perceptions moved closer and the resolution was passed but the gap between the rich and poor nations was still very wide. For example, the USA wanted very little control to be exercised over multinational companies, many of which are North American; but the poor nations wanted a greater degree of control as they believe that the companies of the west exploit their resources. Many other issues were influenced by major differences between rich and poor and the resulting resolution which established the format for Rio was extremely wide. Given the complexity of UNCED and the weeks of preparation that went into it; it is commendable that 38 chapters of Agenda 21 were agreed, along with two conventions, a set of guidelines and a Rio declaration.

In retrospect, there are two observations that stand out as to what happened in Rio. Firstly, this was not a conference about the environment at all, it concerned the world's economy and how the environment affects it. This in itself is a mammoth step forward as politicians come to understand that the issues do not just concern plants and animals, but life itself. Secondly, this was the first meeting of world leaders since the end of the Cold War. The old East/West agenda is dead, attention is now focused on North and South. Rio not only marked the beginning of a new era but a triumph for that small band of campaigners who set out at Stockholm. Twenty years on their issues of environment and development have taken centre stage in a new age.

An Environmental Revolution

Lester R. Brown

Lester R. Brown founded the Worldwatch Institute in 1974, a research institute devoted to the analysis of global environment issues. Ten years later he launched the State of the World reports and in 1988 launched World Watch, a bimonthly magazine focusing on the Institute's research. He is the recipient of a MacArthur Foundation award, winner of the UN 1989 environment prize and author of numerous books on environmental and development issues. He published *Launching the Environmental Revolution: State of the World 1992* this year.

If the degradation of the planet is to be halted then a major shift has to take place socially, economically and politically. A revolution is necessary to reverse the deterioration which has occurred in the last twenty years. Such a revolution will involve a dramatic change in lifestyle, a major shift in human reproductive behaviour and a restructuring of the global economy.

In early June 1992, the United Nations convened its Conference on Environment and Development in Rio de Janeiro. Coming 20 years after the UN meeting in Stockholm that officially launched the environmental movement, this so-called Earth Summit dwarfed its predecessor. With close to 10,000 official delegates from 150 or more countries and perhaps 15,000 concerned citizens and activists participating in a parallel Global Forum, it was the largest UN conference ever held.

The 116 national political leaders gathered in Rio was the largest such gathering in history. The 7,000 journalists accredited to the conference may have been the largest gathering of representatives of the global communications media ever assembled.

As part of their preparation for the meeting, governments prepared reports on the state of their environments. Most focused on national achievements – a reduction in air pollution here or a successful reforestation programme there. But overall, global environmental trends were not reassuring. The health of the planet had deteriorated dangerously during the 20 years since Stockholm.

Our world of the mid-nineties faces potentially convulsive change. The question is, in what direction will it take us? Will the change come from strong worldwide initiatives that reverse the degradation of the planet and restore hope for the future, or will it come from continuing environmental deterioration that leads to economic decline and social instability?

Muddling through will not work. Either we turn things around quickly or the self-reinforcing internal dynamic of the deterioration-and-decline scenario will take over. The policy decisions we make in the years immediately ahead will determine whether our children live in a world of development or decline.

There is no precedent for the change in prospect. Building an environmentally sustainable future depends on restructuring the global economy, major shifts in human reproductive behaviour, and dramatic changes in values and life-styles. Doing all this quickly adds up to a revolution, one defined by the need to restore and preserve the Earth's environmental systems. If this Environmental Revolution succeeds, it will rank with the Agricultural and Industrial Revolutions as one of the great economic and social transformations in human history.

Like the Agricultural Revolution, it will dramatically alter population trends. While the former set the stage for enormous increases in human numbers, this revolution will succeed only if it stabilizes population size, re-establishing a balance between people and the natural systems on which they depend. In contrast to the Industrial Revolution, which was based on a shift to fossil fuels, this new transformation will be based on a shift away from fossil fuels.

The two earlier revolutions were driven by technological advances – the first by the discovery of farming and the second by the inventions of the steam engine, which converted the energy in coal into mechanical power. The Environmental Revolution, while it will obviously use new technologies, will be driven primarily by the restructuring of the global economy so that it does not destroy its natural support systems.

The pace of the Environmental Revolution will be far faster than that of its predecessors. The Agricultural Revolution began some 10,000 years ago and the Industrial Revolution has been under way for two centuries. But if the Environmental Revolution is to succeed, it must be compressed into a few decades.

Progress in the Agricultural Revolution was measured almost exclusively in the growth in food output that eventually enabled farmers to produce a surplus that could feed city dwellers. Similarly, industrial progress was gauged by success in expanding the output of raw materials and manufactured goods. The Environmental Revolution will be judged by whether it can

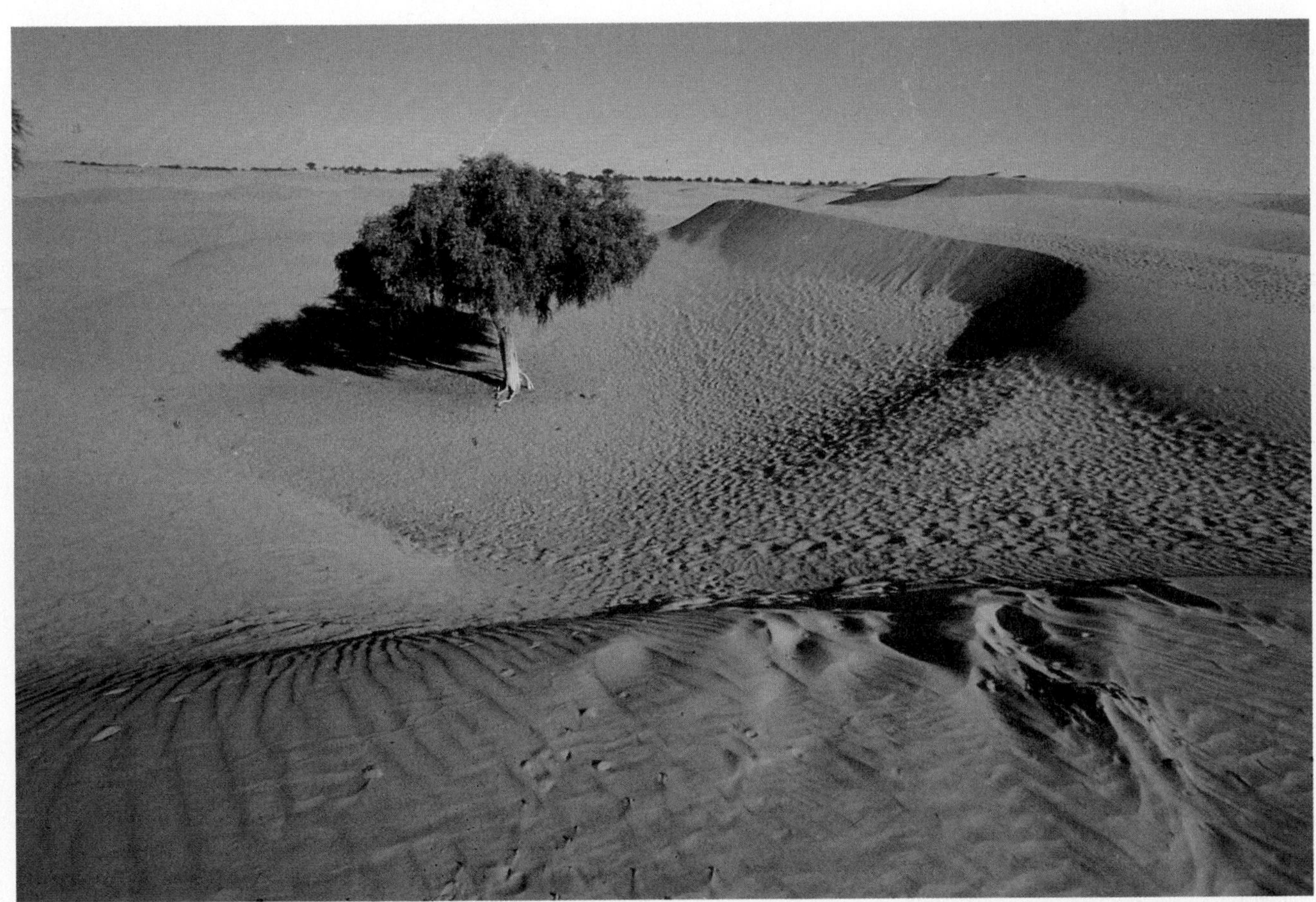

shift the world economy on to an environmentally sustainable development path, one that leads to greater economic security, healthier life-styles, and a worldwide improvement in the human condition.

Many still do not see the need for such an economic and social transformation. They see the Earth's deteriorating physical condition as a peripheral matter that can be dealt with by minor policy adjustments. But 20 years of effort have failed to stem the tide of environmental degradation. There is now too much evidence on too many fronts to take these issues lightly.

Already the planet's degradation is damaging human health, slowing the growth in world food production, and reversing economic progress in dozens of countries. By the age of 10, thousands of children living in southern California's Los Angeles basin have respiratory systems that are permanently impaired by polluted air. Some 300,000 Soviet citizens are being treated for radiation sickness. The accelerated depletion of the stratospheric ozone layer in the northern hemisphere will lead to an estimated additional 200,000 skin cancer fatalities over the next half-century in the United States alone. Worldwide, millions of lives are at stake. These examples, and countless others, show that our health is closely linked to that of the planet.

A scarcity of new cropland and fresh water plus the negative effects of soil erosion, air pollution, and hotter summers on crop yields is slowing growth of the world grain harvest. Combined with continuing rapid population growth, this has reversed the steady rise in grain output per person to which the world has become accustomed. Between 1950 and 1984, the historical peak year, world grain production per person climbed by nearly 40 per cent. Since then, it has fallen roughly one per cent a year, with the drop concentrated in poor countries. With food imports in these nations restricted by rising external debt, there are far more hungry people today than ever before.

On the economic front, the signs are equally ominous: soil erosion, deforestation and overgrazing are adversely affecting productivity in the farming, forestry and livestock sectors, slowing overall economic growth in agriculturally based economies. The World Bank reports that after three decades of broad-based economic gains, incomes fell during the eighties in more than 40 developing countries. Collectively, these nations contain more than 800 million people – almost three times the population of North America and nearly one sixth that of the world. In Nigeria, the most populous country in the ill-fated group, the incomes

of its 123 million people fell a painful 20 per cent, exceeding the fall in US incomes during the depression decade of the thirties.

Anyone who thinks these environmental, agricultural and economic trends can easily be reversed need only look at population projections. Those of us born before the middle of this century have seen world population double to five billion. We have witnessed the environmental effects of adding 2.5 billion people, especially in the Third World. We can see the loss of tree cover, the devastation of grasslands, the soil erosion, the crowding and poverty, the land hunger, and the water pollution associated with this addition. But what if 4.7 billion more people are added by 2050, over 90 per cent of them in the Third World, as now projected by UN demographers?

The decline in living conditions that was once predicted by some ecologists from the combination of continuing rapid population growth, spreading environmental degradation, and rising external debt has become a reality for one sixth of humanity. Moreover, if a more comprehensive system of national economic accounting were used – one that incorporated losses of natural capital, such as topsoil and forest, the destruction of productive grasslands, the extinction of plant and animal species, or the health costs of air and water pollution, nuclear radiation, and increased ultraviolet radiation – it might well show that most of humanity suffered a decline in living conditions during the eighties.

Today we study the archaeological sites of civilisations that were undermined by environmental deterioration. The wheat lands that made North Africa the granary of the Roman Empire are now largely desert. The early civilizations of the Tigris-Euphrates Basin declined as the waterlogging and salting of irrigation systems slowly shrank their food supply. And the collapse of the Mayan civilization that flourished in the Guatemalan lowlands from the third century BC to the ninth century AD may have been triggered by deforestation and soil erosion.

No one knows for certain why the centres of Mayan culture and art fell into neglect, nor whether the population of one million to three million moved or died off, bur recent progress in deciphering hieroglyphs in the area adds credence to an environmental decline hypothesis. One of those involved with the project, Linda Schele of the University of Texas, observes: "They were worried about war at the end. Ecological disasters, too. Deforestation and starvation. I think the population rose to the limits that their technology could bear. They were so close to the edge, if anything went wrong, it was all over."

Whether the Mayan economy had become environmentally unsustainable before it actually began to decline, we do not know. What we do know is that our economy has, and that unless we harness the knowledge, information and technology available to us in halting that decline, we are destined to follow the same route as those ancient civilisations.

Living in a Time of Change

Chris Church

Chris Church qualified as an environmental biologist in 1977 and since then has been active in the environment field. After working for Friends of the Earth UK he now works independently. He acted as UK coordinator for the Earth Summit Tree of Life project, worked as an advisor to the BBC-TV One World season of programmes and launched the Environmental Law Foundation. He is currently Development Director for Global Action Plan - UK which aims to empower individuals to take effective environmental action in their homes, workplaces and communities.

Individuals are at the forefront of change whether it is through political or economic pressure or by example. In the past, particularly where environmental and development issues are concerned, individual effort has often been portrayed as eccentric or even dangerous. Yet many of the changes which have taken place over the last twenty years must be accredited to the efforts of individuals who have demanded through positive action, that those in a position of power take note of their views and instigate change.

As nation states and international organisations seem to become ever more powerful, it is easy to forget how many of the key social changes throughout history have been down to the inspiration and commitment of just a few people.

As the power and scope of the international bodies reach further and further, so an individual now has access to ever more information and can make direct contact with other people around the world in a way that would have been inconceivable fifty years ago. Rather than being swept away, the power of individuals to bring about change is as great or greater than it was when the United Nations was created.

The growth of the non-governmental organisations (NGOs) has been one of the most important social developments of this century. In 1900 there were just a handful of independent groups working for change at an international level – now there are over 5000. There is no doubt that their influence on policy, especially in the fields of environment and development, has been profound. In the northern nations citizen action groups have scored some impressive victories using a variety of tactics.

The first major international victory for the environmental groups – the campaign to save the great whales of the world – started at the 1972 UN Conference on the Human Environment. That campaign brought together coordinated political lobbying, high-profile direct action, action by workers in whaling-product industries demanding the development of alternatives, and individual consumers, who would no longer buy the products that contributed to the destruction. These tactics have been repeated again and again.

Action in the south has been every bit as impressive. Groups who have lacked the financial resources, and in some cases, the multi-party systems that make effective political lobbying possible, have built people-based campaigns that through their simplicity and commitment have caught the attention of the world's media. From high-profile activities such as the Narmada Dam campaign or the Altamira gathering of the indigenous peoples of the Brazilian rainforest to lower-profile urban or rural development projects, activities across the poorer parts of the world have shown how individuals everywhere can mobilise and be effective.

This flowering of activity was never clearer than at the Global Forum when groups of every shape and size imaginable came together to monitor the Earth Summit, to plan joint campaigns and above all to learn more about each other. Out of the Forum, and out of the flawed but crucially important declarations of the Summit has emerged a new basis for action. With that comes a whole new range of challenges, both for individuals and NGOs.

NGOs need to develop better ways of working together and to look beyond policy change to effective implementation. They also need, in many cases, to examine how they can help their individual supporters to become more effective. For here is one of the challenges for individuals: as NGOs become larger, more effective and more concerned with the global agenda, so less attention is paid to resolving the more mundane day-to-day problems. Some individuals now find themselves being offered little to do in support of their chosen cause other than to provide funds.

Yet the lesson that has been learnt from so many effective development projects is that involving people at all stages is crucial to success. When this does not happen so people may become alienated and feel unable to contribute. And many do feel distant from the need for change – in western nations never more than a small part of the population has been actively involved in campaigning on environment or development issues. There are passive

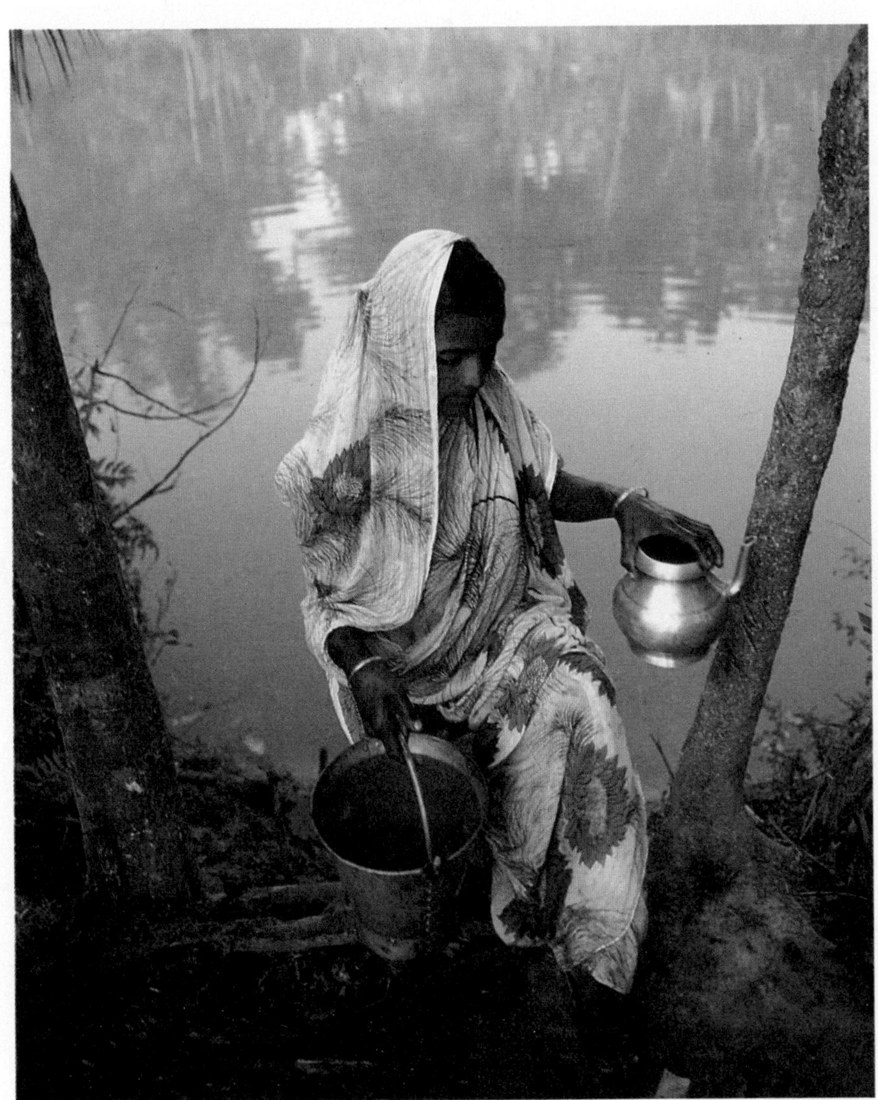

supporters who will donate or may change their purchasing habits, but the radical agenda that is emerging out of the Rio meetings will need more active citizens than ever before, especially in those rich nations where patterns of resource use must change.

So why do people not get involved? It is easy to point to lack of time or funds, but at the root of much of the apathy is a feeling that it is all someone else's problem. People may refuse to tackle a problem because:

The Government will take care of it

It is what we pay our taxes for, after all ... In fact the experience of the last twenty years is that governments only take action on environmental issues when pushed into it by public opinion. Despite the recognition of the growing importance of these issues they rarely get far up the agenda, and in battles between short-term profit and longer-term environmental health, the short-term all too often wins out. But it has been said, and shown to be true on many occasions, that when the people lead, the leaders follow.

For any individual, helping maintain the pressure on their government is one of the most important ways to secure a sustainable environment.

The NGOs will take care of it

There is no doubt that the environment and development groups have won some important battles, changed many damaging policies and are widely trusted by the public. The damage would be far worse were it not for those victories, but the destruction continues. More fundamentally, there is the challenge of putting those new policies to work and that needs action at the community and individual level.

Agenda 21 may have set new national targets; local agenda 21s are now needed for communities around the world that can involve everyone in turning them from words into action.

The United Nations will take care of it

Some of these problems – desertification or climate change – seem so large that it is hard to see how any one nation can make a difference. The idea that the UN can mobilise the resources needed for effective change is a tempting one for many, but the states that make up the UN all have their own agenda, and its ability to act is constrained by those agendas. The UN can act as the focus for the transfer and spread of information and ideas, and over the next few years a key role must be to ensure that its member governments give due priority to citizen-based initiatives.

There is one more idea that many people cling on to:

The planet will take care of itself

The planet has indeed looked after itself for millions of years, but in the last few decades humanity has done damage that will take centuries to repair. If this process continues much longer the damage will be irreversible – for that reason alone the next few years are crucial ones. A person may get ill because of disease but often it is because of an unhealthy lifestyle. Restoring the planet to good health means accepting responsibility for the unhealthy behaviour by people around the world that has caused the problems.

At the root of all these excuses for inaction is one more underlying problem, fear. Be it fear of the unknown, fear that things will change for the worse or simply fear of change, for many individuals that fear outweighs the concerns they may have about the long-term future for their community or their planet. Fear can paralyse: in society it is

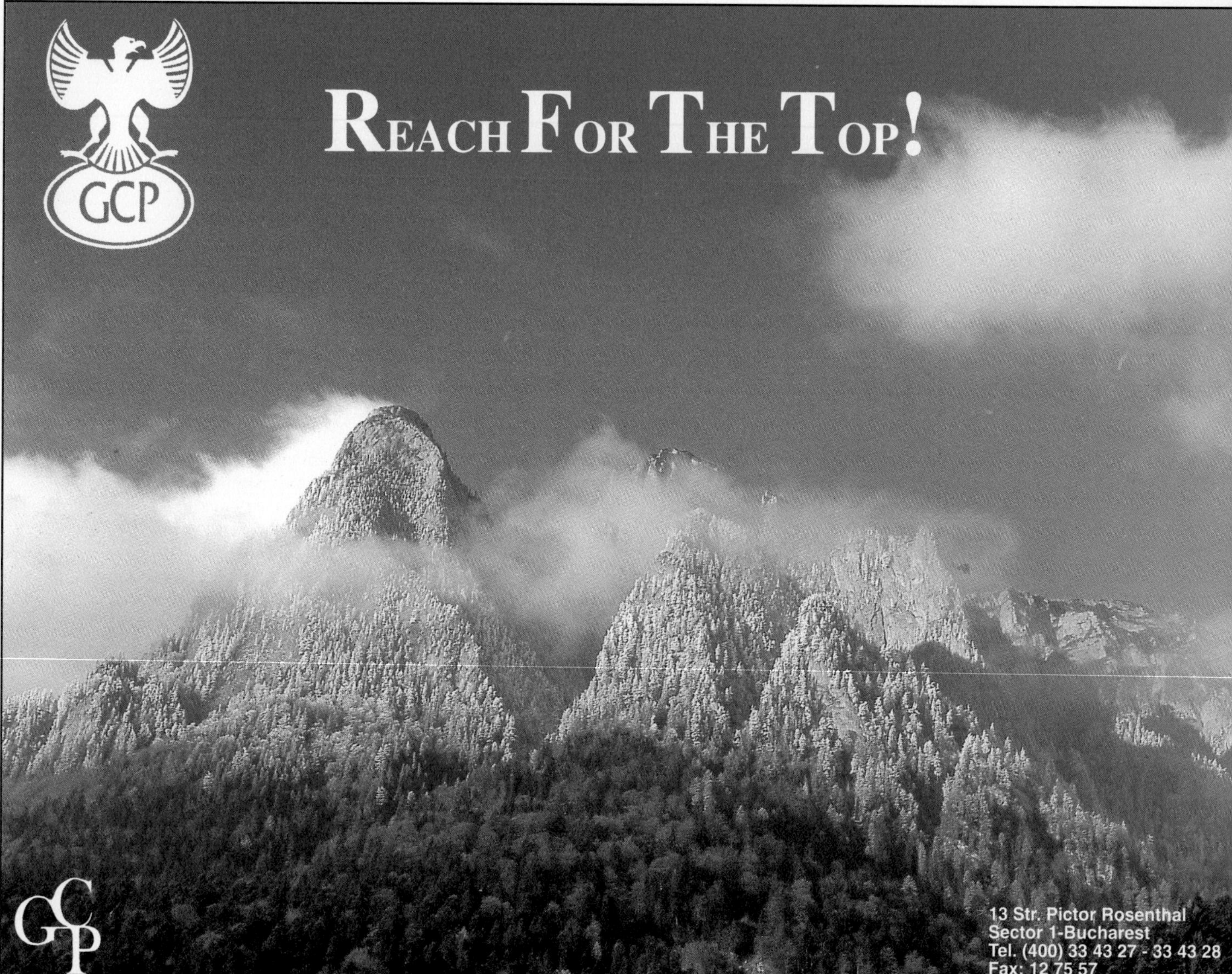

UNCED opened the eyes of the world to the issues of environment and development. Heads of States and governments from around the world pledged their support to the principles involved.

GCP – GENERAL CONSULTING AND PROCUREMENT SA agrees with these principles and looks forward to working in the future with companies throughout the world dedicated to the same goals.

Dr. Ec. George C. Paunescu
Chairman
G.C.P. S.A.

manifest in a desire to focus on safeguarding individual interest and in so doing to encourage isolation.

In America and Western Europe that isolation has been particularly emphasised by an increasingly car-dependent culture that leads to widely-scattered communities with no central focus; the images of poverty and environmental destruction that enter uninvited through the television often reinforce that fear and isolation. In poorer nations the environmental crisis itself can create isolation – Kenyan writer Celestous Juma tells of an Africa "full of lonely peasants; millions of people alienated from one another by the destruction of nature."

If individuals are to use their power for change to good effect, then part of that power must go to overcoming that numbing isolation and developing new ways of collective and participative working – ways in which individuality is recognised and valued but in which the whole must be much greater than the parts. The ultimate lesson of all this is that it is, in the last resort, up to all of us – an over-repeated truism, but one that will not go away.

Organisations, from the United Nations or the World Bank down to a tiny village, are usually slow to change. When change does come it is usually due to people – the only effective agents of positive change. The change can be brought about by political or economic pressure, but it is sometimes easy to forget the third means of change – change by example.

Politicians, business managers and community leaders all have a key role to play: not through pontificating abut the need for change or about what should be done, but by involving themselves in the change and by being seen to take an active lead. At a local level this means not merely attending the first planting of a community woodland, but putting time aside to make a regular commitment.

The very concept of leadership has become devalued during the last century: the leader as one who leads, who takes risks who is exposed but in so doing sets a powerful example is a rare model these days. Today's leader is more likely to be seen surrounded by aides walking from the limousine to the boardroom to take decisions affecting the lives of people he or she will never meet.

The starting point for any individual keen to bring about change has been and will be, time and time again, to reclaim that role of leadership from the administrators, the directors and the managers. This is no easy task, for any high-profile leader who challenges the status quo is bound to be a target for criticism and mockery. In rich nations in the 1970s environmentalists were portrayed as eccentric, dangerous or frequently both, yet the first faltering policies of some of those pioneers are now embedded in international policy.

Any individual can take on leadership at this level: this can be done through initiating a practical project or a new organisation, through bringing new energy and direction into existing structures or by using any of the media tools to publicise issues and ideas. The ultimate function of any such leader-by-example must of course be two-fold: to make themselves redundant by solving the problem that they set out to tackle, and most importantly, to inspire and empower new leaders.

In the aftermath of the Summit, all organisations from governments downwards face new challenges. But whatever their agenda, one priority for those organisations committed to making sustainable policies a reality must be to encourage and empower those individuals who support them to take a positive lead in bringing change to their communities. The real question is how can that best be done?

The need for participation has already been mentioned, as have some of the personal barriers that prevent that participation. The most effective way in which organisations can help remove those barriers is by making sure that the participation is not a top-down directed exercise, but that all concerned come together at the same level and that the national or international bodies recognise the needs and values of the communities where they are working. Change will only be successful if it meets the perceived needs of those affected by it.

The Earth Summit itself stood accused of failing on this issue: it was suggested by southern nations that the central items on the agenda – forests, biodiversity and climate change – represented the priorities of the richer nations, and that the root causes of environmental degradation and poverty were being ignored. Hopefully this lesson is starting to permeate international decision-making processes: there is now a need to apply the same process at a local level throughout the world.

A good model for this has been the Primary Environmental Care (PEC) programme developed by OXFAM and other groups. This approach has three key elements: popular empowerment, securing basic rights and needs, and caring for the environment. Real lasting environmental improvement will only come about by dealing with the first two issues. The logic behind it is inevitable and not surprising: what is perhaps surprising is the way in which it has been ignored in so many cases.

PEC attempts to integrate these concerns and has already demonstrated an impressive track record, from rubber tappers developing extractive reserves in Amazonian forest to NGOs working with the landless poor in Bangladesh. OXFAM 's role in these projects is to supply resources and education to help with both environmental care and social reform.

It is also clear that PEC is as relevant in the northern nations as in the south – in fact the need to emphasise basic rights may be even more important in some northern industrial cities that are drifting into decay after decades of prosperity. Despite high levels of consumption, millions in European and American inner city areas face long-term unemployment and relative poverty yet lack the community organisation that can stimulate self-help. In poorer countries it is often different. Dominican Republic activist Dionisia Acosta puts it succinctly: "We, the poor, have to organise because we have no alternative. The poor must help the poor and hope that society will change." Primary Environmental Care offers an important tool for effective urban regeneration.

Even the most motivated individuals can drive themselves into the ground in attempting to improve their environment if no support is available. How best to deliver

Banco Nacional de México

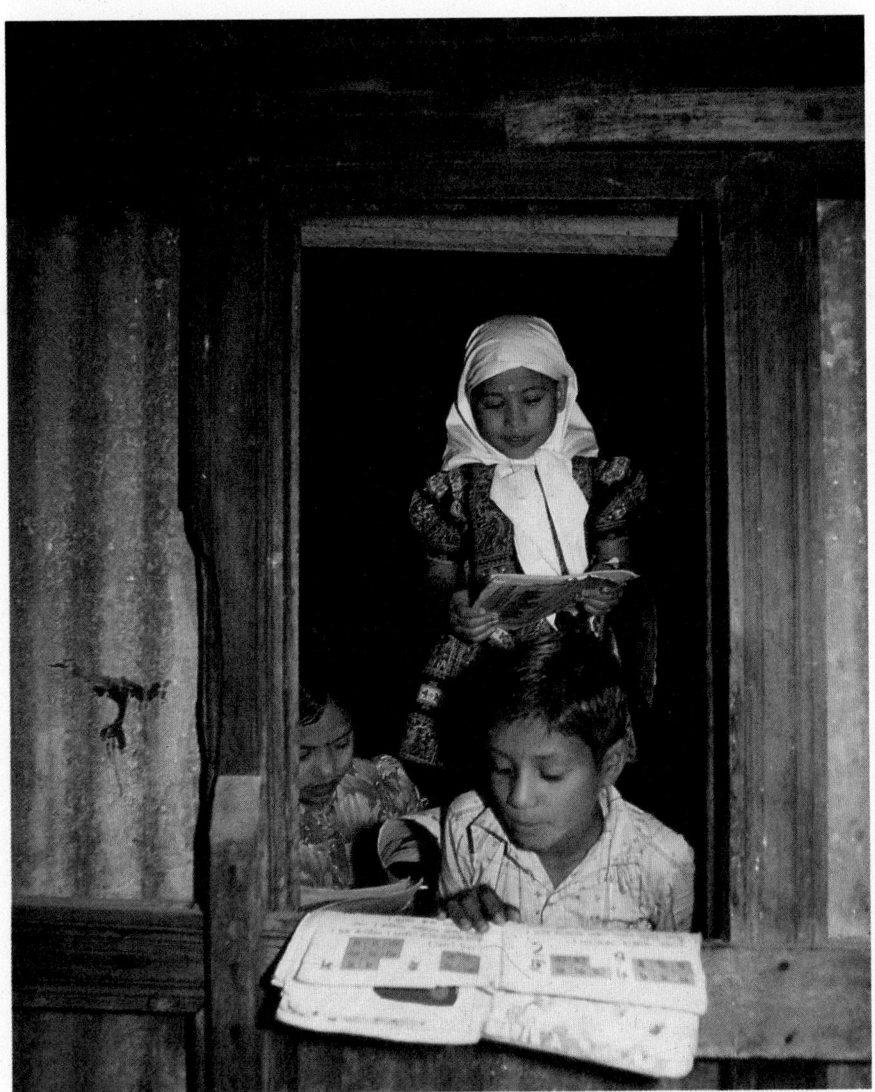

that support is the key to people-centred sustainable development, but the first step must be a commitment to genuinely provide support rather than management. In this way small innovative projects that may not fit in with some centrally generated strategy can nevertheless come to fruition to meet the needs of those who initiated them.

Good examples can be seen in certain Latin American *favelas* or shanty-towns. Some authorities see *favelas* as unplanned problem areas to be bulldozed in the name of planned developments: the more far-sighted are now, where appropriate, encouraging and supporting the initiators of these new communities by providing water, sewage, health care and other essential services, and in this way encouraging the self-development from shanty-town to suburb.

Another pioneering way forward in Amazonia has been the work of the Gaia Foundation where a small central fund-raising office works with a network of individuals who can in turn work with villagers on developing and funding 'micro-projects' – small scale developments that meet the needs of communities but are often too small to qualify for funding from larger agencies. The Foundation does not run projects but has an impressive record of assessing requests for support and providing funding on a time-scale that would be impossible for larger agencies.

Standing back and letting innovators innovate is one way forward: another is to provide a framework for that energy. In the wake of the Summit many nations are starting to develop national targets for sustainability and looking to see how these targets can be met. Yet national targets of this nature may be meaningless to community organisations struggling with their own problems or to individuals looking to make changes in their lives but unsure of what to do for the best. An effective way to stimulate individual action will be turning those targets into a local framework for action. Communities can then see how resolving their local priorities also contributes to national objectives.

One organisation – Global Action Plan for the Earth (GAP) – is already working on this in Europe and North America. Individuals are encouraged to examine how they can cut waste and limit consumption with the aim of meeting specific targets – regional and national offices assist by running a feedback system that shows each individual what they have saved (be it litres of water or tonnes of CO_2) and the total amount saved. Through projects like this, those people around the world who made pledges of personal action for the Tree of Life at the Global Forum will be able to monitor their own progress while seeing how individual drops really do fill the global bucket.

From cutting wasteful consumption in the richer regions to planning strategies for survival in the poorest ones, individuals are at the forefront of change. Yet personal contributions are often ignored, not least because the mechanisms do not exist to record or value them. Just as women's labour in agricultural communities throughout the world has been consistently undervalued, so little recognition has been given to the voluntary efforts of countless individuals. If empowerment is to mean anything it must involve not just helping people plan to take action but also helping them to see how they have made a difference.

Changing Business Attitudes

Lloyd Timberlake

Lloyd Timberlake is the director of external affairs at the International Institute for Environment and Development. He has written numerous articles and books on environment and development issues including *Africa in Crisis* which won the World Hunger Media Award and *Only One Earth* the book of the international television series. He was closely involved with the work of the World Commission on Environment and Development and the publication of *Our Common Future* as well as *Changing Course* for the Business Council for Sustainable Development.

Eco-efficiency is the way forward for corporations who want to achieve success in business whilst taking account of environmental and development issues. This term describes the production of goods and services whilst reducing resource consumption and pollution. It is a vital component in linking business, the environment and the needs of this and future generations.

In mid-1990, Maurice Strong, Secretary-General of UNCED, asked Stephan Schmidheiny to be his principal adviser for business and industry. He was given a double mandate by Mr Strong: to prepare a report which reflected a business view on environmental and development issues, and one which encouraged the private sector to become more knowledgeable about and enthusiastic over the Earth Summit's main theme of sustainable development.

In order to accomplish both mandates, Mr Schmidheiny set up the Business Council for Sustainable Development (BCSD)which he invited chief executive officers to join. Almost all who were asked accepted. These included the leaders of chemical companies such as Dow, duPont and Ceiba-Geigy, heads of energy companies such as Shell, Chevron, Norsk Hydro and TransAlta Utilities, metal companies including Nippon Steel and ALCOA and car companies such as Volkswagen and Nissan. The BCSD included representatives from Europe, North and South America, Asia, Africa and Australia.

The members all believed in the efficiency of the marketplace and decided to target fellow business leaders, politicians, environmental leaders and the concerned public through a commercially published book. This would fulfil the first part of the original mandate, to produce a report reflecting the business view of environmental and development issues, and reach a wide audience at a low cost.

Changing Course: a Global Business Perspective on Development and the Environment was published in seven languages prior to the Earth Summit. It combines convictions and examples with case studies of business success.

Although the book is accredited to Stephan Schmidheiny with the BCSD, each member signed his or her name to a three page declaration. Reviews worldwide have praised its combination of vision and practicality.

But what of the second mandate, to raise business awareness of the concept of sustainable development? To address this issue the BCSD organised over 50 meetings in 20 countries, particularly in the developing world. There are now national or regional business groups examining issues of sustainable development in Asia, Africa and Latin America.

Difficult though it is to precis the themes of such a complex work, this was the task undertaken by Mr Schmidheiny and US Council members when presenting a copy of the publication to US President George Bush shortly before the Earth Summit. President Bush had expressed concern that environmental treaties reached at Rio might hurt the competitiveness of US business. Council members urged him to take a different view of business and the environment, emphasising that their report was not of gloom and doom but good news. Good news both for business and for the political leaders attempting to establish a framework in which business can prosper.

The good news is that business excellence and environmental concern can be combined.

In fact, in the near future it will be impossible to separate the two.

The BCSD came to this conclusion after searching for a link between the two ideals of business and environmental excellence. It found that link in the concept of efficiency, which connects business, the environment, and the increasing human needs of this generation and the larger generations to come. Efficiency keeps companies competitive; it adds most value with the least use of natural resources; and it is crucial in the fight against mass poverty in the world.

The Council thus coined the term eco-efficiency to describe the method of production of those corporations that produce ever more useful goods and services while continuously reducing resource consumption and pollution. The members all agreed, after studying world-wide business trends, that tomorrow's winners will be those who make the most and the fastest progress in improving their eco-efficiency. Why? Because:

- customers are demanding cleaner products, as well as products and services which support the development goals of poorer countries. This customer concern comes in rising and falling waves, but there is an overall upwards movement;
- insurance companies are more amenable to covering clean companies;
- employees, particularly the best and the brightest, prefer to work for environmentally responsible corporations;
- environmental regulations are getting tougher, and will continue to get tougher;
- new economic instruments – taxes, charges and trade permits – are rewarding clean companies. Business in general, and the BCSD in particular, is calling for the increased use of such instruments;
- banks are more willing to lend to companies which prevent pollution rather than having to pay for expensive clean-ups, for two main reasons. First, there is growing concern among bankers regarding their liability for the environmental misdeeds of borrowers. Second, a company which is unlikely to become entangled in an environmental lawsuit or unlikely to be liable for large clean-up bills, is a company more likely to be able to repay its loans on schedule.

All these trends, which will accelerate as science offers more evidence of environmental damage, mean that investments in eco-efficiency will help, rather than hurt, profitability. It is the eco-efficient companies – and the eco-efficient nations – which will emerge as the most competitive as these trends take hold.

The BCSD wrote that business has had the advantage of already coping with the quality revolution. As long as it focused only on the end of the assembly line, then improving quality meant discarding or fixing rejects – and thus it meant increased costs. But once it examined the total system from design on through, it found it could design quality in at the beginning, minimise rejects and actually save money. Having done the unthinkable in one area – improving quality while cutting costs – business can now at least begin to think the unthinkable in another area: decreasing resource use and improving environmental management, while cutting costs.

Taking advantage of the trends discussed above will require changes by both business and governments. Businesses will have to seek close and open cooperation with all of their stakeholders in introducing policies aimed at sustainable progress. Stakeholders include not only the obvious ones such as customers, employers, investors, suppliers and clients, but also pressure groups, neighbours and governments.

Business must actively participate in the legislative process so that the most efficient mix of government regulation, market instruments and self-regulation may be developed. Command-and-control regulation has its place, especially where health is endangered or where damage might be serious and permanent. But self-regulation and market instruments are usually more cost-effective for both business and society, and the BCSD encourages the greater use of both.

In order for markets to give the right signals, prices of resources and products should increasingly reflect both the cost of their production and the cost of their environmental impact. Over the longer term, the basis for charges, taxes and incentives should be shifted to discourage environmental damage while encouraging the process of saving, investing, and adding value. National and all other accounts must be redesigned to reflect both damages to and improvements in stocks of natural resources and in ecosystems.

Economic growth in all parts of the world is an essential prerequisite both for sustainable development in the developing world and the continuing prosperity of the more industrialised nations. Both open, competitive international trade and international cooperation are essential for growth and for the efficient distribution of environmentally sound technologies. It is in the long-term interest of industrialised countries to trade with and invest in poorer countries, seeking forms of trade and investment mutually beneficial to both sides and providing equitable access to markets for all.

During their debates, the BCSD members often confronted the huge uncertainty of these sustainability issues. How much more aid do developing countries need to reach this level of sustainable development? How much must the price of carbon-based energy increase in order to prevent disastrous global warming and to encourage the development of new technologies? These are unknown quantities but when an important trend in business is identified, it is at the least short-sighted and certainly uneconomic not to take advantage of it. In business there are never any final destinations, but continuous processes and constant adjustment. So too in sustainable development. The detailed route may be indistinct but the direction of travel is obvious.

The book *Changing Course*, is divided largely into tasks for business and tasks for governments. By the time the BCSD took its message to Rio, many of the tasks were well known. What was less well known is how business can take a leadership role in working with governments to establish new economic instruments, new terms of international trade and new international treaties which reflect both economic and environmental realities.

This was why, in plenary session at Rio, Mr Schmidheiny called for a bold new partnership between business and governments. As he put it, business must move beyond the traditional approach of back door lobbying: governments must move beyond traditional over-reliance on command-and-control regulations.

Such a partnership is needed in developing countries to establish the enabling conditions for progress and investment, to open markets and opportunities to all. Open negotiations between business and governments are also essential to achieve the optimal mix of economic instruments, regulations and self-regulation required to make markets reflect environmental as well as economic truth.

The BCSD has paid a great deal of attention to the businesses of farming and forestry, because they sustain the livelihoods of almost half this planet's people and because of their obvious environmental impact. Both are often influenced by market signals working against efficient resource use – and thus against the environment. As a first step, distorting subsidies should be removed, to reflect the full costs of environmental resources. New partnerships are needed here as well, to create the right market signals and regulations to enable business to be a more effective manager of forests, including the genetic resource and the environmental and social services of forests.

And a new, effective business/government partnership will be crucial for technological cooperation – moving and using technology so as to integrate economic development and environmental protection in developing countries. Technology must be moved from those who developed it and have the know-how to train others in its use, to those who see a need for it and are committed to its effective use. This means business, company-to-company transactions, and of course increased investment.

Governments in both industrial and developing countries must work together to establish the required legal, social and economic frameworks to facilitate this process of technical cooperation. It requires of both business and government a long-term commitment to business development, training of the people involved, upgrading the technology to remain competitive, and the introduction of new management systems.

The BCSD's participation in Rio was well received. Thus in the space of only two years, Mr Schmidheiny and his fellow BCSD members established their organisation and guided its efforts to produce a report for a major UN conference and to interest business leaders everywhere in sustainable development. In years to come the Summit may be regarded as a success not least because it represented the first time business and industry played a thoughtful and organised role in deliberating environment and development issues.

Priorities for the Future

Reg Green

Reg Green is the occupational health, safety and environment officer for the International Federation of Chemical, Energy and General Workers' Unions (ICEF). He occupied the same position in the International Confederation of Free Trade Unions (ICFTU) leading up to and during the UNCED process and was responsible for coordinating the trade unions at the Earth Summit. The ICEF works closely with the ICFTU in matters of health, safety and the environment and represents workers worldwide in the chemical and process sectors of the industry.

Trade Unions have been at the forefront of change for over a century, striving to improve and enhance working standards and conditions on behalf of workers. They are now addressing environmental issues on behalf of their members and working with environmental groups to improve the workplace and move away from the unsustainable development path which has been followed in the past.

The Earth Summit was convened to address ways of tackling two of the world's most pressing and difficult problems; its burgeoning environmental difficulties and the economic development and security of its citizens, known collectively as sustainable development. Two key components contribute to sustainable development.

First, addressing the political and economic needs and aspirations of people – including working people – worldwide. Second – and most important – it depends upon the efforts of working people for its success.

Working people have an overriding interest in encouraging and promoting sustainable development and play a pivotal role in bringing it about. This point bears stressing as the environmental and developmental debate has shown little regard to date for the views of working people and their representative organisations. Listening to the comments of some of the protagonists in the debate, including the vast majority of those addressing the Earth Summit, one could be forgiven for thinking that economic development – sustainable or otherwise – is something which occurs separately from human and worker involvement. Workers and their trade unions will continue to oppose this thinking and ensure that they are fully involved in the future political processes dealing with the environment, particularly where it relates to the workplace and its immediate environs.

Even had the Earth Summit ended on a more positive note, with rich and poor nations recognising their mutual rights and responsibilities, the resulting high level political statements and commitments would still have to be put into effect at the national, local and, ultimately, workplace level. Fine words would (and will) have to be translated into meaningful action.

Workers and their trade unions know only too well the cost of lengthy government deliberations or of international government agreements. They understand only too well the relationships between politics and their broader interest.

Workers and trade unions know that polluting plants and processes are socially and environmentally unacceptable. They are aware of the unsustainable values and unacceptable morals of a world where a minority live in relative comfort and security and the great majority are compelled to eke out a living devoid of any social safety net and all too frequently bereft of legal and human, including trade union, rights. Trade unions have been fighting these injustices for over one hundred years.

Workers know what can be done to help eradicate or alleviate problems whether in connection with health and safety protection or pollution prevention and mitigation. However, their demands are frequently met with the response that raising health and safety standards or that introducing stricter controls would be too expensive or threaten and/or cost jobs. Indeed, in a world where transnational corporations are able to shift capital and production to countries with lower standards of worker and environmental protection, this is now a very real threat.

These are the political realities facing many workers. As individuals their power is limited, but as members of trade unions they have learned their effectiveness. Workers organised in trade unions have taken a leading role in achieving protective legislation such as enhanced social security, medical cover, protection against arbitrary decisions and victimisation and the promotion of international solidarity. It has been organised workers who have fought for and won improvements in health and safety standards and, increasingly, in broader environmental standards. Indeed, trade unions are now fighting for environmental issues to form part of the normal collective bargaining process, for workers' representatives to be included on joint management/worker environment committees and to be included in workplace

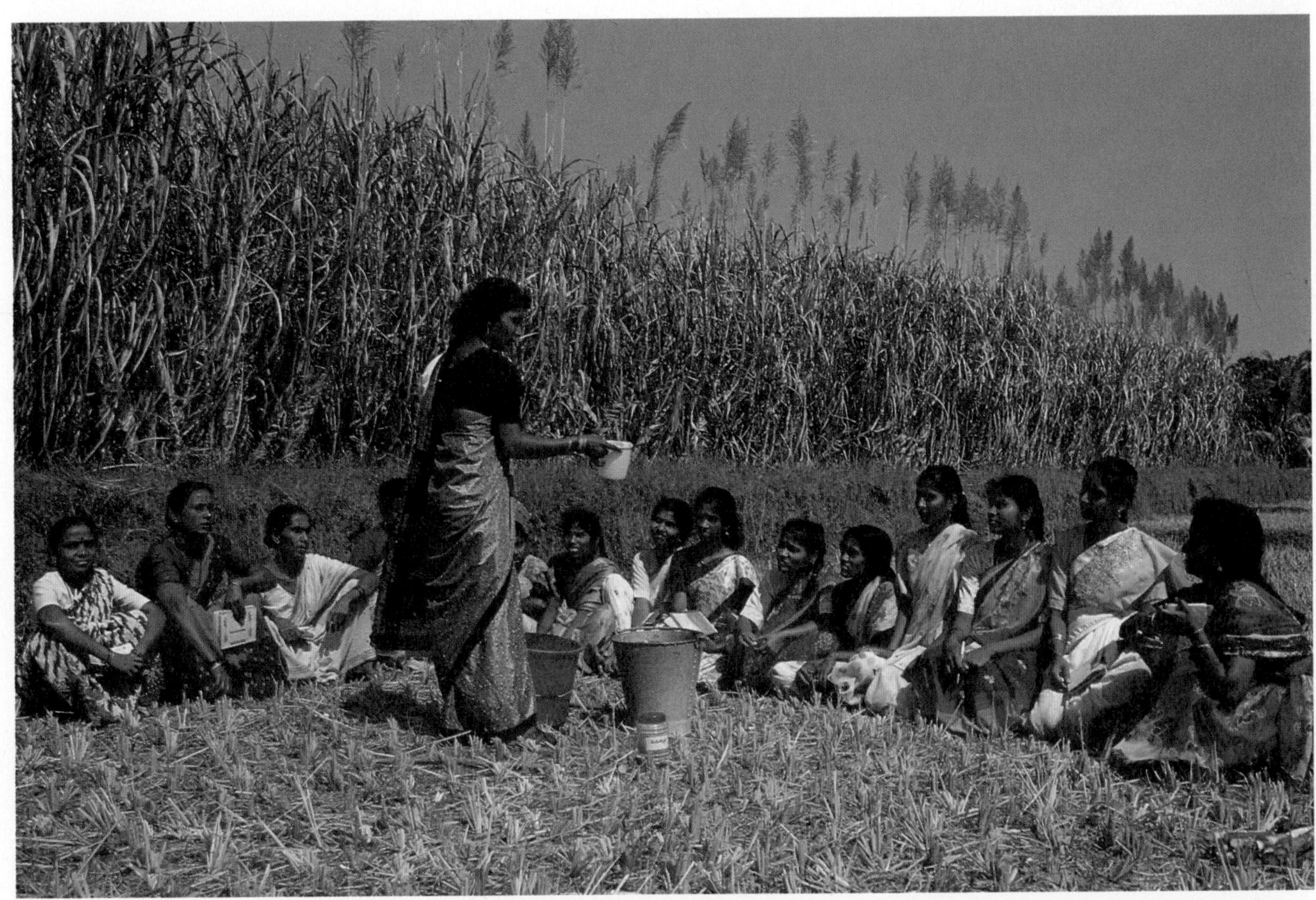

environmental audits. Organised labour has a long and noble history of achieving progressive change, no other group has been more active in defending these changes.

Workers are in the front line when it comes to industrial accidents and illness; workers and their families are the most likely to be exposed to the effects of pollution, directly or indirectly. Terrible as its consequences were, Bhopal was no different in many ways from the risks to which countless millions of other workers all over the world are exposed – both at home and in the workplace; it is workers who are the first to spot a dangerous or damaging aspect of their work environment; it is workers who have the first hand knowledge and experience to formulate solutions; and it is workers who rely on a secure income for their survival and that of their families, and who therefore have a vested interest in the long term viability and sustainability of their work activity.

Why, therefore, is it that those who have the single biggest interest in sustainable development and those upon whom its achievement will succeed or fail are largely excluded from participating in the decision-making processes? Because organised workers are effective and, by extension, inconvenient in the eyes of many governments and employers. Organised workers do not content themselves with making statements or calling for action. They are both prepared and able to take action in pursuit of their demands.

It was no coincidence that the few trade union representatives included in the government delegations at the Earth Summit came from those countries where organised labour is strong, legal and at least politically tolerated. It was with a strong sense of irony that these trade union representatives listened to speeches about democracy and equality from some of the most oppressive, anti-union, undemocratic countries.

Increasingly, organised workers are joining with environmental groups to tackle workplace related environmental problems. The relationship between the two groups is still somewhat tentative, but there have been good examples of cooperation leading to improvements in both the workplace and the wider environment, together with the development of politically effective coalitions. This is an increasing recognition on the part of both groups that together they are more effective than apart.

The Earth Summit addressed a number of vital issues and must be considered an important milestone in the development of environmental thinking and the broader recognition of the close link between environment and development. At the same

time it served to highlight the substantially different and divergent standpoints which exist in the world.

In particular, it showed the extent of the gulf between the rich and the poor nations. Charges of 'environmental neo-colonialism' and of a massive lack of political will on the part of the highly industrialised countries were being made by the less developed countries. At the same time, many less developed countries were criticized by those in the highly industrialised world as being unwilling to recognise that, in a world of finite resources and exploding population, it will not be possible to follow the same unsustainable development path which has been pursued in the past.

The Earth Summit showed that unless one deals with political reality, the most impressive statements, agendas and manifestos will come to nothing. Unfortunately, it was precisely at the political level that the Summit was least successful. Getting agreement, in principle, on protecting the environment, on saving human life, on increasing the share of global prosperity to the poorer peoples of the world is relatively simple. This was proved in Rio de Janeiro in June 1992. The difficulty lies in achieving action. It is at this stage that one hears the global version of the old workplace argument, it is too expensive, it will cost jobs, the electorate would not stand for it. The message, despite grand speeches, appears to be 'business as usual' for many governments and businesses.

For workers and their trade unions the Earth Summit demonstrated once again that one cannot rely on others to make the decisions. Real change is unlikely to be generated from the top down, real change occurs from the bottom up. Responsibility for sustainable development is too important an issue to be left exclusively in the hands of governments thinking no further than the next election or with businesses whose principal concern is a favourable financial dividend at the end of each year.

Sustainable development is, above all, about the workplace and work activities. It is concerned with the needs of workers and their families, ensuring that their voices are presented in the decision making processes. Trade unions understand the political reasons why these rights are not automatically granted to workers as they also understand the limitations of international conferences such as the Earth Summit.

It is in the workplace where real and progressive changes can be made. Only a handful of governments who attended the Earth Summit recognised the important contribution to be made to sustainable development by organised labour. Other governments would do well to reflect on the tragic environmental and developmental legacy of Central and Eastern Europe and realise that hope for the future in this part of the world exists largely because workers gathered together in independent trade union organisations to defeat the corrupt, undemocratic and unsustainable governments of the region.

For all the work put into the Earth Summit by the UNCED secretariat, and for all the effort that the secretariat made to try to gather as many views as possible, there will be no positive outcome for either the environment or for development unless the political realities are addressed. Sustainable development is not only about the environment and economic development, it is about human – including trade union – rights, widespread democratic political enfranchisement, participation, accountability, and an understanding and acceptance of cultural differences.

The trade union movement has followed the whole UNCED process with interest and participated where possible. It intends to continue to participate where practicable. But the post-Earth Summit feeling within trade unions is that the future lies with those who are capable of organising the necessary changes at the level of the individual and in the workplace and building on this foundation.

Trade unions are already including environmental protection in their collective bargaining with employers; they are demanding rights for workers and their trade union representatives to sit on joint management/worker environment committees; they are insisting on the right to take place in workplace environmental audits and on the right to refuse to undertake dangerous or environmentally damaging work. They are not short of ideas and are willing to work with those who are genuinely interested in making the world a better place for all its citizens.

A Growing Strength

Wangari Maathi

Wangari Maathi is a leading voice in the Greenbelt Movement of Kenya. She delivered a speech on behalf of non-governmental organisations at the Earth Summit after consultation with many other groups.

Non-governmental organisations (NGOs) have been a major force of change in the past twenty years; many of the most well known and active of them at work today were formed as a direct result of the Stockholm Conference in 1972. At the Earth Summit NGOs organised their own parallel event, the Global Forum, which featured representatives from thousands of diverse organisations world-wide.

The environment and development NGOs have followed the UNCED process from its inception. Some tirelessly walked the halls of the United Nations for two years, making serious proposals for action to the governments of the world. Others watched the process from afar hoping that political leaders and government officials would rise and meet the challenges presently confronting the human species.

Three different governmental approaches were distinguishable in the UNCED process: that which seeks the urgently needed structural changes in the way it manages its resources and share its benefits; that which makes merely cosmetic adjustments in a hopelessly unsustainable economic, social and environmental order; and that which is simply bent on preventing progress.

UNCED has brought about a leap in public awareness of key environment and development issues, and its failure or success must be assessed on the basis of the progress it makes on issues that are vital to building environmentally sound and socially equitable societies. These include: eliminating poverty; fair and environmentally sound trade; reversal of the net flow of resources from South to North; clear recognition of the responsibilities of business and industry; changes in wasteful patterns of consumption; internalisation of the costs of environmental and natural resource use; equitable access to environmentally sound technology and its benefits; redirection of military expenditures to environmental and social goals; and democratization of local, national and international political institutions and decision-making structures.

Without progress on these issues policies and actions agreed to at UNCED and elsewhere will be seriously undermined. Solutions must be found to growing North/South inequities and increasing ecological degradation. But changing inequitable social structures within countries is equally important.

New patterns of international cooperation are required to address global concerns but, unfortunately, negotiations so far have often been compromised by the paralysing logic and narrow interests of traditional power politics.

However, the nature of the environment and development debate has changed forever. UNCED has achieved the first step in the integration of the two key components. Issues such as poverty, trade and debt were put on the negotiating table and, as never before, discussed by such a broad range of governmental and non-governmental actors.

However what has been gained through UNCED risks being sabotaged by the failure of governments to make commitments to concrete actions on certain key issues. We recognize the collective responsibility of all governments, and in fact of all sectors of society, in this failure.

The important, indeed vital, role which NGOs and social movements have to play in international negotiations has been broadened through the UNCED process. UN procedures will never be the same again.

One of the most positive results of the Earth Summit process is the growing strength of the international environment and development movement. NGOs have been meeting for over two years now and have been building bridges between the North and South, East and West.

We will continue our struggle towards a democratic, socially equitable and ecologically sustainable world. We are empowered through our own networks, and have developed cooperation treaties for concrete action.

We recognise the progress made in many areas in UNCED and we will continue to push vigorously and relentlessly for the steps yet to be taken. We will fight to ensure that those tools that UNCED created to achieve a new pattern of civilisation are used democratically, fully and effectively. We urge the elected leaders and governments to do the same.

The Institutions Debate

Lee A. Kimball

Lee A. Kimball is a senior associate at the World Resources Institute in Washington, DC. Her WRI report, *Forging International Agreement: Strengthening Inter-Governmental Institutions for Environment and Development* was published in April 1992.

In order to achieve the goal of sustainable development recognition must be given to the interaction between economic, social and environmental trends. Institutions will need to be established which can expose policy and programme needs and requirements in order to integrate environmental considerations into plans at all levels. International institutions will play a key role.

If the UN Conference on Environment and Development accomplished anything, it was to force people worldwide to re-think how their lives affect natural environments and resources and to confront anew what determines the surrounds in which they live. But the world is still in the conceptual stages of putting that legacy into practice. As much as individual choices remain the bottom line, those choices will have to be mustered and channelled so that collectively they support sustainable development. Without common structures where agreements can be forged and commitments made to stick, and where resources can be pooled to achieve shared goals, individual choices may work at cross purposes. Both nationally and internationally, our institutions of government serve those functions.

The institutions debate at UNCED can be seen from two perspectives: the tasks to be performed, and the structural settings used to define and organize those tasks. It comes as no surprise that Agenda 21 applied these perspectives to particular sectors, such as agriculture and human settlements.

Where the Rio Conference took a quantum leap forward, however, was in recognizing that the interactions among sectors, and the intertwined nature of economic, social and environmental trends warranted a new approach to defining and organizing tasks, both at the national level and internationally. The 1972 Stockholm Conference launched efforts to integrate environmental considerations into development sector-by-sector and project-by-project, and these responsibilities were left largely in the hands of the managers. The Rio Conference has called for institutions that can expose policy and programme interactions in the planning stages, in order to anticipate and avoid conflicts that might arise later. It has also sought to open these processes to all affected constituencies and major groups[1], so as to better 'ground-truth' the policies and increase the stake of those who can make them work. The challenge now is getting these institutions to take root.

From the perspective of tasks to be performed, Agenda 21 will require regular environmental monitoring and data collection programmes to identify trends and patterns in social, economic and environmental conditions. More resources will have to be devoted to expert analysis to establish what combination of human activities and natural forces produced these conditions, and to evaluate the costs, benefits, and risks posed by different policies, technologies or development projects and strategies. Building consensus among multiple constituencies and reconciling the policies (and budgets) that govern their activities will place unprecedented demands on institutional structures and processes and a new order of magnitude of transparency and accountability will be necessary to maintain that consensus, verifying that responsibilities are equitable shared and effectively carried out.

This focus on the institutions debate at UNCED will concentrate on the international institutional arrangements, and the next steps that can put them into practice. The building blocks for international institutions, however are the decisions and activities undertaken at the national level. After Rio, it is up to each country to translate UNCED 's Agenda 21 into a national strategy, tailored to its particular conditions and development objectives and updated regularly. National structures should be set up to coordinate their preparation, and funding, and to review them based on consultative processes in which all major groups have access to information and can contribute to the outcome. These national Agenda 21s should ensure that policies and programmes complement and reinforce each other. Ideally, when national actions have transboundary, regional or global consequences, the national agenda would reflect agreed international policies and objectives. Thus each nation would be responsible for integrating country programmes and action plans prepared under

1 The major groups identified in the UNCED process included business and industry, trade and labour associations, scientific and other professional organizations, women and youth, religious groups, indigenous peoples, local communities, farmers, etc.

the ozone, climate and biodiversity treaties, for example, into national sustainable development strategies.

The initiative for forging these strategies does not rest with governments alone. The engagement of major groups is vital in convening the process and designing and carrying out the strategies. And where international development assistance plays a role, donor consortia – whether based on the round tables employed by the UN Development Programme (UNDP), the consultative group sponsored by the World Bank, or other alternatives – should adjust their membership and reorient their operations to better support the formulation and implementation of broadly-based, well-integrated national strategies.

The implications of Agenda 21 for international institutions are legion. And they are complicated by the fact that the structures of international governance are less well developed and more dispersed than those at the national level. The great achievements of Rio were to focus the next stages of institutional reform and renovation, and to create in Agenda 21 a conceptual framework within which policy and programme initiatives can be related and upon which priorities can be agreed. That framework sets forth objectives and timetables in sectoral and cross-sectoral areas, and links these to the need for data and information, scientific and technological means, capacity-building initiatives, regional and international cooperation and financial resources.

The decisions on international institutions taken at Rio can be summarized as follows:

First, UNCED called for the establishment of a high-level UN Commission on Sustainable Development, which will begin meeting in 1993. Its mandate is to review progress in the implementation of Agenda 21 and to rationalize inter-governmental decision-making on environment and development issues. The Commission is to draw on information provided by governments, reports from relevant UN system organizations, information on progress in implementing international environmental conventions, and input from non- governmental organizations (NGOs). The organizational details of the new Commission, which is to report to the UN Economic and Social Council (ECOSOC), has been determined by the UN General Assembly this autumn, including its membership, relationship to other UN bodies, and the frequency, duration and location of its meetings. Staffing decisions for both the Commission and the inter-agency coordinating mechanism noted below are left up to UN Secretary-General Boutros-Ghali.

Second, UNCED provided for regular oversight by the UN General Assembly and suggested that no later than 1997 it convene a special session to review and appraise Agenda 21. At the 1992 session of the Assembly, countries are requested to report their plans and commitments for making financial resources available to support the decisions of the Rio Conference. This sets a precedent for annual pledging sessions on environment and development, reinforced by the Commission's mandate to track commitments of financial resources.

Third, ECOSOC, consistent with its mandate, is given responsibility for coordinating the different UN agencies and programmes, while the Administrative Committee on Coordination (ACC), composed of the directors of each agency and headed by the UN Secretary-General, is to be 'revitalized' to promote effective inter-agency collaboration on environment and development. It may establish a special task force for this purpose. An important aspect of both the Commission and the inter-agency process is the effort to better link the UN system with the international financial institutions – the World Bank, the International Monetary Fund, and the regional development banks – and with the growing number of regional and multilateral organizations that are not UN organs *per se* (e.g. the Association of Southeast Asian Nations, the South Pacific Forum, the European Community, the Latin American Economic System). Following UNCED, Secretary-General Boutros-Ghali established an inter-agency task force to report back to him in preparation for the autumn General Assembly on the system-wide institutional implications of the Conference.

Fourth, in the area of data collection, environmental monitoring, and expert assessment, Agenda 21 in virtually every chapter underscores the need for better information and analysis to underpin sustainable development policies and programmes. On the institutional side, it has encouraged the strengthening of Earthwatch, the inter-agency environmental monitoring programme coordinated by UNEP, and called for the establishment of a similar

THE ENVIRONMENT : A TRADITION AT RENAULT.

Concern for the environment is a tradition at Renault. The company has never ceased to implement innovative solutions in the fight against pollution and for protection of the environment : recycling of cardboards, oils and metals from the start of the company in 1900, processing of polluted water and vapours from painting cells (in the fifties), purifying of gases and monitoring of quality of the air (in the seventies and eighties).

Today, thanks to the workforce of 350 people and an investment of 950 MF in 1991, Renault is working towards and proposing concrete solutions for every phase of a vehicle's life, from its conception through manufacture and use and at the end of its service life.

This means that our vehicles are increasingly environmentally friendly. For example :

- they are designed to be easily disassembled and use recyclable materials and identifiable parts (all of the plastic parts of the Espace and Safrane are marked with the main ingredients from which they are made).
- Our vehicles are manufactured in clean factories where, for example, waste is systematically recycled and paint lines use water based paints without solvents, etc.

Furthermore, Renault vehicles are used in perfect harmony with the environment.

In concrete terms that means setting up, for the first time in Europe and throughout the continent, the means for collecting and recycling waste produced in our networks by vehicle maintenance and repair.

- Other concrete results are the large volume of research work on cleaning up exhaust gases and, in particular, the introduction of the air injection engine (giving a reduction of 8% in fuel consumption).

Renault is also developing technologies aiming to lower diesel engine emission, to reduce the volatility of fuels as well as working on the design of engines for the future; electric car, two-stroke engine or hybrid electric/turbine vehicle, etc.

And finally, when Renault vehicles come to the end of their life, they can be disposed of without harmful effects on the environment.

In order to solve the present problem of the scrapping of 25% of vehicle components (plastics, glass, rubber, minerals, etc.), our company has been engaging in numerous actions for several years, as well as acting in partnership with our suppliers. These actions have led to the creation in 1991 - for first time in France - of an experimental vehicle dismantle and recycling plant at our factory at Flins. The experience gained will allow us, from September 1992, and for the first time in Europe, to set up a semi-industrial used-vehicle recycling plant (handling capacity 200 vehicles/day). This project will give viable form to our global know-how in the area of vehicle processing :

- draining of all fluids,
- removal of mechanical components and parts,
- shredding of the vehicle,
- waste-to-energy conversion of shredding residue.

For many years Renault has included concern for the environment as part of its industrial strategy, a concern shared by all those who work with us.

The "green" car, the product of a "clean" plant, is in the process of creation at Renault.

Development Watch to coordinate economic and social statistics and assessments. These would be linked by an 'appropriate' UN office. In addition, the UN Secretary-General is to make recommendations to the General Assembly at its autumn session on the appointment of a high-level board of eminent persons, who in their personal capacity would provide expertise in environment and development, including scientific expertise. Finally, drawing on the model of the Inter-governmental Panel on Climate Change (IPCC), Agenda 21 encourages the establishment of inter-governmental scientific and technical panels on different environment and development issues.

Fifth, regional and sub-regional initiatives are highlighted throughout Agenda 21. They cover information networks and other capacity-building programmes, as well as formulating integrated policies and programmes for dealing with transboundary issues and ecosystems. While UNEP, ENDP, the UN regional economic commissions, and the regional development banks feature prominently, Agenda 21 recognizes that there are many autonomous regional institutions and conferences that may take the lead in particular efforts and with which collaboration is essential. It suggests establishing regional consultative mechanisms that include NGOs and all relevant bilateral and multilateral donors for exchanging experience and reviewing progress in implementing Agenda 21, and for harmonizing donor programmes. Its most concrete proposal is for the new UN Commission to consider an 'expeditious' survey, prepared by the UN Secretary-General, summarizing UNCED's recommendations for regional and sub-regional undertakings.

Sixth, the General Assembly is specifically requested to examine ways of enhancing the involvement of non-governmental organizations and major groups in the UN system to follow up UNCED, and to make available to them information, reports, and other data produced within the system. The more open accreditation procedures applied during UNCED are to serve as a model for expanding NGO roles and access. Beyond the UN system itself, Agenda 21 calls on all inter-governmental organizations, including the international finance and development agencies, to reconsider their procedures so that NGOs can better contribute to policy design, decision-making, implementation and evaluation. It notes in addition the proposal for a non-governmental Earth Council. The April 1992 report of the reconvened Brundtland Commission goes further in stating that "we attach particular significance to there being a new, independent, international body outside the UN system to monitor, assess and report on environmental trends."

When the General Assembly meets to sort out the details of the Commission on Sustainable Development, it will have to consider carefully how to monitor progress in a manner that advances Agenda 21. If the Commission engages too much in finger-pointing, it will undermine its ability to constructively review and update the objectives and timetables set forth. It should follow closely the emphasis in Agenda 21 on the problems encountered by governments in implementing commitments and legal obligations, and the need for partnerships to overcome them. At the same time, the mere existence of a regular, well-publicized forum on environment and development, whose documentation clearly juxtaposes programme objectives, targets and commitments against results, means visibility and notoriety. This alone entails progress. And it underscores the importance of the data collection, assessment and expert review functions noted above. Without accurate, objective, and transparent information, progress review will be meaningless.

The General Assembly could request that the group of eminent persons first concentrate on the expert capacity needed by the UN secretariat offices and high-level positions. More changes are likely in 1992, with this phase of 'renewal' to be completed in 1995, the fiftieth anniversary of the United Nations. This provides the opportunity to sort out the respective roles and staffing of the Commission, the UN Environment Programme, and other economic and social programmes.

With respect to 'hands-on operational' assistance programmes, UNCED has recommended that UNDP act as the lead agency in organizing UN system efforts, strengthening its in-country system of resident representatives to coordinate agencies and programmes in the field. Current UN debates stress improving the links between the policies articulated by different UN system agencies and the technical cooperation they support. As these initiatives gain substance and as the policies themselves are revised to integrate environment and development goals, this should reinforce unfolding events in other fora, such as the Global Environment Facility and the OECD Development Assistance Committee, where guidelines and programmes are being designed specifically to finance the implementation of international legal obligations to protect the environment. As national structures are refined to define and organise an integrated programme for sustainable development, this will allow the Commission to concentrate on the big picture mobilizing support to achieve it from UN system technical assistance and the more substantial capital assistance programmes of the banks, and on how both can leverage private sector investment and co-financing.

The counterpart to achieving greater coherence among, and maximum benefit from, the programmes of international institutions is for individual governments to coordinate their national positions so that they are consistently reflected in the different inter-governmental organizations in which they participate. If the Commission in its relationship with ECOSOC and subject to the Agenda 21 framework can induce governments to set integrated goals, it will become far easier for the different institutional agencies and organizations to direct their efforts in mutually reinforcing initiatives. Governments will have to ensure that the representatives they send to the Commission are well versed in the issues before it, familiar with its work from year to year, and well connected to power and influence at home. They must be willing to use it to set new goals and update old ones. And the non-governmental community must find new ways to inform and inspire the Commission in its vision of sustainable development.

Conflicts and Dilemmas

David Lascelles

David Lascelles is natural resources editor of the UK based Financial Times newspaper, specialising in environment and energy issues. He covered the Earth Summit for the Financial Times.

The old East/West confrontation has shifted to one between North and South and environment and development have become fixtures on this new agenda. Some of the most acrimonious debates during the UNCED process focused on the North/South debate and the marked divisions of wealth and poverty between the two.

It came to be called the Earth Summit. But its official title was the United Nations Conference on the Environment and Development – a form of words which gave it a much wider brief than vanishing rain forests or greenhouse gases. This was meant to stress the close connection between the two themes – how they come together in the concept of sustainable development which states that growth should take place without impoverishing future generations.

But by adding development to the agenda, the conference organisers opened the floodgates and risked drowning the event in words and argument. Many of the issues that came pouring through were legitimate: the role that poverty plays in degrading the environment, population control, the need to transfer efficient new technologies to the Third World. But a lot of them were more remote: the need for freer trade, vast increases in aid to poor countries, and more rights for women.

Above all, the stress on development highlighted the gap between the rich countries of the north and the poor of the south. It showed the sharp contrast in their priorities, with the rich countries concerned about cleaning up the world, and the poor hankering after the basic necessities of life. As Pakistan's environment minister, Mr Anwar Saifullah, put it, "Eighty per cent of our water is untreated. That's our biggest problem. When I have to worry about such basic provisions of life, it's a luxury to talk about the environment."

It also pitted rich against poor on matters of conservation: should the rain forests be preserved as a global good, or chopped down to serve pressing local economic needs? And inevitably it raised the age-old question of aid, dressed up this time in a newly fashionable green garb. All this proved deeply divisive in Rio, though whether it added a useful extra dimension to the debate or merely sidetracked the conference from the real environmental issues must be a matter of opinion.

The growing focus of UNCED on Third World issues became evident well ahead of the summit itself. More than a year earlier, the conference organisers headed by Maurice Strong in Geneva identified the Third World's backwardness as the greatest threat to the environment. Explosive population growth, the huge imbalances in consumption between North and South, and the growing demands that the Third World will place on "environmental space" as they develop in the years ahead – all these emerged as the major issues. Mr Strong's team prepared estimates of the amount of money needed to get the Third World into a sustainable development mode – more than $700 billion a year. This delighted the Third World, in particular the Group of 77 developing countries. But it alarmed the industrialised nations who had accepted the need for more aid in principle, but could see frighteningly large demands building up.

In the months before Rio, the G77 met in Peking and issued a call for a massive "Green Fund" to be financed by the industrialised countries – but dispensed by Third World countries. The rich North quickly moved to try and stifle this idea. At a meeting hosted by Malaysia, one of the most vociferous of the G77 members, Mr David MacLean the G7UK environment minister, said: "To persuade our taxpayers to accept new and additional burdens, we have to be able to point to new commitments and additional global benefits."

The G77 soon dropped the Green Fund idea, but still headed for Rio planning to make ambitious aid demands. Since the rich countries were equally prepared to resist, the conference gathered in a confrontational mood.

It was clear from the start that the centre of negotiation would be the size of the aid commitment that the North was prepared to make. Allied to this was how tightly new money would be linked specifically to environmental work, and how it would be dispensed. Of the $700 billion identified by Mr Strong, over $500 billion was to come from the developing countries themselves.

This left $175 billion to come in the form of aid. Since the rich countries were already giving $55 billion a year, the remaining target was $120 billion. But as the two week event progressed, it became obvious that a mere fraction of this sum would be offered. One by one, the leaders of the industrial countries came forward to make their pledges, George Bush, John Major, Francois Mitterand, Helmut Kohl. The final tally, according to Mr Strong, was $6-7 billion a year. The major single donor was Japan with $7.5 billion spread over five years. All this money is to be channelled through the Global Environment Facility (GEF), the fund administered jointly by the UN and the World Bank for projects of global, as opposed to merely national, environmental importance. The G77 was hostile to the GEF which it saw as a rich nations club. But the donor countries agreed to "democratise" it by giving recipient countries a say in how its money is spent.

The industrial countries were also reluctant to firm up their commitments to the UN target of raising aid to the equivalent of 0.7 per cent of GNP. Only France felt able to do it. Thus, in terms of aid, UNCED must be judged to have failed in its aim of generating major new flows of funds. On the other hand, it reinforced the concept of environmental aid as more rich countries earmarked money specifically for this purpose for the first time.

The bitterness of the wrangling over aid spilled over into other areas of tension between North and South and undoubtedly made them harder to resolve. The most conspicuous was the emotive subject of rain forests.

The UNCED organisers had originally hoped to pull together an international treaty on the conservation of rain forests, reflecting the high level of concern about deforestation in the industrial countries. But this proved impossible. The industrial countries argued that although forests belonged to individual countries, they served the global good by absorbing carbon from the atmosphere, and by preserving plant and animal species. But the Third World countries resented being told by rich countries how to manage their natural resources, particularly ones which played such a major part in their economies. Dr Lim Kent Yaik, Malaysia's minister of primary industries, said: "We feel offended that the whole discussion on the environment in the last few years has been a finger-pointing exercise centred on countries who are commercially exploiting their forest."

With a treaty clearly out of the question, the Summit compromised instead on a Declaration of Principles on Forests, which has no legal force. This was a carefully crafted document which recognised every country's right to manage its own resources, but asserted that forests are "essential to the ecology as a whole". It also requires all signatories to strive for the "greening of the world", placing a responsibility for afforestation on rich as well as poor countries.

The strongest point won by the Third World was the inclusion of a "ban on bans", a reference to the boycotts of tropical hardwoods which have occurred in Europe and the US. But the Third World had to accept a commitment to a stronger agreement on forests some time in the future.

Just as forests had raised the question of how far global interest could limit a country's right to exploit its resources, the Summit's proposed treaty on bio-diversity exposed sensitivities about national rights. This treaty was designed to protect the diversity of the planet's plant and animal life. But the real issue was not so much conservation as commercialisation. Who had the right to exploit these riches, could they be patented, how should the owning nation be recompensed? These were pressing questions for Third World countries since they possess the greatest natural endowments. Mr Marcos Azambuja, the Brazilian ambassador to the conference said: "Suppose someone develops a medicine from a rare plant in the Amazon. Who should have the rights to that?" The Third World essentially got its way with this treaty – so much so that George Bush refused to sign it because he maintained that it would undermine the patent rights acquired at great cost by US companies.

The second and only other treaty agreed in Rio – on climate change – produced less North/South tension. Here, the industrial countries committed themselves to devising ways of reducing their emissions of gases which are harmful to the atmosphere. They also pledged financial aid to the Third World to help them clean up their air – though as has already been mentioned, this was far from generous.

International trade issues cropped up in many of the debates about specific Rio documents. Three in particular worried Third World delegates. One was

protectionism. As the industrialised countries raise their environmental standards through regulation, the likelihood grows that goods produced in poor countries will fail to meet them, and will be excluded. Although no decisions were taken about this in Rio, it was recognised as a problem to be solved by GATT.

Another was the enforced migration – again through regulation – of "dirty" industries from rich to poorer countries. This was denounced as unacceptable. In fact a number of countries, including the US, announced plans to require their industries to comply with US environmental regulations when they set up plants abroad.

A third was the transfer of environmentally friendly technology. There was no doubting the need for this: much of the world's atmospheric problem could be solved if China installed new industrial boilers, for example. And many industrial countries are keen to sell know-how and hardware, notably Japan which sees the environment as a major selling opportunity. But again, the problem was money. The GEF funds will help, but almost certainly not enough.

What all this adds up to is a clear recognition at Rio that economic backwardness damages the environment, that the resources to overcome it must come, at least in part, from the developed world, and that until progress is made, environmentalism will be a low priority in the majority of the world's countries. Much of this was summed up in the Rio Declaration, the over-arching document expressing the spirit of the Rio gathering. Among the 27 principles it endorses is Principle Six which says "The special situation and needs of developing countries, particularly the least developed and those most environmentally vulnerable, shall be given special priority. International actions in the field of environment and development should also address the interest and needs of all countries."

This statement, along with the South's success in resisting a forestry treaty, mark some success by the Third World in establishing its priorities. On the other hand, the industrial countries showed, in their reluctance to make substantial financial commitments, that they have a separate set of priorities in which environmental aid plays only a small part. In the end, therefore, the Third World probably came out of Rio badly, but the final judgment may not be feasible for several years as the results of this unique event trickle slowly through.

Agenda 21

Chapter 1

Preamble

This is an abridged version of Agenda 21. Each programme area comprises four sections: basis for action, objectives, activities and means of implementation. To allow maximum space for factual information the following revisions to the text have been made. Basis for action: listing of programme areas edited. Objectives: full text. Activities: abridged in some chapters to management-related activites. Means of implementation: abridged to financing and cost evaluation. The full text for financing and cost evaluation is carried in chapter 2, page 51. In following sections it has been contracted to a minimum. The unabridged text of Agenda 21 is available from the United Nations.

Humanity stands at a defining moment in history. We are confronted with a perpetuation of disparities between and within nations, a worsening of poverty, hunger, ill health and illiteracy, and the continuing deterioration of the ecosystems on which we depend for our well-being. However, integration of environment and development concerns and greater attention to them will lead to the fulfilment of basic needs, improved living standards for all, better protected and managed ecosystems and a safer, more prosperous future. No nation can achieve this on its own; but together we can – in a global partnership for sustainable development.

This global partnership must build on the premises of General Assembly resolution 44/228 of 22 December 1989, which was adopted when the nations of the world called for the United Nations Conference on Environment and Development, and on the acceptance of the need to take a balanced and integrated approach to environment and development questions.

Agenda 21 addresses the pressing problems of today and also aims at preparing the world for the challenges of the next century. It reflects a global consensus and political commitment at the highest level on development and environment cooperation. Its successful implementation is first and foremost the responsibility of Governments.[1] National strategies, plans, policies and processes are crucial in achieving this. International cooperation should support and supplement such national efforts. In this context, the United Nations system has a key role to play. Other international, regional and subregional organizations are also called upon to contribute to this effort. The broadest public participation and the active involvement of the non-governmental organizations and other groups should also be encouraged.

The developmental and environmental objectives of Agenda 21 will require a substantial flow of new and additional financial resources to developing countries, in order to cover the incremental costs for the actions they have to undertake to deal with global environmental problems and to accelerate sustainable development. Financial resources are also required for strengthening the capacity of international institutions for the implementation of Agenda 21. An indicative order of magnitude assessment of costs is included in each of the programme areas. This assessment will need to be examined and refined by the relevant implementing agencies and organizations.

In the implementation of the relevant programme areas identified in Agenda 21, special attention should be given to the particular circumstances facing the economies in transition. It must also be recognized that these countries are facing unprecedented challenges in transforming their economies, in some cases in the midst of considerable social and political tension.

The programme areas that constitute Agenda 21 are described in terms of the basis for action, objectives, activities and means of implementation. Agenda 21 is a dynamic programme. It will be carried out by the various actors according to the different situations, capacities and priorities of countries and in full respect of all the principles contained in the Rio Declaration on Environment and Development. It could evolve over time in the light of changing needs and circumstances. This process marks the beginning of a new global partnership for sustainable development.

Throughout Agenda 21 the term "environmentally sound" means "environmentally safe and sound", in particular when applied to the terms "energy sources", "energy supplies", "energy systems", or "technology/technologies".

1 When the term Governments is used, it will be deemed to include the European Economic Community within its areas of competence.

Social and Economic Dimensions

Section I

Chapter 2

International cooperation to accelerate sustainable development in developing countries and related domestic policies

In order to meet the challenges of environment and development, States decided to establish a new global partnership. This partnership commits all States to engage in a continuous and constructive dialogue, inspired by the need to achieve a more efficient and equitable world economy, keeping in view the increasing interdependence of the community of nations, and that sustainable development should become a priority item on the agenda of the international community. It is recognized that, for the success of this new partnership, it is important to overcome confrontation and to foster a climate of genuine cooperation and solidarity. It is equally important to strengthen national and international policies and multinational cooperation to adapt to the new realities.

Economic policies of individual countries and international economic relations both have great relevance to sustainable development. The reactivation and acceleration of development requires both a dynamic and a supportive international economic environment and determined policies at the national level. It will be frustrated in the absence of either of these requirements. A supportive external economic environment is crucial. The development process will not gather momentum if the global economy lacks dynamism and stability and is beset with uncertainties. Neither will it gather momentum if the developing countries are weighted down by external indebtedness, if development finance is inadequate, if barriers restrict access to markets and if commodity prices and the terms of trade of developing countries remain depressed. The record of the 1980s was essentially negative on each of these counts and needs to be reversed. The policies and measures needed to create an international environment that is strongly supportive of national development efforts are thus vital. International cooperation in this area should be designed to complement and support – not to diminish or subsume – sound domestic economic policies, in both developed and developing countries, if global progress towards sustainable development is to be achieved.

The international economy should provide a supportive international climate for achieving environment and development goals.

Governments recognize that there is a new global effort to relate the elements of the international economic system and mankind's need for a safe and stable natural environment. Therefore, it is the intent of Governments that consensus-building at the intersection of the environmental and trade and development areas will be ongoing in existing international forums, as well as in the domestic policy of each country.

A Promoting sustainable development through trade

Basis for action An open, equitable, secure, non-discriminatory and predictable multilateral trading system that is consistent with the goals of sustainable development and leads to the optimal distribution of global production in accordance with comparative advantage is of benefit to all trading partners. Moreover, improved market access for developing countries' exports in conjunction with sound macroeconomic and environmental policies would have a positive environmental impact and therefore make an important contribution towards sustainable development.

Experience has shown that sustainable development requires a commitment to sound economic policies and management, an effective and predictable public administration, the integration of environmental concerns into decision-making and progress towards democratic government, in the light of country-specific conditions, which allows for full participation of all parties concerned. These attributes are essential for the fulfilment of the policy directions and objectives listed below.

The commodity sector dominates the economies of many developing countries in terms of production, employment and export earnings. An important feature of the world commodity economy in the 1980s was the prevalence of very low and declining real prices for most commodities in international markets and a resulting substantial contraction in commodity export earnings for many producing countries. The ability of those countries to mobilize, through international trade, the resources needed to finance investments required for sustainable development may be impaired by this development and by tariff and non-tariff impediments, including tariff escalation, limiting their access to export markets. The removal of existing distortions in international trade is essential. In particular, the achievement of this objective requires that there be substantial and progressive reduction in the

Harvesting cocoa in Indonesia. The commodity sector dominates the economies of many developing countries but has suffered from low and declining prices during the 1980s.

support and protection of agriculture – covering internal regimes, market access and export subsidies – as well as of industry and other sectors, in order to avoid inflicting large losses on the more efficient producers, especially in developing countries. Thus, in agriculture, industry and other sectors, there is scope for initiatives aimed at trade liberalization and at policies to make production more responsive to environment and development needs. Trade liberalization should therefore be pursued on a global basis across economic sectors so as to contribute to sustainable development.

The international trading environment has been affected by a number of developments that have created new challenges and opportunities and have made multilateral economic cooperation of even greater importance. World trade has continued to grow faster than world output in recent years. However, the expansion of world trade has been unevenly spread, and only a limited number of developing countries have been capable of achieving appreciable growth in their exports. Protectionist pressures and unilateral policy actions continue to endanger the functioning of an open multilateral trading system, affecting particularly the export interests of developing countries. Economic integration processes have intensified in recent years and should impart dynamism to global trade and enhance the trade and development possibilities for developing countries. In recent years, a growing number of these countries have adopted courageous policy reforms involving ambitious autonomous trade liberalization, while far-reaching reforms and profound restructuring processes are taking place in Central and Eastern European countries, paving the way for their integration into the world economy and the international trading system. Increased attention is being devoted to enhancing the role of enterprises and promoting competitive markets through adoption of competitive policies. The GSP has proved to be a useful trade policy instrument, although its objectives will have to be fulfilled, and trade facilitation strategies relating to electronic data interchange (EDI) have been effective in improving the trading efficiency of the public and private sectors. The interactions between environment policies and trade issues are manifold and have not yet been fully assessed. An early, balanced, comprehensive and successful outcome of the Uruguay Round of multilateral trade negotiations would bring about further liberalization and expansion of world trade, enhance the trade and development possibilities of developing countries and provide greater security and predictability to the international trading system.

Objectives In the years ahead, and taking into account the results of the Uruguay Round of multilateral trade negotiations, Governments should continue to strive to meet the following objectives:

a To promote an open, non-discriminatory and equitable multilateral trading system that will enable all countries – in particular, the developing countries – to improve their economic structures and improve the standard of living of their populations through sustained economic development;

b To improve access to markets for exports of developing countries;

c To improve the functioning of commodity markets and achieve sound, compatible and consistent commodity policies at national and international levels with a view to optimizing the contribution of the commodity sector to sustainable development, taking into account environmental considerations;

d To promote and support policies, domestic and international, that make economic growth and environmental protection mutually supportive.

Activities

A *International and regional cooperation and coordination: Promoting an international trading system that takes account of the needs of developing countries*

Accordingly the international community should:

a Halt and reverse protectionism in order to bring about further liberalization and expansion of world trade, to the benefit of all countries, in particular the developing countries;

b Provide for an equitable, secure, non-discriminatory and predictable international trading system;

c Facilitate, in a timely way, the integration of all countries into the world economy and the international trading system;

d Ensure that environment and trade policies are mutually supportive, with a view to achieving sustainable development;

e Strengthen the international trade policies system through an early, balanced, comprehensive and successful outcome of the Uruguay Round of multilateral trade negotiations.

The international community should aim at finding ways and means of achieving a better functioning and enhanced transparency of commodity markets, greater diversification of the commodity sector in developing economies within a macroeconomic framework that takes into consideration a country's economic struct-ure, resource endowments and market opportunities, and better management of natural resources that takes into account the necessities of sustainable development.

Therefore, all countries should implement previous commitments to halt and reverse protectionism and further expand market access, particularly in areas of interest to developing countries. This improvement of market access will be facilitated by appropriate structural adjustment in developed countries. Developing countries should continue the trade-policy reforms and structural adjustment they have undertaken. It is thus urgent to achieve an improvement in market access conditions for commodities, notably through the progressive removal of barriers that restrict imports, particularly from developing countries, of commodity products in primary and processed forms, as well as the substantial and progressive reduction of types of support that induce uncompetitive production, such as production and export subsidies.

B *Management-related activities: Developing domestic policies that maximize the benefits of trade liberalization for sustainable development*

For developing countries to benefit from the liberalization of trading systems, they should implement the following policies, as appropriate:

a Create a domestic environment supportive of an optimal balance between production for the domestic and export markets and remove biases against exports and discourage inefficient import-substitution;

b Promote the policy framework and the infrastructure required to improve the efficiency of export and import trade as well as the functioning of domestic markets.

The following policies should be adopted by developing countries with respect to commodities consistent with market efficiency:

a Expand processing, distribution and improve marketing practices and the competitiveness of the commodity sector;

b Diversify in order to reduce dependence on commodity exports;

c Reflect efficient and sustainable use of factors of production in the formation of commodity prices, including the reflection of environmental, social and resources costs.

Financing and cost evaluation The Conference secretariat has estimated the average total annual cost (1993-2000) of implementing the activities in this programme area to be about $8.8 billion from the international community on grant or concessional terms. These are indicative and order of magnitude estimates only and have not been reviewed by governments. Actual costs and financial terms, including any that are non-concessional, will depend upon, *inter alia*, the specific strategies and programmes governments decide upon for implementation.

B Making trade and environment mutually supportive

Basis for action. Environment and trade policies should be mutually supportive. An open, multilateral trading system makes possible a more efficient allocation and use of resources and thereby contributes to an increase in production and incomes and to lessening demands on the environment. It thus provides additional resources needed for economic growth and development and improved environmental protection. A sound environment, on the other hand, provides the ecological and other resources needed to sustain growth and underpin a continuing expansion of trade. An open, multilateral trading system, supported by the adoption of sound environmental policies, would have a positive impact on the environment and contribute to sustainable development.

International cooperation in the environmental field is growing, and in a number of cases trade provisions in multilateral environment agreements have played a role in tackling global environmental challenges. Trade measures have thus been used in certain specific instances, where considered necessary, to enhance the effectiveness of environmental regulations for the protection of the environment. Such regulations should address the root causes of environmental degradation so as not to result in unjustified restrictions on trade. The challenge is to ensure that trade and environment policies are consistent and reinforce the process of sustainable development. However, account should be taken of the fact that environmental standards valid for developed countries may have unwarranted social and economic costs in developing countries.

Objectives. Governments should strive to meet the following objectives, through relevant multilateral forums, including GATT, UNCTD and other international organizations:

a To make international trade and environment policies mutually supportive in favour of sustainable development;

b To clarify the role of GATT, UNCTD and other international organizations in dealing with trade and environment-related issues, including, where relevant, conciliation procedure and dispute settlement;

c To encourage international productivity and competitiveness and encourage a constructive role on the part of industry in dealing with environment and development issues.

Activities *Developing an environment/trade and development agenda*

Governments should encourage GATT, UNCTD and other relevant international and regional economic institutions to examine, in accordance with their respective mandates and competences, the following propositions and principles:

a Elaborate adequate studies for the better understanding of the relationship between trade and environ-

Expansion of world trade has been unevenly spread with only a limited number of developing countries achieving an appreciable growth in exports.

The Rio message was of solidarity pronouncing the equality and partnership of all people, their common responsibility for one world. Industrial countries bear a special responsibility. Germany has set a goal to reduce CO_2 emissions by 23-30 per cent by the year 2005. In order to formulate more far-reaching global measures the signatories to the Climate Convention have been invited to Germany for the first Signatory States Conference. The reconstruction of eastern Germany and the rehabilitation of the former communist countries in Europe make great demands. But we are strongly committed to the developing countries and to breaking the vicious circle of poverty, population growth and environmental destruction. A dynamic process was begun in Rio.
Dr Helmut Kohl
Chancellor
Federal Republic of Germany

ment for the promotion of sustainable development;
b Promote a dialogue between trade, development and environment communities;
c In those cases when trade measures related to environment are used, ensure transparency and compatibility with international obligations;
d Deal with the root causes of environment and development problems in a manner that avoids the adoption of environmental measures resulting in unjustified restrictions on trade;
e Seek to avoid the use of trade restrictions or distortions as a means to offset differences in cost arising from differences in environmental standards and regulations, since their application could lead to trade distortions and increase protectionist tendencies;
f Ensure that environment-related regulations or standards, including those related to health and safety standards, do not constitute a means of arbitrary or unjustifiable discrimination or a disguised restriction on trade;
g Ensure that special factors affecting environment and trade policies in the developing countries are borne in mind in the application of environmental standards, as well as in the use of any trade measures. It is worth noting that standards that are valid in the most advanced countries may be inappropriate and of unwarranted social cost for the developing countries;
h Encourage participation of developing countries in multilateral agreements through such mechanisms as special transitional rules;
i Avoid unilateral actions to deal with environmental challenges outside the jurisdiction of the importing country. Environmental measures addressing transborder or global environmental problems should, as far as possible, be based on an international consensus. Domestic measures targeted to achieve certain environmental objectives may need trade measures to render them effective. Should trade policy measures be found necessary for the enforcement of environmental policies, certain principles and rules should apply. These could include, *inter alia*, the principle of non-discrimination; the principle that the trade measure chosen should be the least trade-restrictive necessary to achieve the objectives; an obligation to ensure transparency in the use of trade measures related to the environment and to provide adequate notification of national regulations; and the need to give consideration to the special conditions and developmental requirements of developing countries as they move towards internationally agreed environmental objectives;
j Develop more precision, where necessary, and clarify the relationship between GATT provisions and some of the multilateral measures adopted in the environment area;
k Ensure public input in the formation, negotiation and implementation of trade policies as a means of fostering increased transparency in the light of country-specific conditions;
l Ensure that environmental policies provide the appropriate legal and institutional framework to respond to new needs for the protection of the environment that may result from changes in production and trade specialization.

C Providing adequate financial resources to developing countries

Basis for action Investment is critical to the ability of developing countries to achieve needed economic growth to improve the welfare of their populations and to meet their basic needs in a sustainable manner, all without deteriorating or depleting the resource base that underpins development. Sustainable development requires increased investment, for which domestic and external financial resources are needed. Foreign private investment and the return of flight capital, which depend on a healthy investment climate, are an important source of financial resources. Many developing countries have experienced a decade-long situation of negative net transfer of financial resources, during which their financial receipts were exceeded by payments they had to make, in particular for debt-servicing. As a result, domestically mobilized resources had to be transferred abroad instead of being invested locally in order to promote sustainable economic development.

For many developing countries, the reactivation of development will not take place without an early and durable solution to the problems of external indebtedness, taking into account the fact that, for many developing countries, external debt burdens are a significant problem. The burden of debt-service payments on those countries has imposed severe constraints on their ability to accelerate growth and eradicate poverty and has led to a contraction in imports, investment and consumption. External indebtedness has emerged as a main factor in the economic stalemate in the developing countries. Continued vigorous implementation of the evolving international debt strategy is aimed at restoring debtor countries' external financial viability, and the resumption of their growth and development would assist in achieving sustainable growth and development. In this context, additional financial resources in favour of developing countries and the efficient utilization of such resources are essential.

Objectives The specific requirements for the implementation of the sectoral and cross-sectoral programmes included in Agenda 21 are dealt with in the relevant programme areas and in Chapter 33.

Activities
A *Meeting international targets of official development assistance funding*
As discussed in Chapter 33, new and additional resources should be provided to support Agenda 21 programmes.
B *Addressing the debt issue*
In regard to the external debt incurred with commercial banks, the progress being made under the strengthened debt strategy is recognized and a more rapid implementation of this strategy is encouraged. Some countries have already benefited from the combination of sound adjustment policies and commercial bank debt reduction or equivalent measures. The international community encourages:
a Other countries with heavy debts to banks to negotiate similar commercial bank debt reduction with their creditors;
b The parties to such a negotiation to take due account of both the medium-term debt reduction and new money requirements of the debtor country;
c Multilateral institutions actively engaged in the strengthened international debt strategy to continue to support debt-reduction packages related to commercial bank debt with a view to ensuring that the magnitude of such financing is consonant with the evolving debt strategy;
d Creditor banks to participate in debt and debt-service reduction;
e Strengthened policies to attract direct investment, avoid unsustainable levels of debt and foster the return of flight capital.

With regard to debt owed to official bilateral creditors, the recent measures taken by the Paris Club with regard to more generous terms of relief to the poorest most indebted countries are welcomed. Ongoing efforts to implement these "Trinidad terms" measures in a manner commensurate with the

Section I

Tin and iron ore mining in Brazil. Above: at Bom Futuro of the 2,500 prospectors who mine tin, 80 per cent of them suffer from malaria. Below: the Carajas mountains which contain not only the largest iron ore deposits in the world but the purest.

payments capacity of those countries and in a way that gives additional support to their economic reform efforts are welcomed. The substantial bilateral debt reduction undertaken by some creditor countries is also welcomed, and others which are in a position to do so are encouraged to take similar action.

The actions of low-income countries with substantial debt burdens which continue, at great cost, to service their debt and safeguard their creditworthiness are commended. Particular attention should be paid to their resource needs. Other debt-distressed developing countries which are making great efforts to continue to service their debt and meet their external financial obligations also deserve due attention.

In connection with multilateral debt, it is urged that serious attention be given to continuing to work towards growth-oriented solutions to the problem of developing countries with serious debt-servicing problems, including those whose debt is mainly to official creditors or to multilateral financial institutions. Particularly in the case of low-income countries in the process of economic reform, the support of the multilateral financial institutions in the form of new disbursements and the use of their concessional funds is welcomed. The use of support groups should be continued in providing resources to clear arrears of countries embarking upon vigorous economic reform programmes supported by IMF and the World Bank. Measures by the multilateral financial institutions such as the refinancing of interest on non-concessional loans with IDA reflows – "fifth dimension" – are noted with appreciation.

Financing and cost evaluation See Chapter 33.

D Encouraging economic policies conducive to sustainable development

Basis for action The unfavourable external environment facing developing countries makes domestic resource mobilization and efficient allocation and utilization of domestically mobilized resources all the more important for the promotion of sustainable development. In a number of countries, policies are necessary to correct misdirected public spending, large budget deficits and other macroeconomic imbalances, restrictive policies and distortions in the areas of exchange rates, investment and finance, and obstacles to entrepreneurship. In developed countries, continuing policy reform and adjustment, including appropriate savings rates, would help generate resources to support the transition to sustainable development both domestically and in developing countries.

Good management that fosters the association of effective, efficient, honest, equitable and accountable public administration with individual rights and opportunities is an essential element for sustainable, broadly based development and sound economic performance at all development levels. All countries should increase their efforts to eradicate mismanagement of public and private affairs, including corruption, taking into account the factors responsible for, and agents involved in, this phenomenon. Many indebted developing countries are undergoing structural adjustment programmes relating to debt rescheduling or new loans. While such programmes are necessary for improving the balance in fiscal budgets and balance-of-payments accounts, in some cases they have resulted in adverse social and environmental effects, such as cuts in allocations for health care, education and environmental protection. It is important to ensure that structural adjustment programmes do not have negative impacts on the environment and social development so that such programmes can be more in line with the objectives of sustainable development.

Objectives It is necessary to establish, in the light of the country-specific conditions, economic policy reforms that promote the efficient planning and utilization of resources for sustainable development through sound economic and social policies, foster entrepreneurship and the incorporation of social and environmental costs in resource pricing, and remove sources of distortion in the area of trade and investment.

Management-related activities *Promoting sound economic policies*

A The industrialized countries and other countries in a position to do so should strengthen their efforts:

a To encourage a stable and predictable international economic environment, particularly with regard to monetary stability, real rates of interest and fluctuations in key exchange rates;

b To stimulate savings and reduce fiscal deficits;

c To ensure that the processes of policy coordination take into account the interests and concerns of the developing countries, including the need to promote positive action to support the efforts of the least developed countries to halt their marginalization in the world economy;

d To undertake appropriate national macroeconomic and structural policies aimed at promoting non-inflationary growth, narrowing their major external imbalances and increasing the adjustment capacity of their economies.

B Developing countries should consider strengthening their efforts to implement sound economic policies:

a That maintain the monetary and fiscal discipline required to promote price stability and external balance;

b That result in realistic exchange rates;

c That raise domestic savings and investment, as well as improve returns to investment.

More specifically, all countries should develop policies that improve efficiency in the allocation of resources and take full advantage of the opportunities offered by the changing global economic environment. In particular, wherever appropriate, and taking into account national strategies and objectives, countries should:

i Remove the barriers to progress caused by bureaucratic inefficiencies, administrative strains, unnecessary controls and the neglect of market conditions;

Small scale enterprises such as this coffee business in Cameroon can assist indigenous populations and local communities to contribute to the attainment of sustainable development.

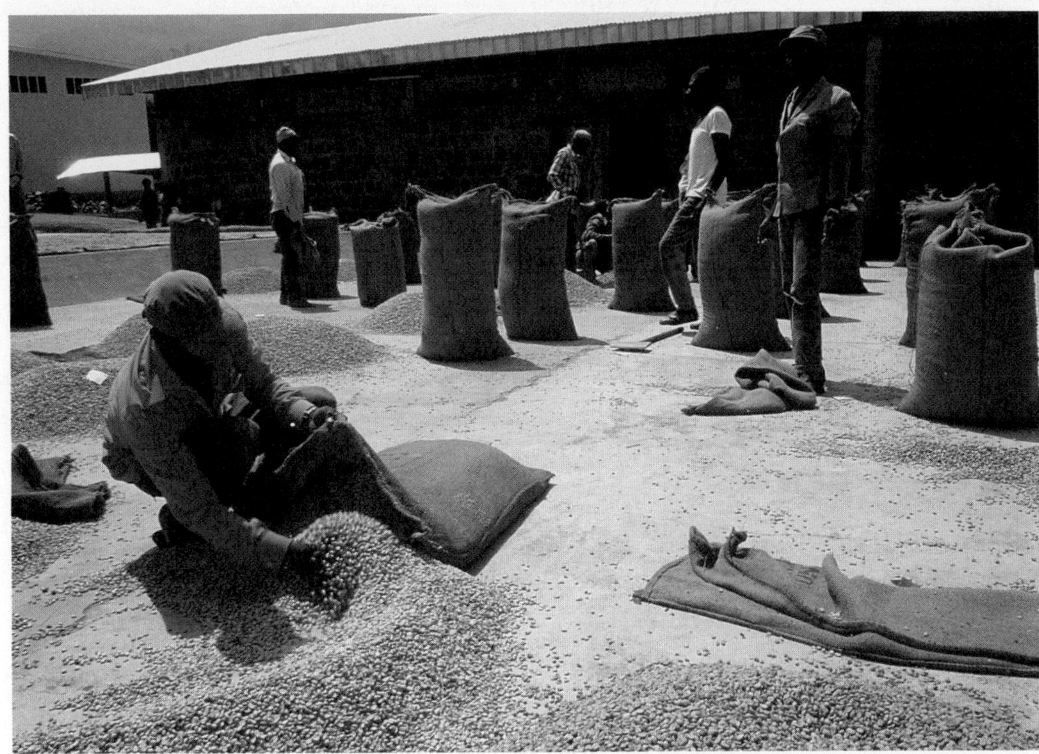

AN ICBP PROJECT

ii Promote transparency in administration and decision-making;
iii Encourage the private sector and foster entrepreneurship by improving institutional facilities for enterprise creation and market entry. The essential objective would be to simplify or remove the restrictions, regulations and formalities that make it more complicated, costly and time-consuming to set up and operate enterprises in many developing countries;
iv Promote and support the investment and infrastructure required for sustainable economic growth and diversification on an environmentally sound and sustainable basis;
v Provide scope for appropriate economic instruments, including market mechanisms, in harmony with the objectives of sustainable development and fulfilment of basic needs;
vi Promote the operation of effective tax systems and financial sectors;
vii Provide opportunities for small-scale enterprises, both farm and non-farm, and for the indigenous population and local communities to contribute fully to the attainment of sustainable development;
viii Remove biases against exports and in favour of inefficient import substitution and establish policies that allow them to benefit fully from the flows of foreign investment, within the framework of national, social, economic and developmental goals;
ix Promote the creation of a domestic economic environment supportive of an optimal balance between production for the domestic and export markets.

Financing and cost evaluation $50 million from the international community on grant or concessional terms.

Chapter 3

Combating poverty

Enabling the poor to achieve sustainable livelihoods

Basis for action. Poverty is a complex multidimensional problem with origins in both the national and international domains. No uniform solution can be found for global application. Rather, country-specific programmes to tackle poverty and international efforts supporting national efforts, as well as the parallel process of creating a supportive international environment, are crucial for a solution to this problem. The eradication of poverty and hunger, greater equity in income distribution and human resource development remain major challenges everywhere. The struggle against poverty is the shared responsibility of all countries.

While managing resources sustainably, an environmental policy that focuses mainly on the conservation and protection of resources must take due account of those who depend on the resources for their livelihoods. Otherwise it could have an adverse impact both on poverty and on chances for long-term success in resource and environmental conservation. Equally, a development policy that focuses mainly on increasing the production of goods without addressing the sustainability of the resources on which production is based will sooner or later run into declining productivity, which could also have an adverse impact on poverty. A specific anti-poverty strategy is therefore one of the basic conditions for ensuring sustainable development. An effective strategy for tackling the problems of poverty, development and environment simultaneously should begin by focusing on resources, production and people and should cover demographic issues, enhanced health care and education, the rights of women, the role of youth and of indigenous people and local communities and a democratic participation process in association with improved governance.

Integral to such action is, together with international support, the promotion of economic growth in developing countries that is both sustained and sustainable and direct action in eradicating poverty by strengthening employment and income-generating programmes.

Objectives The long-term objective of enabling all people to achieve sustainable livelihoods should provide an integrating factor that allows policies to address issues of development, sustainable resource management and poverty eradication simultaneously. The objectives of this programme area are:
a To provide all persons urgently with the opportunity to earn a sustainable livelihood;
b To implement policies and strategies that promote adequate levels of funding and focus on integrated

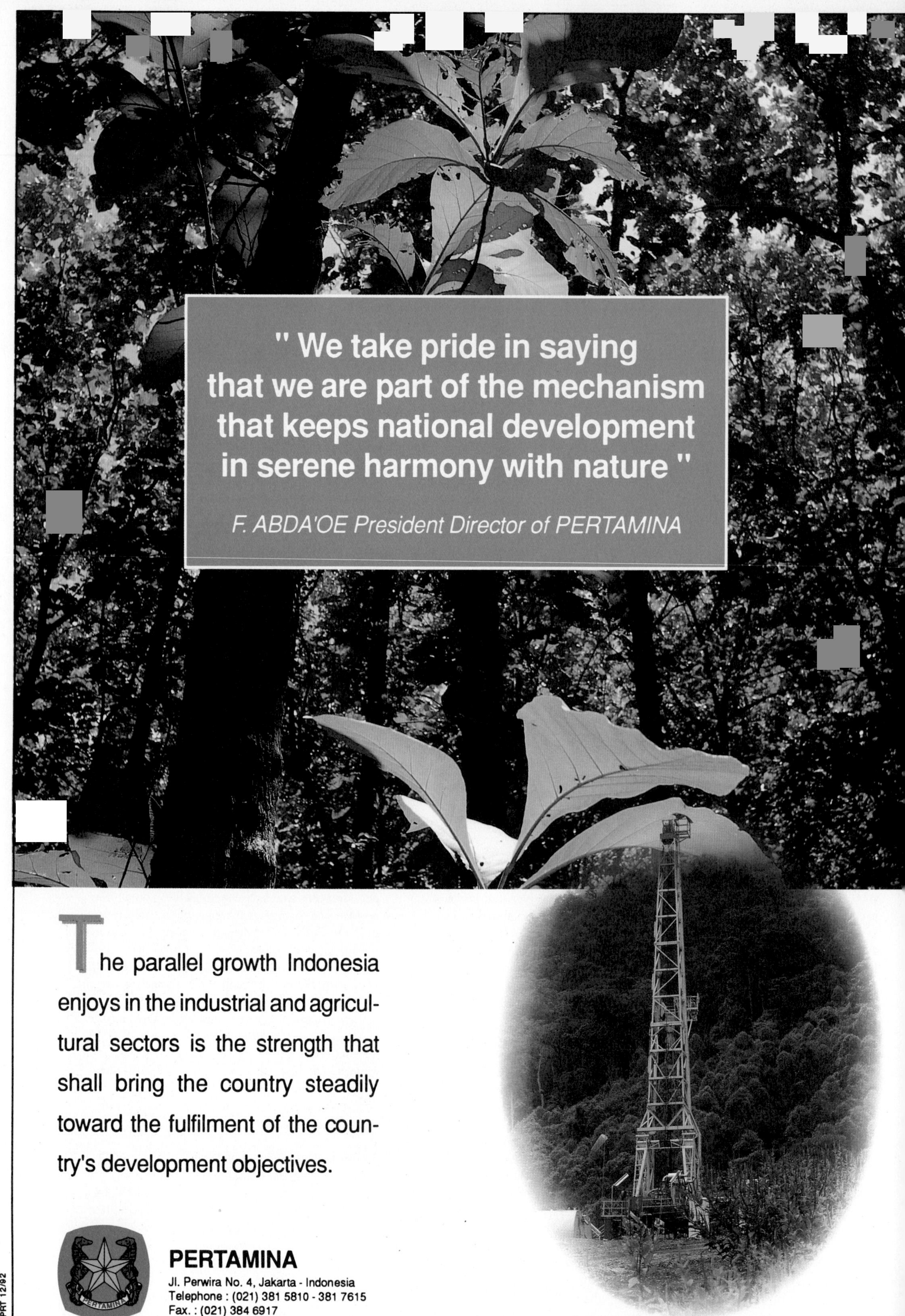
" We take pride in saying
that we are part of the mechanism
that keeps national development
in serene harmony with nature "
F. ABDA'OE President Director of PERTAMINA
The parallel growth Indonesia enjoys in the industrial and agricultural sectors is the strength that shall bring the country steadily toward the fulfilment of the country's development objectives.
PERTAMINA
PERTAMINA
Jl. Perwira No. 4, Jakarta - Indonesia
Telephone : (021) 381 5810 - 381 7615
Fax. : (021) 384 6917
ADP/PRT 12/92

human development policies, including income generation, increased local control of resources, local institution-strengthening and capacity-building and greater involvement of non-governmental organizations and local levels of government as delivery mechanisms;

c To develop for all poverty-stricken areas integrated strategies and programmes of sound and sustainable management of the environment, resource mobilization, poverty eradication and alleviation, employment and income generation;

d To create a focus in national development plans and budgets on investment in human capital, with special policies and programmes directed at rural areas, the urban poor, women and children.

Activities Activities that will contribute to the integrated promotion of sustainable livelihoods and environmental protection cover a variety of sectoral interventions involving a range of actors, from local to global, and are essential at every level, especially the community and local levels. Enabling actions will be necessary at the national and international levels, taking full account of regional and subregional conditions to support a locally driven and country-specific approach. In general design, the programmes should:

a Focus on the empowerment of local and community groups through the principle of delegating authority, accountability and resources to the most appropriate level to ensure that the programme will be geographically and ecologically specific;

b Contain immediate measures to enable those groups to alleviate poverty and to develop sustainability;

c Contain a long-term strategy aimed at establishing the best possible conditions for sustainable local, regional and national development that would eliminate poverty and reduce the inequalities between various population groups. It should assist the most disadvantaged groups – in particular, women, children and youth within those groups – and refugees. The groups will include poor smallholders, pastoralists, artisans, fishing communities, landless people, indigenous communities, migrants and the urban informal sector.

The focus here is on specific cross-cutting measures – in particular, in the areas of basic education, primary/maternal health care, and the advancement of women.

A *Empowering communities*

Sustainable development must be achieved at every level of society. Peoples' organizations, women's groups and non-governmental organizations are important sources of innovation and action at the local level and have a strong interest and proven ability to promote sustainable livelihoods. Governments, in cooperation with appropriate international and non-governmental organizations, should support a community-driven approach to sustainability, which would include, *inter alia*:

a Empowering women through full participation in decision-making;

b Respecting the cultural integrity and the rights of indigenous people and their communities;

c Promoting or establishing grass-roots mechanisms to allow for the sharing of experience and knowledge between communities;

d Giving communities a large measure of participation in the sustainable management and protection of the local natural resources in order to enhance their productive capacity;

e Establishing a network of community-based learning centres for capacity-building and sustainable development.

B *Management-related activities*

Governments, with the assistance of and in cooperation with appropriate international, non-governmental and local community organizations, should establish measures that will directly or indirectly:

a Generate remunerative employment and productive occupational opportunities compatible with country-specific factor endowments, on a scale sufficient to take care of prospective increases in the labour force and to cover backlogs;

b With international support, where necessary, develop adequate infrastructure, marketing systems, technology systems, credit systems and the like and the human resources needed to support the above actions and to achieve a widening of options for resource-poor people. High priority should be given to basic education and professional training;

c Provide substantial increases in economically efficient resource productivity and measures to ensure that the local population benefits in adequate measure from resource use;

d Empower community organizations and people to enable them to achieve sustainable livelihoods;

Section I

AN ICBP PROJECT

Mount Oku, Cameroon. Local villagers have formed a fire patrol to combat forest fires. Empowering communities allows them to participate in the management and protection of their local natural resources.

Cameroon. Women and children working with plants in a local tree nursery project. Local organisations and women's groups have a strong local interest and a proven ability to promote sustainable livelihoods.

Section I

e Set up an effective primary health care and maternal health care system accessible to all;
f Consider strengthening/developing legal frameworks for land management, access to land resources and land ownership – in particular, for women – and for the protection of tenants;
g Rehabilitate degraded resources, to the extent practicable, and introduce policy measures to promote sustainable use of resources for basic human needs;
h Establish new community-based mechanisms and strengthen existing mechanisms to enable communities to gain sustained access to resources needed by the poor to overcome their poverty;
i Implement mechanisms for popular participation – particularly by poor people, especially women – in local community groups, to promote sustainable development;
j Implement, as a matter of urgency, in accordance with country-specific conditions and legal systems, measures to ensure that women and men have the same right to decide freely and responsibly on the number and spacing of their children and have access to the information, education and means, as appropriate, to enable them to exercise this right in keeping with their freedom, dignity and personally held values, taking into account ethical and cultural considerations. Governments should take active steps to implement programmes to establish and strengthen preventive and curative health facilities, which include women-centred, women-managed, safe and effective reproductive health care and affordable, accessible services, as appropriate, for the responsible planning of family size, in keeping with freedom, dignity and personally held values, taking into account ethical and cultural considerations. Programmes should focus on providing comprehensive health care, including pre-natal care, education and information on health and responsible parenthood and should provide the opportunity for all women to breast-feed fully, at least during the first four months post-partum. Programmes should fully support women's productive and reproductive roles and well-being, with special attention to the need for providing equal and improved health care for all children and the need to reduce the risk of maternal and child mortality and sickness;
k Adopt integrated policies aiming at sustainability in

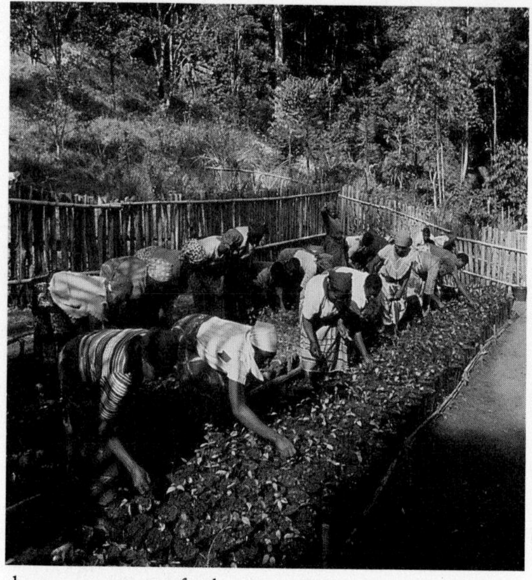
AN ICBP PROJECT

the management of urban centres;
l Undertake activities aimed at the promotion of food security and, where appropriate, food self-sufficiency within the context of sustainable agriculture;
m Support research on and integration of traditional methods of production that have been shown to be environmentally sustainable;
n Actively seek to recognize and integrate informal-sector activities into the economy by removing regulations and hindrances that discriminate against activities in those sectors;
o Consider making available lines of credit and other facilities for the informal sector and improved access to land for the landless poor so that they can acquire the means of production and reliable access to natural resources. In many instances special considerations for women are required. Strict feasibility appraisals are needed for borrowers to avoid debt crises;
p Provide the poor with access to fresh water and sanitation;
q Provide the poor with access to primary education.

Financing and cost evaluation \$30 billion including about \$15 billion from the international community on grant or concessional terms.

Chapter 4

Changing consumption patterns

Since the issue of changing consumption patterns is very broad, it is addressed in several parts of Agenda 21, notably those dealing with energy, transportation and wastes, and in the chapters on economic instruments and the transfer of technology. The present chapter should also be read in conjunction with chapter 5.

A Focusing on unsustainable patterns of production and consumption

Basis for action. Poverty and environmental degradation are closely interrelated. While poverty results in certain kinds of environmental stress, the major cause of the continued deterioration of the global environment is the unsustainable pattern of consumption and production, particularly in industrialized countries, which is a matter of grave concern, aggravating poverty and imbalances.

Measures to be undertaken at the international level for the protection and enhancement of the environment must take fully into account the current imbalances in the global patterns of consumption and production.

Special attention should be paid to the demand for natural resources generated by unsustainable consumption and to the efficient use of those resources consistent with the goal of minimizing depletion and reducing pollution.

Although consumption patterns are very high in certain parts of the world, the basic consumer needs of a large section of humanity are not being met. This results in excessive demands and unsustainable lifestyles among the richer segments, which place immense stress on the environment. The poorer segments, meanwhile, are unable to meet food, health care, shelter and educational needs. Changing consumption patterns will require a multipronged strategy focusing on demand, meeting the basic needs of the poor, and reducing wastage and the use of finite resources in the production process.

Growing recognition of the importance of addressing consumption has also not yet been matched by an understanding of its implications. Some economists are questioning traditional concepts of economic growth and underlining the importance of pursuing economic objectives that take account of the full value of natural resource capital. More needs to be known about the role of consumption in relation to economic growth and population dynamics in order to formulate coherent international and national policies.

Objectives

a To promote patterns of consumption and production that reduce environmental stress and will meet the basic needs of humanity;

b To develop a better understanding of the role of consumption and how to bring about more sustainable consumption patterns.

Management-related activities *Adopting an international approach to achieving sustainable consumption patterns*

In principle, countries should be guided by the following basic objectives in their efforts to address consumption and lifestyles in the context of environment and development:

a All countries should strive to promote sustainable consumption patterns;

b Developed countries should take the lead in achieving sustainable consumption patterns;

c Developing countries should seek to achieve sustainable consumption patterns in their development process, guaranteeing the provision of basic needs for the poor, while avoiding those unsustainable patterns, particularly in industrialized countries, generally recognized as unduly hazardous to the environment, inefficient and wasteful, in their development processes. This requires enhanced technological and other assistance from industrialized countries.

In the follow-up of the implementation of Agenda 21 the review of progress made in achieving sustainable consumption patterns should be given high priority.

Financing and cost evaluation The Conference secretariat has estimated that implementation of this programme is not likely to require significant new financial resources.

B Developing national policies and strategies to encourage changes in unsustainable consumption patterns

Basis for action Achieving the goals of environmental quality and sustainable development will require efficiency in production and changes in consumption patterns in order to emphasize optimization of resource use and minimization of waste. In many instances, this will require reorientation of existing production and consumption patterns that have developed in industrial societies and are in turn emulated in much of the world.

Progress can be made by strengthening positive trends and directions that are emerging, as part of a process aimed at achieving significant changes in the consumption patterns of industries, Governments, households and individuals.

Objectives In the years ahead, Governments, working with appropriate organizations, should strive to meet the following broad objectives:

a To promote efficiency in production processes and reduce wasteful consumption in the process of economic growth, taking into account the development needs of developing countries;

b To develop a domestic policy framework that will encourage a shift to more sustainable patterns of production and consumption;

c To reinforce both values that encourage sustainable production and consumption patterns and policies that encourage the transfer of environmentally sound technologies to developing countries.

Activities

A *Encouraging greater efficiency in the use of energy and resources*

Reducing the amount of energy and materials used per unit in the production of goods and services can contribute both to the alleviation of environmental stress and to greater economic and industrial productivity and competitiveness. Governments, in cooperation with industry, should therefore intensify efforts to use energy and resources in an economically efficient and environmentally sound manner by:

a Encouraging the dissemination of existing environmentally sound technologies;

b Promoting research and development in environmentally sound technologies;

c Assisting developing countries to use these technologies efficiently and to develop technologies suited to their particular circumstances;

d Encouraging the environmentally sound use of new

Harvest time in Perth. Each pound of bread produced in Australia costs the loss of seven pounds of topsoil forever. Soil is now less workable with low water retention,a decline in organic content, salinization and soil erosion - all direct results of deforestation.

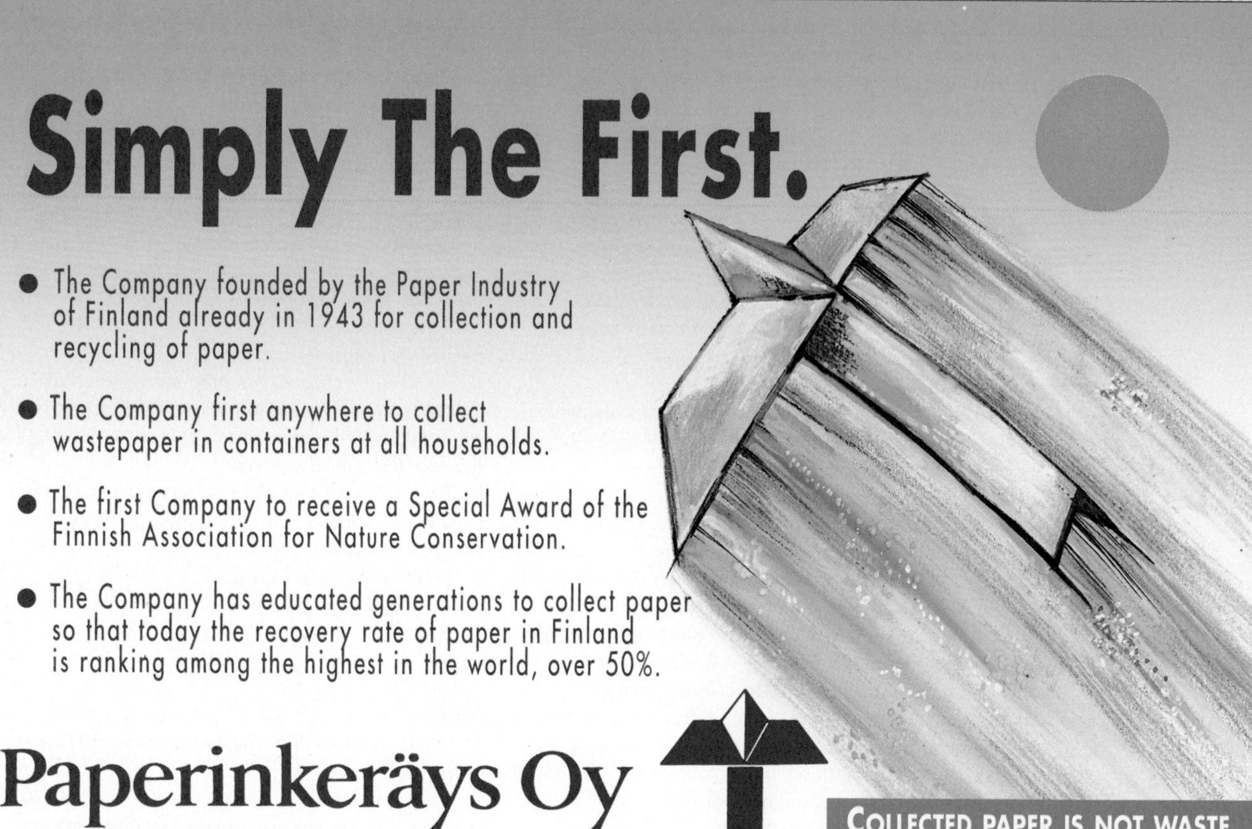
Simply The First.
The Company founded by the Paper Industry of Finland already in 1943 for collection and recycling of paper.
The Company first anywhere to collect wastepaper in containers at all households.
The first Company to receive a Special Award of the Finnish Association for Nature Conservation.
The Company has educated generations to collect paper so that today the recovery rate of paper in Finland is ranking among the highest in the world, over 50%.
Paperinkeräys Oy
The Paper Industry owned National Wastepaper Company of Finland.
A pioneer in Recycling of Paper.
COLLECTED PAPER IS NOT WASTE,
BUT VALUABLE RAW MATERIAL.

Aluminium is easily recycled without losing its inherent properties. Recycling saves 95 per cent of the energy required to produce new aluminium from bauxite. It is also a source of income for groups and individuals who collect the empty containers.

and renewable sources of energy;

e Encouraging the environmentally sound and sustainable use of renewable natural resources.

B *Minimizing the generation of wastes*

At the same time, society needs to develop effective ways of dealing with the problem of disposing of mounting levels of waste products and materials. Governments, together with industry, households and the public, should make a concerted effort to reduce the generation of wastes and waste products by:

a Encouraging recycling in industrial processes and at the consumed level;

b Reducing wasteful packaging of products;

c Encouraging the introduction of more environmentally sound products.

C *Assisting individuals and households to make environmentally sound purchasing decisions*

The recent emergence in many countries of a more environmentally conscious consumer public, combined with increased interest on the part of some industries in providing environmentally sound consumer products, is a significant development that should be encouraged. Governments and international organizations, together with the private sector, should develop criteria and methodologies for the assessment of environmental impacts and resource requirements throughout the full life cycle of products and processes. Results of those assessments should be transformed into clear indicators in order to inform consumers and decision makers.

Governments, in cooperation with industry and other relevant groups, should encourage expansion of environmental labelling and other environmentally related product information programmes designed to assist consumers to make informed choices.

They should also encourage the emergence of an informed consumer public and assist individuals and households to make environmentally informed choices by:

a Providing information on the consequences of consumption choices and behaviour so as to encourage demand for environmentally sound products and use of products;

b Making consumers aware of the health and environmental impact of products, through such means as consumer legislation and environmental labelling;

c Encouraging specific consumer-oriented programmes, such as recycling and deposit/refund systems.

D *Exercising leadership through government purchasing*

Governments themselves also play a role in consumption, particularly in countries where the public sector plays a large role in the economy and can have a considerable influence on both corporate decisions and public perceptions. They should therefore review the purchasing policies of their agencies and departments so that they may improve, where possible, the environmental content of government procurement policies, without prejudice to international trade principles.

E *Moving towards environmentally sound pricing*

Without the stimulus of prices and market signals that make clear to producers and consumers the environmental costs of the consumption of energy, materials and natural resources and the generation of wastes, significant changes in consumption and production patterns seem unlikely to occur in the near future.

Some progress has begun in the use of appropriate economic instruments to influence consumer behaviour. These instruments include environmental charges and taxes, deposit/refund systems, etc. This process should be encouraged in the light of country-specific conditions.

F *Reinforcing values that support sustainable consumption*

Governments and private-sector organizations should promote more positive attitudes towards sustainable consumption through education, public awareness programmes and other means, such as positive advertising of products and services that utilize environmentally sound technologies or encourage sustainable production and consumption patterns. In the review of the implementation of Agenda 21, an assessment of the progress achieved in developing these national policies and strategies should be given due consideration.

Section I

Chapter 5

Demographic dynamics and sustainability

A Developing and disseminating knowledge concerning the links between demographic trends and factors and sustainable development

Basis for action Demographic trends and factors and sustainable development have a synergistic relationship.

The growth of world population and production combined with unsustainable consumption patterns places increasingly severe stress on the life-supporting capacities of our planet. These interactive processes affect the use of land, water, air, energy and other resources. Rapidly growing cities, unless well-managed, face major environmental problems. The increase in both the number and size of cities calls for greater attention to issues of local government and municipal management.

The human dimensions are key elements to consider in this intricate set of relationships and they should be adequately taken into consideration in comprehensive policies for sustainable development. Such policies should address the linkages of demographic trends and factors, resource use, appropriate technology dissemination, and development. Population policy should also recognize the role played by human beings in environ-

The Regency Press Corporation

The Regency Press Corporation is an exclusive publishing company specialising in commemorative and special event publications.

Based in London, The Regency Press Corporation offers a complete publishing service from concept to publication. Projects are individually tailored to create a unique publication with no financial outlay on the part of the client.

From start to finish quality is the key. Experienced staff conceptualise the project through close client liaison; top designers create the individual look necessary for each publication, and experienced editorial staff monitor the project through to production. Only the very best quality in paper, print and production facilities is used. Specialised staff market and distribute the publication worldwide through carefully sourced and researched mailing lists, often individually compiled, tailored to suit the individual needs of the client and the publication.

The Regency Press Corporation offers many years of experience in publishing and marketing. The maximum amount of time and effort is invested in researching, planning and targeting advertising sales to produce the most complementary publicity within each publication. Profits from copy sales are made available to the client either for their own use or to be donated to an organisation or charity of their choice.

For further information on how The Regency Press Corporation can help you with your specialised publication needs please contact:
The Regency Press Corporation
Gordon House
6 Lissenden Gardens
London NW5 1LX
Telephone: (71) 284 4858
Facsimile: (71) 267 5505

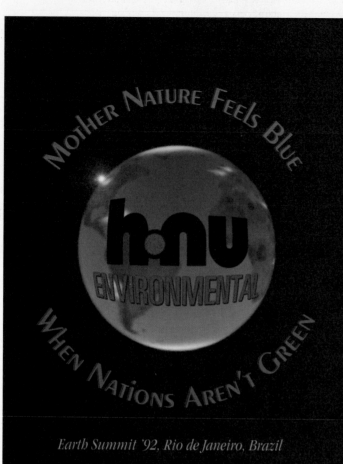

mental and development concerns. There is a need to increase awareness of this issue among decision makers at all levels and to provide both better information on which to base national and international policies and a framework against which to interpret this information.

There is a need to develop strategies to mitigate both the adverse impact on the environment of human activities and the adverse impact of environmental change on human populations. The world's population is expected to exceed 8 billion by the year 2020. Sixty percent of the world's population already live in coastal areas, while 65 per cent of cities with populations above 2.5 million are located along the world coasts; several of them are already at or below the present sea level.

Objectives The following objectives should be achieved as soon as practicable:

a To incorporate demographic trends and factors in the global analysis of environment and development issues;

b To develop a better understanding of the relationships among demographic dynamics, technology, cultural behaviour, natural resources and life support systems;

c To assess human vulnerability in ecologically sensitive areas and centres of population to determine the priorities for action at all levels, taking full account of community defined needs.

Activities *Research on the interaction between demographic trends and factors and sustainable development*

Relevant international, regional and national institutions should consider undertaking the following activities:

a Identifying the interactions between demographic processes, natural resources and life support systems, bearing in mind regional and subregional variations deriving from, *inter alia*, different levels of development;

b Integrating demographic trends and factors into the ongoing study of environmental change, using the expertise of international, regional and national research networks and of local communities, first, to study the human dimensions of environmental change and, second, to identify vulnerable areas;

c Identifying priority areas for action and developing strategies and programmes to mitigate the adverse impact of environmental change on human populations, and vice versa.

Financing and cost evaluation $10 million from the international community on grant or concessional terms.

B Formulating integrated national policies for environment and development, taking into account demographic trends and factors

Basis for action Existing plans for sustainable development have generally recognized demographic trends and factors as elements that have a critical influence on consumption patterns, production, lifestyles and long-term sustainability. But in future, more attention will have to be given to these issues in general policy formulation and the design of development plans. To do this, all countries will have to improve their own capacities to assess the environment and development implications of their demographic trends and factors. They will also need to formulate and implement policies and action programmes where appropriate. Policies should be designed to address the consequences of population growth built into population momentum, while at the same time incorporating measures to bring about demographic transition. They should combine environmental concerns and population issues within a holistic view of development whose primary goals include the alleviation of poverty; secure livelihoods; good health; quality of life; improvement of the status and income of women and their access to schooling and professional training, as well as fulfilment of their personal aspirations; and empowerment of individuals and communities. Recognizing that large increases in the size and number of cities will occur in developing countries under any likely population scenario, greater attention should be given to preparing for the needs, in particular of women and children, for improved municipal management and local government.

Objective Full integration of population concerns into national planning, policy and decision-making processes should continue. Population policies and programmes should be considered, with full recognition of women's rights.

Activities Governments and other relevant actors could, *inter alia*, undertake the following activities, with appropriate assistance from aid agencies, and report on their status of implementation to the International

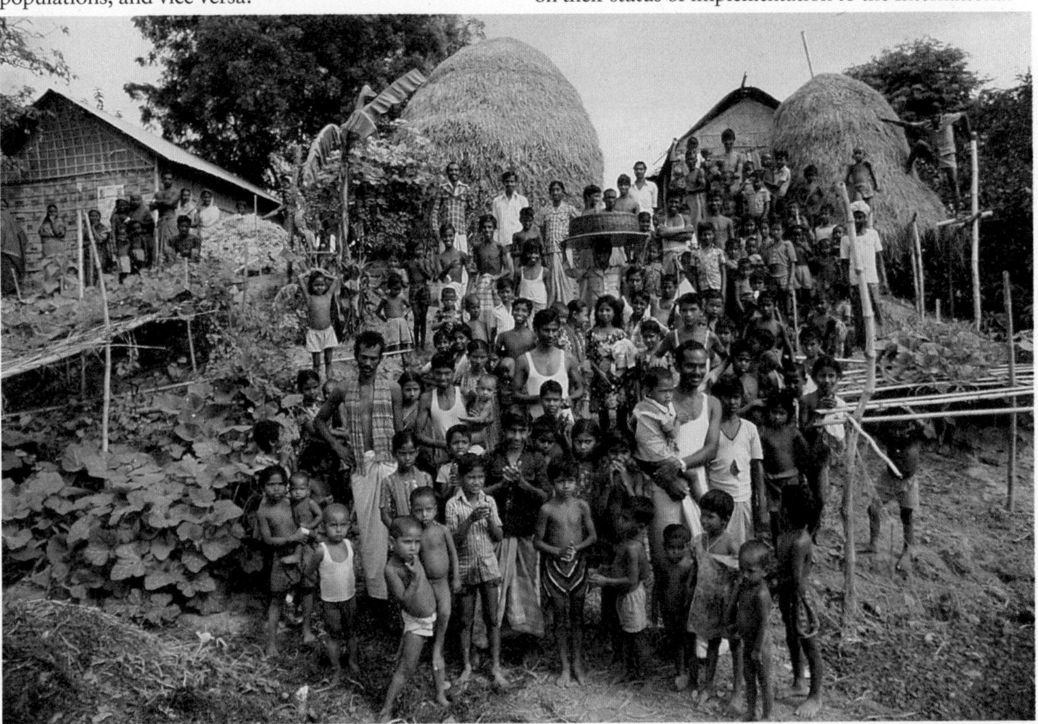

Portrait of a village – Mobarakdi in the Matlab district of Bangladesh. The human dimensions of settlements is a key element in population policies as are their environmental and development concerns.

Section I

Countries need to incorporate demographic trends into national policies. Addressing population growth issues should include improving the status and income of women through access to schooling and professional training.

JORGEN SCHYTTE/STILL PICTURES

Conference on Population and Development to be held in 1994, especially to its committee on population and environment.

A *Assessing the implications of national demographic trends and factors*

The relationships between demographic trends and factors and environmental change and between environmental degradation and the components of demographic change should be analysed.

Research should be conducted on how environmental factors interact with socio-economic factors as a cause of migration.

Vulnerable population groups (such as rural landless workers, ethnic minorities, refugees, migrants, displaced people, women heads of household) whose changes in demographic structure may have specific impacts on sustainable development should be identified.

An assessment should be made of the implications of the age structure of the population on resource demand and dependency burdens, ranging from educational expenses for the young to health care and support for the elderly, and on household income generation.

An assessment should also be made of national population carrying capacity in the context of satisfaction of human needs and sustainable development, and special attention should be given to critical resources, such as water and land, and environmental factors, such as ecosystem health and biodiversity.

The impact of national demographic trends and factors on the traditional livelihoods of indigenous groups and local communities, including changes in traditional land use because of internal population pressures, should be studied.

B *Building and strengthening a national information base*

National databases on demographic trends and factors and environment should be built and/or strengthened, disaggregating data by ecological region (ecosystem approach), and population/environment profiles should be established by region.

Methodologies and instruments should be developed to identify areas where sustainability is, or may be, threatened by the environmental effects of demographic trends and factors, incorporating both current and projected demographic data linked to natural environmental processes.

Case-studies of local level responses by different groups to demographic dynamics should be developed, particularly in areas subject to environmental stress and in deteriorating urban centres.

Population data should be disaggregated by, *inter alia*, sex and age in order to take into account the implications of the gender division of labour for the use and management of natural resources.

C *Incorporating demographic features into policies and plans*

In formulating human settlements policies, account should be taken of resource needs, waste production and ecosystem health.

The direct and induced effects of demographic changes on environment and development programmes should, where appropriate, be integrated, and the impact on demographic features assessed.

National population policy goals and programmes that are consistent with national environment and development plans for sustainability and in keeping with the freedom, dignity and personally held values of individuals should be established and implemented.

Appropriate socio-economic policies for the young and the elderly, both in terms of family and state support systems, should be developed.

Policies and programmes should be developed for handling the various types of migrations that result from or induce environmental disruptions, with special attention to women and vulnerable groups.

Demographic concerns, including concerns for environmental migrants and displaced people, should be incorporated in the programmes for sustainable development of relevant international and regional institutions.

National reviews should be conducted and the integration of population policies in national development and environment strategies should be monitored nationally.

Financing and cost evaluation $90 million from the international community on grant or concessional terms.

C Implementing integrated environment and development programmes at the local level, taking into account demographic trends and factors

Basis for action Population programmes are more effective when implemented together with appropriate cross-sectoral policies. To attain sustainability at the local level, a new framework is needed that integrates demographic trends and factors with such

Education and training empowers individuals. Places are restricted at this village school in Kalsaka, Burkima Faso, and children are only admitted in alternate years. Those born in the in-between years miss out for life.

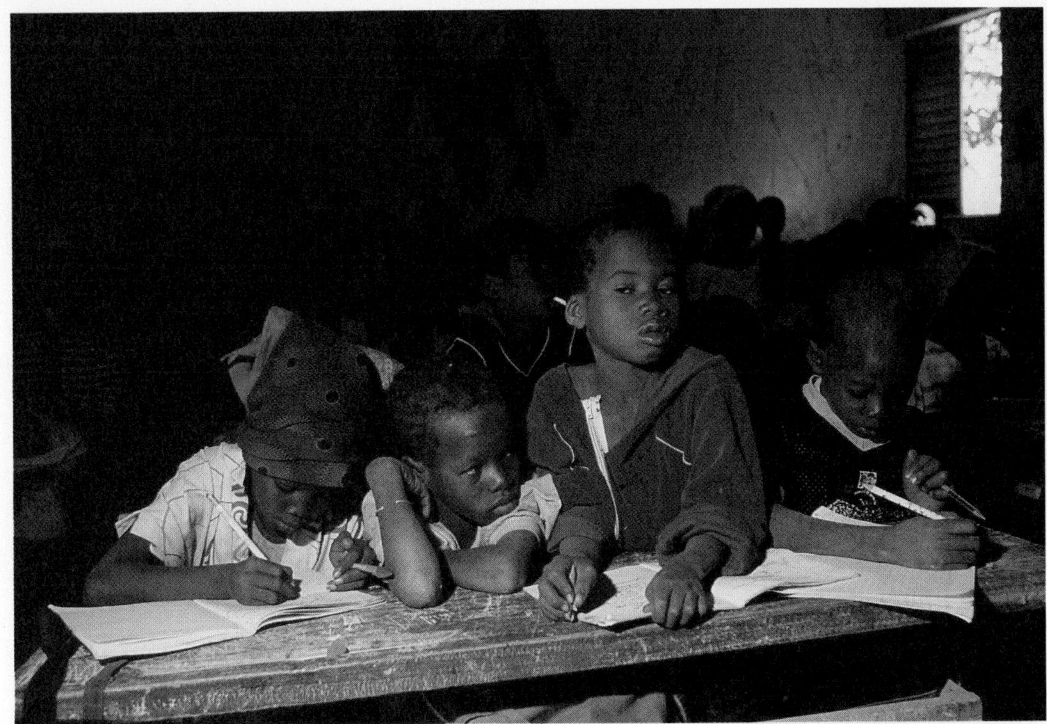

factors as ecosystem health, technology and human settlements, and with socio-economic structures and access to resources. Population programmes should be consistent with socio-economic and environmental planning. Integrated sustainable development programmes should closely correlate action on demographic trends and factors with resource management activities and development goals that meet the needs of the people concerned.

Objective Population programmes should be implemented along with natural resource management and development programmes at the local level that will ensure sustainable use of natural resources, improve the quality of life of the people and enhance environmental quality.

Activities Governments and local communities, including community-based women's organizations and national non-governmental organizations, consistent with national plans, objectives, strategies and priorities, could, *inter alia*, undertake the activities set out below with the assistance and cooperation of international organizations, as appropriate. Governments could share their experience in the implementation of Agenda 21 at the International Conference on Population and Development, to be held in 1994, especially its committee on population and environment.

A *Developing a framework for action*

An effective consultative process should be established and implemented with concerned groups of society where the formulation and decision-making of all components of the programmes are based on a nationwide consultative process drawing on community meetings, regional workshops and national seminars, as appropriate. This process should ensure that views of women and men on needs, perspective and constraints are equally well reflected in the design of programmes, and that solutions are rooted in specific experience. The poor and underprivileged should be priority groups in this process.

Nationally determined policies for integrated and multifaceted programmes, with special attention to women, to the poorest people living in critical areas and to other vulnerable groups should be implemented, ensuring the involvement of groups with a special potential to act as agents for change and sustainable development. Special emphasis should be placed on those programmes that achieve multiple objectives, encouraging sustainable economic development, and mitigating adverse impacts of demographic trends and factors, and avoiding long-term environmental damage. Food security, access to secure tenure, basic shelter, and essential infrastructure, education, family welfare, women's reproductive health, family credit schemes, reforestation programmes, primary environmental care, women's employment should, as appropriate, be included among other factors.

An analytical framework should be developed to identify complementary elements of sustainable development policies as well as the national mechanisms to monitor and evaluate their effects on population dynamics.

Special attention should be given to the critical role of women in population/environment programmes and in achieving sustainable development. Projects should take advantage of opportunities to link social, economic and environmental gains for women and their families. Empowerment of women is essential and should be assured through education, training and policies to accord and improve women's right and access to assets, human and civil rights, labour-saving measures, job opportunities and participation in decision-making. Population/environment programmes must enable women to mobilize themselves to alleviate their burden and improve their capacity to participate in and benefit from socio-economic development. Specific measures should be undertaken to close the gap between female and male illiteracy rates.

B *Supporting programmes that promote changes in demographic trends and factors towards sustainability*

Reproductive health programmes and services, should, as appropriate, be developed and enhanced to reduce maternal and infant mortality from all causes and enable women and men to fulfil their personal aspirations in terms of family size, in a way in keeping with their freedom and dignity and personally held values.

Governments should take active steps to implement, as a matter of urgency, in accordance with country-specific conditions and legal systems, measures to ensure that women and men have the same right to decide freely and responsibly on the number and spacing of their children, to have access to the information, education and means, as appropriate, to enable them to exercise this right in keeping with their freedom, dignity and personally held values taking into account ethical and cultural considerations.

Governments should take active steps to implement

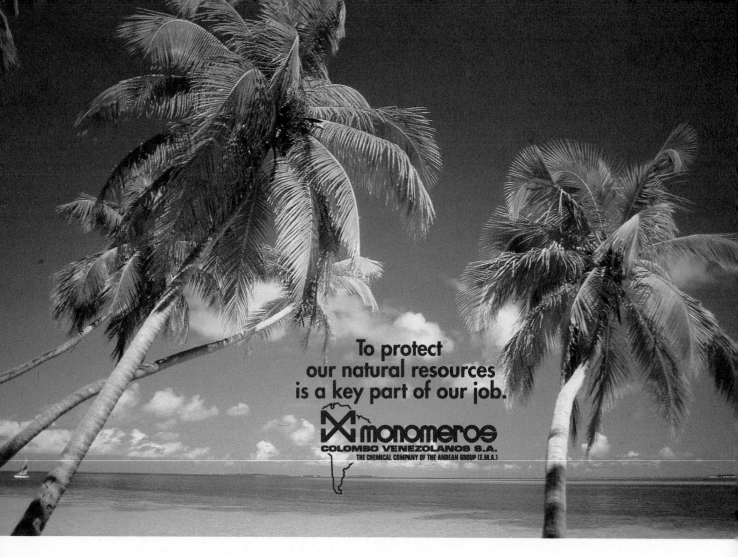

To integrate programmes at local levels special attention should be paid to vulnerable groups, poor people and women, using media such as community meetings, regional workshops and national seminars.

Section I

programmes to establish and strengthen preventive and curative health facilities that include women-centred, women-managed, safe and effective reproductive health care and affordable, accessible services, as appropriate, for the responsible planning of family size, in keeping with freedom, dignity and personally held values and taking into account ethical and cultural considerations. Programmes should focus on providing comprehensive health care, including pre-natal care, education and information on health and responsible parenthood and should provide the opportunity for all women to breast-feed fully, at least during the first four months post-partum. Programmes should fully support women's productive and reproductive roles and well being, with special attention to the need for providing equal and improved health care for all children and the need to reduce the risk of maternal and child mortality and sickness.

Consistent with national priorities, culturally based information and education programmes that transmit reproductive health messages to men and women that are easily understood should be developed.

C *Creating appropriate institutional conditions* Constituencies and institutional conditions to facilitate the implementation of demographic activities should, as appropriate, be fostered. This requires support and commitment from political, indigenous, religious and traditional authorities, the private sector and the national scientific community. In developing these appropriate institutional conditions, countries should closely involve established national machinery for women.

Population assistance should be coordinated with bilateral and multilateral donors to ensure that population needs and requirements of all developing countries are addressed, fully respecting the overall coordinating responsibility and the choice and strategies of the recipient countries.

Coordination should be improved at local and international levels. Working practices should be enhanced in order to make optimum use of resources, draw on collective experience and improve the implementation of programmes. UNFPA and other relevant agencies should strengthen the coordination of international cooperation activities with recipient and donor countries in order to ensure that adequate funding is available to respond to growing needs.

Proposals should be developed for local, national and international population/environment programmes in line with specific needs for achieving sustainability. Where appropriate, institutional changes must be implemented so that old-age security does not entirely depend on input from family members.

Financing and cost evaluation $7 billion including about $3.5 billion from the international community on grant or concessional terms.

Chapter 6

Protection and promotion of human health

Health and development are intimately interconnected. Both insufficient development leading to poverty and inappropriate development resulting in over-consumption, coupled with an expanding world population, can result in severe environmental health problems in both developing and developed nations. Action items under Agenda 21 must address the primary health needs of the world's population, since they are integral to the achievement of the goals of sustainable development and primary environmental care. The linkage of health, environmental and socio-economic improvements requires intersectoral efforts. Such efforts, involving education, housing, public works and community groups, including businesses, schools and universities and religious, civic and cultural organizations, are aimed at enabling people in their communities to ensure sustainable development. Particularly relevant is the inclusion of prevention programmes rather than relying solely on remediation and treatment. Countries ought to develop plans for priority actions, drawing on the programme areas in this chapter, which are based on cooperative planning by the various levels of government, non-governmental organizations and local communities. An appropriate international organization, such as WHO, should coordinate these activities.

A Meeting primary health care needs, particularly in rural areas

Basis for action Health ultimately depends on the ability to manage successfully the interaction between the physical, spiritual, biological and economic/social environment. Sound development is not possible

The Caribbean Development Bank (CDB) is a regional financial institution which was established in October 1969, began operations in January 1970, and has its Headquarters at Wildey, St. Michael, Barbados, West Indies.

Regional members are Anguilla, Antigua and Barbuda, Bahamas, Barbados, Belize, British Virgin Islands, Cayman Islands, Colombia, Dominica, Grenada, Guyana, Jamaica, Mexico, Montserrat, St. Kitts and Nevis, St. Lucia, St. Vincent and the Grenadines, Trinidad and Tobago, Turks and Caicos Islands, Venezuela.

Non-regional members are Canada, France, Germany, Italy, United Kingdom.

Subscribed share capital is US$648.4 million, comprising US$505 million callable capital and US$143.4 million paid-up capital. The United States, as a non-member, has no share in CDB's Ordinary Capital Resources (OCR), but is the largest contributor to the Bank's Special Funds Resources (SFR). The Kingdom of the Netherlands is also a substantial contributor to the SFR.

CDB is committed to contributing to the harmonious economic growth and development of the member countries in the Caribbean and promoting economic cooperation and integration among them, having special and urgent regard to the needs of the less developed member countries of the Region.

In its operations to December 31, 1991, CDB had total net approvals (loans, contingent loans, equity and grants) in the equivalent of US$1,009 million.

The Bank has sought to increase the integration of environmental considerations in its operational policies. In this regard, it requires borrowers to undertake an environmental impact assessment of project proposals to ensure that they are environmentally sound and sustainable. In circumstances where borrowers are not themselves equipped to undertake such assessment, CDB staff/consultants carry out the task during project preparation/appraisal.

Over the past two years, CDB has sought to increase the awareness and technical competence of its own staff and that of staff of public organisations of the Borrowing Member Countries through short term intensive training programmes on Environmental Impact Assessment at the project level.

CDB supported "Earth Summit" as a critical intensification of global efforts towards a more environmentally sustainable development future.

For its part, the Bank is committed to further expanding its project activities to meet the growing needs of its Borrowing Member Countries in the field of Environment/Development.

ENVIRONMENT PROTECTION AND ECONOMIC GROWTH IN THE EGYPTIAN PETROLEUM SECTOR

The Petroleum Industry and Environment Enhancement should be a major subject in the dialogue between Oil Producers and Consumers and the International Cooperation. Fossil fuels will remain to represent 85% of the Energy demands and is an essential element in the economic development.

Consequently the challenge that will face the world is to reach a balance between Environment Enhancement and the continuity of the economical development.

During the last ten years the Egyptian Petroleum Sector has been one of the major earners of foreign exchange for the country.

Accordingly, the Ministry of Petroleum has set strategic targets for the Egyptian General Petroleum Corporation (EGPC) and has been closely followed over the past Decade.

Annual production has always topped local demand by about 50%, the rest is being exported.

Securing the remaining reserves of oil and gas is no less important than stepping up production.

We are encouraging foreign companies to invest in oil and gas exploration in Egypt. To increase the nation's reserve base, the petroleum sector adopted different, simultaneous approaches. One is to modify the concession agreements to encourage more companies to explore for oil and gas.

The second approach is to add the gas clause to the new agreements.

The third approach to increase oil reserves is to discover new fields.

A national grid is also expanding to carry gas from its production, collection and treatment points to preset Domestic and Industrial Destinations. The main consumers are power stations.

All this is being managed through a cautious feeling of environmental development planning.

without a healthy population; yet most developmental activities affect the environment to some degree, which in turn causes or exacerbates many health problems. Conversely, it is the very lack of development that adversely affects the health condition of many people, which can be alleviated only through development. The health sector cannot meet basic needs and objectives on its own; it is dependent on social, economic and spiritual development, while directly contributing to such development. It is also dependent on a healthy environment, including the provision of a safe water supply and sanitation and the promotion of a safe food supply and proper nutrition. Particular attention should be directed towards food safety, with priority placed on the elimination of food contamination; comprehensive and sustainable water policies to ensure safe drinking water and sanitation to preclude both microbial and chemical contamination; and promotion of health education, immunization and provision of essential drugs. Education and appropriate services regarding responsible planning of family size, with respect for cultural, religious and social aspects, in keeping with freedom, dignity and personally held values and taking into account ethical and cultural considerations, also contribute to these intersectoral activities.

Objectives Within the overall strategy to achieve health for all by the year 2000, the objectives are to meet the basic health needs of rural peri-urban and urban populations; to provide the necessary specialized environmental health services; and to coordinate the involvement of citizens, the health sector, the health-related sectors and relevant non-health sectors (business, social, educational and religious institutions) in solutions to health problems. As a matter of priority, health service coverage should be achieved for population groups in greatest need, particularly those living in rural areas.

Activities National Governments and local authorities, with the support of relevant non-governmental organizations and international organizations, in the light of countries' specific conditions and needs, should strengthen their health sector programmes, with special attention to rural needs, to:

a Build basic health infrastructures, monitoring and planning systems:
i Develop and strengthen primary health care systems that are practical, community-based, scientifically sound, socially acceptable and appropriate to their needs and that meet basic health needs for clean water, safe food and sanitation;
ii Support the use and strengthening of mechanisms that improve coordination between health and related sectors at all appropriate levels of government, and in communities and relevant organizations;
iii Develop and implement rational and affordable approaches to the establishment and maintenance of health facilities;
iv Ensure and, where appropriate, increase provision of social services support;
v Develop strategies, including reliable health indicators, to monitor the progress and evaluate the effectiveness of health programmes;
vi Explore ways to finance the health system based on the assessment of the resources needed and identify the various financing alternatives;
vii Promote health education in schools, information exchange, technical support and training;
viii Support initiatives for self-management of services by vulnerable groups;
ix Integrate traditional knowledge and experience into national health systems, as appropriate;
x Promote the provisions for necessary logistics for outreach activities, particularly in rural areas;
xi Promote and strengthen community-based rehabilitation activities for the rural handicapped.
b Support research and methodology development:
i Establish mechanisms for sustained community involvement in environmental health activities, including optimization of the appropriate use of community financial and human resources;
ii Conduct environmental health research, including behaviour research and research on ways to increase coverage and ensure greater utilization of services by peripheral, underserved and vulnerable populations, as appropriate to good prevention services and health care;
iii Conduct research into traditional knowledge of prevention and curative health practices.

Section I

Pauline Sawadogo feeds her new born baby, left, whilst, right, a less healthy child is treated in a field hospital for diarrhoea, one of the main causes of childhood death in many developing countries.

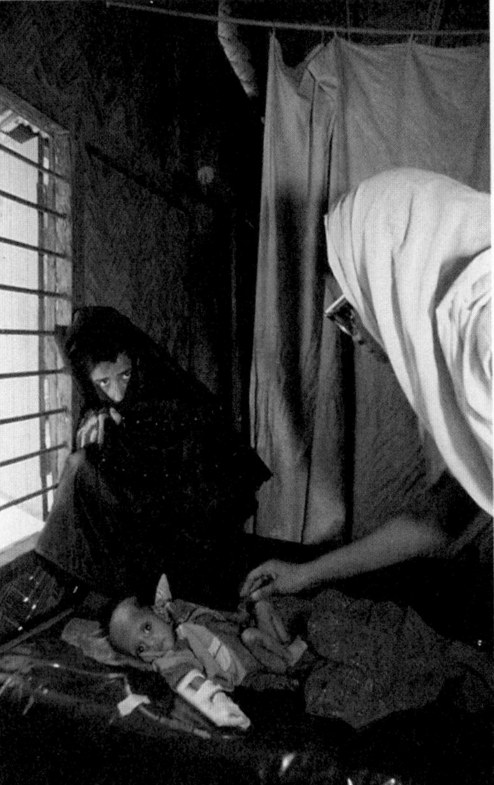

Primary health care includes food safety and child care. Above: monks from Bjakar Ozong, Bhutan give women lectures in child care. Below: food and nutrition lessons are given to mothers by a health worker in Rutiyay, India.

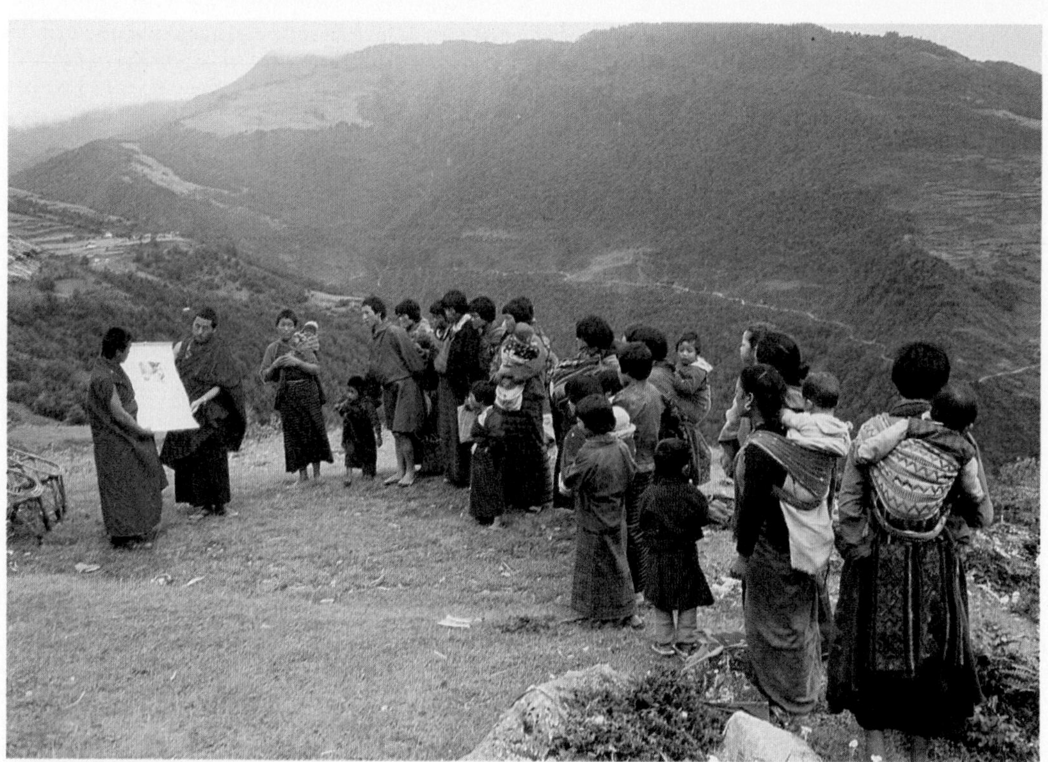

JORGEN SCHYTTE/STILL PICTURES

Financing and cost evaluation $40 billion, including about $5 billion from the international community on grant or concessional terms.

B Control of communicable diseases

Basis for action. Advances in the development of vaccines and chemotherapeutic agents have brought many communicable diseases under control. However, there remain many important communicable diseases for which environmental control measures are indispensable, especially in the field of water supply and sanitation. Such diseases include cholera, diarrhoeal diseases, leishmaniasis, malaria and schistosomiasis. In all such instances, the environmental measures, either as an integral part of primary health care or undertaken outside the health sector, form an indispensable component of overall disease control strategies, together with health and hygiene education, and in some cases, are the only component.

With HIV infection levels estimated to increase to 30-40 million by the year 2000, the socio-economic impact of the pandemic is expected to be devastating for all countries, and increasingly for women and children. While direct health costs will be substantial, they will be dwarfed by the indirect costs of the pandemic – mainly costs associated with the loss of income and decreased productivity of the workforce. The pandemic will inhibit growth of the service and industrial sectors and significantly increase the costs of human capacity-building and retraining. The agricultural sector is particularly affected where production is labour-intensive.

Objectives A number of goals have been formulated through extensive consultations in various inter-

My government is committed to the huge task of reversing the trend of increasing degradation of the ecosystems of this region. With the help of the Caribbean Conservation Association, the United States Agency for International Development and the local Environmental Awareness Group, we have begun to tackle the many problems in a determined effort to achieve sound national environmental development. We hail the resolve of UNCED with the specific aim of strengthening national and international efforts to promote sustainable and environmental development in all countries.
Rt.Hon. V. C. Bird
Prime Minister
Antigua and Barbuda

national forums attended by virtually all Governments, relevant United Nations organizations (including WHO, UNICEF, UNFPA, UNESCO, UNDP and the World Bank) and a number of non-governmental organizations. Goals (including but not limited to those listed below) are recommended for implementation by all countries where they are applicable, with appropriate adaptation to the specific situation of each country in terms of phasing, standards, priorities and availability of resources, with respect for cultural, religious and social aspects, in keeping with freedom, dignity and personally held values and taking into account ethical considerations. Additional goals that are particularly relevant to a country's specific situation should be added in the country's national plan of action (Plan of Action for Implementing the World Declaration on the Survival, Protection and Development of Children in the 1990s[1]). Such national level action plans should be coordinated and monitored from within the public health sector. Some major goals are:

a By the year 2000, to eliminate guinea worm disease (dracunculiasis);
b By the year 2000, eradicate polio;
c By the year 2000, to effectively control onchocerciasis (river blindness) and leprosy;
d By 1995, to reduce measles deaths by 95 per cent and reduce measles cases by 90 per cent compared with pre-immunization levels;
e By continued efforts, to provide health and hygiene education and to ensure universal access to safe drinking water and universal access to sanitary measures of excreta disposal, thereby markedly reducing waterborne diseases such as cholera and schistosomiasis and reducing:
i By the year 2000, the number of deaths from childhood diarrhoea in developing countries by 50 to 70 per cent;
ii By the year 2000, the incidence of childhood diarrhoea in developing countries by at least 25 to 50 per cent;
iii By the year 2000, to initiate comprehensive programmes to reduce mortality from acute respiratory infections in children under five years by at least one third, particularly in countries with high infant mortality;
g By the year 2000, to provide 95 per cent of the world's child population with access to appropriate care for acute respiratory infections within the community and at first referral level;
h By the year 2000, to institute anti-malaria programmes in all countries where malaria presents a significant health problem and maintain the transmission-free status of areas freed from endemic malaria;
i By the year 2000, to implement control programmes in countries where major human parasitic infections are endemic and achieve an overall reduction in the prevalence of schistosomiasis and of other trematode infections by 40 per cent and 25 per cent, respectively, from a 1984 baseline, as well as a marked reduction in incidence, prevalence and intensity of filarial infections;
j To mobilize and unify national and international efforts against AIDS to prevent infection and to reduce the personal and social impact of HIV infection;
k To contain the resurgence of tuberculosis, with particular emphasis on multiple antibiotic resistant forms;
l To accelerate research on improved vaccines and implement to the fullest extent possible the use of vaccines in the prevention of disease.

Activities Each national Government, in accordance with national plans for public health, priorities and objectives, should consider developing a national health action plan with appropriate international assistance and support, including, at a minimum, the following components:
a National public health systems:
i Programmes to identify environmental hazards in the causation of communicable diseases;
ii Monitoring systems of epidemiological data to ensure adequate forecasting of the introduction, spread or aggravation of communicable diseases;
iii Intervention programmes, including measures consistent with the principles of the global AIDS strategy;
iv Vaccines for the prevention of communicable diseases;
b Public information and health education: Provide education and disseminate information on the risks of endemic communicable diseases and build awareness on environmental methods for control of communicable diseases to enable communities to play a role in the control of communicable diseases;
c Intersectoral cooperation and coordination:
i Second experienced health professionals to relevant sectors, such as planning, housing and agriculture;
ii Develop guidelines for effective coordination in the areas of professional training, assessment of risks and development of control technology;
d Control of environmental factors that influence the spread of communicable diseases:

Apply methods for the prevention and control of communicable diseases, including water supply and sanitation control, water pollution control, food quality control, integrated vector control, garbage collection and disposal and environmentally sound irrigation practices;
e Primary health care system:
i Strengthen prevention programmes, with particular emphasis on adequate and balanced nutrition;
ii Strengthen early diagnostic programmes and improve capacities for early preventative/treatment action;
iii Reduce the vulnerability to HIV infection of women and their offspring;
f Provide support for research and methodology development:
i Intensify and expand multidisciplinary research, including focused efforts on the mitigation and environmental control of tropical diseases;
ii Carry out intervention studies to provide a solid epidemiological basis for control policies and to evaluate the efficiency of alternative approaches;
iii Undertake studies in the population and among health workers to determine the influence of cultural, behavioural and social factors on control policies;
g Development and dissemination of technology:
i Develop new technologies for the effective control of communicable diseases;
ii Promote studies to determine how to optimally disseminate results from research;
iii Ensure technical assistance, including the sharing of knowledge and know-how.

Financing and cost evaluation $4 billion, including about $900 million from the international community on grant or concessional terms.

C Protecting vulnerable groups

Basis for action In addition to meeting basic health needs, specific emphasis has to be given to protecting and educating vulnerable groups, particularly infants, youth, women, indigenous people and the very poor as a prerequisite for sustainable development. Special attention should also be paid to the health needs of the elderly and disabled population.

Infants and children. Approximately one third of

CVRD – AN EXAMPLE OF SUSTAINABLE DEVELOPMENT

Companhia Vale do Rio Doce – CVRD – a Brazilian company with worldwide operations and one of the world's major producers and exporters of iron ore, celebrates its Fiftieth Anniversary in 1992. Its activities also extend to the mining of gold, bauxite and manganese ore and the production of aluminium and pulp, as well as railroad and ocean transportation. CVRD operates two major systems, each one integrating mines, railroad and port facilities: the Southern System in the States of Minas Gerais and Espírito Santo and the Northern System in the Amazon Area, in the States of Para and Maranhão.

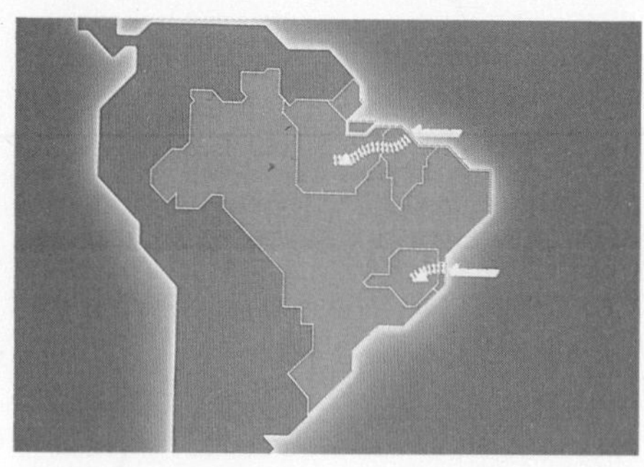

Tubarão Marine Terminal

The quality of the environment is a permanent and important concern in all CVRD's projects and operations. In the last decade, the company has invested around US$600 million in programmes for environmental control, conservation and recuperation of natural forests, as well as in environmental research, technology and education. Between 1991 and 1995 CVRD will spend a further US$300 million on such programmes.

For more than thirty years CVRD has been maintaining the 22,000 hectares of natural forest in its Linhares Reservation in the State of Espírito Santo. Because of the research which the corporation has undertaken, it now holds the most detailed knowledge available anywhere on the Atlantic Forest Belt, an eco-system that in the sixteenth century covered a total of one million km^2, which has now been reduced to a mere 4% of its original dimensions. This knowledge is being deployed to the full in the recuperation of impaired watersheds and land areas and in the replanting of sloping terrain.

Linhares Forest Reserve

Carajás Mining operation in tropical forest

In the Amazon Region, occupation of which got under way in the Sixties, hence a good deal prior to the inception of its activities there, CVRD had already defined a line of preventative activity, planning and implementing the Carajas Iron Ore Project in such a manner as to cause the least possible harm to the environment. Of the aggregate area under its responsibility, totalling some 412,000 hectares of natural forest, CVRD actually uses only 1.6% for its mining and infra-structural activities. CVRD also looks after surveillance and maintenance of neighbouring areas protected by legislation and belonging to federal agencies and can justly claim to protect in that region, over 1,000,000 hectares of natural forest in terms of uninterrupted area. CVRD is also engaged in a vast programme of forestry research, using native and exotic species, and avails itself of all-encompassing technology for the recuperation of downgraded areas so as to re-integrate them into the primary forest resources and permit rational application, based on achieving compatibility between regional development on the one hand and strict environmental precautions on the other. Indigenous communities receive specific assistance in the fields of health care, education and farming techniques, and three reservations for the native population have already been marked out in the region covered by the project.

Communicable diseases can be controlled or restricted. Above, the International Centre for Diarrhoeal Disease Research, Dacca, Bangladesh. Below, Workers in a water-testing and purification laboratory in Mangua, Nicaragua.

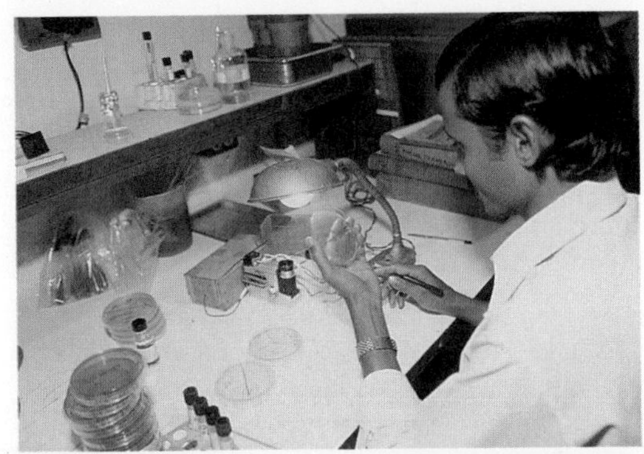

JORGEN SCHYTTE/STILL PICTURES

the world's population are children under 15 years old. At least 15 million of these children die annually from such preventable causes as birth trauma, birth asphyxia, acute respiratory infections, malnutrition, communicable diseases and diarrhoea. The health of children is affected more severely than other population groups by malnutrition and adverse environmental factors, and many children risk exploitation as cheap labour or in prostitution.

Youth. As has been the historical experience of all countries, youth are particularly vulnerable to the problems associated with economic development, which often weakens traditional forms of social support essential for the healthy development, of young people. Urbanization and changes in social mores have increased substance abuse, unwanted pregnancy and sexually transmitted diseases, including AIDS. Currently more than half of all people alive are under the age of 25 and 4 out of every 5 live in developing countries. Therefore it is important to ensure that historical experience is not replicated.

Women. In developing countries, the health status of women remains relatively low, and during the 1980s poverty, malnutrition and general ill-health in women were even rising. Most women in developing countries still do not have adequate basic educational opportunities and they lack the means of promoting their health, responsibly controlling their reproductive life and improving their socio-economic status. Particular attention should be given to the provision of pre-natal care to ensure healthy babies.

Indigenous people and their communities. Indigenous people and their communities make up a significant percentage of global population. The outcomes of their experience have tended to be very similar in that the basis of their relationship with traditional lands has been fundamentally changed. They tend to feature disproportionately in unemployment, lack of housing, poverty and poor health. In many countries the number of indigenous people is growing faster than the general population. Therefore it is important to target health initiatives for indigenous people.

Objectives The general objectives of protecting vulnerable groups are to ensure that all such individuals should be allowed to develop to their full potential (including healthy physical, mental and spiritual development); to ensure that young people can develop, establish and maintain healthy lives; to allow women to perform their key role in society; and to support indigenous people through educational, economic and technical opportunities.

Specific major goals for child survival, development and protection were agreed upon at the World Summit for Children and remain valid also for Agenda 21. Supporting and sectoral goals cover women's health and education, nutrition, child health, water and sanitation, basic education and children in difficult circumstances.

Governments should take active steps to implement, as a matter of urgency, in accordance with country specific conditions and legal systems, measures to ensure that women and men have the same right to decide freely and responsibly on the number and spacing of their children, to have access to the information, education and means, as appropriate, to enable them to exercise this right in keeping with their freedom, dignity and personally held values, taking into account ethical and cultural considerations.

Governments should take active steps to implement programmes to establish and strengthen preventive and curative health facilities which include women-centred, women-managed, safe and effective reproductive health care and affordable, accessible services, as appropriate, for the responsible planning of family size, in keeping with freedom, dignity and personally held values and taking into account ethical and cultural considerations. Programmes should focus on providing comprehensive health care, including pre-natal care, education and information on health and responsible parenthood and should provide the opportunity for all women to breast-feed fully, at least during the first four months post-partum. Programmes should fully support women's productive and reproductive roles and well being, with special attention to the need for providing equal and improved health care for all children and the need to reduce the risk of maternal and child mortality and sickness.

Activities National Governments, in cooperation with local and non-governmental organizations, should initiate or enhance programmes in the following areas:

a Infants and children:

i Strengthen basic health-care services for children in the context of primary health-care delivery, including prenatal care, breast-feeding, immunization and nutrition programmes;

ii Undertake widespread adult education on the use of oral rehydration therapy for diarrhoea, treatment of respiratory infections and prevention of communicable diseases;

iii Promote the creation, amendment and enforcement of a legal framework protecting children from sexual and workplace exploitation;

iv Protect children from the effects of environmental and occupational toxic compounds;

b Youth: Strengthen services for youth in health, education and social sectors in order to provide better information, education, counselling and treatment for specific health problems, including drug abuse;

c Women:

i Involve women's groups in decision-making at the national and community levels to identify health risks and incorporate health issues in national action programmes on women and development;

ii Provide concrete incentives to encourage and maintain attendance of women of all ages at school and adult education courses, including health

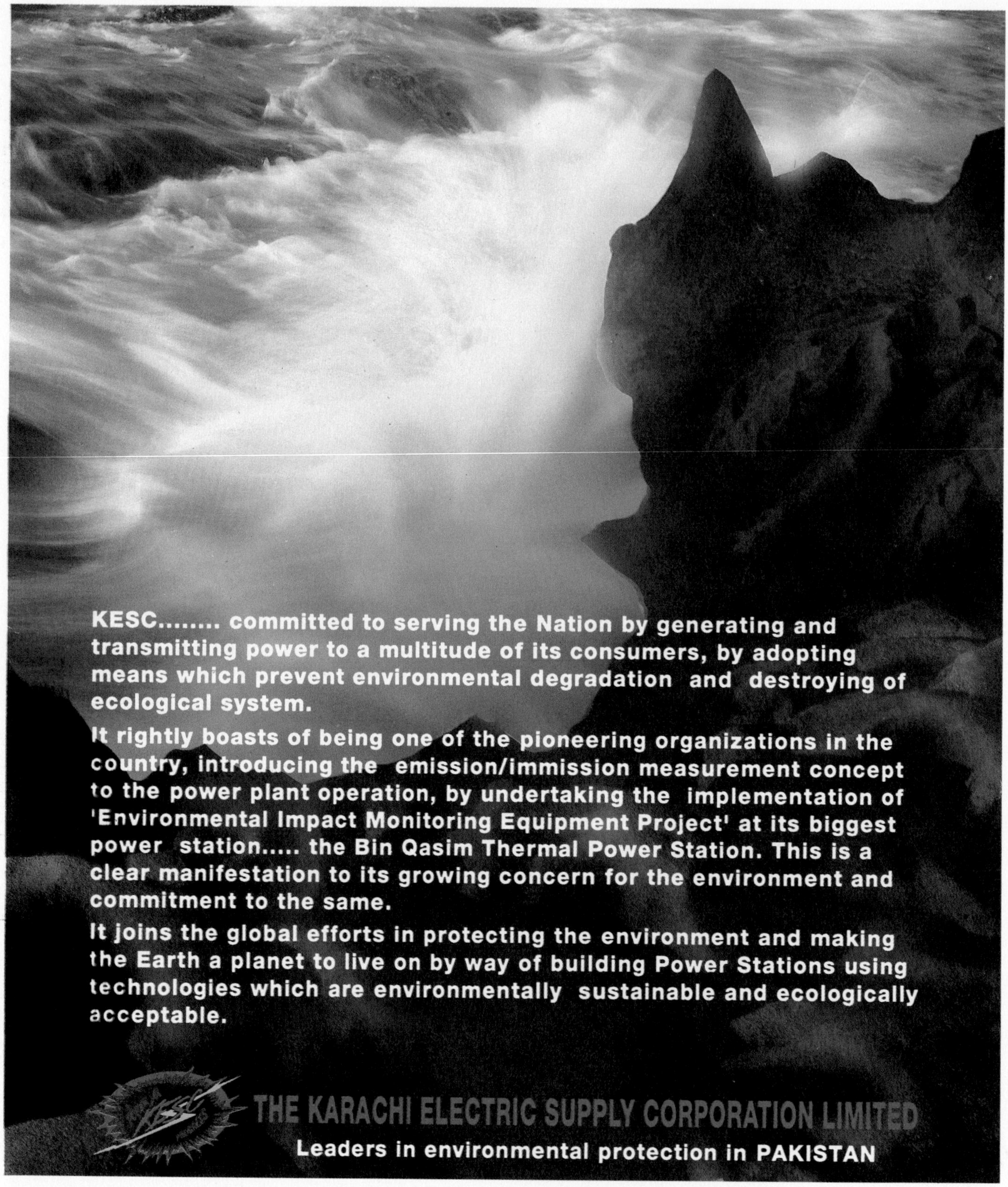
KESC........ committed to serving the Nation by generating and transmitting power to a multitude of its consumers, by adopting means which prevent environmental degradation and destroying of ecological system.
It rightly boasts of being one of the pioneering organizations in the country, introducing the emission/immission measurement concept to the power plant operation, by undertaking the implementation of 'Environmental Impact Monitoring Equipment Project' at its biggest power station..... the Bin Qasim Thermal Power Station. This is a clear manifestation to its growing concern for the environment and commitment to the same.
It joins the global efforts in protecting the environment and making the Earth a planet to live on by way of building Power Stations using technologies which are environmentally sustainable and ecologically acceptable.
THE KARACHI ELECTRIC SUPPLY CORPORATION LIMITED
Leaders in environmental protection in PAKISTAN

UNCED provided all nations with a unique opportunity to establish a framework for ecologically sustainable development. Australia participated actively in the UNCED process to ensure practical outcomes that would provide the basis for effective international action and cooperation into the next century. Australia is now moving to ensure the prompt ratification of the framework convention on climate change and the convention on biological diversity and examining the implications of Agenda 21 for domestic and global environmental policies. The international community must maximise the opportunity given to it by UNCED for the benefit of both present and future generations.
Hon J. E. Keating
Prime Minister
Australia

education and training in primary, home and maternal health care;
iii Carry out baseline surveys and knowledge, attitude and practice studies on the health and nutrition of women throughout their life cycle, especially as related to the impact of environmental degradation and adequate resources;
d Indigenous people and their communities:
i Strengthen, through resources and self-management, preventative and curative health services;
ii Integrate traditional knowledge and experience into health systems.

Financing and cost evaluation $3.7 billion, including about $400 million from the international community on grant or concessional terms.

D Meeting the urban health challenge

Basis for action For hundreds of millions of people, the poor living conditions in urban and peri-urban areas are destroying lives, health, and social and moral values. Urban growth has outstripped society's capacity to meet human needs, leaving hundreds of millions of people with inadequate incomes, diets, housing and services. Urban growth exposes populations to serious environmental hazards and has outstripped the capacity of municipal and local governments to provide the environmental health services that the people need. All too often, urban development is associated with destructive effects on the physical environment and the resource base needed for sustainable development. Environmental pollution in urban areas is associated with excess morbidity and mortality. Overcrowding and inadequate housing contribute to respiratory diseases, tuberculosis, meningitis and other diseases. In urban environments, many factors that affect human health are outside the health sector. Improvements in urban health therefore will depend on coordinated action by all levels of government, health care providers, businesses, religious groups, social and educational institutions and citizens.

Objectives The health and well-being of all urban dwellers must be improved so that they can contribute to economic and social development. The global objective is to achieve a 10 to 40 per cent improvement in health indicators by the year 2000. The same rate of improvement should be achieved for environmental, housing and health service indicators. These include the development of quantitative objectives for infant mortality, maternal mortality, percentage of low birth weight newborns and specific indicators (e.g. tuberculosis as an indicator of crowded housing, diarrhoeal diseases as indicators of inadequate water and sanitation, rates of industrial and transportation accidents that indicate possible opportunities for prevention of injury, and social problems such as drug abuse, violence and crime that indicate underlying social disorders).

Activities Local authorities, with the appropriate support of national Governments and international organizations should be encouraged to take effective measures to initiate or strengthen the following activities:
a Develop and implement municipal and local health plans:
i Establish or strengthen intersectoral committees at both the political and technical level, including active collaboration on linkages with scientific, cultural, religious, medical, business, social and other city institutions, using networking arrangements;
ii Adopt or strengthen municipal or local "enabling strategies" that emphasize "doing with" rather than "doing for" and create supportive environments for health;
iii Ensure that public health education in schools, workplace, mass media etc. is provided or strengthened;
iv Encourage communities to develop personal skills and awareness of primary health care;
v Promote and strengthen community-based rehabilitation activities for the urban and peri-urban disabled and the elderly;
b Survey, where necessary, the existing health, social and environmental conditions in cities, including documentation of intra-urban differences;
c Strengthen environmental health services:
i Adopt health impact and environmental impact assessment procedures;
ii Provide basic and in-service training for new and existing personnel;
d Establish and maintain city networks for collaboration and exchange of models of good practice.

Financing and cost evaluation $222 million, including about $22 million from the international community on grant or concessional terms.

E Reducing health risks from environmental pollution and hazards

Basis for action In many locations around the world the general environment (air, water and land), workplaces and even individual dwellings are so badly polluted that the health of hundreds of millions of people is adversely affected. This is, *inter alia*, due to past and present developments in consumption and production patterns and lifestyles, in energy production and use, in industry, in transportation etc., with little or no regard for environmental protection. There have been notable improvements in some countries, but deterioration of the environment continues. The ability of countries to tackle pollution and health problems is greatly restrained because of lack of resources. Pollution control and health protection measures have often not kept pace with economic development. Considerable development-related environmental health hazards exist in the newly industrializing countries. Furthermore, the recent analysis of WHO has clearly established the interdependence among the factors of health, environment and development and has revealed that most countries are lacking such integration as would lead to an effective pollution control mechanism.[1] Without prejudice to such criteria as may be agreed upon by the international community, or to standards which will have to be determined nationally, it will be essential in all cases to consider the systems of values prevailing in each country and the extent of the applicability of standards that are valid for the most advanced countries but may be inappropriate and of unwarranted social cost for the developing countries.

Objectives The overall objective is to minimize hazards and maintain the environment to a degree that human health and safety is not impaired or endangered and yet encourage development to proceed. Specific programme objectives are:
a By the year 2000, to incorporate appropriate environmental and health safeguards as part of national development programmes in all countries;
b By the year 2000, to establish, as appropriate, adequate national infrastructure and programmes for providing environmental injury, hazard surveillance and the basis for abatement in all countries;
c By the year 2000, to establish, as appropriate, integrated programmes for tackling pollution at the source and at the disposal site, with a focus on abatement actions in all countries;

d To identify and compile, as appropriate, the necessary statistical information on health effects to support cost/benefit analysis, including environmental health impact assessment for pollution control, prevention and abatement measures.

Activities Nationally determined action programmes, with international assistance, support and coordination, where necessary, in this area should include:

a Urban air pollution:
i Develop appropriate pollution control technology on the basis of risk assessment and epidemiological research for the introduction of environmentally sound production processes and suitable safe mass transport;
ii Develop air pollution control capacities in large cities, emphasizing enforcement programmes and using monitoring networks, as appropriate;
b Indoor air pollution:
i Support research and develop programmes for applying prevention and control methods to reducing indoor air pollution, including the provision of economic incentives for the installation of appropriate technology;
ii Develop and implement health education campaigns, particularly in developing countries, to reduce the health impact of domestic use of biomass and coal;
c Water pollution:
i Develop appropriate water pollution control technologies on the basis of health risk assessment;
ii Develop water pollution control capacities in large cities;
d Pesticides: Develop mechanisms to control the distribution and use of pesticides in order to minimize the risks to human health by transportation, storage, application and residual effects of pesticides used in agriculture and preservation of wood;
e Solid waste:
i Develop appropriate solid waste disposal technologies on the basis of health risk assessment;
ii Develop appropriate solid waste disposal capacities in large cities;
f Human settlements: Develop programmes for improving health conditions in human settlements, in particular within slums and non-tenured settlements, on the basis of health risk assessment;
g Noise: Develop criteria for maximum permitted safe noise exposure levels and promote noise assessment and control as part of environmental health programmes;
h Ionizing and non-ionizing radiation: Develop and implement appropriate national legislation, standards and enforcement procedures on the basis of existing international guidelines;
i Effects of ultraviolet radiation:
i Undertake, as a matter of urgency, research on the effects on human health of the increasing ultraviolet radiation reaching the earth's surface as a consequence of depletion of the stratospheric ozone layer;
ii On the basis of the outcome of this research, consider taking appropriate remedial measures to mitigate the above-mentioned effects on human beings;
j Industry and energy production:
i Establish environmental health impact assessment procedures for the planning and development of new industries and energy facilities;
ii Incorporate appropriate health risk analysis in all national programmes for pollution control and management, with particular emphasis on toxic compounds such as lead;
iii Establish industrial hygiene programmes in all major industries for the surveillance of workers' exposure to health hazards;
iv Promote the introduction of environmentally sound technologies within the industry and energy sectors;
k Monitoring and assessment: Establish, as appropriate, adequate environmental monitoring capacities for the surveillance of environmental quality and the health status of populations;
l Injury monitoring and reduction:
i Support, as appropriate, the development of systems to monitor the incidence and cause of injury to allow well-targeted intervention/prevention strategies;
ii Develop, in accordance with national plans, strategies in all sectors (industry, traffic and others) consistent with the WHO safe cities and safe communities programmes, to reduce the frequency and severity of injury;
iii Emphasize preventive strategies to reduce occupationally derived diseases and diseases caused by environmental and occupational toxins to enhance worker safety;
m Research promotion and methodology development:
i Support the development of new methods for the quantitative assessment of health benefits and cost associated with different pollution control strategies;
ii Develop and carry out interdisciplinary research on the combined health effects of exposure to multiple environmental hazards, including epidemiological investigations of long-term exposures to low levels of pollutants and the use of biological markers capable of estimating human exposures, adverse effects and susceptibility to environmental agents.

Financing and cost evaluation $3 billion, including about $115 million from the international community on grant or concessional terms.

1 Report of the WHO Commission on Health and Environment (Geneva, forthcoming).

Chapter 7 Promoting sustainable human settlement development

In industrialized countries, the consumption patterns of cities are severely stressing the global ecosystem, while settlements in the developing world need more raw material, energy, and economic development simply to overcome basic economic and social problems. Human settlement conditions in many parts of the world, particularly the developing countries, are deteriorating mainly as a result of the low levels of investment in the sector attributable to the overall resource constraints in these countries. In the low-income countries for which recent data are available, an average of only 5.6 per cent of central government expenditure went to housing, amenities, social security and welfare.[1] Expenditure by international support and finance organizations is equally low. For example, only 1 per cent of the United Nations system's total grant-financed expenditures in 1988 went to human settlements,[2] while in 1991, loans from the World Bank and the International Development Association (IDA) for urban development and water supply and sewerage amounted to 5.5 and 5.4 per cent, respectively, of their total lending.[3] On the other hand, available information indicates that technical cooperation activities in the human settlement sector generate considerable public and private sector investment. For example, every dollar of UNDP technical cooperation expenditure on human settlements in 1988 generated a follow-up investment of $122, the highest of all UNDP sectors of assistance.[4] This is the foundation of the "enabling approach" advocated for the human settlement sector. External assistance will help to generate the internal resources needed to improve the living and working environments of all people by the year 2000 and beyond, including the growing number of unemployed – the no-income group. At the same time the environmental implications of urban development should be recognized and addressed in an integrated fashion by all countries, with high priority being given to the needs of the urban and rural poor, the unemployed and the growing number of people without any source of income.

Human settlement objective

The overall human settlement objective is to improve the social, economic and environmental quality of human settlements and the living and working environments of all people, in particular the urban and rural poor. Such improvement should be based on technical cooperation activities, partnerships among the public, private and community sectors and participation in the decision-making process by community groups and special interest groups such as women, indigenous people, the elderly and the disabled. These approaches should form the core principles of national settlement strategies. In developing these strategies, countries will need to set priorities among the eight programme areas in this chapter in accordance with their national plans and objectives, taking fully into account their social and cultural capabilities. Furthermore, countries should make appropriate provision to monitor the impact of their strategies on marginalized and disenfranchised groups, with particular reference to the needs of women.

A Providing adequate shelter for all

Basis for action Access to safe and healthy shelter is essential to a person's physical, psychological, social and economic well-being and should be a fundamental part of national and international action. The right to adequate housing as a basic human right is enshrined in the Universal Declaration of Human Rights and the International Covenant on Economic, Social and Cultural Rights. Despite this, it is estimated that at the present time, at least 1 billion people do not have access to safe and healthy shelter and that if appropriate action is not taken, this number will increase dramatically by the end of the century and beyond.

A major global programme to address this problem is the Global Strategy for Shelter to the Year 2000, adopted by the General Assembly in December 1988 (resolution 43/181, annex). Despite its widespread endorsement, the Strategy needs a much greater level of political and financial support to enable it to reach its goal of facilitating adequate shelter for all by the end of the century and beyond.

Objective The objective is to achieve adequate shelter for rapidly growing populations and for the currently deprived urban and rural poor through an enabling approach to shelter development and improvement that is environmentally sound.

Activities

a As a first step towards the goal of providing adequate shelter for all, all countries should take immediate measures to provide shelter to their homeless poor, while the international community and financial institutions should undertake actions to support the efforts of the developing countries to provide shelter to the poor;
b All countries should adopt and/or strengthen national shelter strategies, with targets based, as appropriate, on the principles and recommendations contained in the Global Strategy for Shelter to the Year 2000. People should be protected by law against unfair eviction from their homes or land;
c All countries should, as appropriate, support the shelter efforts of the urban and rural poor, the unemployed and the no-income group by adopting and/or adapting existing codes and regulations, to facilitate their access to land, finance and low-cost building materials and by actively promoting the regularization and upgrading of informal settlements and urban slums as an expedient measure and pragmatic solution to the urban shelter deficit;
d All countries should, as appropriate, facilitate access of urban and rural poor to shelter by adopting and utilizing housing and finance schemes and new innovative mechanisms adapted to their circumstances;
e All countries should support and develop environmentally compatible shelter strategies at national, state/provincial and municipal levels through partnerships among the private, public and community sectors and with the support of community-based organizations;
f All countries, especially developing ones, should, as appropriate, formulate and implement programmes to reduce the impact of the phenomenon of rural to urban drift by improving rural living conditions;
g All countries, where appropriate, should develop

The Chalco district of Mexico City. Most of this district was constructed in less than a year in order to house migrant workers who had been forced to leave their land because of the effects of soil erosion.

Section I

The international community has now realized the need to address collectively the global environment degradation problem. The basic ingredients of human life – land, water and atmosphere – are gravely threatened. Environmental problems should not be dealt with in isolation but alongside development by integrating environmental issues with the dynamics of economic growth and development. Bangladesh is deeply concerned over the global environmental problems and has adopted a national environmental policy. UNCED offers an historic opportunity for world leaders to move towards new forms of international co-operation to make this planet healthier and safer for the present and future generations.
H.E. Mr. Abdur Rahman Biswas
President
The People's Republic of Bangladesh

and implement resettlement programmes that address the specific problems of displaced populations in their respective countries;

h All countries should, as appropriate, document and monitor the implementation of their national shelter strategies by using, *inter alia*, the monitoring guidelines adopted by the Commission on Human Settlements and the shelter performance indicators being produced jointly by the United Nations Centre for Human Settlements (Habitat) and the World Bank;

i Bilateral and multilateral cooperation should be strengthened in order to support the implementation of the national shelter strategies of developing countries;

j Global progress reports covering national action and the support activities of international organizations and bilateral donors should be produced and disseminated on a biennial basis, as requested in the Global Strategy for Shelter to the Year 2000.

Financing and cost evaluation $75 billion, including about $10 billion from the international community on grant or concessional terms.

B Improving human settlement management

Basis for action. By the turn of the century, the majority of the world's population will be living in cities. While urban settlements, particularly in developing countries, are showing many of the symptoms of the global environment and development crisis, they nevertheless generate 60 per cent of gross national product and, if properly managed, can develop the capacity to sustain their productivity, improve the living conditions of their residents and manage natural resources in a sustainable way.

Some metropolitan areas extend over the boundaries of several political and/or administrative entities (counties and municipalities) even though they conform to a continuous urban system. In many cases this political heterogeneity hinders the implementation of comprehensive environmental management programmes.

Objective The objective is to ensure sustainable management of all urban settlements, particularly in developing countries, in order to enhance their ability to improve the living conditions of residents, especially the marginalized and disenfranchised, thereby contributing to the achievement of national economic development goals.

Activities

A *Improving urban management*

One existing framework for strengthening management is in the United Nations Development Programme/World Bank/United Nations Centre for Human Settlements (Habitat) Urban Management Programme (UMP), a concerted global effort to assist developing countries in addressing urban management issues. Its coverage should be extended to all interested countries during the period 1993-2000. All countries should, as appropriate and in accordance with national plans, objectives and priorities and with the assistance of non-governmental organizations and representatives of local authorities, undertake the following activities at the national, state/provincial and local levels, with the assistance of relevant programmes and support agencies:

a Adopting and applying urban management guidelines in the areas of land management, urban environmental management, infrastructure management and municipal finance and administration;

b Accelerating efforts to reduce urban poverty through a number of actions, including:

i Generating employment for the urban poor, particularly women, through the provision, improvement and maintenance of urban infrastructure and services and the support of economic activities in the informal sector, such as repairs, recycling, services and small commerce;

ii Providing specific assistance to the poorest of the urban poor through, *inter alia*, the creation of social infrastructure in order to reduce hunger and homelessness, and the provision of adequate community services;

iii Encouraging the establishment of indigenous community-based organizations, private voluntary organizations and other forms of non-governmental entities that can contribute to the efforts to reduce poverty and improve the quality of life for low-income families;

c Adopting innovative city planning strategies to address environmental and social issues by:

i Reducing subsidies on, and recovering the full costs of, environmental and other services of high standard (e.g. water supply, sanitation, waste collection, roads, telecommunications) provided to higher income neighbourhoods;

ii Improving the level of infrastructure and service provision in poorer urban areas;

d Developing local strategies for improving the quality of life and the environment, integrating decisions on land use and land management, investing in the public and private sectors and mobilizing human and material resources, thereby promoting employment generation that is environmentally sound and protective of human health.

B *Strengthening urban data systems*

During the period 1993-2000 all countries should undertake, with the active participation of the business sector as appropriate, pilot projects in selected cities for the collection, analysis and subsequent dissemination of urban data, including environmental impact analysis, at the local, state/provincial, national and international levels and the establishment of city data management capabilities.[5] United Nations organizations, such as Habitat, UNEP and UNDP, could provide technical advice and model data management systems.

C *Encouraging intermediate city development*

In order to relieve pressure on large urban agglomerations of developing countries, policies and strategies should be implemented towards the development of intermediate cities that create employment opportunities for unemployed labour in the rural areas and support rural-based economic activities, although sound urban management is essential to ensure that urban sprawl does not expand resource degradation over an ever wider land area and increase pressures to convert open space and agricultural/buffer lands for development.

Therefore all countries should, as appropriate, conduct reviews of urbanization processes and policies in order to assess the environmental impacts of growth and apply urban planning and management approaches specifically suited to the needs, resource capabilities and characteristics of their growing intermediate-sized cities. As appropriate, they should also concentrate on activities aimed at facilitating the transition from rural to urban lifestyles and settlement patterns and at promoting the development of small-scale economic activities, particularly the production of food, to support local income generation and the production of intermediate goods and services for rural hinterlands.

All cities, particularly those characterized by severe sustainable development problems, should, in accordance with national laws, rules and regulations, develop and strengthen programmes aimed at addressing such problems and guiding their development along a sustainable path. Some international initiatives in support

An overcrowded *favela* housing migrants on the outskirts of Caracas. The urban poor are a high priority group as the inhabitants of many urban areas include a high number of people with low or no income.

of such efforts, as in the Sustainable Cities Programme of Habitat and the Healthy Cities Programme of WHO, should be intensified. Additional initiatives involving the World Bank, the regional development banks and bilateral agencies, as well as other interested stakeholders, particularly international and national representatives of local authorities, should be strengthened and coordinated. Individual cities should, as appropriate:

a Institutionalize a participatory approach to sustainable urban development, based on a continuous dialogue between the actors involved in urban development (the public sector, private sector and communities), especially women and indigenous people;

b Improve the urban environment by promoting social organization and environmental awareness through the participation of local communities in the identification of public services needs, the provision of urban infrastructure, the enhancement of public amenities and the protection and/or rehabilitation of older buildings, historic precincts and other cultural artifacts. In addition, "green works" programmes should be activated to create self-sustaining human development activities and both formal and informal employment opportunities for low-income urban residents;

c Strengthen the capacities of their local governing bodies to deal more effectively with the broad range of developmental and environmental challenges associated with rapid and sound urban growth through comprehensive approaches to planning that recognize the individual needs of cities and are based on ecologically sound urban design practices;

d Participate in international "sustainable city networks" to exchange experiences and mobilize national and international technical and financial support;

e Promote the formulation of environmentally sound and culturally sensitive tourism programmes as a strategy for sustainable development of urban and rural settlements and as a way of decentralizing urban development and reducing discrepancies among regions;

f Establish mechanisms, with the assistance of relevant international agencies, to mobilize resources for local initiatives to improve environmental quality;

g Empower community groups, non-governmental organizations and individuals to assume the authority and responsibility for managing and enhancing their immediate environment through participatory tools, techniques and approaches embodied in the concept of environmental care.

Cities of all countries should reinforce cooperation among themselves and cities of the developed countries, under the aegis of non-governmental organizations active in this field, such as the International Union of Local Authorities (IULA), the International Council for Local Environmental Initiatives (ICLEI) and the World Federation of Twin Cities.

Financing and cost evaluation \$100 billion, including about \$15 billion from the international community on grant or concessional terms.

Section I

C Promoting sustainable land-use planning and management

Basis for action. Access to land resources is an essential component of sustainable low-impact lifestyles. Land resources are the basis for (human) living systems and provide soil, energy, water and the opportunity for all human activity. In rapidly growing urban areas, access to land is rendered increasingly difficult by the conflicting demands of industry, housing, commerce, agriculture, land tenure structures and the need for open spaces. Furthermore, the rising costs of urban land prevent the poor from gaining access to suitable land. In rural areas, unsustainable practices, such as the exploitation of marginal lands and the encroachment on forests and ecologically fragile areas by commercial interests and landless rural populations, result in environmental degradation, as well as in diminishing returns for impoverished rural settlers.

Objective The objective is to provide for the land requirements of human settlement development through environmentally sound physical planning and land use so as to ensure access to land to all households and, where appropriate, the encouragement of communally and collectively owned and managed land.[6] Particular attention should be paid to the needs of women and indigenous people for economic and cultural reasons.

Activities All countries should consider, as appropriate, undertaking a comprehensive national inventory of their land resources in order to establish a land information system in which land resources will be classified according to their most appropriate uses and environmentally fragile or disaster-prone areas will be identified for special protection measures.

Subsequently, all countries should consider developing national land-resource management plans to guide land-resource development and utilization and, to that end, should:

a Establish, as appropriate, national legislation to guide the implementation of public policies for environmentally sound urban development, land utilization, housing and for the improved management of urban expansion;

b Create, where appropriate, efficient and accessible land markets that meet community development needs by, *inter alia*, improving land registry systems and streamlining procedures in land transactions;

c Develop fiscal incentives and land-use control measures, including land-use planning solutions for a more rational and environmentally sound use of limited land resources;

d Encourage partnerships among the public, private and community sectors in managing land resources for human settlements development;

The protection of the environment being a concern shared by all nations, this issue is a joint responsibility. Therefore, the environmental problems can best be solved through the integration of environmental concerns in all measures to be taken at the local, national and international levels.
Mr. Jean-Luc Dehaene
Prime Minister
Belgium

e Strengthen community-based land-resource protection practices in existing urban and rural settlements;
f Establish appropriate forms of land tenure that provide security of tenure for all land-users, especially indigenous people, women, local communities, the low-income urban dwellers and the rural poor;
g Accelerate efforts to promote access to land by the urban and rural poor, including credit schemes for the purchase of land and for building/acquiring or improving safe and healthy shelter and infrastructure services;
h Develop and support the implementation of improved land-management practices that deal comprehensively with potentially competing land requirements for agriculture, industry, transport, urban development, green spaces, preserves and other vital needs;
i Promote understanding among policy makers of the adverse consequences of unplanned settlements in environmentally vulnerable areas and of the appropriate national and local land-use and settlements policies required for this purpose.

At the international level, global coordination of land-resource management activities should be strengthened by the various bilateral and multilateral agencies and programmes, such as UNDP, FAO, the World Bank, the regional development banks, other interested organizations and the UNDP/World Bank/Habitat Urban Management Programme, and action should be taken to promote the transfer of applicable experience on sustainable land-management practices to and among developing countries.

Financing and cost evaluation \$3 billion, including about \$300 million from the international community on grant or concessional terms.

D Promoting the integrated provision of environmental infrastructure: water, sanitation, drainage and solid-waste management

Basis for action The sustainability of urban development is defined by many parameters relating to the availability of water supplies, air quality and the provision of environmental infrastructure for sanitation and waste management. As a result of the density of users, urbanization, if properly managed, offers unique opportunities for the supply of sustainable environmental infrastructure through adequate pricing policies, educational programmes and equitable access mechanisms that are economically and environmentally sound. In most developing countries, however, the inadequacy and lack of environmental infrastructure is responsible for widespread ill-health and a large number of preventable deaths each year. In those countries conditions are set to worsen due to growing needs that exceed the capacity of Governments to respond adequately.

An integrated approach to the provision of environmentally sound infrastructure in human settlements, in particular for the urban and rural poor, is an investment in sustainable development that can improve the quality of life, increase productivity, improve health and reduce the burden of investments in curative medicine and poverty alleviation.

Most of the activities whose management would be improved by an integrated approach, are covered in Agenda 21 as follows: chapter 6 (Protecting and promoting human health conditions), chapters 9 (Protecting the atmosphere), 18 (Protecting the quality and supply of freshwater resources) and 21 (Environmentally sound management of solid wastes and sewage-related issues).

Objective The objective is to ensure the provision of adequate environmental infrastructure facilities in all settlements by the year 2025. The achievement of this objective would require that all developing countries incorporate in their national strategies programmes to build the necessary technical, financial and human resource capacity aimed at ensuring better integration of infrastructure and environmental planning by the year 2000.

Activities All countries should assess the environmental suitability of infrastructure in human settlements, develop national goals for sustainable management of waste, and implement environmentally sound technology to ensure that the environment, human health and quality of life are protected. Settlement infrastructure and environmental programmes designed to promote an integrated human settlements approach to the planning, development, maintenance and management of environmental infrastructure (water supply, sanitation, drainage, solid-waste management) should be strengthened with the assistance of bilateral and multilateral agencies. Coordination among these agencies and with collaboration from international and national representatives of local authorities, the private sector and community groups should also be strengthened. The activities of all agencies engaged in providing environmental infrastructure should, where possible, reflect an ecosystem or metropolitan area approach to settlements and should include monitoring, applied research, capacity-building, transfer of appropriate technology and technical cooperation among the range of programme activities.

Developing countries should be assisted at the national and local levels in adopting an integrated approach to the provision of water supply, energy, sanitation, drainage and solid-waste management, and external funding agencies should ensure that this approach is applied in particular to environmental infrastructure improvement in informal settlements based on regulations and standards that take into account the living conditions and resources of the communities to be served.

All countries should, as appropriate, adopt the following principles for the provision of environmental infrastructure:
a Adopt policies that minimize if not altogether avoid environmental damage, whenever possible;
b Ensure that relevant decisions are preceded by environmental impact assessments and also take into account the costs of any ecological consequences;
c Promote development in accordance with indigenous practices and adopt technologies appropriate to local conditions;
d Promote policies aimed at recovering the actual cost of infrastructure services, while at the same time recognizing the need to find suitable approaches (including subsidies) to extend basic services to all households;
e Seek joint solutions to environmental problems that affect several localities.

The dissemination of information from existing programmes should be facilitated and encouraged among interested countries and local institutions.

Financing and cost evaluation The Conference secretariat has estimated most of the costs of implementing the activities of this programme in other chapters. The secretariat estimates the average total annual cost (1993-2000) of technical assistance from the international community on grant or concessional terms to be about \$50 million.

E Promoting sustainable energy and transport systems in human settlements

Basis for action. Most of the commercial and non-

THE ENLIGHTENED SERVICE OF ENERGY

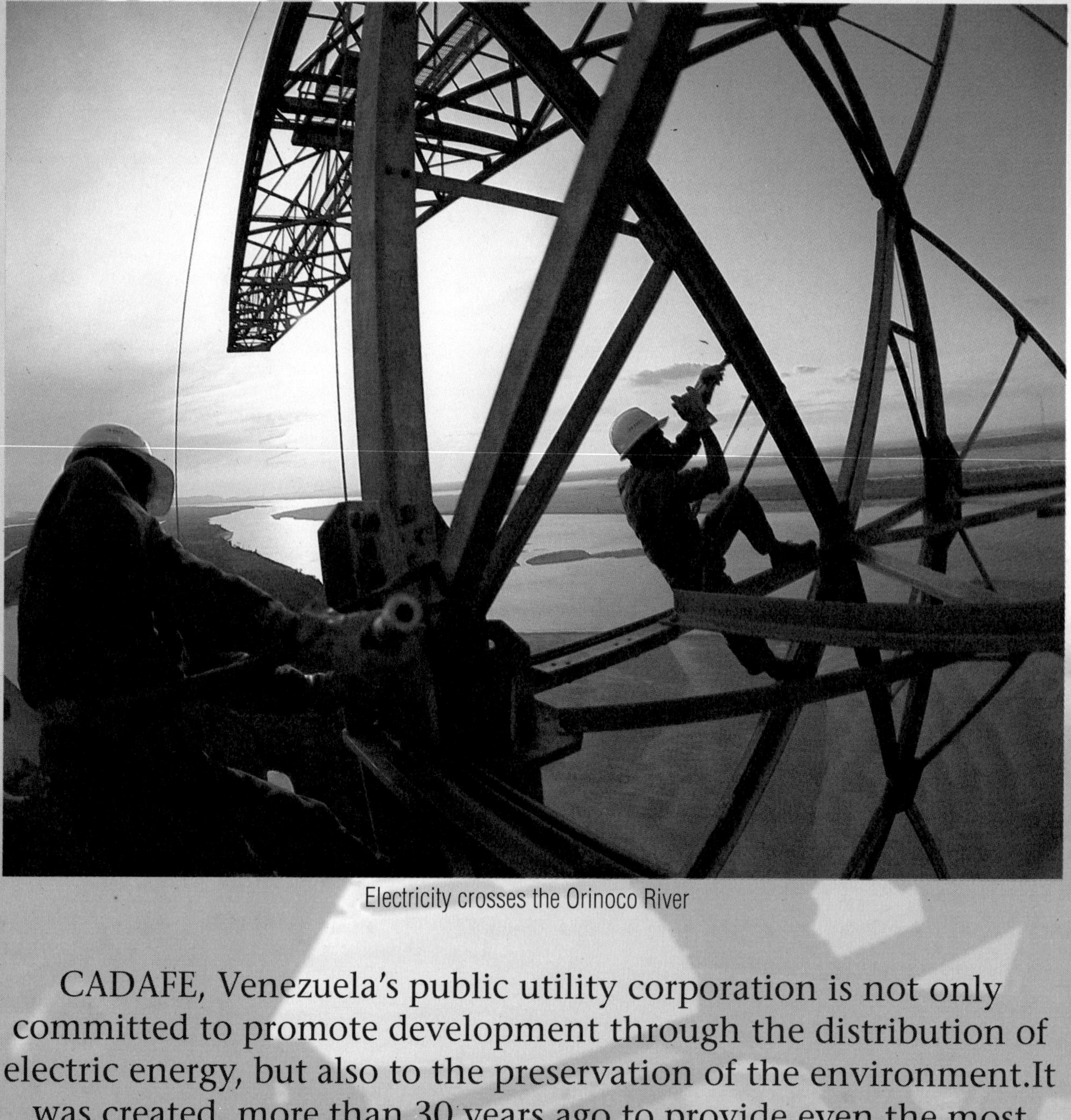

Electricity crosses the Orinoco River

CADAFE, Venezuela's public utility corporation is not only committed to promote development through the distribution of electric energy, but also to the preservation of the environment.It was created more than 30 years ago to provide even the most remote regions of the land with reliable electric service and environmental benefits while promoting economic growth and holding down customers' energy costs. Cadafe provides electric energy to more than 93 % of the land. In Venezuela we say that "Cadafe reaches the limits of the country" and even beyond them since it services parts of Colombia.

CADAFE
empresa de energía eléctrica del estado venezolano

Transport accounts for some 60 per cent of petroleum consumption and contributes to pollution, health and noise problems. Developing alternative transport, such as the electric car, would help improve the quality of life of many urban populations.

commercial energy produced today is used in and for human settlements, and a substantial percentage of it is used by the household sector. Developing countries are at present faced with the need to increase their energy production to accelerate development and raise the living standards of their populations, while at the same time reducing energy production costs and energy-related pollution. Increasing the efficiency of energy use to reduce its polluting effects and to promote the use of renewable energies must be a priority in any action taken to protect the urban environment.

Developed countries, as the largest consumers of energy, are faced with the need for energy planning and management, promoting renewable and alternate sources of energy, and evaluating the life-cycle costs of current systems and practices as a result of which many metropolitan areas are suffering from pervasive air quality problems related to ozone, particulate matters and carbon monoxide. The causes have much to do with technological inadequacies and with an increasing fuel consumption generated by inefficiencies, high demographic and industrial concentrations and a rapid expansion in the number of motor vehicles.

Transport accounts for about 30 per cent of commercial energy consumption and for about 60 per cent of total global consumption of liquid petroleum. In developing countries, rapid motorization and insufficient investments in urban-transport planning, traffic management and infrastructure, are creating increasing problems in terms of accidents and injury, health, noise, congestion and loss of productivity similar to those occurring in many developed countries. All of these problems have a severe impact on urban populations, particularly the low-income and no-income groups.

Objectives The objectives are to extend the provision of more energy-efficient technology and alternative/renewable energy for human settlements and to reduce negative impacts of energy production and use on human health and on the environment.

Activities The principal activities relevant to this programme area are included in chapter 9 (Protecting the atmosphere), programme area B, subprogramme 1 (Energy development, efficiency and consumption) and subprogramme 2 (Transportation).

A comprehensive approach to human settlement development should include the promotion of sustainable energy development in all countries, as follows:

a Developing countries, in particular, should:

i Formulate national action programmes to promote and support reafforestation and national forest regeneration with a view to achieving sustained provision of the biomass energy needs of the low-income groups in urban areas and the rural poor, in particular women and children;

ii Formulate national action programmes to promote integrated development of energy-saving and renewable energy technologies, particularly for the use of solar, hydro, wind and biomass sources;

iii Promote wide dissemination and commercialization of renewable energy technologies through suitable measures, *inter alia*, fiscal and technology transfer mechanisms;

iv Carry out information and training programmes directed at manufacturers and users in order to promote energy-saving techniques and energy-efficient appliances;

b International organizations and bilateral donors should:

i Support developing countries in implementing national energy programmes in order to achieve widespread use of energy-saving and renewable energy technologies, particularly the use of solar, wind, biomass and hydro sources;

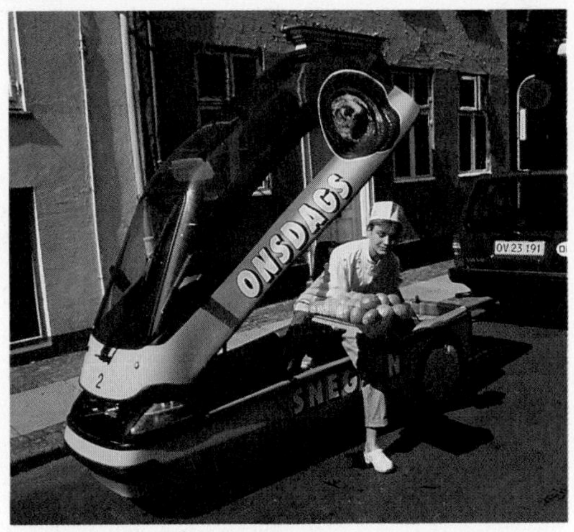

ii Provide access to research and development results to increase energy-use efficiency levels in human settlements.

Promoting efficient and environmentally sound urban transport systems in all countries should be a comprehensive approach to urban-transport planning and management. To this end, all countries should:

a Integrate land-use and transportation planning to encourage development patterns that reduce transport demand;

b Adopt urban-transport programmes favouring high-occupancy public transport in countries, as appropriate;

c Encourage non-motorized modes of transport by providing safe cycleways and footways in urban and suburban centres in countries, as appropriate;

d Devote particular attention to effective traffic management, efficient operation of public transport and maintenance of transport infrastructure;

e Promote the exchange of information among countries and representatives of local and metropolitan areas;

f Re-evaluate the present consumption and production patterns in order to reduce the use of energy and national resources.

Financing and cost evaluation The Conference secretariat has estimated the costs of implementing the activities of this programme in chapter 9.

F Promoting human settlement planning and management in disaster-prone areas

Basis for action. Natural disasters cause loss of life, disruption of economic activities and urban productivity, particularly for highly susceptible low-income groups, and environmental damage, such as loss of fertile agricultural land and contamination of water resources, and can lead to major resettlement of populations. Over the past two decades, they are estimated to have caused some 3 million deaths and affected 800 million people. Global economic losses have been estimated by the Office of the United Nations Disaster Relief Coordinator to be in the range of $30-50 billion per year.[7]

The General Assembly, in resolution 44/236, proclaimed the 1990s as the International Decade for Natural Disaster Reduction. The goals of the Decade[8] bear relevance to the objectives of the present programme area.

In addition, there is an urgent need to address the prevention and reduction of man-made disasters and/or disasters caused by, *inter alia*, industries, unsafe nuclear power generation and toxic wastes (see chapter 6 of Agenda 21).

Objective The objective is to enable all countries, in

Mankind is under threat in the global drive for progress at the expense of the Earth's natural resources. The Earth must be saved from further degradation. The convening of UNCED could not have been more timely. The international community must use the opportunity to take appropriate action to rehabilitate the destruction we have inflicted on our world and to conserve our natural resource base. This will need global goodwill and determination. With such a commitment UNCED will succeed and mankind will remove itself from potential listing as an endangered species.
H.E. Sir Ketumile Masire
President
Botswana

particular those that are disaster-prone, to mitigate the negative impact of natural and man-made disasters on human settlements, national economies and the environment.

Activities Three distinct areas of activity are foreseen under this programme area, namely, the development of a "culture of safety", pre-disaster planning and post-disaster reconstruction.

A *Developing a culture of safety*
To promote a "culture of safety" in all countries, especially those that are disaster-prone, the following activities should be carried out:
a Completing national and local studies on the nature and occurrence of natural disasters, their impact on people and economic activities, the effects of inadequate construction and land use in hazard-prone areas, and the social and economic advantages of adequate pre-disaster planning;
b Implementing nationwide and local awareness campaigns through all available media, translating the above knowledge into information easily comprehensible to the general public and to the populations directly exposed to hazards;
c Strengthening, and/or developing global, regional, national and local early warning systems to alert populations to impending disasters;
d Identifying industrially based environmental disaster areas at the national and international levels and implementing strategies aimed at the rehabilitation of these areas through, *inter alia*:
i Restructuring of the economic activities and promoting new job opportunities in environmentally sound sectors;
ii Promoting close collaboration between governmental and local authorities, local communities and non-governmental organizations and private business;
iii Developing and enforcing strict environmental control standards.

B *Developing pre-disaster planning*
Pre-disaster planning should form an integral part of human settlement planning in all countries. The following should be included:
a Undertaking complete multi-hazard research into risk and vulnerability of human settlements and settlement infrastructure, including water and sewerage, communication and transportation networks, as one type of risk reduction may increase vulnerability to another (e.g., an earthquake-resistant house made of wood will be more vulnerable to wind storms);
b Developing methodologies for determining risk and vulnerability within specific human settlements and incorporating risk and vulnerability reduction into the human settlement planning and management process;
c Redirecting inappropriate new development and human settlements to areas not prone to hazards;
d Preparing guidelines on location, design and operation of potentially hazardous industries and activities;
e Developing tools (legal, economic etc.) to encourage disaster-sensitive development, including means of ensuring that limitations on development options are not punitive to owners, or incorporate alternative means of compensation;
f Further developing and disseminating information on disaster-resistant building materials and construction technologies for buildings and public works in general;
g Developing training programmes for contractors and builders on disaster-resistant construction methods. Some programmes should be directed particularly to small enterprises, which build the great majority of housing and other small buildings in the developing countries, as well as to the rural populations, which build their own houses;
h Developing training programmes for emergency site managers, non-governmental organizations and community groups which cover all aspects of disaster mitigation, including urban search and rescue, emergency communications, early warning techniques, and pre-disaster planning;
i Developing procedures and practices to enable local communities to receive information about hazardous installations or situations in these areas, and facilitate their participation in early warning and disaster abatement and response procedures and plans;
j Preparing action plans for the reconstruction of settlements, especially the reconstruction of community life-lines.

C *Initiating post-disaster reconstruction and rehabilitation planning*
The international community, as a major partner in post-reconstruction and rehabilitation, should ensure that the countries involved derive the greatest benefits from the funds allocated by undertaking the following activities:
a Carrying out research on past experiences on the social and economic aspects of post-disaster reconstruction and adopting effective strategies and guidelines for post-disaster reconstruction, with particular focus on development-focused strategies in the allocation of scarce reconstruction resources, and on the opportunities that post-disaster reconstruction provides to introduce sustainable settlement patterns;
b Preparing and disseminating international guidelines for adaptation to national and local needs;
c Supporting efforts of national Governments to initiate contingency planning, with participation of affected communities, for post-disaster reconstruction and rehabilitation.

Financing and cost evaluation $50 million from the international community on grant or concessional terms.

G Promoting sustainable construction industry activities

Basis for action The activities of the construction sector are vital to the achievement of the national socio-economic development goals of providing shelter, infrastructure and employment. However, they can be a major source of environmental damage through depletion of the natural resource base, degradation of fragile eco-zones, chemical pollution and the use of building materials harmful to human health.

Objectives The objectives are, first, to adopt policies and technologies and to exchange information on them in order to enable the construction sector to meet human settlement development goals, while avoiding harmful side-effects on human health and on the biosphere, and, second, to enhance the employment-generation capacity of the construction sector. Governments should work in close collaboration with the private sector in achieving these objectives.

Activities All countries should, as appropriate and in accordance with national plans, objectives and priorities:
a Establish and strengthen indigenous building materials industry, based, as much as possible, on inputs of locally available natural resources;
b Formulate programmes to enhance the utilization of local materials by the construction sector by expanding technical support and incentive schemes for increasing the capabilities and economic viability of small-scale and informal operatives which make use of these

Section I

The Million Homes project, Sri Lanka. A government scheme lends money to local groups and communities enabling people to build and improve homes. Repayment of loans is high. Recouped capital is re-invested into the scheme.

materials and traditional construction techniques;

c Adopt standards and other regulatory measures which promote the increased use of energy-efficient designs and technologies and sustainable utilization of natural resources in an economically and environmentally appropriate way;

d Formulate appropriate land-use policies and introduce planning regulations specially aimed at the protection of eco-sensitive zones against physical disruption by construction and construction-related activities;

e Promote the use of labour-intensive construction and maintenance technologies which generate employment in the construction sector for the underemployed labour force found in most large cities, while at the same time promoting the development of skills in the construction sector;

f Develop policies and practices to reach the informal sector and self-help housing builders by adopting measures to increase the affordability of building materials on the part of the urban and rural poor, through, *inter alia*, credit schemes and bulk procurement of building materials for sale to small-scale builders and communities.

All countries should:

a Promote the free exchange of information on the entire range of environmental and health aspects of construction, including the development and dissemination of databases on the adverse environmental effects of building materials through the collaborative efforts of the private and public sectors;

b Promote the development and dissemination of databases on the adverse environmental and health effects of building materials and introduce legislation and financial incentives to promote recycling of energy-intensive materials in the construction industry and conservation of waste energy in building-materials production methods;

c Promote the use of economic instruments, such as product charges, to discourage the use of construction materials and products that create pollution during their life cycle;

d Promote information exchange and appropriate technology transfer among all countries, with particular attention to developing countries, for resource management in construction, particularly for non-renewable resources;

e Promote research in construction industries and related activities, and establish and strengthen institutions in this sector.

Financing and cost evaluation $40 billion, including about $4 billion from the international community on grant or concessional terms.

H Promoting human resource development and capacity-building for human settlements development

Basis for action Most countries, in addition to shortcomings in the availability of specialized expertise in the areas of housing, settlement management, land management, infrastructure, construction, energy, transport, and pre-disaster planning and reconstruction, face three cross-sectoral human resource development and capacity-building shortfalls. First is the absence of an enabling policy environment capable of integrating the resources and activities of the public sector, the private sector and the community, or social sector; second is the weakness of specialized training and research institutions; and third is the insufficient capacity for technical training and assistance for low-income communities, both urban and rural.

Objective The objective is to improve human resource development and capacity-building in all countries by enhancing the personal and institutional capacity of all actors, particularly indigenous people and women, involved in human settlement development. In this regard, account should be taken of traditional cultural practices of indigenous people and their relationship to the environment.

Activities Specific human resource development and capacity-building activities have been built into each of the programme areas of this chapter. More generally, however, additional steps should be taken to reinforce those activities. In order to do so, all countries, as appropriate, should take the following action:

a Strengthening the development of human resources and of capacities of public sector institutions through technical assistance and international cooperation so as to achieve by the year 2000 substantial improvement in the efficiency of governmental activities;

b Creating an enabling policy environment supportive of the partnership between the public, private and community sectors;

c Providing enhanced training and technical assistance to institutions providing training for technicians, professionals and administrators, and appointed, elected and professional members of local governments and strengthening their capacity to address priority training needs, particularly in regard to social, economic and environmental aspects of human settlements development;

d Providing direct assistance for human settlement development at the community level, *inter alia*, by:

i Strengthening and promoting programmes for social mobilization and raising awareness of the potential of women and youth in human settlement activities;

ii Facilitating coordination of the activities of women, youth, community groups and non-governmental organizations in human settlements development;

iii Promoting research on women's programmes and other groups, and evaluating progress made with a view to identifying bottlenecks and needed assistance;

e Promoting the inclusion of integrated environmental management into general local government activities.

Both international organizations and non-governmental organizations should support the above activities by, *inter alia*, strengthening subregional training institutions, providing updated training materials and disseminating the results of successful human resource and capacity-building activities, programmes and projects.

Financing and cost evaluation $65 million from the international community on grant or concessional terms.

1 No aggregate figures are available on internal expenditure or official development assistance on human settlements. However, data available in the World Development Report, 1991, for 16 low-income developing countries shows that the percentage of central government expenditure on housing, amenities and social security and welfare for 1989 averaged 5.6 per cent, with a high of 15.1 per cent in the case of Sri Lanka, which has embarked on a vigorous housing programme. In OECD industrialized countries, during the same year, the percentage of central government expenditure on housing, amenities and social security and welfare ranged from a minimum of 29.3 per cent to a maximum of 49.4 per cent, with an average of 39 per cent (World Bank, World Development Report, 1991, World Development Indicators, table 11 (Washington, D.C., 1991)).

2 See the report of the Director-General for Development and International Economic Cooperation containing preliminary statistical data on operational activities of the United Nations system for 1988 (A/44/324-E/1989/106/Add.4, annex).

3 World Bank, Annual Report, 1991 (Washington, D.C., 1991).

4 UNDP, "Reported investment commitments related to UNDP-assisted projects, 1988", table 1, "Sectoral distribution of investment commitment in 1988-1989".

5 A pilot programme of this type, the City Data Programme (CDP), is already in operation in the United Nations Centre on Human Settlements (Habitat) aimed at the production and dissemination to participating cities of micro-computer application software designed to store, process and retrieve city data for local, national and international exchange and dissemination.

6 This calls for integrated land-resource management policies, which are also addressed in chapter 10 of Agenda 21.

7 Estimates of the Office of the United Nations Disaster Relief Coordinator.

8 The goals of the International Decade for Natural Disaster Reduction, set out in the annex to General Assembly resolution 44/236, are as follows:

a To improve the capacity of each country to mitigate the effects of natural disasters expeditiously and effectively, paying special attention to assisting developing countries in the assessment of disaster damage potential and in the establishment of early warning systems and disaster-resistant structures when and where needed;

b To devise appropriate guidelines and strategies for applying existing scientific and technical knowledge, taking into account the cultural and economic diversity among nations;

c To foster scientific and engineering endeavours aimed at closing critical gaps in knowledge in order to reduce loss of life and property;

d To disseminate existing and new technical information related to measures for the assessment, prediction and mitigation of natural disasters;

e To develop measures for the assessment, prediction, prevention and mitigation of natural disasters through programmes of technical assistance and technology transfer, demonstration projects, and education and training, tailored to specific disasters and locations, and to evaluate the effectiveness of those programmes.

Chapter 8 Integrating environment and development in decision-making

A Integrating environment and development at the policy, planning and management levels

Basis for action Prevailing systems for decision-making in many countries tend to separate economic, social and environmental factors at the policy, planning and management levels. This influences the actions of all groups in society, including Governments, industry and individuals, and has important implications for the efficiency and sustainability of development. An adjustment or even a fundamental reshaping of decision-making, in the light of country-specific conditions, may be necessary if environment and development is to be put at the centre of economic and political decision-making, in effect achieving a full integration of these factors. In recent years, some Governments have also begun to make significant changes in the institutional structures of government in order to enable more systematic consideration of the environment when decisions are made on economic, social, fiscal, energy, agricultural, transportation, trade and other policies, as well as the implications of policies in these areas for the environment. New forms of dialogue are also being developed for achieving better integration among national and local government, industry, science, environmental groups and the public in the process of developing effective approaches to environment and development. The responsibility for bringing about changes lies with Governments in partnership with the private sector and local authorities, and in collaboration with national, regional and inter-national organizations, including in particular UNEP, UNDP and the World Bank. Exchange of experience between countries can also be significant. National plans, goals and objectives, national rules, regulations and law, and the specific situation in which different countries are placed are the overall framework in which such integration takes place. In this context, it must be borne in mind that environmental standards may pose severe economic and social costs if they are uniformly applied in developing countries.

Objectives The overall objective is to improve or restructure the decision-making process so that consideration of socio-economic and environmental issues is fully integrated and a broader range of public participation assured. Recognizing that countries will develop their own priorities in accordance with their prevailing conditions, needs, national plans, policies and programmes, the following objectives are proposed:

a To conduct a national review of economic, sectoral

and environmental policies, strategies and plans to ensure the progressive integration of environmental and developmental issues;

b To strengthen institutional structures to allow the full integration of environmental and developmental issues, at all levels of decision-making;

c To develop or improve mechanisms to facilitate the involvement of concerned individuals, groups and organizations in decision-making at all levels;

d To establish domestically determined procedures to integrate environment and development issues in decision-making.

Activities

A *Improving decision-making processes*

The primary need is to integrate environmental and developmental decision-making processes. To do this, Governments should conduct a national review and, where appropriate, improve the processes of decision-making so as to achieve the progressive integration of economic, social and environmental issues in the pursuit of development that is economically efficient, socially equitable and responsible and environmentally sound. Countries will develop their own priorities in accordance with their national plans, policies and programmes for the following activities:

a Ensuring the integration of economic, social and environmental considerations in decision-making at all levels and in all ministries;

b Adopting a domestically formulated policy framework that reflects a long-term perspective and cross-sectoral approach as the basis for decisions, taking account of the linkages between and within the various political, economic, social and environmental issues involved in the development process;

c Establishing domestically determined ways and means to ensure the coherence of sectoral, economic, social and environmental policies, plans and policy instruments, including fiscal measures and the budget; these mechanisms should apply at various levels and bring together those interested in the development process;

d Monitoring and evaluating the development process systematically, conducting regular reviews of the state of human resources development, economic and social conditions and trends, the state of the environment and natural resources; this could be complemented by annual environment and development reviews, with a view to assessing sustainable development achievements by the various sectors and departments of government;

e Ensuring transparency of, and accountability for, the environmental implications of economic and sectoral policies;

f Ensuring access by the public to relevant information, facilitating the reception of public views and allowing for effective participation.

B *Improving planning and management systems*

To support a more integrated approach to decision-making, the data systems and analytical methods used to support such decision-making processes may need to be improved. Governments, in collaboration, where appropriate, with national and international organizations, should review the status of the planning and management system and, where necessary, modify and strengthen procedures so as to facilitate the integrated consideration of social, economic and environmental issues. Countries will develop their own priorities in accordance with their national plans, policies and programmes for the following activities:

a Improving the use of data and information at all stages of planning and management, making systematic and simultaneous use of social, economic, developmental, ecological and environmental data; analysis should stress inter-actions and synergisms; a broad range of analytical methods should be encouraged so as to provide various points of view;

b Adopting comprehensive analytical procedures for prior and simultaneous assessment of the impacts of decisions, including the impacts within and among the economic, social and environmental spheres; these procedures should extend beyond the project level to policies and programmes; analysis should also include assessment of costs, benefits and risks;

c Adopting flexible and integrative planning approaches that allow the consideration of multiple goals and enable adjustment of changing needs; integrative area approaches at the ecosystem or watershed level can assist in this approach;

d Adopting integrated management systems, particularly for the management of natural resources; traditional or indigenous methods should be studied and considered wherever they have proved effective; women's traditional roles should not be marginalized as a result of the introduction of new management systems;

e Adopting integrated approaches to sustainable development at the regional level, including trans-boundary areas, subject to the requirements of particular circumstances and needs;

f Using policy instruments (legal/regulatory and economic) as a tool for planning and management, seeking incorporation of efficiency criteria in decisions; instruments should be regularly reviewed and adapted to ensure that they continue to be effective;

g Delegating planning and management responsibilities to the lowest level of public authority consistent with effective action; in particular the advantages of effective and equitable opportunities for participation by women should be discussed;

h Establishing procedures for involving local communities in contingency planning for environmental and industrial accidents, and maintaining an open exchange of information on local hazards.

Financing and cost evaluation $50 million from the international community on grant or concessional terms.

JORGEN SCHYTTE/STILL PICTURES

Bangladesh. A Danida-sponsored project to generate income for women. Such schemes provide funds for low income groups as well as allowing them to become involved in decision making processes.

Nature in Bulgaria is beautiful, diverse and unique in many respects. Its conservation requires a judicious environmental and development strategy. In addressing environmental issues Bulgaria will also rely on the cooperation, assistance and expertise of advanced industrial states. The Earth Summit was a forum which discussed global environmental problems and outlined further concerted actions based on the sustainable development concept. It is our moral obligation to do something now, so that the coming generations may live in a better and friendlier environment.
Zhelyu Zhelev
President
Republic of Bulgaria

B Providing an effective legal and regulatory framework

Basis for action Laws and regulations suited to country-specific conditions are among the most important instruments for transforming environment and development policies into action, not only through "command and control" methods, but also as a normative framework for economic planning and market instruments. Yet, although the volume of legal texts in this field is steadily increasing, much of the law-making in many countries seems to be *ad hoc* and piecemeal, or has not been endowed with the necessary institutional machinery and authority for enforcement and timely adjustment.

While there is continuous need for law improvement in all countries, many developing countries have been affected by shortcomings of laws and regulations. To effectively integrate environment and development in the policies and practices of each country, it is essential to develop and implement integrated, enforceable and effective laws and regulations that are based upon sound social, ecological, economic and scientific principles. It is equally critical to develop workable programmes to review and enforce compliance with the laws, regulations and standards that are adopted. Technical support may be needed for many countries to accomplish these goals. Technical cooperation requirements in this field include legal information, advisory services and specialized training and institutional capacity-building.

The enactment and enforcement of laws and regulations (at the regional, national, state/provincial or local/municipal level) are also essential for the implementation of most international agreements in the field of environment and development, as illustrated by the frequent treaty obligation to report on legislative measures. The survey of existing agreements undertaken in the context of conference preparations has indicated problems of compliance in this respect, and the need for improved national implementation and, where appropriate, related technical assistance. In developing their national priorities, countries should take account of their international obligations.

Objectives The overall objective is to promote, in the light of country-specific conditions, the integration of environment and development policies through appropriate legal and regulatory policies, instruments and enforcement mechanisms at the national, state, provincial and local level. Recognizing that countries will develop their own priorities in accordance with their needs and national and, where appropriate, regional plans, policies and programmes, the following objectives are proposed:

a To disseminate information on effective legal and regulatory innovations in the field of environment and development, including appropriate instruments and compliance incentives, with a view to encouraging their wider use and adoption at the national, state, provincial and local level;

b To support countries that request it in their national efforts to modernize and strengthen the policy and legal framework of governance for sustainable development, having due regard for local social values and infrastructures;

c To encourage the development and implementation of national, state, provincial and local programmes that assess and promote compliance and respond appropriately to non-compliance.

Activities

A *Making laws and regulations more effective*
Governments, with the support, where appropriate, of competent international organizations, should regularly assess the laws and regulations enacted and the related institutional/administrative machinery established at the national/state and local/municipal level in the field of environment and sustainable development, with a view to rendering them effective in practice. Programmes for this purpose could include the promotion of public awareness, preparation and distribution of guidance material, and specialized training, including workshops, seminars, education programmes and conferences, for public officials who design, implement, monitor and enforce laws and regulations.

B *Establishing judicial and administrative procedures*
Governments and legislators, with the support, where appropriate, of competent international organizations, should establish judicial and administrative procedures for legal redress and remedy of actions affecting environment and development that may be unlawful or infringe on rights under the law, and should provide access to individuals, groups and organizations with a recognized legal interest.

C *Providing legal reference and support services*
Competent intergovernmental and non-governmental organizations could cooperate to provide Governments and legislators, upon request, with an integrated programme of environment and development law (sustainable development law) services, carefully adapted to the specific requirements of the recipient legal and administrative systems. Such systems could usefully include assistance in the preparation of comprehensive inventories and reviews of national legal systems. Past experience has demonstrated the usefulness of combining specialized legal information services with legal expert advice. Within the United Nations system, closer cooperation among all agencies concerned would avoid duplication of databases and facilitate division of labour. These agencies could examine the possibility and merit of performing reviews of selected national legal systems.

D *Establishing a cooperative training network for sustainable development law*
Competent international and academic institutions could, within agreed frameworks, cooperate to provide, especially for trainees from developing countries, postgraduate programmes and in-service training facilities in environment and development law. Such training should address both the effective application and the progressive improvement of applicable laws, the related skills of negotiating, drafting and mediation, and the training of trainers. Intergovernmental and non-governmental organizations already active in this field could cooperate with related university programmes to harmonize curriculum planning and to offer an optimal range of options to interested Governments and potential sponsors.

E *Developing effective national programmes for reviewing and enforcing compliance with national, state, provincial and local laws on environment and development*
Each country should develop integrated strategies to maximize compliance with its laws and regulations relating to sustainable development, with assistance from international organizations and other countries as appropriate. The strategies could include:

a Enforceable, effective laws, regulations and standards that are based on sound economic, social and environmental principles and appropriate risk assessment, incorporating sanctions designed to punish violations, obtain redress and deter future violations;

b Mechanisms for promoting compliance;

c Institutional capacity for collecting compliance data, regularly reviewing compliance, detecting violations, establishing enforcement priorities, undertaking effective enforcement, and conducting periodic evaluations of the effectiveness of compliance and enforcement programmes;

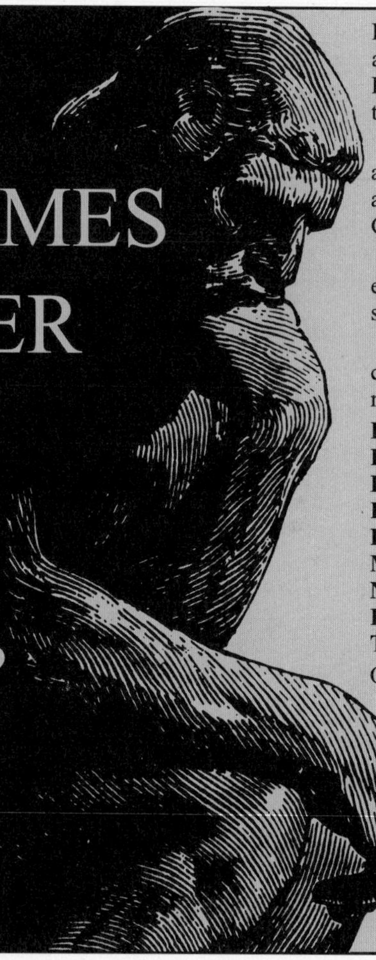

Mechanics in a workshop in the Noakhali District, Bangladesh. Industry and business should incorporate social, economic and environmental dimensions into economic management of projects.

JORGEN SCHYTTE/STILL PICTURES

d Mechanisms for appropriate involvement of individuals and groups in the development and enforcement of laws and regulations on environment and development.

F *National monitoring of legal follow-up to international instruments*

Contracting parties to international agreements, in consultation with the appropriate secretariats of relevant international conventions as appropriate, should improve practices and procedures for collecting information on legal and regulatory measures taken. Contracting parties to international agreements could undertake sample surveys of domestic follow-up action subject to agreement by the sovereign States concerned.

Financing and cost evaluation $6 million from the international community on grant or concessional terms.

C Making effective use of economic instruments and market and other incentives

Basis for action. Environmental law and regulation are important but cannot alone be expected to deal with the problems of environment and development. Prices, markets and governmental fiscal and economic policies also play a complementary role in shaping attitudes and behaviour towards the environment.

During the past several years, many Governments, primarily in industrialized countries but also in Central and Eastern Europe and in developing countries, have been making increasing use of economic approaches, including those that are market-oriented. Examples include the polluter-pays principle and the more recent natural-resource-user-pays concept.

Within a supportive international and national economic context and given the necessary legal and regulatory framework, economic and market-oriented approaches can in many cases enhance capacity to deal with the issues of environment and development. This would be achieved by providing cost-effective solutions, applying integrated pollution prevention control, promoting technological innovation and influencing environmental behaviour, as well as providing financial resources to meet sustainable development objectives.

What is needed is an appropriate effort to explore and make more effective and widespread use of economic and market-oriented approaches within a broad framework of development policies, law and regulation suited to country-specific conditions as part of a general transition to economic and environmental policies that are supportive and mutually reinforcing.

Objectives Recognizing that countries will develop their own priorities in accordance with their needs and national plans, policies and programmes, the challenge is to achieve significant progress in the years ahead in meeting three fundamental objectives:

a To incorporate environmental costs in the decisions of producers and consumers, to reverse the tendency to treat the environment as a "free good" and to pass these costs on to other parts of society, other countries, or to future generations;

b To move more fully towards integration of social and environmental costs into economic activities, so that prices will appropriately reflect the relative scarcity and total value of resources and contribute towards the prevention of environmental degradation;

c To include, wherever appropriate, the use of market principles in the framing of economic instruments and policies to pursue sustainable development.

Activities

A *Improving or reorienting governmental policies*

In the near term, Governments should consider gradually building on experience with economic instruments and market mechanisms by undertaking to reorient their policies, keeping in mind national plans, priorities and objectives, in order to:

a Establish effective combinations of economic, regulatory and voluntary (self-regulatory)approaches;

b Remove or reduce those subsidies that do not conform with sustainable development objectives;

c Reform or recast existing structures of economic and fiscal incentives to meet environment and development objectives;

d Establish a policy framework that encourages the creation of new markets in pollution control and environmentally sounder resource management;
e Move towards pricing consistent with sustainable development objectives.

In particular, Governments should explore, in cooperation with business and industry, as appropriate, how effective use can be made of economic instruments and market mechanisms in the following areas:
i Issues related to energy, transportation, agriculture and forestry, water, wastes, health, tourism and tertiary services;
ii Global and transboundary issues;
iii The development and introduction of environmentally sound technology and its adaptation, diffusion and transfer to developing countries, in conformity with chapter 34.

B *Taking account of the particular circumstances of developing countries and countries with economies in transition*
A special effort should be made to develop applications of the use of economic instruments and market mechanisms geared to the particular needs of developing countries and countries with economies in transition, with the assistance of regional and international economic and environmental organizations and, as appropriate, non-governmental research institutes, by:
a Providing technical support to those countries on issues relating to the application of economic instruments and market mechanisms;
b Encouraging regional seminars and, possibly, the development of regional centres of expertise.

C *Creating an inventory of effective uses of economic instruments and market mechanisms*
Given the recognition that the use of economic instruments and market mechanisms is relatively recent, exchange of information about different countries' experiences with such approaches should be actively encouraged. In this regard, Governments should encourage the use of existing means of information exchange to look at effective uses of economic instruments.

D *Increasing understanding of the role of economic instruments and market mechanisms*
Governments should encourage research and analysis on effective uses of economic instruments and incentives with the assistance and support of regional and international economic and environmental organizations, as well as non-governmental research institutes, with a focus on such key issues as:
a The role of environmental taxation suited to national conditions;
b The implications of economic instruments and incentives for competitiveness and international trade, and potential needs for appropriate future international cooperation and coordination;
c The possible social and distributive implications of using various instruments.

E *Establishing a process for focusing on pricing*
The theoretical advantages of using pricing policies, where appropriate, need to be better understood, and accompanied by greater understanding of what it means to take significant steps in this direction. Processes should therefore be initiated, in cooperation with business, industry, large enterprises, transnational corporations, as well as other social groups, as appropriate, at both the national and international levels, to examine:
a The practical implications of moving towards greater reliance on pricing that internalize environmental costs appropriate to help achieve sustainable development objectives;
b The implications for resource pricing in the case of resource-exporting countries, including the implications of such pricing policies for developing countries;
c The methodologies used in valuing environmental costs.

F *Enhancing understanding of sustainable development economics*
Increased interest in economic instruments, including market mechanisms, also requires a concerted effort to improve understanding of sustainable development economics by:
a Encouraging institutions of higher learning to review their curricula and strengthen studies in sustainable development economics;
b Encouraging regional and international economic organizations and non-governmental research institutes with expertise in this area to provide training sessions and seminars for government officials;
c Encouraging business and industry, including large industrial enterprises and transnational corporations with expertise in environmental matters, to organize training programmes for the private sector and other groups.

Financing and cost evaluation $5 million from the international community on grant or concessional terms.

D Establishing systems for integrated environmental and economic accounting

Basis for action. A first step towards the integration of sustainability into economic management is the establishment of better measurement of the crucial role of the environment as a source of natural capital and as a sink for by-products generated during the production of man-made capital and other human activities. As sustainable development encompasses social, economic and environmental dimensions, it is also important that national accounting procedures are not restricted to measuring the production of goods and services that are conventionally remunerated. A common framework needs to be developed whereby the contributions made by all sectors and activities of society, that are not included in the con-ventional national accounts, are included, to the extent consistent with sound theory and practicability, in satellite accounts. A programme to develop national systems of integrated environmental and economic accounting in all countries is proposed.

Objectives. The main objective is to expand existing systems of national economic accounts in order to integrate environment and social dimensions in the accounting framework, including at least satellite systems of accounts for natural resources in all member States. The resulting systems of integrated environmental and economic accounting (IEEA) to be established in all member States at the earliest date should be seen as a complement to, rather than a substitute for, traditional national accounting practices for the foreseeable future. IEEAs would be designed to play an integral part in the national development decision-making process. National accounting agencies should work in close collaboration with national environmental statistics as well as the geographic and natural resources departments. The definition of economically active could be expanded to include people performing productive but unpaid tasks in all countries. This would enable their contribution to be adequately measured and taken into account in decision-making.

Activities

A *Strengthening international cooperation*

The Statistical Office of the United Nations Secretariat should:

a Make available to all member States the methodologies contained in the SNA Handbook on Integrated Environmental and Economic Accounting;

b In collaboration with other relevant United Nations organizations, further develop, test, refine and then standardize the provisional concepts and methods such as those proposed by the SNA Handbook, keeping member States informed of the status of the work throughout this process;

c Coordinate, in close cooperation with other international organizations, the training of national accountants, environmental statisticians and national technical staff in small groups for the establishment, adaptation and development of national IEEAs.

The Department of Economic and Social Development of the United Nations Secretariat, in close collaboration with other relevant United Nations organizations, should:

i Support, in all member States, the utilization of sustainable development indicators in national economic and social planning and decision-making practices, with a view to ensuring that IEEAs are usefully integrated in economic development planning at the national level;

ii Promote improved environmental and economic and social data collection.

B *Strengthening national accounting systems*

At the national level, the programme could be adopted mainly by the agencies dealing with national accounts, in close cooperation with environmental statistics and natural resource departments, with a view to assisting national economic analysts and decision makers in charge of national economic planning. National institutions should play a crucial role not only as the depositary of the system but also in its adaptation, establisment and continuous use. Unpaid productive work such as domestic work and child care should be included, where appropriate, in satellite national accounts and economic statistics. Time-use surveys could be a first step in the process of developing these satellite accounts.

C *Establishing an assessment process*

At the international level, the Statistical Commission should assemble and review experience and advise member States on technical and methodological issues related to the further development and implementation of IEEAs in member States.

Governments should seek to identify and consider measures to correct price distortions arising from environmental programmes affecting land, water, energy and other natural resources.

Governments should encourage corporations:

a To provide relevant environmental information through transparent reporting to shareholders, creditors, employees, governmental authorities, consumers and the public;

b To develop and implement methods and rules for accounting for sustaining development.

D *Strengthening data and information collection*

National Governments could consider implementing the necessary enhancement in data collection to set in place national IEEAs with a view to contributing pragmatically to sound economic management. Major efforts should be made to augment the capacity to collect and analyse environmental data and information and to integrate it with economic data, including gender disaggregated data. Efforts should also be made to develop physical environmental accounts. International donor agencies should consider financing the development of intersectoral data banks to help ensure that national planning for sustainable development is based on precise, reliable and effective information and is suited to national conditions.

E *Strengthening technical cooperation*

The Statistical Office of the United Nations Secretariat, in close collaboration with relevant United Nations organizations, should strengthen existing mechanisms for technical cooperation among countries. This should also include exchange of experience in the establishment of IEEAs, particularly in connection with the valuation of non-marketed natural resources and standardization in data collection. The cooperation of business and industry, including large industrial enterprises and transnational corporations with experience in valuation of such resources, should also be sought.

Financing and cost evaluation $2 million from the international community on grant or concessional terms.

JØRGEN SCHYTTE/STILL PICTURES

Women receiving instruction in the use of pesticides as part of farming skills training in Hesaragatta, India. Environment standards can pose severe economic and social costs if they are uniformly applied in developing countries.

Section II

Conservation and Management of Resources for Development

Chapter 9 Protection of the atmosphere

Protection of the atmosphere is a broad and multi-dimensional endeavour involving various sectors of economic activity. The options and measures described in this chapter are recommended for consideration and, as appropriate, implementation by governments and other bodies in their efforts to protect the atmosphere.

It is recognized that many of the issues discussed in this chapter are also addressed in such international agreements as the 1985 Vienna Convention for the Protection of the Ozone Layer, the 1987 Montreal Protocol on Substances that Deplete the Ozone Layer as amended, the 1992 Framework Convention on Climate Change, and other international, including regional, instruments. In the case of activities covered by such agreements, it is understood that the recommendations contained in this chapter do not oblige any government to take measures which exceed the provisions of these legal instruments. However, within the framework of this chapter, governments are free to carry out additional measures which are consistent with those legal instruments.

It is also recognized that activities that may be undertaken in pursuit of the objectives of this chapter should be coordinated with social and economic development in an integrated manner with a view to avoiding adverse impacts on the latter, taking into full account the legitimate priority needs of developing countries for the achievement of sustained economic growth and the eradication of poverty.

In this context particular reference is also made to Programme Area A of Chapter 2 of Agenda 21.

A Addressing the uncertainties: improving the scientific basis for decision-making

Basis for action Concern about climate change and climate variability, air pollution and ozone depletion has created new demands for scientific, economic and social information to reduce the remaining uncertainties in these fields. Better understanding and prediction of the various properties of the atmosphere and of the affected ecosystems, as well as health impacts and their interactions with socio-economic factors, are needed.

Objectives The basic objective of this programme area is to improve the understanding of processes that influence and are influenced by the Earth's atmosphere on a global, regional and local scale, including, *inter alia*, physical, chemical, geological, biological, oceanic, hydrological, economic and social processes; to build capacity and to enhance international cooperation; and to improve understanding of the economic and social

DAVID HOFFMAN/STILL PICTURES

Industry is essential for production but the activities of industry often result in harmful emissions into the atmosphere and environment. Industrial development should be encouraged to minimize adverse impacts.

11,000 tons of pollutant hangs over Mexico City. 83 per cent of this brown haze is produced by cars; the balance is made up of human excrement, which dries to dust, and factory emissions.

consequences of atmospheric changes and of mitigation and response measures addressing such changes.

Activities Governments at the appropriate level, with the cooperation of the relevant United Nations bodies and, as appropriate, intergovernmental and non-governmental organizations, and the private sector, should:

a Promote research related to the natural processes affecting and being affected by the atmosphere, as well as the critical linkages between sustainable development and atmospheric changes, including impacts on human health, ecosystems, economic sectors, and society.

b Ensure a more balanced geographical coverage of the Global Climate Observing System and its components, including the Global Atmosphere Watch, by facilitating, *inter alia*, the establishment and operation of additional systematic observation stations, and by contributing to the development, utilization and accessibility of these databases;

c Promote cooperation in

i the development of early detection systems concerning changes and fluctuations in the atmosphere, and

ii the establishment and improvement of capabilities to predict such changes and fluctuations and to assess the resulting environmental and socio-economic impacts;

d Cooperate in research to develop methodologies and identify threshold levels of atmospheric pollutants, as well as atmospheric levels of greenhouse gas concentrations, that would cause dangerous anthropogenic interference with the climate system and the environment as a whole, and the associated rates of change that would not allow ecosystems to adapt naturally.

e Promote, and cooperate in the building of scientific capacities, the exchange of scientific data and information, and the facilitation of the participation and training of experts and technical staff, particularly of developing countries, in the fields of research, data assembly, collection and assessment, and systematic observation related to the atmosphere.

B. Promoting sustainable development

A *Energy development, efficiency and consumption*

Basis for action Energy is essential to economic and social development and improved quality of life. Much of the world's energy, however, is currently produced and consumed in ways that could not be sustained if technology were to remain constant and if overall quantities were to increase substantially. The need to control atmospheric emissions of greenhouse and other gases and substances will increasingly need to be based on efficiency in energy production, transmission, distribution and consumption, and on growing reliance on environmentally sound energy systems, particularly new and renewable sources of energy.[1] All energy sources will need to be used in ways that respect the atmosphere, human health, and the environment as a whole.

The existing constraints to increasing the environmentally sound energy supplies required for pursuing the path towards sustainable development, particularly in developing countries, need to be removed.

Objectives The basic and ultimate objective of this programme area is to reduce adverse effects on the atmosphere from the energy sector by promoting policies or programmes, as appropriate, to increase the contribution of environmentally safe and sound and cost effective energy systems, particularly new and renewable ones, through less polluting and more efficient energy production, transmission, distribution and use. This objective should reflect the need for equity, adequate energy supplies and increasing energy consumption in developing countries, and the need to take into consideration the situations of countries that are highly dependent on income generated from the production, processing and export, and/or consumption of fossil fuels and associated energy-intensive products and/or the use of fossil fuels for which countries have serious difficulties in switching to alternatives, and of countries highly vulnerable to adverse effects of climate change.

Activities Governments at the appropriate level, with the cooperation of the relevant United Nations bodies and, as appropriate, intergovernmental and non-governmental organizations, and the private sector, should:

a Cooperate in identifying and developing economically viable, and environmentally sound energy sources to promote the availability of increased energy supplies to support sustainable development efforts, in particular in developing countries;

b Promote the development at the national level of appropriate methodologies for making integrated energy, environment and economic policy decisions for

UNCED confirmed that environmental problems must be addressed in a global context. For Canada, sustainable development is a prerequisite of our prosperity and a safeguard of our identity and we were proud to be one of the original co-sponsors of the United Nations resolution calling for UNCED. The main challenge of UNCED was to bring the North and South together to work towards the goal of sustainable development. The Summit's conventions on climate change and biodiversity were indicative of the great strides we have made in achieving our objective. However, success will be measured not in words, but in actions. Our children's future depends on the steadfastness of our commitment.
Brian Mulroney
Prime Minister
Canada

sustainable development, *inter alia* through environmental impact assessments;
c Promote the research, development, transfer and use of improved energy-efficient technologies and practices, including endogenous technologies in all relevant sectors, giving special attention to the rehabilitation and modernization of power systems, with particular attention to developing countries;
d Promote the research, development, transfer and use of technologies and practices for environmentally sound energy systems, including new and renewable energy systems, with particular attention to developing countries;
e Promote the development of institutional, scientific, planning and management capacities, particularly in developing countries, to develop, produce, and use increasingly efficient and less polluting forms of energy;
f Review current energy supply mixes to determine how the contribution of environmentally sound energy systems as a whole, particularly new and renewable energy systems, could be increased in an economically efficient manner, taking into account respective countries' unique social, physical, economic and political characteristics, and examining and implementing, where appropriate, measures to overcome any barriers to their development and use;
g Coordinate energy plans regionally and sub-regionally, where applicable, and study the feasibility of efficient distribution of environmentally sound energy from new and renewable energy sources;
h In accordance with national socio-economic development and environment priorities, evaluate and, as appropriate, promote cost-effective policies or programmes, including administrative, social and economic measures, in order to improve energy efficiency;
i Build capacity for energy planning and programme management in energy efficiency, as well as for the development, introduction, and promotion of new and renewable sources of energy;
j Promote appropriate energy efficiency and emission standards or recommendations at the national level[2], aimed at the development and use of technologies that minimize adverse impacts on the environment.
k Encourage education and awareness-raising programmes at the local, national, subregional and regional levels concerning energy efficiency and environmentally sound energy systems;
l Establish or enhance, as appropriate, in cooperation with the private sector, labelling programmes for products to provide decision makers and consumers with information on opportunities for energy efficiency.

B *Transportation*

Basis for action The transport sector has an essential and positive role to play in economic and social development, and transportation needs will undoubtedly increase. However, since the transport sector is also a source of atmospheric emissions, there is need for a review of existing transport systems, and the more effective design and management of traffic and transport systems.

Objectives The basic objective of this programme area is to develop and promote cost-effective policies or programmes, as appropriate, to limit, reduce or control, as appropriate, harmful emissions into the atmosphere and other adverse environmental effects of the transport sector, taking into account development priorities as well as the specific local and national circumstances and safety aspects.

Activities Governments at the appropriate level, with the cooperation of the relevant United Nations bodies and, as appropriate, intergovernmental and nongovernmental organizations, and the private sector, should:
a Develop and promote, as appropriate, cost effective, more efficient, less polluting and safer transport systems, particularly integrated rural and urban mass transit, as well as environmentally sound road networks, taking into account the needs for sustainable social, economic and development priorities, particularly in developing countries;
b Facilitate at the international, regional, subregional and national levels the access to and the transfer of safe, efficient, including resource-efficient, and less polluting transport technologies, particularly to the developing countries, including the implementation of appropriate training programmes;
c Strengthen, as appropriate, their efforts at collecting, analysing and exchanging relevant information on the relation between environment and transport, with particular emphasis on the systematic observation of emissions and the development of a transport database;
d In accordance with national socio-economic development and environment priorities, evaluate and, as appropriate, promote cost effective policies or programmes, including administrative, social and economic measures, in order to encourage use of transportation modes that minimize adverse impacts on the atmosphere;
e Develop or enhance, as appropriate, mechanisms to integrate transport planning strategies and urban and regional settlement planning strategies, with a view to reducing the environmental impacts of transport;
f Study, within the framework of the United Nations and its regional economic commissions, the feasibility of convening regional conferences on transport and the environment.

C *Industrial development*

Basis for action Industry is essential for the production of goods and services and is a major source of employment and income, and industrial development as such is essential for economic growth. At the same time, industry is a major resource and materials user and consequently industrial activities result in emissions into the atmosphere and the environment as a whole. Protection of the atmosphere can be enhanced, *inter alia*, by increasing resource and materials efficiency in industry, installing or improving pollution abatement technologies and replacing chlorofluorocarbons (CFCs) and other ozone-depleting substances with appropriate substitutes, as well as by reducing wastes and by-products.

Objectives The basic objective of this programme area is to encourage industrial development in ways that minimize adverse impacts on the atmosphere by, *inter alia*, increasing efficiency in the production and consumption by industry of all resources and materials, by improving pollution-abatement technologies, and by developing new environmentally sound technologies.

Activities Governments at the appropriate level, with the cooperation of the relevant United Nations bodies and, as appropriate, intergovernmental and non-governmental organizations, and the private sector, should:
a In accordance with national socio-economic development and environment priorities, evaluate and, as appropriate, promote cost effective policies or programmes, including administrative, social and economic measures, in order to minimize industrial pollution and adverse impacts on the atmosphere;
b Encourage industry to increase and strengthen its capacity to develop technologies, products and processes which are safe, less polluting, and make more efficient use of all resources and materials, including energy;

Leaf loss on a beech tree in Knole Park, United Kingdom illustrates the impact atmospheric emissions can have on trees. Freshwater and marine ecosystems and biodiversity are also affected. Right: Sweden. Lime is dumped into a lake to neutralize the acid which is killing it.

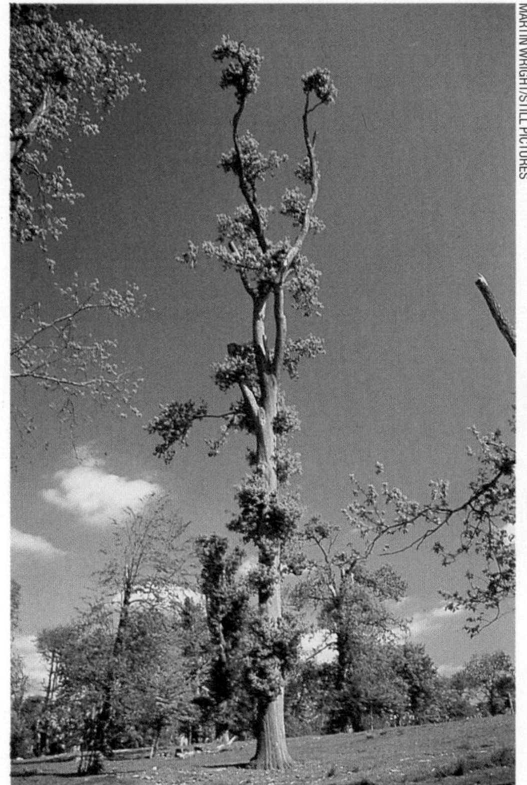

MARTIN WRIGHT/STILL PICTURES

Section II

c Cooperate in development and transfer of such industrial technologies and in development of capacities to manage and use such technologies, particularly with respect to developing countries;
d Develop, improve and apply environmental impact assessments to foster sustainable industrial development;
e Promote efficient use of materials and resources, taking into account the life cycles of products, in order to realize the economic and environmental benefits of using resources more efficiently and producing less wastes;
f Support the promotion of less polluting and more efficient technologies and processes in industries, taking into account area-specific accessible potentials for energy, particularly safe and renewable sources of energy, with a view to limiting industrial pollution and adverse impacts on the atmosphere.

D *Terrestrial and marine resource development and land use*

Basis for action Land-use and resource policies will both affect and be affected by changes in the atmosphere. Certain practices related to terrestrial and marine resources and land use can decrease greenhouse gas sinks and increase atmospheric emissions. The loss of biological diversity may reduce the resilience of ecosystems to climatic variations and air pollution damage. Atmospheric changes can have important impacts on forests, biodiversity, and freshwater and marine ecosystems, as well as on economic activities, such as agriculture. Policy objectives in different sectors may often diverge and will need to be handled in an integrated manner.

Objectives The objectives of this programme area are:
a To promote terrestrial and marine resource utilization and appropriate land-use practices that contribute to:
i Reducing atmospheric pollution and/or limiting anthropogenic emissions of greenhouse gases;
ii The conservation, sustainable management and enhancement, where appropriate, of all sinks for greenhouse gases;
iii The conservation and sustainable use of natural and environmental resources;
b To ensure that actual and potential atmospheric changes and their socio-economic and ecological impacts are fully taken into account in planning and implementing policies and programmes concerning terrestrial and marine resources utilization and land-use practices.

Activities Governments at the appropriate level, with the cooperation of the relevant United Nations bodies and, as appropriate, intergovernmental and non-governmental organizations, and the private sector, should:
a In accordance with national socio-economic development and environment priorities, evaluate and, as appropriate, promote cost effective policies or programmes, including administrative, social and economic measures, in order to encourage environmentally sound land-use practices.
b Implement policies and programmes that will discourage inappropriate and polluting land-use practices and promote sustainable utilization of terrestrial and marine resources;
c Consider promoting the development and use of terrestrial and marine resources and land-use practices that will be more resilient to atmospheric changes and fluctuations;
d Promote sustainable management and cooperation in the conservation and enhancement, as appropriate, of sinks and reservoirs of greenhouse gases, including biomass, forests and oceans, as well as other terrestrial, coastal and marine ecosystems.

C Preventing stratospheric ozone depletion

Basis for action Analysis of recent scientific data has confirmed the growing concern about the continuing depletion of the Earth's stratospheric ozone layer by reactive chlorine and bromine from man-made CFCs, halons and related substances. While the 1985 Vienna Convention for the Protection of the Ozone Layer and the 1987 Montreal Protocol on Substances that Deplete the Ozone Layer (as amended in London in 1990) were important steps in international action, the total chlorine loading of the atmosphere of ozone-depleting substances has continued to rise. This can be changed through compliance with the control measures identified within the Protocol.

Objectives The objectives of this programme area are:

a To realize the objectives defined in the Vienna Convention and the Montreal Protocol and its 1990 amendments, including the consideration in those instruments of the special needs and conditions of the developing countries and the availability to them of alternatives to substances that deplete the ozone layer. Technologies and natural products that reduce demand for these substances should be encouraged;

b To develop strategies aimed at mitigating the adverse effects of ultraviolet radiation reaching the Earth's surface as a consequence of depletion and modification of the stratospheric ozone layer.

Activities Governments at the appropriate level, with the cooperation of the relevant United Nations bodies and, as appropriate, intergovernmental and non-governmental organizations, and the private sector, should:

a Ratify, accept or approve the Montreal Protocol and its 1990 amendments; pay their contributions towards the Vienna/Montreal trust funds and the interim multilateral ozone fund promptly; and contribute, as appropriate, towards ongoing efforts under the Montreal Protocol and its implementing mechanisms, including making available substitutes for CFCs and other ozone-depleting substances and facilitating the transfer of the corresponding technologies to developing countries in order to enable them to comply with the obligations of the Protocol;

b Support further expansion of the Global Ozone Observing System by facilitating – through bilateral and multilateral funding – the establishment and operation of additional systematic observation stations, especially in the tropical belt in the southern hemisphere.

c Participate actively in the continuous assessment of scientific information and the health and environmental effects, as well as of the technological/economic implications of stratospheric ozone depletion; and consider further actions that prove warranted and feasible on the basis of these assessments;

d Based on the results of research on the effects of the additional ultraviolet radiation reaching the Earth's surface, consider taking appropriate remedial measures in the fields of human health, agriculture and marine environment;

Above: the Australian Slip Slap Slop campaign educates the public on the dangers of sun exposure and its link to skin cancer. Below: A traffic policeman in Bangkok protects himself from harmful emissions with a mask.

e Replace CFCs and other ozone-depleting substances, consistent with the Montreal Protocol, recognizing that a replacement's suitability should be evaluated holistically and not simply based on its contribution to solving one atmospheric or environmental problem.

D Transboundary atmospheric pollution

Basis for action Transboundary air pollution has adverse health impacts on humans and other detrimental environmental impacts, such as tree and forest loss and the acidification of water bodies. The geographical distribution of atmospheric pollution monitoring networks is uneven, with the developing countries severely underrepresented. The lack of reliable emissions data outside Europe and North America is a major constraint to measuring transboundary air pollution. There is also insufficient information on the environmental and health effects of air pollution in other regions.

The 1979 Economic Commission for Europe Convention on Long-range Transboundary Air Pollution, and its protocols, have established a regional regime in Europe and North America, based on a review process and cooperative programmes for systematic observation of air pollution, assessment and information exchange. These programmes need to be continued and enhanced, and their experience needs to be shared with other regions of the world.

Objectives The objectives of this programme area are:

a To develop and apply pollution control and measurement technologies for stationary and mobile sources of air pollution and to develop alternative environmentally sound technologies;

b To observe and assess systematically the sources and extent of transboundary air pollution resulting from natural processes and anthropogenic activities;

c To strengthen the capabilities, particularly of developing countries, to measure, model and assess the fate and impacts of transboundary air pollution, through, *inter alia*, exchange of information and training of experts;

d To develop capabilities to assess and mitigate transboundary air pollution resulting from industrial and nuclear accidents, natural disasters and the deliberate and/or accidental destruction of natural resources;

e To encourage the establishment of new and the implementation of existing regional agreements for limiting transboundary air pollution;

f To develop strategies aiming at the reduction of emissions causing transboundary air pollution and their effects.

Activities Governments at the appropriate level, with the cooperation of the relevant United Nations bodies and, as appropriate, intergovernmental and non-governmental organizations, the private sector and financial institutions, should:

a Establish and/or strengthen regional agreements for transboundary air pollution control and cooperate, particularly with developing countries, in the areas of systematic observations and assessment, modelling and the development and exchange of emission control technologies of mobile and stationary sources of air pollution. In this context, greater emphasis should be put on addressing the extent, causes, health and socio-economic impacts of ultraviolet radiation, acidification of the environment and photo-oxidant damage to forests and other vegetation;

b Establish or strengthen early warning systems and response mechanisms for transboundary air pollution resulting from industrial accidents and natural disasters and the deliberate and/or accidental destruction of natural resources;

c Facilitate training opportunities and exchange of data, information and national and/or regional experiences;

d Cooperate on regional, multilateral and bilateral bases to assess transboundary air pollution, and elaborate and implement programmes identifying specific actions to reduce atmospheric emissions and to address their environmental, economic, social and other effects.

Financial and cost evaluation For programme Area A about $640 million from the international community on grant or concessional terms. For the four-part programme under Programme Area B about $20 billion from the international community on grant or concessional terms. For programme Area C in the range of $160-590 million on grant or concessional terms.

1 New and renewable energy sources are solar thermal, solar photovoltaic, wind, hydro, biomass, geothermal, ocean, animal and human power, as referred to in the reports of the Committee on the Development and Utilization of New and Renewable Sources of Energy, prepared specifically for the Conference (see A/CONF.151/PC/119 and A/AC.218/1992/5).

2 This includes standards or recommendations promoted by regional economic integration organizations.

Section II

Chapter 10

Integrated approach to the planning and management of land resources

Land is normally defined as a physical entity in terms of its topography and spatial nature; a broader integrative view also includes natural resources: the soils, minerals, water and biota that the land comprises. These components are organized in ecosystems which provide a variety of services essential to the maintenance of the integrity of life-support systems and the productive capacity of the environment. Land resources are used in ways that take advantage of all these characteristics. Land is a finite resource, while the natural resources it supports can vary over time and according to management conditions and uses. Expanding human requirements and economic activities are placing ever increasing pressures on land resources, creating competition and conflicts and resulting in suboptimal use of both land and land resources. If, in the future, human requirements are to be met in a sustainable manner, it is now essential to resolve these conflicts and move towards more effective and efficient use of land and its natural resources. Integrated physical and land-use planning and management is an eminently practical way to achieve this. By examining all uses of land in an integrated manner, it makes it possible to minimize conflicts, to make the most efficient trade-offs and to link social and economic development with environmental protection and enhancement, thus helping to achieve the objectives of sustainable development. The essence of the integrated approach finds expression in the coordination of the sectoral planning and management activities concerned with the various aspects of land use and land resources.

The present chapter consists of one programme area, the integrated approach to the planning and management of land resources, which deals with the reorganization and, where necessary, some strengthening of the decision-making structure, including existing policies, planning and management procedures and methods that can assist in putting in place an integrated approach to land resources. It does not deal with the operational aspects of planning and management, which are more appropriately dealt with under the relevant sectoral programmes. Since the programme deals with an important cross-sectoral aspect of decision-making for sustainable development, it is closely related to a number of other programmes that deal with that issue directly.

Integrated approach to the planning and management of land resources

Basis for action Land resources are used for a variety of purposes which interact and may compete with one another; therefore, it is desirable to plan and manage all uses in an integrated manner. Integration should take place at two levels, considering, on the one hand, all environmental, social and economic factors (including, for example, impacts of the various economic and social sectors on the environment and natural resources) and, on the other, all environmental

AN ICBP PROJECT

Harvesting potatoes on recently deforested land in Cameroon. In this hilly territory the topsoil will rapidly be washed away by rain unless soil conservation measures are taken.

Bauxite mines in Western Australia which have been reforested by Alcoa of Australia. The rehabiliation included the construction of waterways to control both the run-off and soil erosion, which might affect the river system.

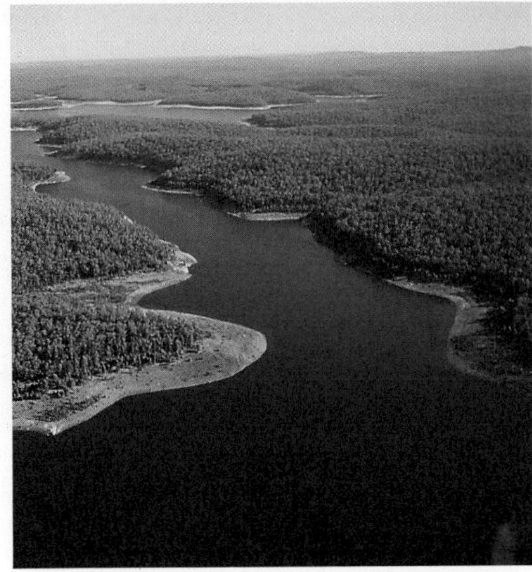

and resource components together (i.e., air, water, biota, land, geological and natural resources). Integrated consideration facilitates appropriate choices and trade-offs, thus maximizing sustainable productivity and use. Opportunities to allocate land to different uses arise in the course of major settlement or development projects or in a sequential fashion as lands become available on the market. This in turn provides opportunities to support traditional patterns of sustainable land management or to assign protected status for conservation of biological diversity or critical ecological services.

A number of techniques, frameworks and processes can be combined to facilitate an integrated approach. They are the indispensable support for the planning and management process, at the national and local level, ecosystem or area levels and for the development of specific plans of action. Many of its elements are already in place but need to be more widely applied, further developed and strengthened. This programme area is concerned primarily with providing a frame-work that will coordinate decision-making; the content and operational functions are therefore not included here but are dealt with in the relevant sectoral programmes of Agenda 21.

Objectives The broad objective is to facilitate allocation of land to the uses that provide the greatest sustainable benefits and to promote the transition to a sustainable and integrated management of land resources. In doing so, environmental, social and economic issues should be taken into consideration. Protected areas, private property rights, the rights of indigenous people and their communities and other local communities and the economic role of women in agriculture and rural development, among other issues, should be taken into account. In more specific terms, the objectives are as follows:

a To review and develop policies to support the best possible use of land and the sustainable management of land resources, by not later than 1996;

b To improve and strengthen planning, management and evaluation systems for land and land resources, by not later than 2000;

c To strengthen institutions and coordinating mechanisms for land and land resources, by not later than 1998;

d To create mechanisms to facilitate the active involvement and participation of all concerned, particularly communities and people at the local level, in decision-making on land use and management, by not later than 1996.

Management-related activities

A *Developing supportive policies and policy instruments*
Governments at the appropriate level, with the support of regional and international organizations, should ensure that policies and policy instruments support the best possible land use and sustainable management of land resources. Particular attention should be given to the role of agricultural land. To do this, they should:

a Develop integrated goal-setting and policy formulation at the national, regional and local levels that takes into account environmental, social, demographic and economic issues;

b Develop policies that encourage sustainable land use and management of land resources and take the land resource base, demographic issues and the interests of the local population into account;

c Review the regulatory framework, including laws, regulations and enforcement procedures, in order to identify improvements needed to support sustainable land use and management of land resources and restricts the transfer of productive arable land to other uses;

d Apply economic instruments and develop institutional mechanisms and incentives to encourage the best possible land use and sustainable management of land resources;

e Encourage the principle of delegating policy-making to the lowest level of public authority consistent with effective action and a locally driven approach.

B *Strengthening planning and management systems*
Governments at the appropriate level, with the support of regional and international organizations, should review and, if appropiate, revise planning and management systems to facilitate an integrated approach. To do this, they should:

a Adopt planning and management systems that facilitate the integration of environmental components such as air, water, land and other natural resources, using landscape ecological planning (LANDEP) or other approaches that focus on, for example, an ecosystem or a watershed;

b Adopt strategic frameworks that allow the integration of both developmental and environmental goals; examples of these frameworks include sustainable livelihood systems, rural development, the World Conservation Strategy/Caring for the Earth, primary environmental care (PEC) and others;

c Establish a general framework for land-use and physical planning within which specialized and more detailed sectoral plans (e.g., for protected areas, agriculture, forests, human settlements, rural development) can be developed; establish intersectoral consultative bodies to streamline project planning and implementation;

d Strengthen management systems for land and natural resources by including appropriate traditional and indigenous methods; examples of these practices include pastoralism, Hema reserves (traditional Islamic land reserves) and terraced agriculture;

e Examine and, if necessary, establish innovative and flexible approaches to programme funding;

f Compile detailed land capability inventories to guide sustainable land resources allocation, management and use at the national and local levels.

C *Promoting application of appropriate tools for planning and management*
Governments at the appropriate level, with the support of national and international organizations, should promote the improvement, further development and widespread application of planning and management tools that facilitate an integrated and sustainable approach to land and resources. To do this, they should:

a Adopt improved systems for the interpretation and integrated analysis of data on land use and land resources;

b Systematically apply techniques and procedures for assessing the environmental, social and economic

Portugal, a land of forests

Of the 88, 705 Km2 of mainland Portugal, more than one third is forested. The cork oak is one of the country's main forest species, covering 670, 000 hectares which represents 30 % of the world's total area of cork forest. Thanks to the cork oak, Portugal is the world leader in the cork industry, producing more and better than any of its competitors and boasting the largest industrial and marketing structure, responsible for 54 % of the world's cork production and 70 % of manufactured products. Cork is the name given to the bark of the cork oak (Quercus Suber L.) which is stripped every nine years during the Summer months, without causing lasting damage to the tree, which regenerates itself during a life cycle which can last 150 years. Cork is the basis of an industry of vital economic importance, with wide ranging applications in manufacturing industry, from cork stoppers to flooring tiles and which has been used as the protective heat shield in missiles and space craft, including the Space Shuttle.

The Amorim Group, started by António Alves Amorim in 1870, is today by far the world's biggest corporate group in the cork sector, established over five continents. Exports from the Group account for a substantial part of Portugal's trade. The Amorim Group has always maintained a different idea of progress:

-'With loving care and attention, respect for Nature is always repaid by her best fruits'.We owe our success to our long established partnership with Nature and we continually defend our partnership through an aggressive policy, which includes legislative measures that cover four major areas : - Protection of forest land, protection of the cork oak, cork production and protection of the cork farmer. Through experience and steady investment we have developed highly efficient production processes which include the use of waste materials (cork dust) as fuel for our boilers. We consider ourselves a living example of the communion between man and nature, the life of the land and the life of man, with cork as a product taking its place in the natural ecological heritage of Portugal and the planet.

Considering how important the environmental issue is to our company's policies and decision making and how successful we have been in combining the need for economic development with respect and fellowship with Nature, I therefore unreservedly endorse the UNCED historic initiative to promote the international cooperation which is so urgently required, in order to protect the environment of our planet and thus ensure the long term future of all its inhabitants.

Américo Ferreira de Amorim
(President)

Amorim Group

impacts, risks, costs and benefits of specific actions;

c Analyse and test methods to include land and ecosystem functions and land resources values in national accounts.

D *Raising awareness*

Governments at the appropriate level, in collaboration with national institutions and interest groups and with the support of regional and international organizations, should launch awareness-raising campaigns to alert and educate people on the importance of integrated land and land resources management and the role that individuals and social groups can play in it. This should be accompanied by provision of the means to adopt improved practices for land use and sustainable management.

E *Promoting public participation*

Governments at the appropriate level, in collaboration with national organizations and with the support of regional and international organizations, should establish innovative procedures, programmes, projects and services that facilitate and encourage the active participation of those affected in the decision-making and implementation process, especially of groups that have, hitherto, often been excluded, such as women, youth, indigenous people and their communities and other local communities.

Financing and cost evaluation Sources of funds and concessional financing $50 million from the international community on grant or concessional terms.

Chapter 11 Combating deforestation

This chapter refers to the four programme areas resulting from the negotiations held at the fourth session of the Preparatory Committee.

A Sustaining the multiple roles and functions of all types of forests, forest lands and woodlands

Basis for action There are major weaknesses in the policies, methods and mechanisms adopted to support and develop the multiple ecological, economic, social and cultural roles of trees, forests and forest lands. Many developed countries are confronted with the effects of air pollution and fire damage on their forests. More effective measures and approaches are often required at the national level to improve and harmonize policy formulation, planning and programming; legislative measures and instruments; development patterns; participation of the general public, especially women and indigenous people; involvement of youth; roles of the private sector, local organizations, non-governmental organizations and cooperatives; development of technical and multidisciplinary skills and quality of human resources; forestry extension and public education; research capability and support; administrative structures and mechanisms, including intersectoral coordination, decentralization and responsibility and incentive systems; and dissemination of information and public relations. This is especially important to ensure a rational and holistic approach to the sustainable and environmentally sound development of forests. The need for securing the multiple roles of forests and forest lands through adequate and appropriate institutional strengthening has been repeatedly emphasized in many of the reports, decisions and recommendations of FAO, ITTO, UNEP, the World Bank, IUCN and other organizations.

Objectives

a To strengthen forest-related national institutions, to enhance the scope and effectiveness of activities related to the management, conservation and sustainable development of forests, and to effectively ensure the sustainable utilization and production of forests' goods and services in both the developed and the developing countries; by the year 2000, to strengthen the capacities and capabilities of national institutions to enable them to acquire the necessary knowledge for the protection and conservation of forests, as well as to expand their scope and, correspondingly, enhance the effectiveness of programmes and activities related to the management and development of forests;

b To strengthen and improve human, technical and professional skills, as well as expertise and capabilities to effectively formulate and implement policies, plans, programmes, research and projects on management, conservation and sustainable development of all types of forests and forest-based resources, and forest lands inclusive, as well as other areas from which forest benefits can be derived.

Management-related activities Governments at the appropriate level, with the support of regional, subregional and international organizations, should, where necessary, enhance institutional capability to promote the multiple roles and functions of all types of forests and vegetation inclusive of other related lands and forest-based resources in supporting sustainable development and environmental conservation in all sectors. This should be done, wherever possible and necessary, by strengthening and/or modifying the existing structures and arrangements, and by improving cooperation and coordination of their respective roles. Some of the major activities in this regard are as follows:

a Rationalizing and strengthening administrative structures and mechanisms, including provision of adequate levels of staff and allocation of responsibilities, decentralization of decision-making, provision of infrastructural facilities and equipment, intersectoral coordination and an effective system of communication;

b Promoting participation of the private sector, labour unions, rural cooperatives, local communities, indigenous people, youth, women, user groups and non-governmental organizations in forest-related activities, and access to information and training programmes within the national context;

c Reviewing and, if necessary, revising measures and programmes relevant to all types of forests and vegetation, inclusive of other related lands and forest-based resources, and relating them to other land uses and development policies and legislation; promoting adequate legislation and other measures as a basis against uncontrolled conversion to other types of land uses;

d Developing and implementing plans and programmes, including definition of national and, if necessary, regional and subregional goals, programmes and criteria for their implementation and subsequent improvement;

e Establishing, developing and sustaining an effective system of forest extension and public education to ensure better awareness, appreciation and management of forests with regard to the multiple roles and values of trees, forests and forest lands;

f Establishing and/or strengthening institutions for forest education and training, as well as forestry industries, for developing an adequate cadre of trained and skilled staff at the professional, technical and vocational levels, with emphasis on youth and women;

g Establishing and strengthening capabilities for research related to the different aspects of forests and forest products, for example, on the sustainable management of forests, research on biodiversity, on the effects of air-borne pollutants, on traditional uses of

forest resources by local populations and indigenous people, and on improving market returns and other non-market values from the management of forests.

Financial and cost evaluation $2.5 billion, including about $860 million from the international community on grant or concessional terms.

B Enhancing the protection, sustainable management and conservation of all forests, and the greening of degraded areas, through forest rehabilitation, afforestation, reforestation and other rehabilitative means

Basis for action Forests world-wide have been and are being threatened by uncontrolled degradation and conversion to other types of land uses, influenced by increasing human needs; agricultural expansion; and environmentally harmful mismanagement, including, for example, lack of adequate forest-fire control and anti-poaching measures, unsustainable commercial logging, overgrazing and unregulated browsing, harmful effects of airborne pollutants, economic incentives and other measures taken by other sectors of the economy. The impacts of loss and degradation of forests are in the form of soil erosion; loss of biological diversity, damage to wildlife habitats and degradation of watershed areas, deterioration of the quality of life and reduction of the options for development.

The present situation calls for urgent and consistent action for conserving and sustaining forest resources. The greening of suitable areas, in all its component activities, is an effective way of increasing public awareness and participation in protecting and managing forest resources. It should include the consideration of land use and tenure patterns and local needs and should spell out and clarify the specific objectives of the different types of greening activities.

Objectives

a To maintain existing forests through conservation and management, and sustain and expand areas under forest and tree cover, in appropriate areas of both developed and developing countries, through the conservation of natural forests, protection, forest rehabilitation, regeneration, afforestation, reforestation and tree planting, with a view to maintaining or restoring the ecological balance and expanding the contribution of forests to human needs and welfare;
b To prepare and implement, as appropriate, national forestry action programmes and/or plans for the management, conservation and sustainable development of forests. These programmes and/or plans should be integrated with other land uses. In this context, country-driven national forestry action programmes and/or plans under the Tropical Forestry Action Programme are currently being implemented in more than 80 countries, with the support of the international community;
c To ensure sustainable management and, where appropriate, conservation of existing and future forest resources;
d To maintain and increase the ecological, biological, climatic, socio-cultural and economic contributions of forest resources;
e To facilitate and support the effective implementation of the non-legally binding authoritative statement of principles for a global consensus on the managament, conservation and sustainable development of all types of forests, adopted by the United Nations Conference on Environment and Development, and on the basis of the implementation of these principles to consider the need for and the feasibility of all kinds of appropriate internationally agreed arrangements to promote international cooperation on forest management, conservation and sustainable development of all types of forests including afforestation, reforestation, and rehabilitation.

Management-related activities Governments should recognize the importance of categorizing forests, within the framework of long-term forest conservation and management policies, into different forest types and setting up sustainable units in every region/watershed with a view to securing the conservation of forests. Governments, with the participation of the private sector, non-governmental organizations, local community groups, indigenous people, women, local government units and the public at large, should act to maintain and expand the existing vegetative cover wherever ecologically, socially and economically feasible, through technical cooperation and other forms of support. Major activities to be considered include:
a Ensuring the sustainable management of all forest ecosystems and woodlands, through improved proper planning, management and timely implementation of silvicultural operations, including inventory and relevant research, as well as rehabilitation of degraded natural forests to restore productivity and environ-

When aborigines used fire to open up this Australian forest land it resulted in trees and shrubs resistant to fire damage colonizing the forests. The fire also assisted some seeds to germinate.

Section II

A stark aerial image of ancient forest in Washington State, USA. Below: This Amazonian land has been forest for 60 million years. It is now barren having suffered the effects of soil erosion when it was cleared.

mental contributions, giving particular attention to human needs for economic and ecological services, wood-based energy, agroforestry, non-timber forest products and services, watershed and soil protection, wildlife management, and forest genetic resources;

b Establishing, expanding and managing, as appropriate to each national context, protected area systems, which includes systems of conservation units for their environmental, social and spiritual functions and values, including conservation of forests in representative ecological systems and landscapes, primary old-growth forests, conservation and management of wildlife, nomination of World Heritage Sites under the World Heritage Convention, as appropriate, conservation of genetic resources, involving in/situ and ex situ measures and undertaking supportive measures to ensure sustainable utilization of biological resources and conservation of biological diversity and the traditional forest habitats of indigenous people, forest dwellers and local communities;

c Undertaking and promoting buffer and transition zone management;

d Carrying out revegetation in appropriate mountain areas, highlands, bare lands, degraded farm lands, arid and semi-arid lands and coastal areas for combating desertification and preventing erosion problems and for other protective functions and national programmes for rehabilitation of degraded lands, including community forestry, social forestry, agroforestry and silvipasture, while also taking into account the role of forests as national carbon reservoirs and sinks;

e Developing industrial and non-industrial planted forests in order to support and promote national ecologically sound afforestation and reforestation/regeneration programmes in suitable sites, including upgrading of existing planted forests of both industrial and non-industrial and commercial purpose to increase their contribution to human needs and to offset pressure on primary/old growth forests. Measures should be taken to promote and provide intermediate yields and to improve the rate of returns on investments in planted forests, through interplanting and underplanting valuable crops;

f Developing/strengthening a national programme and/or master plan for planted forests as a priority, indicating, *inter alia*, the location, scope and species, and specifying areas of existing planted forests requiring rehabilitation, taking into account the economic aspect for future planted forest development, giving emphasis to native species;

g Increasing the protection of forests from pollutants, fire, pests and diseases and other human-made interferences such as forest poaching, mining and unmitigated shifting cultivation, the uncontrolled introduction of exotic plant and animal species, as well as developing and accelerating research for a better understanding of problems relating to the management and regeneration of all types of forests; strengthening and/or establishing appropriate measures to assess and/or check inter-border movement of plants and related materials;

h Stimulating development of urban forestry for the greening of urban, peri-urban and rural human settlements for amenity, recreation and production purposes and for protecting trees and groves;

i Launching or improving opportunities for participation of all people, including youth, women, indigenous people and local communities in the formulation, development and implementation of forest-related programmes and other activities, taking due account of the local needs and cultural values;

j Limiting and aiming to halt destructive shifting cultivation by addressing the underlying social and ecological causes.

DANIEL DANCER/STILL PICTURES

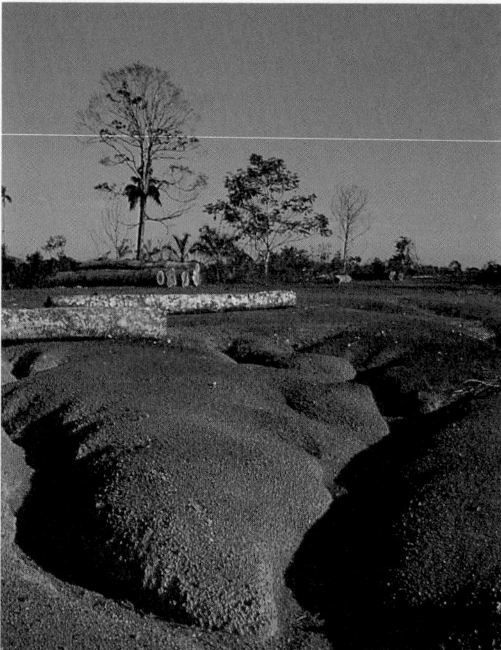

Financial and cost evaluation $10 billion, including about $3.7 billion from the international community on grant or concessional terms.

C Promoting efficient utilization and assessment to recover the full valuation of the goods and services provided by forests, forest lands and woodlands

Basis for action The vast potential of forests and forest lands as a major resource for development is not yet fully realized. The improved management of forests can increase the production of goods and services and, in particular, the yield of wood and non-wood forest products, thus helping to generate additional employment and income, additional value through processing and trade of forest products, increased contribution to foreign exchange earnings, and increased return on investment. Forest resources, being renewable, can be sustainably managed in a manner that is compatible with environmental conservation. The implications of the harvesting of forest resources for the other values of the forest should be taken fully into consideration in the development of forest policies. It is also possible to increase the value of forests through non-damaging uses such as eco-tourism and the managed supply of

For the developing countries, environmental protection is closely linked with the fight against poverty. When we speak of sustainable development, we are thinking of economic growth with social equity and preservation and care for natural resources. In the last dec ade the world has shown its capacity to reach agreements which only yesterday seemed impossible. It requires awareness, imagination and generosity to harmonize interests and make common welfare prevail. International agreement on the environment is possible and we can and must reach it. The destiny of mankind depends on it.
H.E. Mr Patricio Aywin Azocar
President
The Republic of Chile

genetic materials. Concerted action is needed in order to increase people's perception of the value of forests and of the benefits they provide. The survival of forests and their continued contribution to human welfare depends to a great extent on succeeding in this endeavour.

Objectives

a To improve recognition of the social, economic and ecological values of trees, forests and forest lands, including the consequences of the damage caused by the lack of forests; to promote methodologies with a view to incorporating social, economic and ecological values of trees, forests and forest lands into the national economic accounting systems; to ensure their sustainable management in a way that is consistent with land use, environmental considerations and development needs;
b To promote efficient, rational and sustainable utilization of all types of forests and vegetation inclusive of other related lands and forest-based resources, through the development of efficient forest-based processing industries, value-adding secondary processing and trade in forest products, based on sustainably managed forest resources and in accordance with plans that integrate all wood and non-wood values of forests;
c To promote more efficient and sustainable use of forests and trees for fuelwood and energy supplies;
d To promote more comprehensive use and economic contributions of forest areas by incorporating eco-tourism into forest management and planning.

Management-related activities Governments, with the support of the private sector, scientific institutions, indigenous people, non-governmental organizations, cooperatives and entrepreneurs, where appropriate, should undertake the following activities, properly coordinated at the national level, with financial and technical cooperation from international organizations:
a Carrying out detailed investment studies, supply-demand harmonization and environmental impact analysis to rationalize and improve trees and forest utilization and to develop and establish appropriate incentive schemes and regulatory measures, including tenurial arrangements, to provide a favourable investment climate and promote better management;
b Formulating scientifically sound criteria and guidelines for the management, conservation and sustainable development of all types of forests;
c Improving environmentally sound methods and practices of forest harvesting, which are ecologically sound and economically viable, including planning and management, improved use of equipment, storage and transportation to reduce and, if possible, maximize the use of waste and improve value of both wood and non-wood forest products;
d Promoting the better use and development of natural forests and woodlands, including planted forests, wherever possible, through appropriate and environmentally sound and economically viable activities, including silvicultural practices and management of other plant and animal species;
e Promoting and supporting the downstream processing of forest products to increase retained value and other benefits;
f Promoting/popularizing non-wood forest products and other forms of forest resources, apart from fuel-wood (e.g., medicinal plants, dyes, fibres, gums, resins, fodder, cultural products, rattan, bamboo) through programmes and social forestry/participatory forest activities, including research on their processing and uses;
g Developing, expanding and/or improving the effectiveness and efficiency of forest-based processing industries, both wood and non-wood based, involving such aspects as efficient conversion technology and improved sustainable utilization of harvesting and process residues; promoting underutilized species in natural forests through research, demonstration and commercialization; promoting value-adding secondary processing for improved employment, income and retained value; and promoting/improving markets for, and trade in, forest products through relevant institutions, policies and facilities;
h Promoting and supporting the management of wildlife, as well as eco-tourism, including farming, and encouraging and supporting the husbandry and cultivation of wild species, for improved rural income and employment, ensuring economic and social benefits without harmful ecological impacts;
i Promoting appropriate small-scale forest-based enterprises for supporting rural development and local entrepreneurship;
j Improving and promoting methodologies for a comprehensive assessment that will capture the full value of forests, with a view to including that value in the market-based pricing structure of wood and non-wood based products;
k Harmonizing sustainable development of forests with national development needs and trade policies that are compatible with the ecologically sound use of forest resources, using, for example, the ITTO Guidelines for Sustainable Management of Tropical Forests;
l Developing, adopting and strengthening national programmes for accounting the economic and non-economic value of forests.

Financial and cost evaluation $18 billion, including about $880 million from the international community on grant or concessional terms.

D Establishing and/or strengthening capacities for the planning, assessment and systematic observations of forests and related programmes, projects and activities, including commercial trade and processes

Basis for action Assessment and systematic observations are essential components of long-term planning, for evaluating effects, quantitatively and qualitatively, and for rectifying inadequacies. This mechanism, however, is one of the often neglected aspects of forest resources, management, conservation and development. In many cases, even the basic information related to the area and type of forests, existing potential and volume of harvest is lacking. In many developing countries, there is a lack of structures and mechanisms to carry out these functions. There is an urgent need to rectify this situation for a better understanding of the role and importance of forests and to realistically plan for their effective conservation, management, regeneration, and sustainable development.

Objectives

a To strengthen or establish systems for the assessment and systematic observations of forests and forest lands with a view to assessing the impacts of programmes, projects and activities on the quality and extent of forest resources, land available for afforestation, and land tenure, and to integrate the systems in a continuing process of research and in-depth analysis, while ensuring necessary modifications and improve-ments for planning and decision-making. Specific emphasis should be given to the participation of rural people in these processes;
b To provide economists, planners, decision makers and local communities with sound and adequate up-dated information on forests and forest land resources.

Management-related activities Governments and institutions, in collaboration, where necessary, with

Ghana National Petroleum Corporation

Keeping Ghana GREEN

"If people don't have a means of providing fuel for cooking, they will cut down a tree, even if it is the only tree under which they can sit... because they've got to eat, they've got to cook. So they will destroy a tree." (Letitia Obeng)

Concern for the environment, for the sustenance of "Mother Earth" are deeply rooted in Ghanaian culture. The land and its resources are acknowledged to belong to the past, the present and the future generations. Taboos have always sought to prevent the abuse by human beings of the endowments of nature.

As Ghana's rich cultural heritage is a source of inspiration for national development, the Ghana National Petroleum Corporation, a young corporation in a competitive international industry, draws its ability to develop and advance from a firm grounding in these cultural traditions.

For us in Ghana sustaining the environment is a matter of human survival. As the international economic order becomes more adverse, our tropical forests yield to the onslaught of farmers whose incomes are declining from the unjust global reward system. Desperate to survive in the face of falling commodity prices, we tend to look on helplessly as international companies, interested in developing our mineral resources, pay scant attention to issues of the environment. We remain trapped in practices that gravely affect our environment due to our very state of under-development. For instance, more than 75% of the energy used in Ghana has been wood fuels, contributing to severe deforestation.

For us as a national corporation, providing more energy – efficient technology to the majority of our population, is an important contribution to keeping Ghana green. Minimising the use of wood fuels, making liquefied petroleum gas from the refining process at the national refinery useable for domestic purposes, whilst at the same time avoiding problems that developed countries face with the use of fossil fuels, utilising natural gas associated with oil production, are all expressions of our responsibility to "ensure that petroleum operations are conducted in such a manner as to prevent adverse effects on the environment, resources and people of Ghana" [Ghana National Petroleum Corporation Law, 1983, Section 2(2)(e).]

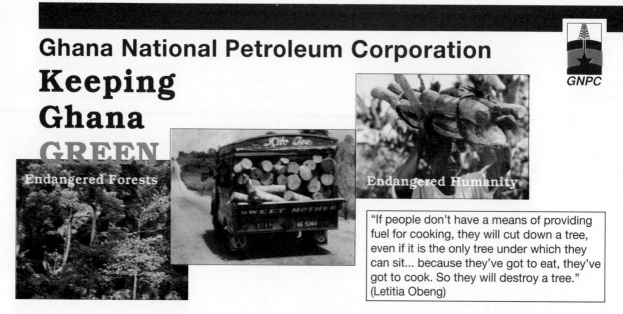

We recognise our responsibility, not only as a Ghanaian entity, but also as a player in the international economic arena, to support the collective objectives of the world community which Earth Summit'92 symbolised.

Protecting the global environment is a shared responsibility of individuals, governments, non-governmental organisations, corporations, churches, families, trade unions, etc; each and every one of us must play our part.

Our corporation is developing its capacity to realise this international commitment.

TSATSU TSIKATA
CHAIRMAN & ACTING CHIEF EXECUTIVE

Top: Food from the forest - just one of the many valuable forest based resources.
Middle: the promotion of efficient, rational and sustainable utilization of all types of forest, and not just for the provision of wood, is essential.
Bottom: demonstrators express their concern over the logging of Brazilian forests outside the Brazilian Embassy in London, England.

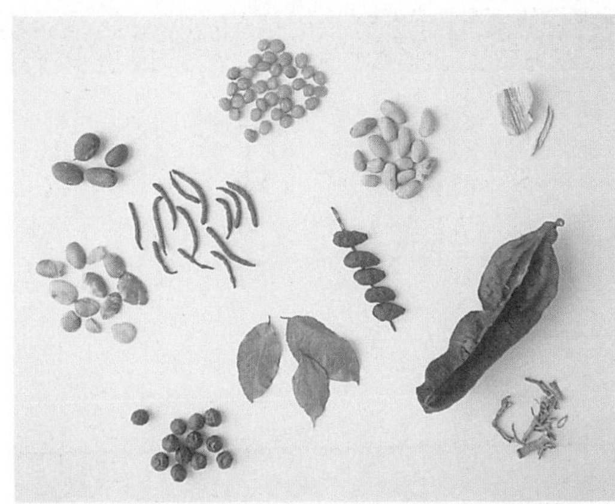

EDWARD PARKER/STILL PICTURES

DAVID HOFFMAN/STILL PICTURES

appropriate international agencies and organizations, universities and non-governmental organizations, should undertake assessments and systematic observations of forests and related programmes and processes with a view to their continuous improvement. This should be linked to related activities of research and management and, wherever possible, be built upon existing systems. Major activities to be considered are:

a Assessing and carrying out systematic observations of the quantitative and qualitative situation and changes of forest cover and forest resources endowments, including land classification, land use and updates of its status, at the appropriate national level, and linking this activity, as appropriate, with planning as a basis for policy and programme formulation;

b Establishing national assessment and systematic observation systems and evaluation of programmes and processes, including establishment of definitions, standards, norms and intercalibration methods, and the capability for initiating corrective actions as well as improving the formulation and implementation of programmes and projects;

c Making estimates of impacts of activities affecting forestry developments and conservation proposals, in terms of key variables such as developmental goals, benefits and costs, contributions of forests to other sectors, community welfare, environmental conditions and biological diversity and their impacts at the local, regional and global levels, where appropriate, to assess the changing technological and financial needs of countries;

d Developing national systems of forest resource assessment and valuation, including necessary research and data analysis, which account for, where possible, the full range of wood and non-wood forest products and services, and incorporating results in plans and strategies and, where feasible, in national systems of accounts and planning;

e Establishing necessary intersectoral and programme linkages, including improved access to information, in order to support a holistic approach to planning and programming.

Financial and cost evaluation $750 million, including about $230 million from the international community on grant or concessional terms.

Section II

Chapter 12

Managing fragile ecosystems: combating desertification and drought

Fragile ecosystems are important ecosystems, with unique features and resources. Fragile ecosystems include deserts, semi-arid lands, mountains, wetlands, small islands and certain coastal areas. Most of these ecosystems are regional in scope, as they transcend national boundaries. This chapter addresses land resource issues in deserts, as well as arid, semi-arid and dry sub-humid areas. Sustainable mountain development is addressed in chapter 13; small islands and coastal areas are discussed in chapter 17.

Desertification is land degradation in arid, semi-arid and dry sub-humid areas resulting from various factors, including climatic variations and human activities. Desertification affects about one sixth of the world's population, 70 per cent of all drylands, amounting to 3.6 billion hectares, and one quarter of the total land area of the world. The most obvious impact of desertification, in addition to widespread poverty, is the degradation of 3.3 billion hectares of the total area of rangeland, constituting 73 per cent of the rangeland with a low potential for human and animal carrying capacity; decline in soil fertility and soil structure on about 47 per cent of the dryland areas constituting marginal rainfed cropland; and the degradation of irrigated cropland, amounting to 30 per cent of the dryland areas with a high population density and agricultural potential.

The priority in combating desertification should be the implementation of preventive measures for lands that are not yet degraded, or which are only slightly degraded. However, the severely degraded areas should not be neglected. In combating desertification and drought, the participation of local communities, rural organizations, national Governments, non-governmental organizations and international and regional organizations is essential.

A Strengthening the knowledge base and developing information and monitoring systems for regions prone to desertification and drought, including the economic and social aspects of these ecosystems

Basis for action The global assessments of the status and rate of desertification conducted by the United Nations Environment Programme (UNEP) in 1977, 1984 and 1991 have revealed insufficient basic knowledge of desertification processes. Adequate world-wide systematic observation systems are helpful for the development and implementation of effective anti-desertification programmes. The capacity of existing international, regional and national institutions, particularly in developing countries, to generate and exchange relevant information is limited. An integrated

LESOTHO HIGHLANDS DEVELOPMENT AUTHORITY

The Lesotho Highlands water project is one of the most ambitious, multipurpose, international water resources development schemes presently being undertaken in the world. The latest engineering methods and tools are being utilised to construct dams, tunnels and a hydropower plant.

Every effort is being made, through implementation of an environmental action plan, to ensure that negative environmental impacts of the project are kept to a minimum, and that the standard of living of those affected by the project is in no way impaired.

Furthermore, Lesotho intends to exploit to the full, the new development opportunities provided by the project, for the sustained benefit of the mountain people in whose midst it is being built.

An independent, internationally renowned expert panel review in 1990 concluded: "There can be few other comparable projects in the world, let alone Africa, where the standard of environmental planning has been as good as in the present case."

A special word of thanks is due to Lesotho's cooperating partners, in particular the World Bank and the European Economic Community, who have given assistance to LHDA in preparing its environmental plans.

The Lesotho Highlands Development Authority (LHDA) will conduct its operations in the spirit of the Earth Summit and Agenda 21, and honour its environmental and development obligations to the Basotho Nation and its natural heritage.

M. E. Sole
Chief Executive

and coordinated information and systematic observation system based on appropriate technology and embracing global, regional, national and local levels is essential for understanding the dynamics of desertification and drought processes. It is also important for developing adequate measures to deal with desertification and drought and improving socio-economic conditions.

Objectives

a To promote the establishment and/or strengthening of national environmental information coordination centres that will act as focal points within Governments for sectoral ministries and provide the necessary standardization and back-up services; to ensure also that national environmental information systems on desertification and drought are linked together through a network at subregional, regional and interregional levels;

b To strengthen regional and global systematic observation networks linked to the development of national systems for the observation of land degradation and desertification caused both by climate fluctuations and by human impact, and to identify priority areas for action;

c To establish a permanent system at both national and international levels for monitoring desertification and land degradation with the aim of improving living conditions in the affected areas.

Management-related activities Governments at the appropriate level, with the support of the relevant international and regional organizations, should:

a Establish and/or strengthen environmental information systems at the national level;

b Strengthen national, state/provincial and local assessment and ensure cooperation/networking between existing environmental information and monitoring systems, such as Earthwatch and the Sahara and Sahel Observatory;

c Strengthen the capacity of national institutions to analyse environmental data so that ecological change can be monitored and environmental information obtained on a continuing basis at the national level.

Financing and cost evaluation $350 million including about $175 million from the international community on grant or concessional terms.

B Combating land degradation through, *inter alia*, intensified soil conservation, afforestation and reforestation activities

Basis for action Desertification affects about 3.6 billion hectares, which is about 70 per cent of the total area of the world's drylands or nearly one quarter of the global land area. In combating desertification on rangeland, rainfed cropland and irrigated land, preventative measures should be launched in areas which are not yet affected or are only slightly affected by desertification; corrective measures should be implemented to sustain the productivity of moderately desertified land; and rehabilitative measures should be taken to recover severely or very severely desertified drylands.

An increasing vegetation cover would promote and stabilize the hydrological balance in the dryland areas and maintain land quality and land productivity. Prevention of not yet degraded land and application of corrective measures and rehabilitation of moderate and severely degraded drylands, including areas affected by sand dune movements, through the introduction of environmentally sound, socially acceptable, fair and economically feasible land-use systems. This will enhance the land carrying capacity and maintenance of biotic resources in fragile ecosystems.

Objectives

a As regards areas not yet affected or only slightly affected by desertification, to ensure appropriate management of existing natural formations (including forests) for the conservation of biodiversity, watershed protection, sustainability of their production and agricultural development, and other purposes, with the full participation of indigenous people;

b To rehabilitate moderately to severely desertified drylands for productive utilization and sustain their productivity for agropastoral/agroforestry development through, *inter alia*, soil and water conservation;

c To increase the vegetation cover and support management of biotic resources in regions affected or prone to desertification and drought, notably through such activities as afforestation/reforestation, agroforestry, community forestry and vegetation retention schemes;

d To improve management of forest resources, including woodfuel, and to reduce woodfuel consumption through more efficient utilization, conservation and the enhancement, development and

ROMANO CAGNONI/STILL PICTURES

Desertification affects about 3.6 billion hectares, one quarter of the global land area. Vegetation cover in areas such as Mali needs to be increased through soil and water conservation.

Collecting woodfuel in (left) Mali, and (right) Burkima Faso, West Africa. The World Bank estimate woodfuel consumption at four and a half times the sustainable production level resulting in progressive deforestation.

ROMANO CAGNONI/STILL PICTURES

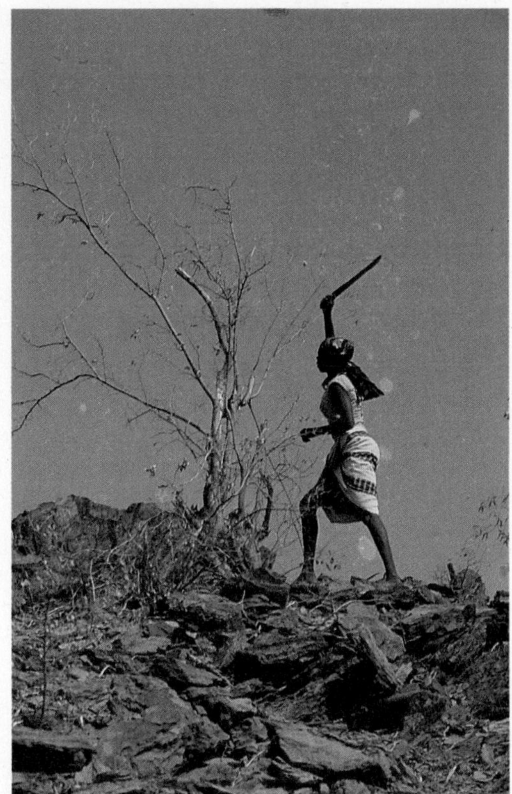

use of other sources of energy, including alternative sources of energy.

Management-related activities Governments at the appropriate level, and with the support of the relevant international and regional organizations, should:

a implement urgent direct preventive measures in drylands that are vulnerable but not yet affected, or only slightly desertified drylands, by introducing:

i improved land-use policies and practices for more sustainable land productivity;

ii appropriate, environmentally sound and economically feasible agricultural and pastoral technologies;

iii improved management of soil and water resources;

b Carry out accelerated afforestation and reforestation programmes, using drought-resistant, fast-growing species, in particular native ones, including legumes and other species, combined with community-based agroforestry schemes. In this regard, creation of large-scale reforestation and afforestation schemes, particularly through the establishment of green belts, should be considered, bearing in mind the multiple benefits of such measures;

c Implement urgent direct corrective measures in moderately to severely desertified drylands with a view to restoring and sustaining their productivity;

d Promote improved land/water/crop-management systems, making it possible to combat salinization in existing irrigated croplands; and to stabilize rainfed croplands and introduce improved soil/crop-management systems into land-use practice;

e Promote participatory management of natural resources, including rangeland, to meet both the needs of rural populations and conservation purposes, based on innovative or adapted indigenous technologies;

f Promote in situ protection and conservation of special ecological areas through legislation and other means for the purpose of combating desertification while ensuring the protection of biodiversity;

g Promote and encourage investment in forestry development in drylands through various incentives, including legislative measures;

h Promote the development and use of sources of energy which will lessen pressure on ligneous resources, including alternative sources of energy and improved stoves.

Financing and cost evaluation $6 billion including about $3 billion from the international community on grant or concessional terms.

C Developing and strengthening integrated development programmes for the eradication of poverty and promotion of alternative livelihood systems in areas prone to desertification

Basis for action In areas prone to desertification and drought, current livelihood and resource-use systems are not able to maintain living standards. In most of the arid and semi-arid areas, the traditional livelihood systems based on agropastoral systems are often inadequate and unsustainable, particularly in view of the effects of drought and increasing demographic pressure. Poverty is a major factor in accelerating the rate of degradation and desertification. Action is therefore needed to rehabilitate and improve the agropastoral systems for sustainable management of rangelands, as well as alternative livelihood systems.

Objectives

a To create the capacity of village communities and pastoral groups to take charge of their development and the management of their land resources on a socially equitable and ecologically sound basis;

b To improve production systems in order to achieve greater productivity within approved programmes for conservation of national resources and in the framework of an integrated approach to rural development;

c To provide opportunities for alternative livelihoods as a basis for reducing pressure on land resources while at the same time providing additional sources of income, particularly for rural populations, thereby improving their standard of living.

Management-related activities Governments at the appropriate level, with the support of the relevant international and regional organizations, should:

a Adopt policies at the national level regarding a decentralized approach to land-resource management, delegating responsibility to rural organizations;

b Create or strengthen rural organizations in charge of village and pastoral land management;

c Establish and develop local, national and

Section II

Demonstrating the use of stone lines to control soil erosion in Kalsaka, Burkima Faso. Stones slow down rain running off the land, allowing it to nourish crops. Using this method crop yields increase by 50 per cent on average, more in dry years.

intersectoral mechanisms to handle environmental and developmental consequences of land tenure expressed in terms of land use and land ownership. Particular attention should be given to protecting the property rights of women and pastoral and nomadic groups living in rural areas;
d Create or strengthen village associations focused on economic activities of common pastoral interest (market gardening, transformation of agricultural products, livestock, herding, etc.);
e Promote rural credit and mobilization of rural savings through the establishment of rural banking systems;
f Develop infrastructure, as well as local production and marketing capacity, by involving the local people to promote alternative livelihood systems and alleviate poverty;
g Establish a revolving fund for credit to rural entrepreneurs and local groups to facilitate the establishment of cottage industries/business ventures and credit for input to agropastoral activities.

Financing and cost evaluation The Conference secretariat has estimated the costs for this programme area in chapter 3 and chapter 14.

D Developing comprehensive anti-desertification programmes and integrating them into national development plans and national environmental planning

Basis for action In a number of developing countries affected by desertification, the natural resource base is the main resource upon which the development process must rely. The social systems interacting with land resources make the problem much more complex, requiring an integrated approach to the planning and management of land resources. Action plans to combat desertification and drought should include management aspects of the environment and development, thus conforming with the approach of integrating national development plans and national environmental action plans.

Objectives
a To strengthen national institutional capabilities to develop appropriate anti-desertification programmes and to integrate them into national development planning;
b To develop and integrate strategic planning frameworks for the development, protection and management of natural resources in dryland areas into national development plans, including national plans to combat desertification, and environmental action plans in countries most prone to desertification;
c To initiate a long-term process for implementing and monitoring strategies related to natural resources management;
d To strengthen regional and international cooperation for combating desertification through, *inter alia*, the adoption of legal and other instruments.

Management-related activities Governments at the appropriate level, and with the support of the relevant international and regional organizations, should:
a Establish or strengthen, national and local anti-desertification authorities within government and local executive bodies, as well as local committees/associations of land users, in all rural communities affected, with a view to organizing working cooperation between all actors concerned, from the grass-roots level (farmers and pastoralists) to the higher levels of government;
b Develop national plans of action to combat desertification and as appropriate, make them integral parts of national development plans and national environmental action plans;
c Implement policies directed towards improving land use, managing common lands appropriately, providing incentives to small farmers and pastoralists, involving women and encouraging private investment in the development of drylands;
d Ensure coordination among ministries and institutions working on anti-desertification programmes at national and local levels.

Financing and cost evaluation $180 million including about $90 million from the international community on grant or concessional terms.

E Developing comprehensive drought preparedness and drought-relief schemes, including self-help arrangements, for drought-prone areas and designing programmes to cope with environmental refugees

Basis for action Drought, in differing degrees of frequency and severity, is a recurring phenomenon throughout much of the developing world, especially Africa. Apart from the human toll (an estimated 3 million people died in the mid-1980s because of drought in sub-Saharan Africa) the economic costs of drought-related disasters are also high in terms of lost production, misused inputs and diversion of development resources.

Early-warning systems to forecast drought will make possible the implementation of drought-preparedness schemes. Integrated packages at the farm and watershed level, such as alternative cropping strategies, soil and water conservation and promotion of water harvesting techniques, could enhance the capacity of land to cope with drought and provide basic necessities, thereby minimizing the number of environmental refugees and the need for emergency drought relief. At the same time, contingency arrangements for relief are needed for periods of acute scarcity.

Objectives
a To develop national strategies for drought preparedness in both the short and long term, aimed at reducing the vulnerability of production systems to drought;
b To strengthen the flow of early-warning information to decision makers and land users to enable nations to implement strategies for drought intervention;
c To develop and integrate drought-relief schemes and means of coping with environmental refugees into national and regional development planning.

Management-related activities In drought-prone areas, Governments at the appropriate level, with the support of the relevant international and regional organizations, should:
a Design strategies to deal with national food deficiencies in periods of production shortfall. These strategies should deal with issues of storage and stocks, imports, port facilities, food storage, transport and distribution;

Jean-Marie Sawadogo with crops from a dry year and a year when rain was plentiful. Right: A mother with her dead child, one of 300 Somalian refugees who died daily due to lack of food. Drought carries a high human cost and in economic terms it often involves diverting resources earmarked for development.

NANA/REIMERS

b Improve national and regional capacity for agrometeorology and contingency crop planning. Agrometeorology links the frequency, content and regional coverage of weather forecasts with the requirements of crop planning and agricultural extension;
c Prepare rural projects for providing short-term rural employment to drought-affected households. The loss of income and entitlement to food is a common source of distress in times of drought. Rural works help to generate the income required to buy food for poor households;
d Establish contingency arrangements, where necessary, for food and fodder distribution and water supply;
e Establish budgetary mechanisms for providing, at short notice, resources for drought relief;
f Establish safety nets for the most vulnerable households.

Financing and cost evaluation $1.2 billion including about $1.1 billion from the international community on grant or concessional terms.

F Encouraging and promoting popular participation and environmental education, focusing on desertification control and management of the effects of drought

Basis for action The experience to date on the successes and failures of programmes and projects points to the need for popular support to sustain activities related to desertification and drought control. But it is necessary to go beyond the theoretical ideal of popular participation and to focus on obtaining actual active popular involvement, rooted in the concept of partnership. This implies the sharing of responsibilities and the mutual involvement of all parties. In this context, this programme area should be considered an essential supporting component of all desertification-control and drought-related activities.

Objectives
a To develop and increase public awareness and knowledge concerning desertification and drought, including the integration of environmental education in the curriculum of primary and secondary schools;
b To establish and promote true partnership between government authorities, at both the national and local levels, other executing agencies, non-governmental organizations and land users stricken by drought and desertification, giving land users a responsible role in the planning and execution processes in order to benefit fully from development projects;
c To ensure that the partners understand one another's needs, objectives and points of view by providing a variety of means such as training, public awareness and open dialogue;
d To support local communities in their own efforts in combating desertification, and to draw on the knowledge and experience of the populations concerned, ensuring the full participation of women and indigenous populations.

Management-related activities Governments at the appropriate level, with the support of the relevant international and regional organizations, should:
a Adopt policies and establish administrative structures for more decentralized decision-making and implementation;
b Establish and utilize mechanisms for the consultation and involvement of land users and for enhancing capability at the grass-roots level to identify and/or contribute to the identification and planning of action;
c Define specific programme/project objectives in cooperation with local communities; design local management plans to include such measures of progress, thereby providing a means of altering project design or changing management practices, as appropriate;
d Introduce legislative, institutional/organizational and financial measures to secure user involvement and access to land resources;
e Establish and/or expand favourable conditions for the provision of services, such as credit facilities and marketing outlets for rural populations;
f Develop training programmes to increase the level of education and participation of people, particularly women and indigenous groups, through, *inter alia*, literacy and the development of technical skills;
g Create rural banking systems to facilitate access to credit for rural populations, particularly women and indigenous groups, and to promote rural savings;
h Adopt appropriate policies to stimulate private and public investment.

Financing and cost evaluation $1.0 billion including about $500 million from the international community on grant or concessional terms.

Chapter 13

Managing fragile ecosystems: sustainable mountain development

Mountains are an important source of water, energy and biological diversity. Furthermore, they are a source of such key resources as minerals, forest products and agricultural products and of recreation. As a major ecosystem representing the complex and interrelated ecology of our planet, mountain environments are essential to the survival of the global ecosystem. Mountain ecosystems are, however, rapidly changing. They are susceptible to accelerated soil erosion, landslides and rapid loss of habitat and genetic diversity. On the human side, there is widespread poverty among mountain inhabitants and loss of indigenous knowledge. As a result, most global mountain areas are experiencing environmental degradation. Hence, the proper management of mountain resources and socio-economic development of the people deserves immediate action.

About 10 per cent of the world's population depends on mountain resources. A much larger percentage draws on other mountain resources, including and especially water. Mountains are a storehouse of biological diversity and endangered species. The two programme areas included in this chapter further elaborate the problem of fragile ecosystems with regard to all mountains of the world.

A Generating and strengthening knowledge about the ecology and sustainable development of mountain ecosystems

Basis for action Mountains are vulnerable to human and natural ecological imbalance. Mountains are the areas most sensitive to all climatic changes in the atmosphere. Specific information on ecology, natural resource potential and socio-economic activities is essential. Mountain and hillside areas hold a rich variety of ecological systems. Because of their vertical dimensions, mountains create gradients of temperature, precipitation and insolation. A given mountain slope may include several climatic systems – such as tropical, subtropical, temperate and alpine – each of which represents a microcosm of a larger habitat diversity. There is, however, a lack of knowledge of mountain ecosystems.The creation of a global mountain database is therefore vital for launching programmes that contribute to the sustainable development of mountain ecosystems.

Objectives

a To undertake a survey of the different forms of soils, forest, water use, crop, plant and animal resources of mountain ecosystems, taking into account the work of existing international and regional organizations;

b To maintain and generate database and information systems to facilitate the integrated management and environmental assessment of mountain ecosystems, taking into account the work of existing international and regional organizations;

c To improve and build the existing land/water ecological knowledge base regarding technologies and agricultural and conservation practices in the mountain regions of the world, with the participation of local communities;

d To create and strengthen the communications network and information clearing-house for existing organizations concerned with mountain issues;

e To improve coordination of regional efforts to protect fragile mountain ecosystems through the consideration of appropriate mechanisms, including regional legal and other instruments;

f To generate information to establish databases and information systems to facilitate an evaluation of environmental risks and natural disasters in mountain ecosystems.

Management-related activities Governments at the appropriate level, with the support of the relevant international and regional organizations, should:

a Strengthen existing institutions or establish new ones at local, national and regional levels to generate a multidisciplinary land/water ecological knowledge base on mountain ecosystems;

b Promote national policies that would provide incentives to local people for the use and transfer of environment-friendly technologies and farming and conservation practices;

c Build up the knowledge base and understanding by creating mechanisms for cooperation and information exchange among national and regional institutions working on fragile ecosystems;

d Encourage policies that would provide incentives to farmers and local people to undertake conservation and regenerative measures;

e Diversify mountain economies, *inter alia*, by creating and/or strengthening tourism, in accordance with integrated management of mountain areas;

f Integrate all forest, rangeland and wildlife activities in such a way that specific mountain ecosystems are maintained;

g Establish appropriate natural reserves in representative species-rich sites and areas.

Financing and cost evaluation $50 million from the international community on grant or concessional terms.

B Promoting integrated watershed development and alternative livelihood opportunities

Basis for action Nearly half of the world's population is affected in various ways by mountain ecology and the degradation of watershed areas. About 10 per cent of the Earth's population lives in mountain areas with higher slopes, while about 40 per cent occupies the adjacent medium- and lower-watershed areas. There are serious problems of ecological deterioration in these watershed areas. For example, in the hillside areas of the Andean countries of South America a large portion of the farming population is now faced with a rapid deterioration of land resources. Similarly, the mountain and upland areas of the Himalayas, South-East Asia and East and Central Africa, which make vital contributions to agricultural production, are threatened by cultivation of marginal lands due to expanding population. In many areas this is accompanied by excessive livestock grazing, deforestation and loss of biomass cover.

Soil erosion can have a devastating impact on the vast numbers of rural people who depend on rainfed agriculture in the mountain and hillside areas. Poverty, unemployment, poor health and bad sanitation are widespread. Promoting integrated watershed development programmes through effective participation of local people is a key to preventing further ecological imbalance. An integrated approach is needed for conserving, upgrading and using the natural resource base of land, water, plant, animal and human resources. In addition, promoting alternative livelihood opportunities, particularly through development of employment schemes that increase the productive base, will have a significant role in improving the standard of living among the large rural population living in mountain ecosystems.

Section II

Mountains are most sensitive to all climatic changes in the atmosphere and often contain several climatic systems. There is a lack of knowledge of mountain ecosystems and a database is a vital component of sustainable mountain development.

Objectives

a By the year 2000, to develop appropriate land-use planning and management for both arable and non-arable land in mountain-fed watershed areas to prevent soil erosion, increase biomass production and maintain the ecological balance;

b To promote income-generating activities, such as sustainable tourism, fisheries and environmentally sound mining, and to improve infrastructure and social services, in particular to protect the livelihoods of local communities and indigenous people;

c To develop technical and institutional arrangements for affected countries to mitigate the effects of natural disasters through hazard-prevention measures, risk zoning, early-warning systems, evacuation plans and emergency supplies.

Management-related activities Governments at the appropriate level, with the support of the relevant international and regional organizations, should:

a Undertake measures to prevent soil erosion and promote erosion-control activities in all sectors;

b Establish task forces or watershed development committees, complementing existing institutions, to coordinate integrated services to support local initiatives in animal husbandry, forestry, horticulture and rural development at all administrative levels;

c Enhance popular participation in the management of local resources through appropriate legislation;

d Support non-governmental organizations and other private groups assisting local organizations and communities in the preparation of projects that would enhance participatory development of local people;

e Provide mechanisms to preserve threatened areas that could protect wildlife, conserve biological diversity or serve as national parks;

f Develop national policies that would provide incentives to farmers and local people to undertake conservation measures and to use environment-friendly technologies;

g Undertake income-generating activities in cottage and agro-processing industries, such as the cultivation and processing of medicinal and aromatic plants;

h Undertake the above activities, taking into account the need for full participation of women, including indigenous people and local communities, in development.

Financial and cost evaluation $13 billion including about $1.9 billion from the international community on grant or concessional terms.

Financing for the promotion of alternative livelihoods in mountain ecosystems should be viewed as part of a country's anti-poverty or alternative livelihoods programme, which is also discussed in chapter 3 and chapter 14.

Chapter 14

Promoting sustainable agriculture and rural development

By the year 2025, 83 per cent of the expected global population of 8.5 billion will be living in developing countries. Yet the capacity of available resources and technologies to satisfy the demands of this growing population for food and other agricultural commodities remains uncertain. Agriculture has to meet this challenge, mainly by increasing production on land already in use and by avoiding further encroachment on land that is only marginally suitable for cultivation.

Major adjustments are needed in agricultural, environmental and macroeconomic policy, at both national and international levels, in developed as well as developing countries, to create the conditions for sustainable agriculture and rural development (SARD). The major objective of SARD is to increase food production in a sustainable way and enhance food security. This will involve education initiatives, utilization of economic incentives and the development of appropriate and new technologies, thus ensuring stable supplies of nutritionally adequate food, access to those supplies by vulnerable groups, and production for markets; employment and income generation to alleviate poverty; and natural resource management and environmental protection.

The priority must be on maintaining and improving the capacity of the higher potential agricultural lands to support an expanding population. However, conserving and rehabilitating the natural resources on lower potential lands in order to maintain sustainable man/land ratios is also necessary. The main tools of SARD are policy and agrarian reform, participation, income diversification, land conservation and improved management of inputs. The success of SARD will depend largely on the support and participation of rural people, national Governments, the private sector and international cooperation, including technical and scientific cooperation.

A Agricultural policy review, planning and integrated programmes in the light of the multifunctional aspect of agriculture, particularly with regard to food security and sustainable development

Basis for action There is a need to integrate sustainable development considerations with agricultural policy analysis and planning in all countries, particularly in developing countries. Recommendations should contribute directly to development of realistic and operational medium- to long-term plans and programmes, and thus to concrete actions. Support to and monitoring of implementation should follow.

The absence of a coherent national policy framework for sustainable agriculture and rural development (SARD) is widespread and is not limited to the developing countries. In particular the economies in transition from planned to market-oriented systems need such a framework to incorporate environmental considerations into economic activities, including agriculture. All countries need to assess comprehensively the impacts of such policies on food and agriculture sector performance, food security, rural welfare and international trading relations as a means for identifying appropriate offsetting measures. The major thrust of food security in this case is to bring about a significant increase in agricultural production in a sustainable way and to achieve a substantial improvement in people's entitlement to adequate food and culturally appropriate food supplies.

Sound policy decisions pertaining to international trade and capital flows also necessitate action to overcome: (a) a lack of awareness of the environmental costs incurred by sectoral and macroeconomic policies and hence their threat to sustainability; (b) insufficient skills and experience in incorporating issues of sustainability into policies and programmes; and (c) inadequacy of tools of analysis and monitoring.[1]

Objectives

a By 1995, to review and, where appropriate, establish a programme to integrate environmental and sustainable development with policy analysis for the food and agriculture sector and relevant macroeconomic policy analysis, formulation and implementation;

b To maintain and develop, as appropriate, operational multisectoral plans, programmes and policy measures, including programmes and measures to enhance sustainable food production and food security within the framework of sustainable development, not later than 1998;

c To maintain and enhance the ability of developing countries, particularly the least developed ones, to themselves manage policy, programming and planning activities, not later than 2005.

Management-related activities Governments at the appropriate level, with the support of the relevant international and regional organizations, should:

a Carry out national policy reviews related to food security, including adequate levels and stability of food supply and access to food by all households;

b Review national and regional agricultural policy in relation, *inter alia*, to foreign trade, price policy, exchange rate policies, agricultural subsidies and taxes, as well as organization for regional economic integration;

c Implement policies to influence land tenure and property rights positively with due recognition of the minimum size of land-holding required to maintain production and check further fragmentation;

d Consider demographic trends and population movements and identify critical areas for agricultural production;

e Formulate, introduce and monitor policies, laws and regulations and incentives leading to sustainable agricultural and rural development and improved food security and to the development and transfer of appropriate farm technologies, including, where appropriate, low-input sustainable agricultural (LISA) systems;

f Support national and regional early warning systems through food-security assistance schemes that monitor food supply and demand and factors affecting household access to food;

g Review policies with respect to improving harvesting, storage, processing, distribution and marketing of products at the local, national and regional levels;

h Formulate and implement integrated agricultural projects that include other natural resource activities, such as management of rangelands, forests, and wildlife, as appropriate;

i Promote social and economic research and policies that encourage sustainable agriculture development, particularly in fragile ecosystems and densely populated areas;

j Identify storage and distribution problems affecting food availability; support research, where necessary, to overcome these problems and cooperate with producers and distributors to implement improved practices and systems.

Financing and cost evaluation $3 billion, including about $450 million from the international community on grant or concessional terms.

B Ensuring people's participation and promoting human resource development for sustainable agriculture

Basis for action This component bridges policy and integrated resource management. The greater the degree of community control over the resources on which it relies, the greater will be the incentive for economic and human resources development. At the same time, policy instruments to reconcile long-run and short-run requirements must be set by national Governments. The approaches focus on fostering self-reliance and cooperation, providing information and supporting user-based organizations. Emphasis should be on management practices, building agreements for changes in resource utilization, the rights and duties associated with use of land, water and forests, the functioning of markets, prices, and the access to information, capital and inputs. This would require training and capacity-building to assume greater responsibilities in sustainable development efforts.[2]

Objectives

a To promote greater public awareness of the role of people's participation and people's organizations, especially women's groups, youth, indigenous people and people under occupation, local communities and small farmers, in sustainable agriculture and rural development;

b To ensure equitable access of rural people, particularly women, small farmers, landless and indigenous people and people under occupation, to land, water and forest resources and to technologies, financing, marketing, processing and distribution;

c To strengthen and develop the management and the internal capacities of rural people's organizations and extension services and to decentralize decision-making to the lowest community level.

Management-related activities Governments at the appropriate level, with the support of the relevant international and regional organizations, should:

a Develop and improve integrated agricultural extension services and facilities and rural organizations and undertake natural resource management and food security activities, taking into account the different needs of subsistence agriculture as well as market-oriented crops;

b Review and refocus existing measures to achieve wider access to land, water and forest resources and ensure equal rights of women and other disadvantaged groups, with particular emphasis on rural populations, indigenous people, people under occupation and local communities;

c Assign clear titles, rights and responsibilities for land and for individuals or communities to encourage investment in land resources;

d Develop guidelines for decentralization policies for rural development through reorganization and strengthening of rural institutions;

e Develop policies in extension, training, pricing, input distribution, credit and taxation to ensure necessary incentives and equitable access by

Environmental Protection and the Agricultural Priorities of Romania's Economic Development

Gheorghe Barbulescu
President Banca Agricola SA

Through its close links with the soil and nature, agriculture should play an important part in the protection and improvement of the quality of the environment.

The latest figures show that out of Romania's total land area of 23,839,000 hectares, agricultural land accounts for 14,798,278 hectares. This total divides into:

Arable land	9,423,503 hectares (2.9 million of which are irrigated)
Pasture	3,309,827 hectares
Hay	1,457,857 hectares
Viticulture	285,839 hectares
Orchards	311,256 hectares

Woodland accounts for a further 6,680,090 hectares (28% of the total land area) and marshland 893,404 hectares (3.75%). The remaining balance is uncultivated.

During the 45 years of communist dictatorship an attempt was made to increase agricultural production and partial success was achieved. Unfortunately, these efforts did not include increasing the land's productivity levels, resulting in relatively large areas of agricultural land with a low fertility level, some of it barren. Uncultivated areas are increasing, through annual soil erosion, lack of water and an increase in acidity levels.

However, programmes and measures are being developed to rectify the damage of the past and provide a competitive agricultural system with a sustainable and healthy future. A domestic strategy for agricultural development is being closely linked with an environment protection plan.

One positive feature has been the creation in 1992 of soil quality monitoring systems. These systems measure the soil elements, irrigation levels, ground water and surface water quality. The monitoring system conforms with European standards as far as soil quality is concerned (Pan-European GEMS-UNEP in a network of 16 x 16 km).

The improvement of natural resources, their protection and their best rational use can only be achieved using top quality food and agricultural products. By this means an efficient and competitive agricultural industry will be developed working in harmony with nature.

These programmes and measures require funding and a large proportion of the necessary finance will be provided by Banca Agricola – SA one of the main supporters of Romanian agriculture. Even since its establishment as a joint stock company Banca Agricola's main area of investment, and one of its major objectives, has been to support loan projects for agriculture.

Through its agricultural loan project programme Banca Agricola grants loans for:

- establishing and improving family farms whilst avoiding land plot splitting and negative environmental effects;
- achieving productive investment objectives which have a positive impact on the environment e.g. plantations, woodland, healthy livestock development;
- soil drainage and desalination projects to render land usable for agriculturally and environmentally sound projects;
- microclimatic and agricultural production microzones mainly to support environmental projects i.e. green areas, crop rotation, livestock objectives;
- the modernization of irrigation and drainage schemes;
- the installation and improvement of water purifying projects.

Not all investment projects are on a large or national scale. It is important to underline the need to achieve small and medium-size investment objectives.

Banca Agricola is well established as a balancing factor in environmentally sound agricultural development by providing the financial resources, investment capital and risk cover necessary for the promotion of a healthy and profitable agricultural economy with a sound environmental base.

the poor to production-support services;

f Provide support services and training, recognizing the variation in agricultural circumstances and practices by location; the optimal use of on-farm inputs and the minimal use of external inputs; optimal use of local natural resources and management of renewable energy sources; and the establishment of networks that deal with the exchange of information on alternative forms of agriculture.

Financing and cost evaluation $4.4 billion, including about $650 million from the international community on grant or concessional terms.

C Improving farm production and farming systems through diversification of farm and non-farm employment and infrastructure development

Basis for action Agriculture needs to be intensified to meet future demands for commodities and to avoid further expansion onto marginal lands and encroachment on fragile ecosystems. Increased use of external inputs and development of specialized production and farming systems tend to increase vulnerability to environmental stresses and market fluctuations. There is, therefore, a need to intensify agriculture by diversifying the production systems for maximum efficiency in the utilization of local resources, while minimizing environmental and economic risks. Where intensification of farming systems is not possible, other on-farm and off-farm employment opportunities should be identified and developed, such as cottage industries, wildlife utilization, aquaculture and fisheries, non-farm activities, such as light village-based manufacturing, farm commodity processing, agribusiness, recreation and tourism, etc.

Objectives

a To improve farm productivity in a sustainable manner, as well as to increase diversification, efficiency, food security and rural incomes, while ensuring that risks to the ecosystem are minimized;

b To enhance the self-reliance of farmers in developing and improving rural infrastructure, and to facilitate the transfer of environmentally sound technologies for integrated production and farming systems, including indigenous technologies and the sustainable use of biological and ecological processes, including agroforestry, sustainable wildlife conservation and management, aquaculture, inland fisheries and animal husbandry;

c To create farm and non-farm employment opportunities, particularly among the poor and those living in marginal areas, taking into account the alternative livelihood proposal *inter alia* in dryland areas.

Management-related activities Governments at the appropriate level, with the support of the relevant international and regional organizations, should:

a Develop and disseminate to farming households integrated farm management technologies, such as crop rotation, organic manuring and other techniques involving reduced use of agricultural chemicals, multiple techniques for sources of nutrients and the efficient utilization of external inputs, while enhancing techniques for waste and by-product utilization and prevention of pre- and post-harvest losses, taking particular note of the role of women;

b Create non-farm employment opportunities through private small-scale agro-processing units, rural service centres and related infrastructural improvements;

c Promote and improve rural financial networks that utilize investment capital resources raised locally;

d Provide the essential rural infrastructure for access to agricultural inputs and services, as well as to national and local markets, and reduce food losses;

e Initiate and maintain farm surveys, on-farm testing of appropriate technologies and dialogue with rural communities to identify constraints and bottlenecks and find solutions;

f Analyse and identify possibilities for economic integration of agricultural and forestry activities, as well as water and fisheries, and to take effective measures to encourage forest management and growing of trees by farmers (farm forestry) as an option for resource development.

Financing and cost evaluation $10 billion, including about $1.5 billion from the international community on grant or concessional terms.

D Land-resource planning, information and education for agriculture

Basis for action Inappropriate and uncontrolled land uses are a major cause of degradation and depletion of land resources. Present land use often disregards the actual potentials, carrying capacities and limitations of

MARTIN WRIGHT/STILL PICTURES

The sunflower fields in the Perigord region of Southern France reflect the growing demand in the western world for sunflower oil products.

BOB

SHARES

THE CONCERN

OF THE

WORLD

ON

ENVIRONMENTAL ISSUES

Bank of Baroda

(A Government of India Undertaking)

CENTRAL OFFICE

3, WALCHAND HIRACHAND MARG

BALLARD PIER

BOMBAY 400 038

INDIA

Agriculture has to meet the challenge of feeding a projected population of 8.5 billion by the year 2025 through increased production on existing agricultural land and by avoiding further encroachment on non-agricultural land, which is often not suitable for cultivation.

JORGEN SCHYTTE/STILL PICTURES

Section II

b To improve and implement programmes to put integrated pest-management practices within the reach of farmers through farmer networks, extension services and research institutions;
c Not later than the year 1998, to establish operational and interactive networks among farmers, researchers and extension services to promote and develop integrated pest management.

Management-related activities Governments at the appropriate level, with the support of the relevant international and regional organizations, should:
a Review and reform national policies and the mechanisms that would ensure the safe and appropriate use of pesticides – for example, pesticide pricing, pest control brigades, price-structure of inputs and outputs and integrated pest-management policies and action plans;
b Develop and adopt efficient management systems to control and monitor the incidence of pests and disease in agriculture and the distribution and use of pesticides at the country level;
c Encourage research and development into pesticides that are target-specific and readily degrade into harmless constituent parts after use;
d Ensure that pesticide labels provide farmers with understandable information about safe handling, application and disposal.

Financing and cost evaluation $1.9 billion, including about $285 million from the international community on grant or concessional terms.

J Sustainable plant nutrition to increase food production

Basis for action Plant nutrient depletion is a serious problem resulting in loss of soil fertility, particularly in developing countries. To maintain soil productivity, the FAO sustainable plant nutrition programmes could be helpful. In sub-Saharan Africa, nutrient output from all sources currently exceeds inputs by a factor of three or four, the net loss being estimated at some 10 million metric tons per year. As a result, more marginal lands and fragile natural ecosystems are put under agricultural use, thus creating further land degradation and other environmental problems. The integrated plant nutrition approach aims at ensuring a sustainable supply of plant nutrients to increase future yields without harming the environment and soil productivity.

In many developing countries, population growth rates exceed 3 per cent a year, and national agricultural production has fallen behind food demand. In these countries the goal should be to increase agricultural production by at least 4 per cent a year, without destroying the soil fertility. This will require increasing agricultural production in high-potential areas through efficiency in the use of inputs. Trained labour, energy supply, adapted tools and technologies, plant nutrients and soil enrichment will all be essential.

Objectives
a Not later than the year 2000, to develop and maintain in all countries the integrated plant nutrition approach, and to optimize availability of fertilizer and other plant nutrient sources;
b Not later than the year 2000, to establish and maintain institutional and human infrastructure to enhance effective decision-making on soil productivity;
c To develop and make available national and international know-how to farmers, extension agents, planners and policy makers on environmentally sound new and existing technologies and soil-fertility management strategies for application in promoting sustainable agriculture.

Management-related activities Governments at the appropriate level, with the support of the relevant international and regional organizations, should:
a Formulate and apply strategies that will enhance soil fertility maintenance to meet sustainable agricultural production and adjust the relevant agricultural policy instruments accordingly;
b Integrate organic and inorganic sources of plant nutrients in a system to sustain soil fertility and determine mineral fertilizer needs;
c Determine plant nutrient requirements and supply strategies and optimize the use of both organic and inorganic sources, as appropriate, to increase farming efficiency and production;
d Develop and encourage processes for the recycling of organic and inorganic waste into the soil structure, without harming the environment, plant growth and human health.

Imaginative recycling of soft drink cans used to make goat-pens in Damaraland, Namibia. Right: Villagers in Tahoua, West Africa get their first glimpse of a more distant world. The television is run by a battery which is powered by solar panels.

MARTIN WRIGHT/STILL PICTURES

Financing and cost evaluation $3.2 billion, including about $475 million from the international community on grant or concessional terms.

K Rural energy transition to enhance productivity

Basis for action Energy supplies in many countries are not commensurate with their development needs and are highly priced and unstable. In rural areas of the developing countries, the chief sources of energy are fuelwood, crop residues and manure, together with animal and human energy. More intensive energy inputs are required for increased productivity of human labour and for income-generation. To this end, rural energy policies and technologies should promote a mix of cost-effective fossil and renewable energy sources that is itself sustainable and ensures sustainable agricultural development. Rural areas provide energy supplies in the form of wood. The full potential of agriculture and agroforestry, as well as common property resources, as sources of renewable energy, is far from being realized. The attainment of sustainable rural development is intimately linked with energy demand and supply patterns.[5]

Objectives

a Not later than the year 2000, to initiate and encourage a process of environmentally sound energy transition in rural communities, from unsustainable energy sources, to structured and diversified energy sources by making available alternative new and renewable sources of energy;

b To increase the energy inputs available for rural household and agro-industrial needs through planning and appropriate technology transfer and development;

c To implement self-reliant rural programmes favouring sustainable development of renewable energy sources and improved energy efficiency.

Management-related activities Governments at the appropriate level, with the support of the relevant international and regional organizations, should:

a Promote pilot plans and projects consisting of electrical, mechanical and thermal power (gasifiers, biomass, solar driers, wind-pumps and combustion systems) that are appropriate and likely to be adequately maintained;

b Initiate and promote rural energy programmes supported by technical training, banking and related infrastructure;

c Intensify research and the development, diversification and conservation of energy, taking into account the need for efficient use and environmentally sound technology.

Financing and cost evaluation $1.8 billion per year, including about $265 million from the international community on grant or concessional terms.

L Evaluation of the effects of ultraviolet radiation on plants and animals caused by the depletion of the stratospheric ozone layer

Basis for action The increase of ultraviolet radiation as a consequence of the depletion of the stratospheric ozone layer is a phenomenon that has been recorded in different regions of the world, particularly in the southern hemisphere. Consequently, it is important to evaluate its effects on plant and animal life, as well as on sustainable agricultural development.

Objective The objective of this programme area is to undertake research to determine the effects of increased ultraviolet radiation resulting from stratospheric ozone layer depletion on the Earth's surface, and on plant and animal life in affected regions, as well as its impact on agriculture, and to develop, as appropriate, strategies aimed at mitigating its adverse effects.

Management-related activities In affected regions, Governments at the appropriate level, with the support of the relevant international and regional organizations, should take the necessary measures, through institutional cooperation, to facilitate the implementation of research and evaluation regarding the effects of enhanced ultraviolet radiation on plant and animal life, as well as on agricultural activities, and consider taking appropriate remedial measures.

1 See chapter 3.
2 See chapter 8 and chapter 37.
3 See chapter 10.
4 See chapter 15.
5 See chapter 9.

Conservation of biological diversity

The objectives and activities in this chapter are intended to improve the conservation of biological diversity and the sustainable use of biological resources, as well as to support the Convention on Biological Diversity.

Our planet's essential goods and services depend on the variety and variability of genes, species, populations and ecosystems. Biological resources feed and clothe us and provide housing, medicines and spiritual nourishment. The natural ecosystems of forests, savannahs, pastures and rangelands, deserts, tundras, rivers, lakes and seas contain most of the Earth's biodiversity. Farmers' fields and gardens are also of great importance as repositories, while gene banks, botanical gardens, zoos and other germplasm repositories make a small but significant contribution. The current decline in biodiversity is largely the result of human activity and represents a serious threat to human development.

Basis for action Despite mounting efforts over the past 20 years, the loss of the world's biological diversity, mainly from habitat destruction, over-harvesting, pollution and the inappropriate introduction of foreign plants and animals, has continued. Biological resources constitute a capital asset with great potential for yielding sustainable benefits. Urgent and decisive action is needed to conserve and maintain genes, species and ecosystems, with a view to the sustainable management and use of biological resources. Capacities for the assessment, study and systematic observation and evaluation of biodiversity need to be reinforced at national and international levels. Effective national action and international cooperation are required for the *in situ* protection of ecosystems, for the *ex situ* conservation of biological and genetic resources and for the enhancement of ecosystem functions. The participation and support of local communities are elements essential to the success of such an approach. Recent advances in biotechnology have pointed up the likely potential for agriculture, health and welfare and for environmental purposes of the genetic material contained in plants, animals and micro-organisms. At the same time, it is particularly important in this context to stress that States have the sovereign right to exploit their own biological resources pursuant to their environmental policies, as well as the responsibility to conserve their biodiversity and use their biological resources sustainably, and to ensure that activities within their jurisdiction or control do not cause damage to the biological diversity of other States or of areas beyond the limits of national jurisdiction.

Objectives Governments at the appropriate level, with the cooperation of the relevant United Nations bodies and regional, intergovernmental and non-governmental organizations, the private sector and financial institutions, and taking into consideration indigenous people and their communities, as well as social and economic factors, should:

a Press for the early entry into force of the Convention on Biological Diversity, with the widest possible participation;

b Develop national strategies for the conservation of biological diversity and the sustainable use of biological resources;

c Integrate strategies for the conservation of biological diversity and the sustainable use of biological resources into national development strategies and/or plans;

d Take appropriate measures for the fair and equitable sharing of benefits derived from research and development and use of biological and genetic resources, including biotechnology, between the sources of those resources and those who use them;

e Carry out country studies, as appropriate, on the conservation of biological diversity and the sustainable use of biological resources, including analyses of relevant costs and benefits, with particular reference to socio-economic aspects;

f Produce regularly updated world reports on biodiversity based upon national assessments;

g Recognize and foster the traditional methods and the knowledge of indigenous people and their communities, emphasizing the particular role of women, relevant to the conservation of biological diversity and the sustainable use of biological resources, and ensure the opportunity for the participation of those groups in the economic and commercial benefits derived from the use of such traditional methods and knowledge;[1]

h Implement mechanisms for the improvement, generation, development and sustainable use of biotechnology and its safe transfer, particularly to

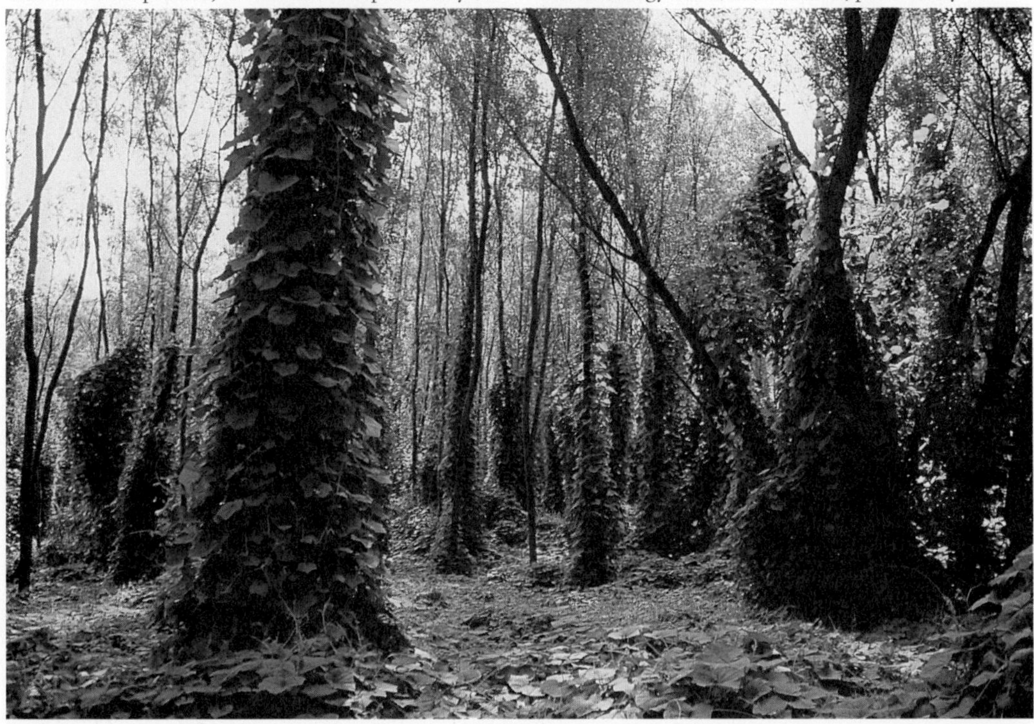

One reason for the loss of the world's biological diversity is the introduction of foreign plants. This Italian woodland is being strangled by a climber seed thought to have been introduced from America mixed with soya seeds.

THE COOPERATIVE CREDIT BANK S.A.

Development Environment in Romania

What do you know about Romania beyond Ceauşecsu, dictatorship, revolution and orphanages.

There are many other things business people should know about Romania. That is why I am taking this opportunity to let you know just what Romania can offer.

The reform process is in progress. In only two and a half years we have put in place a good business environment. The privatisation of the agricultural sector has taken place, the first industrial companies have been offered for sale and expansion of both sectors will continue. Prices have been liberalised and the state monopoly in foreign trade and the banking system has been abolished.

A two tier banking system is now in place, and we are an important part of this new arrangement. BANKCOOP is the leading private bank in Romania. We are strongly involved in developing the economy. We have taken over the financing of the country's consumer and credit cooperatives which represent more than 50 billion lei (approx. $125 million).

We are also involved in the privatisation process; privately owned companies represent over 50 per cent of the activities of the bank.

Romania has a huge economic potential even if, at the moment, we lack certain business infrastructures. Our production and manufacturing capacity is vast but not environmentally sound and we lack certain technological expertise particularly concerning the protection of the environment.

That is why we are striving to finance profitable projects that can lead to the further development of the Romanian economy in a clean and healthy environment. If you are looking for business expansion possibilities in Romania do not hesitate to contact us. We have the expertise and enthusiasm to meet your needs.

Alexandru Dinulescu

President

THE COOPERATIVE CREDIT BANK S.A.
13, Ion Ghica Street, Sector 3 - Bucharest, Romania
Tel. 40.1.312.00.35;40.1.312.00.36
Fax 40.1.312.00.37 Telex 11202

Genetic material contained in plants, animals and micro-organisms can offer great potential to the Earth as well as to its inhabitants. The marine environment is particularly rich in species.

developing countries, taking account of the potential contribution of biotechnology to the conservation of biological diversity and the sustainable use of biological resources;[2]

i Promote broader international and regional cooperation in furthering scientific and economic understanding of the importance of biodiversity and its functions in ecosystems;

j Develop measures and arrangements to implement the rights of countries of origin of genetic resources or countries providing genetic resources, as defined in the Convention on Biological Diversity, particularly developing countries, to benefit from the biotechnological development and the commercial utilisation of products derived from such resources.

Management-related activities Governments at the appropriate levels, consistent with national policies and practices, with the cooperation of the relevant United Nations bodies and, as appropriate, intergovernmental organizations and with the support of indigenous people and their communities, non-governmental organizations and other groups, including the business and scientific communities, and consistent with the requirements of international law, should, as appropriate:

a Develop new or strengthen existing strategies, plans or programmes of action for the conservation of biological diversity and the sustainable use of biological resources, taking account of education and training needs;[3]

b Integrate strategies for the conservation of biological diversity and the sustainable use of biological and genetic resources into relevant sectoral or cross-sectoral plans, programmes and policies, with particular reference to the special importance of terrestrial and aquatic biological and genetic resources for food and agriculture;[4]

c Undertake country studies or use other methods to identify components of biological diversity important for its conservation and for the sustainable use of biological resources, ascribe values to biological and genetic resources, identify processes and activities with significant impacts upon biological diversity, evaluate the potential economic implications of the conservation of biological diversity and the sustainable use of biological and genetic resources, and suggest priority action;

d Take effective economic, social and other appropriate incentive measures to encourage the conservation of biological diversity and the sustainable use of biological resources, including the promotion of sustainable production systems, such as traditional methods of agriculture, agroforestry, forestry, range and wildlife management, which use, maintain or increase biodiversity;[4]

e Subject to national legislation, take action to respect, record, protect and promote the wider application of the knowledge, innovations and practices of indigenous and local communities embodying traditional lifestyles for the conservation of biological diversity and the sustainable use of biological resources, with a view to the fair and equitable sharing of the benefits arising, and promote mechanisms to involve those communities, including women, in the conservation and management of ecosystems;[1]

f Undertake long-term research into the importance of biodiversity for the functioning of ecosystems and the role of ecosystems in producing goods, environmental services and other values supporting sustainable development, with particular reference to the biology and reproductive capacities of key terrestrial and aquatic species, including native, cultivated and cultured species; new observation and inventory techniques; ecological conditions necessary for biodiversity conservation and continued evolution; and social behaviour and nutrition habits dependent on natural ecosystems, where women play key roles. The work should be undertaken with the widest possible participation, especially of indigenous people and their communities, including women;[1]

g Take action where necessary for the conservation of biological diversity through the *in situ* conservation of ecosystems and natural habitats, as well as primitive cultivars and their wild relatives, and the maintenance and recovery of viable populations of species in their natural surroundings, and implement *ex situ* measures, preferably in the source country. *In situ* measures should include the reinforcement of terrestrial, marine and aquatic protected area systems and embrace, *inter alia*, vulnerable freshwater and other wetlands and coastal ecosystems, such as estuaries, coral reefs and mangroves;[5]

h Promote the rehabilitation and restoration of damaged ecosystems and the recovery of threatened and endangered species;

i Develop policies to encourage the conservation of biodiversity and the sustainable use of biological and genetic resources on private lands;

j Promote environmentally sound and sustainable development in areas adjacent to protected areas with a view to furthering protection of these areas;

k Introduce appropriate environmental impact assessment procedures for proposed projects likely to have significant impacts upon biological diversity, providing for suitable information to be made widely available and for public participation, where appropriate, and encourage the assessment of the impacts of relevant policies and programmes on biological diversity;

l Promote, where appropriate, the establishment and strengthening of national inventory, regulation or management and control systems related to biological resources, at the appropriate level;

m Take measures to encourage a greater understanding and appreciation of the value of biological diversity, as manifested both in its component parts and in the ecosystem services provided.

Financing and cost evaluation $3.5 billion including about $1.75 billion from the international community on grant or concessional terms.

1 See chapter 26 and chapter 24.
2 See chapter 16.
3 See chapter 36.
4 See chapter 14 and chapter 11.
5 See chapter 17.

Section II

EN EL PRIMER BANCO ESPAÑOL LA NATURALEZA TIENE CREDITO.

CONSERVAR EL MEDIO AMBIENTE ES UNA LABOR QUE MERECE TODO NUESTRO APOYO. POR ESO, EN EL BANCO CENTRAL HISPANO, LOS PROYECTOS EMPRESARIALES DEDICADOS A LA MEJORA Y CONSERVACION DE LA NATURALEZA TIENEN FINANCIACION PREFERENTE* PORQUE EN EL PRIMER BANCO ESPAÑOL LA NATURALEZA TIENE CREDITO.

*LINEA ESPECIAL "CREDITO VERDE" EN LA DIVISION DE BANCA CORPORATIVA Y DE NEGOCIOS.

Chapter 16

Environmentally sound management of biotechnology

Biotechnology is the integration of the new techniques emerging from modern biotechnology with the well-established approaches of traditional biotechnology. Biotechnology, an emerging knowledge-intensive field, is a set of enabling techniques for bringing about specific man-made changes in deoxyribonucleic acid (DNA), or genetic material, in plants, animals and microbial systems, leading to useful products and technologies. By itself, biotechnology cannot resolve all the fundamental problems of environment and development, so expectations need to be tempered by realism. Nevertheless, it promises to make a significant contribution in enabling the development of, for example, better health care, enhanced food security through sustainable agricultural practices, improved supplies of potable water, more efficient industrial development processes for transforming raw materials, support for sustainable methods of afforestation and reforestation, and detoxification of hazardous wastes. Biotechnology also offers new opportunities for global partnerships, especially between the countries rich in biological resources (which include genetic resources) but lacking the expertise and investments needed to apply such resources through biotechnology and the countries that have developed the technological expertise to transform biological resources so that they serve the needs of sustainable development.[1] Biotechnology can assist in the conservation of those resources through, for example, *ex situ* techniques. The programme areas set out below seek to foster internationally agreed principles to be applied to ensure the environmentally sound management of biotechnology, to engender public trust and confidence, to promote the development of sustainable applications of biotechnology and to establish appropriate enabling mechanisms, especially within developing countries.

A Increasing the availability of food, feed and renewable raw materials

Basis for action To meet the growing consumption needs of the global population, the challenge is not only to increase food supply, but also to improve food distribution significantly while simultaneously developing more sustainable agricultural systems. Much of this increased productivity will need to take place in developing countries. It will require the successful and environmentally safe application of biotechnology in agriculture, in the environment and in human health care. Most of the investment in modern biotechnology has been in the industrialized world. Significant new investments and human resource development will be required in biotechnology, especially in the developing world.

A revolutionary new way of purifying water contaminated with sewage and chemicals developed by MEMTEC of Australia. The liquid is passed through a membrane which filters out impurities.

Objectives The following objectives are proposed, keeping in mind the need to promote the use of appropriate safety measures based on programme area D:

a To increase to the optimum possible extent the yield of major crops, livestock, and aquaculture species, by using the combined resources of modern biotechnology and conventional plant/animal/micro-organism improvement, including the more diverse use of genetic material resources, both hybrid and original.[2] Forest product yields should similarly be increased, to ensure the sustainable use of forests;[3]

b To reduce the need for volume increases of food, feed and raw materials by improving the nutritional value (composition) of the source crops, animals and micro-organisms, and to reduce post-harvest losses of plant and animal products;

c To increase the use of integrated pest, disease and crop management techniques to eliminate over-dependence on agrochemicals, thereby encouraging environmentally sustainable agricultural practices;

d To evaluate the agricultural potential of marginal lands in comparison with other potential uses and to develop, where appropriate, systems allowing for sustainable productivity increases;

e To expand the applications of biotechnology in forestry, both for increasing yields and more efficient utilization of forest products and for improving afforestation and reforestation techniques. Efforts should be concentrated on species and products that are grown in and are of value particularly for developing countries;

f To increase the efficiency of nitrogen fixation and mineral absorption by the symbiosis of higher plants with micro-organisms;

g To improve capabilities in basic and applied sciences and in the management of complex interdisciplinary research projects.

Management-related activities Governments at the appropriate level, with the assistance of international and regional organizations and with the support of non-governmental organizations, the private sector and academic and scientific institutions, should improve both plant and animal breeding and micro-organisms through the use of traditional and modern biotechnologies, to enhance sustainable agricultural output to achieve food security, particularly in developing countries, with due regard to the prior identification of desired characteristics before modification, taking into account the needs of farmers, the socio-economic, cultural and environmental impacts of modifications and the need to promote sustainable social and economic development, paying particular attention to how the use of biotechnology will impact on the maintenance of environmental integrity.

More specifically, these entities should:

a Improve productivity, nutritional quality and shelf-life of food and animal feed products, with efforts including work on pre- and post-harvest losses;

b Further develop resistance to diseases and pests;

These tomatoes are grown in a greenhouse heated using waste water from a power station. In the past the water would have been pumped out, heating up the river and damaging the plant and animal life.

c Develop plant cultivars tolerant and/or resistant to stress from factors such as pests and diseases and from abiotic causes;
d Promote the use of underutilized crops of possible future importance for human nutrition and industrial supply of raw materials;
e Increase the efficiency of symbiotic processes that assist sustainable agricultural production;
f Facilitate the conservation and safe exchange of plant, animal and microbial germ plasm by applying risk assessment and management procedures, including improved diagnostic techniques for detection of pests and diseases by better methods of rapid propagation;
g Develop improved diagnostic techniques and vaccines for the prevention and spread of diseases and for rapid assessment of toxins or infectious organisms in products for human use or livestock feed;
h Identify more productive strains of fast-growing trees, especially for fuel wood, and develop rapid propagation methods to aid their wider dissemination and use;
i Evaluate the use of various biotechnology techniques to improve the yields of fish, algal and other aquatic species;
j Promote sustainable agricultural output by strengthening and broadening the capacity and scope of existing research centres to achieve the necessary critical mass through encouragement and monitoring of research into the development of biological products and processes of productive and environmental value that are economically and socially feasible, while taking safety considerations into account;
k Promote the integration of appropriate and traditional biotechnologies for the purposes of cultivating genetically modified plants, rearing healthy animals and protecting forest genetic resources;
l Develop processes to increase the availability of materials derived from biotechnology for use in food, feed and renewable raw materials production.

Financing and cost evaluation $5 billion including about $50 million from the international community on grant or concessional terms.

B Improving human health

Basis for action The improvement of human health is one of the most important objectives of development. The deterioration of environmental quality, notably air, water and soil pollution owing to toxic chemicals, hazardous wastes, radiation and other sources, is a matter of growing concern. This degradation of the environment resulting from inadequate or inappropriate development has a direct negative effect on human health. Malnutrition, poverty, poor human settlements, lack of good-quality potable water and inadequate sanitation facilities add to the problems of communicable and non-communicable diseases. As a consequence, the health and well-being of people are exposed to increasing pressures.
Objectives The main objective of this programme area is to contribute, through the environmentally sound application of biotechnology, to an overall health programme, to:[4]
a Reinforce or inaugurate (as a matter of urgency) programmes to help combat major communicable diseases;
b Promote good general health among people of all ages;
c Develop and improve programmes to assist in specific treatment of and protection from major non-communicable diseases;
d Develop and strengthen appropriate safety procedures based on programme area D, taking account of ethical considerations;

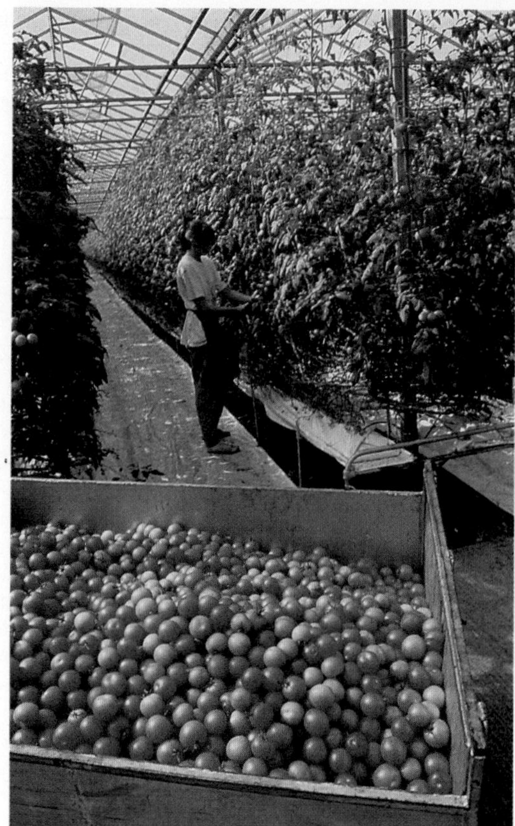

e Create enhanced capabilities for carrying out basic and applied research and for managing interdisciplinary research.

Management-related activities Governments at the appropriate level, with the assistance of international and regional organizations, academic and scientific institutions, and the pharmaceutical industry, should, taking into account appropriate safety and ethical considerations:
a Develop national and international programmes for identifying and targeting those populations of the world most in need of improvement in general health and protection from diseases;
b Develop criteria for evaluating the effectiveness and the benefits and risks of the proposed activities;
c Establish and enforce screening, systematic sampling and evaluation procedures for drugs and medical technologies, with a view to barring the use of those that are unsafe for the purposes of experimentation; ensure that drugs and technologies relating to reproductive health are safe and effective and take account of ethical considerations;
d Improve, systematically sample and evaluate drinking-water quality by introducing appropriate specific measures, including diagnosis of water-borne pathogens and pollutants;
e Develop and make widely available new and improved vaccines against major communicable diseases that are efficient and safe and offer protection with a minimum number of doses, including intensifying efforts directed at the vaccines needed to combat common diseases of children;
f Develop biodegradable delivery systems for vaccines that eliminate the need for present multiple-dose schedules, facilitate better coverage of the population and reduce the costs of immunization;
g Develop effective biological control agents against disease-transmitting vectors, such as mosquitoes and resistant variants, taking account of environmental protection considerations;
h Using the tools provided by modern biotechnology, develop, *inter alia*, improved diagnostics, new drugs and improved treatments and delivery systems;
i Develop the improvement and more effective

We now recognise that environmental protection cannot be achieved outside the wider context of sustainable development and that the war against poverty must be a major part of the task. The success of UNCED is imperative. We need an effective and implementable Agenda 21, the political will to make greater progress in ensuring adequate resources and technical cooperation and in reaching consensus on the responsibilities, obligations and burden-sharing of all countries – developed and developing. I am looking forward to helping the Commonwealth and its members play a positive role in an issue which is crucially important for us all.
Emeka Anyaoku
Commonwealth Secretary-General

utilization of medicinal plants and other related sources;
j Develop processes to increase the availability of materials derived from biotechnology, for use in improving human health.

Financing and cost evaluation $14 billion including about $130 million from the international community on grant or concessional terms.

C Enhancing protection of the environment

Basis for action Environmental protection is an integral component of sustainable development. The environment is threatened in all its biotic and abiotic components: animals, plants, microbes and ecosystems comprising biological diversity; water, soil and air, which form the physical components of habitats and ecosystems; and all the interactions between the components of biodiversity and their sustaining habitats and ecosystems. With the continued increase in the use of chemicals, energy and non-renewable resources by an expanding global population, associated environmental problems will also increase. Despite increasing efforts to prevent waste accumulation and to promote recycling, the amount of environmental damage caused by overconsumption, the quantities of waste generated and the degree of unsustainable land use appear likely to continue growing.

The need for a diverse genetic pool of plant, animal and microbial germ plasm for sustainable development is well established. Biotechnology is one of many tools that can play an important role in supporting the rehabilitation of degraded ecosystems and landscapes. This may be done through the development of new techniques for reforestation and afforestation, germ plasm conservation, and cultivation of new plant varieties. Biotechnology can also contribute to the study of the effects exerted on the remaining organisms and on other organisms by organisms introduced into ecosystems.

Objectives The aim of this programme is to prevent, halt and reverse environmental degradation through the appropriate use of biotechnology in conjunction with other technologies, while supporting safety procedures as an integral component of the programme. Specific objectives include the inauguration as soon as possible of specific programmes with specific targets:
a To adopt production processes making optimal use of natural resources, by recycling biomass, recovering energy and minimizing waste generation;[5]
b To promote the use of biotechnologies, with emphasis on bio-remediation of land and water, waste treatment, soil conservation, reforestation, afforestation and land rehabilitation;[6,7]
c To apply biotechnologies and their products to protect environmental integrity with a view to long-term ecological security.

Management-related activities Governments at the appropriate level and with the support of relevant international and regional organizations, the private sector, non-governmental organizations and academic and scientific institutions, should:
a Develop environmentally sound alternatives and improvements for environmentally damaging production processes;
b Develop applications to minimize the requirement for unsustainable synthetic chemical input and to maximize the use of environmentally appropriate products, including natural products (see programme area A);
c Develop processes to reduce waste generation, treat waste before disposal and make use of biodegradable materials;
d Develop processes to recover energy and provide renewable energy sources, animal feed and raw materials from recycling organic waste and biomass;
e Develop processes to remove pollutants from the environment, including accidental oil spills, where conventional techniques are not available or are expensive, inefficient or inadequate;
f Develop processes to increase the availability of planting materials, particularly indigenous varieties, for use in afforestation and reforestation and to improve sustainable yields from forests;
g Develop applications to increase the availability of stress-tolerant planting material for land rehabilitation and soil conservation;
h Promote the use of integrated pest management based on the judicious use of bio-control agents;
i Promote the appropriate use of bio-fertilizers within national fertilizer programmes;
j Promote the use of biotechnologies relevant to the conservation and scientific study of biological diversity and the sustainable use of biological resources;
k Develop easily applicable technologies for the treatment of sewage and organic waste;
l Develop new technologies for rapid screening of organisms for useful biological properties;
m Promote new biotechnologies for tapping mineral resources in an environmentally sustainable manner.

Financing and cost evaluation $1 billion including about $10 million from the international community on grant or concessional terms.

D Enhancing safety and developing international mechanisms for cooperation

Basis for action There is a need for further development of internationally agreed principles on risk assessment and management of all aspects of biotechnology, which should build upon those developed at the national level. Only when adequate and transparent safety and border-control procedures are in place will the community at large be able to derive maximum benefit from, and be in a much better position to accept the potential benefits and risks of, biotechnology. Several fundamental principles could underlie many of these safety procedures, including: primary consideration of the organism, building on the principle of familiarity, applied in a flexible framework, taking into account national requirements and recognising that the logical progression is to start with a step-by-step and case-by-case approach, but also recognising that experience has shown that in many instances a more comprehensive approach should be used, based on the experiences of the first period, leading *inter alia* to streamlining and categorising; complementary consideration of risk assessment and risk management, and classification into contained use or release to the environment.
Objectives The aim of this programme area is to ensure safety in biotechnology development, application, exchange and transfer through international agreement on principles to be applied on risk assessment and management,* with particular reference to health and environmental considerations, including the widest possible public participation and taking account of ethical considerations.

Activities The proposed activities for this programme area call for close international cooperation. They should build upon planned or existing activities to accelerate the environmentally sound application of biotechnology, especially in developing countries.*

Management-related activities Governments at the appropriate levels and with the support of relevant

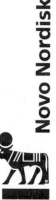

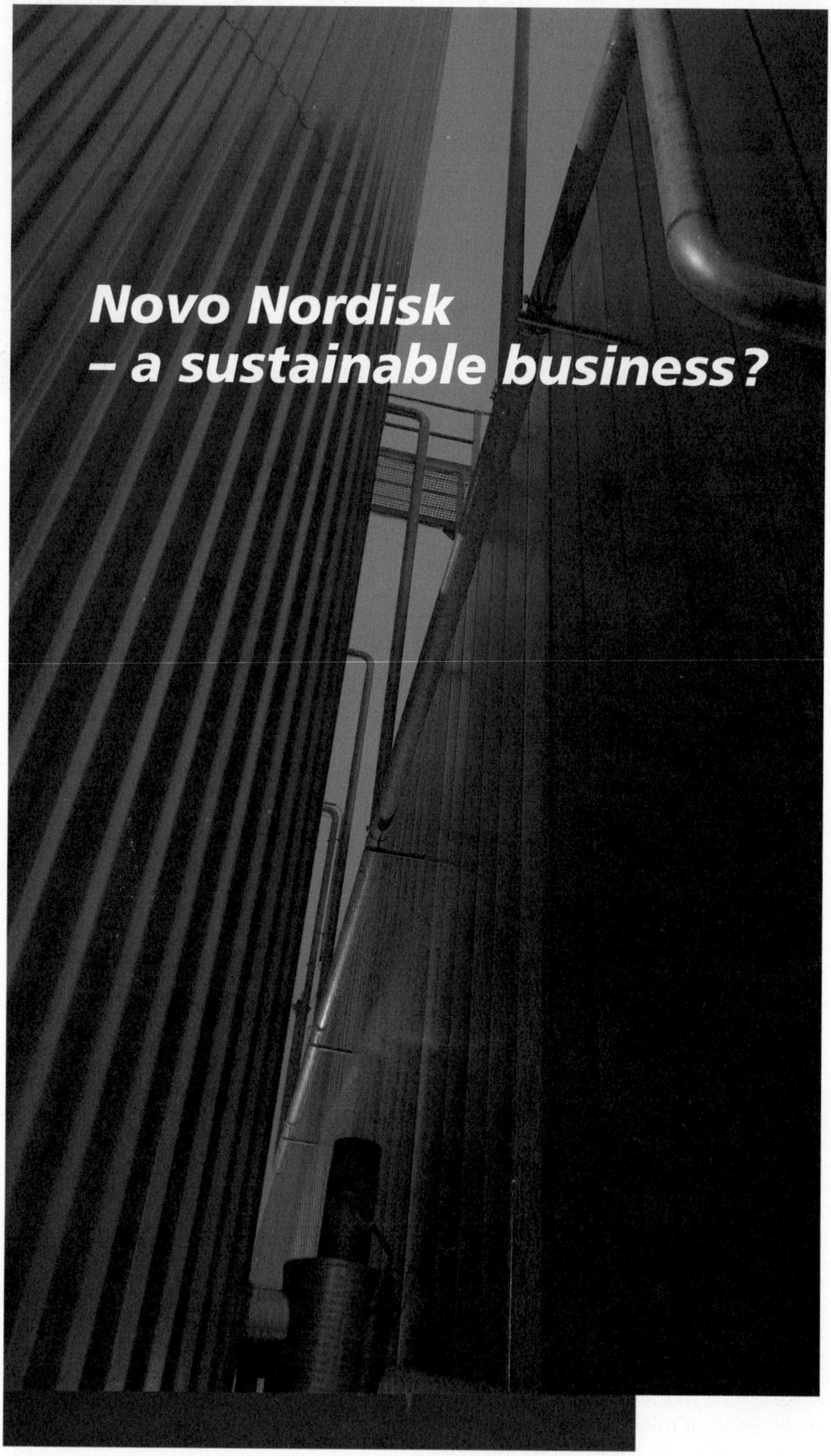
Novo Nordisk
– a sustainable business?

The Borde de Vias Colony in Mexico City. The inhabitants are largely made up of migrants from the country due to land erosion rendering soil unproductive. Such migrants arrive in the city at the rate of 1000 per day.

international and regional organizations, the private sector, non-governmental organizations and academic and scientific institutions, should:

a Make the existing safety procedures widely available by collecting the existing information and adaping it to the specific needs of different countries and regions;

b Further develop, as necessary, the existing safety procedures to promote scientific development and categorization in the areas of risk assessment and risk management (information requirements; databases; procedures for assessing risks and conditions of release; establishment of safety conditions; monitoring and inspections; taking account of ongoing national, regional and international initiatives, avoiding duplication wherever possible);

c Compile, update and develop compatible safety procedures into a framework of internationally agreed principles as a basis for guidelines to be applied on safety in biotechnology, including consideration of the need for and feasibility of an international agreement, and promote information exchange as a basis for further development, drawing on the work already undertaken by international or other expert bodies.

d Undertake training programmes at the national and regional levels on the application of the proposed technical guidelines;

e Assist in exchanging information about the procedures required for safe handling and risk management and about the conditions of release of the products of biotechnology, and cooperate in providing immediate assistance in cases of emergencies that may arise in conjunction with the use of biotechnology products.

Financing and cost evaluation \$2 million from the international community on grant or concessional terms.

E Establishing enabling mechanisms for the development and the environmentally sound application of biotechnology

Basis for action The accelerated development and application of biotechnologies, particularly in developing countries, will require a major effort to build up institutional capacities at the national and regional levels. In developing countries, enabling factors such as training capacity, know-how, research and development facilities and funds, industrial building capacity, capital (including venture capital), protection of intellectual property rights, and expertise in areas such as marketing, research, technology assessment, socio-economic assessment and safety assessment are frequently inadequate. Efforts will therefore need to be made to build up capacities in these and other areas and to match such efforts with appropriate levels of financial support. There is therefore a need to strengthen the endogenous capacities of developing countries by means of new international initiatives to support research in order to speed up the development and application of both new and conventional biotechnologies to serve the needs of sustainable development at the local, national and regional levels. National mechanisms to allow for informed comment by the public with regard to biotechnology research and application should be part of the process.

Some activities at the national, regional and global levels already address the issues outlined in programme areas A, B, C and D, as well as the provision of advice to individual countries on the development of national guidelines and systems for the implementation of those guidelines. These activities are generally uncoordinated, however, involving many different organizations, priorities, constituencies, time-scales, funding sources and resource constraints. There is a need for a much more cohesive and coordinated approach to harness available resources in the most effective manner. As with most new technologies, research in biotechnology and the application of its findings could have significant positive and negative socio-economic as well as cultural impacts. These impacts should be carefully identified in the earliest phases of the development of biotechnology in order to enable appropriate management of the consequences of transferring biotechnology.

Objectives

a To promote the development and application of biotechnologies, with special emphasis on developing countries, by:

i Enhancing existing efforts at the national, regional and global levels;

ii Providing the necessary support for biotechnology, particularly research and product development, at the national, regional and international levels;

iii Raising public awareness regarding the relative beneficial aspects of and risks related to biotechnology, to contribute to sustainable development;

iv Helping to create a favourable climate for

investments, industrial capacity-building and distribution/marketing;

v Encouraging the exchange of scientists among all countries and discouraging the "brain drain";

vi Recognising and fostering the traditional methods and the knowledge of indigenous people and their communities and ensuring the opportunity for their participation in the economic and commercial benefits arising from developments in biotechnology.[9]

b To identify ways and means of enhancing current efforts, building wherever possible on existing enabling mechanisms, particularly regional, to determine the precise nature of the needs for additional initiatives, particularly in respect of developing countries, and to develop appropriate response strategies, including proposals for any new international mechanisms;

c To establish or adapt appropriate mechanisms for safety appraisal and risk assessment at the local, regional and international levels, as appropriate.

Management-related activities Governments at the appropriate level, with the support of international and regional organizations, the private sector, non-governmental organizations and academic and scientific institutions should:

a Develop policies and mobilize additional resources to facilitate greater access to the new biotechnologies, particularly by and among developing countries;

b Implement programmes to create greater awareness of the potential and relative benefits and risks of the environmentally sound application of biotechnology among the public and key decision makers;

c Undertake an urgent review of existing enabling mechanisms, programmes and activities at the national, regional and global levels to identify strengths, weaknesses and gaps, and to assess the priority needs of developing countries;

d Define and implement strategies to overcome constraints identified in the areas of food, feed and renewable raw materials; human health; and environmental protection, building upon existing strengths;

e Undertake an urgent follow-up and critical review to identify ways and means of strengthening endogenous capacities within and among developing countries for the environmentally sound application of biotechnology, including, as a first step, ways to improve existing mechanisms, particularly at the regional level, and, as a subsequent step, the consideration of possible new international mechanisms, such as regional biotechnology centres;

f Develop strategic plans for overcoming targeted constraints by means of appropriate research, product development and marketing;

g Establish additional quality-assurance standards for biotechnology applications and products, where necessary.

Financing and cost evaluation $5 million from the international community on grant or concessional terms.

* See research paper No. 55, entitled "Environmentally sound management of biotechnology: safety in biotechnology – assessment and management of risk" (February 1992), prepared by the United Nations Conference on Environment and Development secretariat to take account of comments made at the third session of the Preparatory Committee for the United Nations Conference on Environment and Development on part II of document A/CONF.151/PC/67, which incorporated the findings of the ad hoc workshop of Senior-level Experts on Assessing and Managing Biotechnology Risks, held in London in June 1991.

1 See chapter 15.
2 See chapter 14.
3 See chapter 11.
4 See chapter 6.
5 See chapter 21.
6 See chapter 10.
7 See chapter 18.

Chapter 17

Protection of oceans, all kinds of seas, including enclosed and semi-enclosed seas, and coastal areas and the protection, rational use and development of their living resources

The marine environment – including the oceans and all seas and adjacent coastal areas – forms an integrated whole that is an essential component of the global life – support system and a positive asset that presents opportunities for sustainable development. International law, as reflected in the provisions of the United Nations Convention on the Law of the Sea[1,2] referred to in this chapter of Agenda 21, sets forth rights and obligations of States and provides the international basis upon which to pursue the protection and sustainable development of the marine and coastal environment and its resources. This requires new approaches to marine and coastal area management and development, at the national, subregional, regional and global levels, approaches that are integrated in content and are precautionary and anticipatory in ambit[3].

A Integrated management and sustainable development of coastal and marine areas, including exclusive economic zones

Basis for action The coastal area contains diverse and productive habitats important for human settlements, development and local subsistence. More than half the world's population lives within 60 km of the shoreline, and this could rise to three quarters by the year 2020. Many of the world's poor are crowded in coastal areas. Coastal resources are vital for many local communities and indigenous people. The exclusive economic zone (EEZ) is also an important marine area where the States manage the development and conservation of natural resources for the benefit of their people. For small island States or countries, these are the areas most available for development activities.

Despite national, subregional, regional and global efforts, current approaches to the management of marine and coastal resources have not always proved capable of achieving sustainable development, and coastal resources and the coastal environment are being rapidly degraded and eroded in many parts of the world.

Objectives Coastal States commit themselves to integrated management and sustainable development of coastal areas and the marine environment under their national jurisdiction. To this end, it is necessary to, *inter alia*:

a Provide for an integrated policy and decision-making process, including all involved sectors, to promote compatibility and a balance of uses;

b Identify existing and projected uses of coastal areas and their interactions;

c Concentrate on well-defined issues concerning coastal management;

d Apply preventive and precautionary approaches in project planning and implementation, including prior

assessment and systematic observation of the impacts of major projects;

e Promote the development and application of methods, such as national resource and environmental accounting, that reflect changes in value resulting from uses of coastal and marine areas, including pollution, marine erosion, loss of resources and habitat destruction;

f Provide access, as far as possible, for concerned individuals, groups and organizations to relevant information and opportunities for consultation and participation in planning and decision-making at appropriate levels.

Management-related activities Each coastal State should consider establishing, or where necessary strengthening, appropriate coordinating mechanisms (such as a high-level policy planning body) for integrated management and sustainable development of coastal and marine areas and their resources, at both the local and national levels. Such mechanisms should include consultation, as appropriate, with the academic and private sectors, non-governmental organizations, local communities, resource user groups, and indigenous people. Such national coordinating mechanisms could provide, *inter alia*, for:

a Preparation and implementation of land and water use and siting policies;

b Implementation of integrated coastal and marine management and sustainable development plans and programmes at appropriate levels;

c Preparation of coastal profiles identifying critical areas, including eroded zones, physical processes, development patterns, user conflicts and specific priorities for management;

d Prior environmental impact assessment, systematic observation and follow-up of major projects, including the systematic incorporation of results in decision-making;

e Contingency plans for human induced and natural disasters, including likely effects of potential climate change and sealevel rise, as well as contingency plans for degradation and pollution of anthropogenic origin, including spills of oil and other materials;

f Improvement of coastal human settlements, especially in housing, drinking water and treatment and disposal of sewage, solid wastes and industrial effluents;

g Periodic assessment of the impacts of external factors and phenomena to ensure that the objectives of integrated management and sustainable development of coastal areas and the marine environment are met;

h Conservation and restoration of altered critical habitats;

i Integration of sectoral programmes on sustainable development for settlements, agriculture, tourism, fishing, ports and industries affecting the coastal area;

j Infrastructure adaptation and alternative employment;

k Human resource development and training;

l Public education, awareness and information programmes;

m Promoting environmentally sound technology and sustainable practices;

n Development and simultaneous implementation of environmental quality criteria.

Coastal States, with the support of international organizations, upon request, should undertake measures to maintain biological diversity and productivity of marine species and habitats under national jurisdiction. *inter alia*, these measures might include: surveys of marine biodiversity, inventories of endangered species and critical coastal and marine habitats; establishment and management of protected areas; and support of scientific research and dissemination of its results.

Financing and cost evaluation $6 billion including about $50 million from the international community on grant or concessional terms.

B Marine environmental protection

Basis for action Degradation of the marine environment can result from a wide range of sources. Land-based sources contribute 70 per cent of marine pollution, while maritime transport and dumping-at-sea activities contribute 10 per cent each. The contaminants that pose the greatest threat to the marine environment are, in variable order of importance and depending on differing national or regional situations: sewage, nutrients, synthetic organic compounds, sediments, litter and plastics, metals, radionuclides, oil/hydrocarbons and polycyclic aromatic hydrocarbons (PAHs). Many of the polluting substances originating from land-based sources are of particular concern to the marine environment since they exhibit at the same time toxicity, persistence and bioaccumulation in the food chain. There is currently no global scheme to address marine pollution from land-based sources.

Degradation of the marine environment can also result from a wide range of activities on land. Human

A significant factor in the degradation and erosion of coastal resources and the coastal environment has been tourism. The seaside resorts of Emilia Romagna are the most intensive tourist centres in the world.

Top: a fisherman with his catch in Mymensingh, Northern Bangladesh where the fishing industry is being monitored and promoted through local government initiatives. Bottom: Esbjerg Harbour, Denmark. Sand eels are over-fished and used for fertilizer and animal feed. As a result a large number of birds who rely on them for food are deprived.

JORGEN SCHYTTE/STILL PICTURES

settlements, land use, construction of coastal infrastructure, agriculture, forestry, urban development, tourism and industry can affect the marine environment. Coastal erosion and siltation are of particular concern.

Marine pollution is also caused by shipping and sea-based activities. Approximately 600,000 tons of oil enter the oceans each year as a result of normal shipping operations, accidents and illegal discharges. With respect to offshore oil and gas activities, currently machinery space discharges are regulated internationally and six regional conventions to control platform discharges have been under consideration. The nature and extent of environmental impacts from offshore oil exploration and production activities generally account for a very small proportion of marine pollution.

A precautionary and anticipatory rather than a reactive approach is necessary to prevent the degradation of the marine environment. This requires, *inter alia*, the adoption of precautionary measures, environmental impact assessments, clean production techniques, recycling, waste audits and minimization, construction and/or improvement of sewage treatment facilities, quality management criteria for the proper handling of hazardous substances, and a comprehensive approach to damaging impacts from air, land and water. Any management framework must include the improvement of coastal human settlements and the integrated management and development of coastal areas.

Objectives States, in accordance with the provisions of the United Nations Convention on the Law of the Sea on protection and preservation of the marine environment, commit themselves, in accordance with their policies, priorities and resources, to prevent, reduce and control degradation of the marine environment so as to maintain and improve its life-support and productive capacities. To this end, it is necessary to:

a Apply preventive, precautionary and anticipatory approaches so as to avoid degradation of the marine environment, as well as to reduce the risk of long-term or irreversible adverse effects upon it;

b Ensure prior assessment of activities that may have significant adverse impacts upon the marine environment;

c Integrate protection of the marine environment into relevant general environmental, social and economic development policies;

d Develop economic incentives, where appropriate, to apply clean technologies and other means consistent with the internalization of environmental costs, such as the polluter pays principle, so as to avoid degradation of the marine environment;

e Improve the living standards of coastal populations, particularly in developing countries, so as to contribute to reducing the degradation of the coastal and marine environment.

States agree that provision of additional financial resources, through appropriate international mechanisms, as well as access to cleaner technologies and relevant research, would be necessary to support action by developing countries to implement this commitment.

Management-related activities

A *Prevention, reduction and control of degradation of the marine environment from land-based activities*
In carrying out their commitment to deal with degradation of the marine environment from land-based activities, States should take action at the national level and, where appropriate, at the regional and subregional levels, in concert with action to implement programme area A, and take account of the Montreal Guidelines for the Protection of the Marine Environment from Land-Based Sources.

To this end, States, with the support of the relevant international environmental, scientific, technical and financial organizations, should cooperate, *inter alia*, to:

a Consider updating, strengthening and extending the Montreal Guidelines, as appropriate;

b Assess the effectiveness of existing regional agreements and action plans, where appropriate, with a view to identifying means of strengthening action, where necessary, to prevent, reduce and control marine degradation caused by land-based activities;

c Initiate and promote the development of new regional agreements, where appropriate;

d Develop means of providing guidance on technologies to deal with the major types of pollution of the marine environment from land-based sources,

according to the best scientific evidence;
e Develop policy guidance for relevant global funding mechanisms;
f Identify additional steps requiring international cooperation.

The UNEP Governing Council is invited to convene, as soon as practicable, an intergovernmental meeting on protection of the marine environment from land-based activities.

As concerns sewage, priority actions to be considered by States may include:
a Incorporating sewage concerns when formulating or reviewing coastal development plans, including human settlement plans;
b Building and maintaining sewage treatment facilities in accordance with national policies and capacities and international cooperation available;
c Locating coastal outfalls so as to maintain an acceptable level of environmental quality and to avoid exposing shell fisheries, water intakes and bathing areas to pathogens;
d Promoting environmentally sound co-treatments of domestic and compatible industrial effluents, with the introduction, where practicable, of controls on the entry of effluents that are not compatible with the system;
e Promoting primary treatment of municipal sewage discharged to rivers, estuaries and the sea, or other solutions appropriate to specific sites;
f Establishing and improving local, national, subregional and regional, as necessary, regulatory and monitoring programmes to control effluent discharge, using minimum sewage effluent guidelines and water quality criteria and giving due consideration to the characteristics of receiving bodies and the volume and type of pollutants.

As concerns other sources of pollution, priority actions to be considered by States may include:
a Establishing or improving, as necessary, regulatory and monitoring programmes to control effluent discharges and emissions, including the development and application of control and recycling technologies;
b Promoting risk and environmental impact assessments to help ensure an acceptable level of environmental quality;
c Promoting assessment and cooperation at the regional level, where appropriate, with respect to the input of point source pollutants from new installations;
d Eliminating the emission or discharge of organohalogen compounds that threaten to accumulate to dangerous levels in the marine environment;
e Reducing the emission or discharge of other synthetic organic compounds that threaten to accumulate to dangerous levels in the marine environment;
f Promoting controls over anthropogenic inputs of nitrogen and phosphorus that enter coastal waters where problems, such as eutrophication threaten the marine environment or its resources;
g Cooperating with developing countries, through financial and technological support, to maximize the best practicable control and reduction of substances and wastes that are toxic, persistent or liable to bioaccumulate and to establish environmentally sound land-based waste disposal alternatives to sea dumping;
h Cooperating in the development and implementation of environmentally sound land-use techniques and practices to reduce run-off to watercourses and estuaries which would cause pollution or degradation of the marine environment;
i Promoting the use of environmentally less harmful pesticides and fertilizers and alternative methods for pest control, and considering the prohibition of those found to be environmentally unsound;
j Adopting new initiatives at national, subregional and regional levels for controlling the input of non-point source pollutants, which require broad changes in sewage and waste management, agricultural practices, mining, construction and transportation.

As concerns physical destruction of coastal and marine areas causing degradation of the marine environment, priority actions should include control and prevention of coastal erosion and siltation due to anthropogenic factors related to, *inter alia*, land-use and construction techniques and practices. Watershed management practices should be promoted so as to prevent, control and reduce degradation of the marine environment.

B *Prevention, reduction and control of degradation of the marine environment from sea-based activities*
States, acting individually, bilaterally, regionally or multilaterally and within the framework of IMO and other relevant international organizations, whether subregional, regional or global, as appropriate, should assess the need for additional measures to address degradation of the marine environment:
a From shipping, by:
i Supporting wider ratification and implementation of relevant shipping conventions and protocols;

EDWARD PARKER/STILL PICTURES

'Nodding donkeys' in Poole Harbour, Dorset, U.K. part of the onshore oil industry. There is no current global scheme addressing marine pollution from land based sources, which account for 70 per cent of the total pollution figure.

THIS BEAUTIFUL
LAND OF OURS
Jamaica – Land of wood and water... Rich with the wholesome beauty of nature... surrounded by the blue waters of the Caribbean sea, rising 2257 metres at the highest peak above sea level. Shaded by majestic mountains filled with an abundance of wildlife and lush vegetation – home of the world-famous Dunn's River Falls, Blue Mountains and Fern Gully ... hundreds of streams, rivers and waterfalls cascading down to white sand beaches. Today – all this is threatened by man's indifference.
In Jamaica, disposing of waste oil is a growing problem. This oil carelessly dumped, contaminates the soil, rivers, streams and beaches.
The Jamaica Public Service Company, suppliers of light and power, now collects waste oil and converts it into fuel for use in JPSCo's operation to produce electricity for the Nation.
The result... reduced environmental pollution; millions of dollars saved; more effective energy management.
The Jamaica Public Service Company, protecting our natural heritage in Jamaica... our watersheds, rivers and beaches for future generations to enjoy.
– We do care.
JAMAICA PUBLIC SERVICE CO. LTD.
Jamaica
Public Service Company, Ltd.
-we do care
6 KNUTSFORD BOULEVARD, P.O. BOX 54
KINGSTON, JAMAICA W.I.
TELEPHONE; (809) 92-63190, TELEX: 2180
CABLE: JAMSERV, TELEFAX: (809) 92-66710

A cormorant suffers from the results of oil pollution whilst right the outflow from an aluminum factory empties into the sea. A precautionary and anticipatory rather than a reactive approach is necessary to address the problems of marine environment degradation.

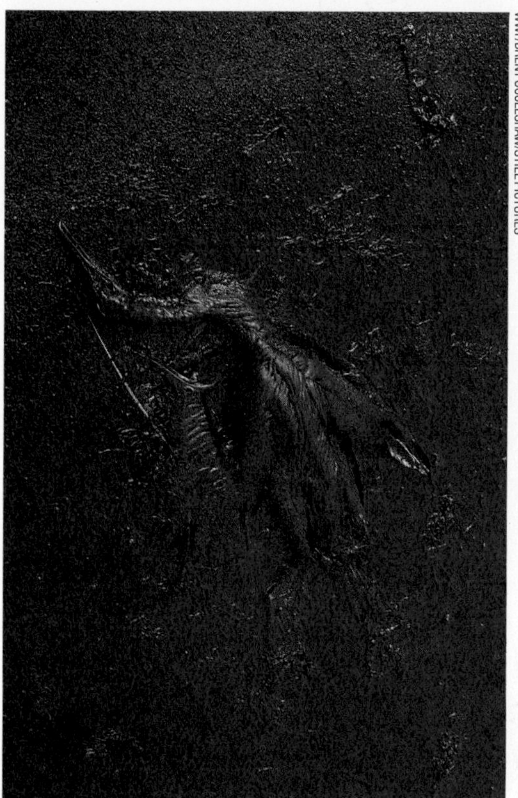

WWF/BRENT OCCLESHAW/STILL PICTURES

Section II

ii Facilitating the processes in (i), providing support to individual States upon request to help them overcome the obstacles identified by them;
iii Cooperating in monitoring marine pollution from ships, especially from illegal discharges, (e.g., aerial surveillance), and enforcing MARPOL discharge, provisions more rigorously;
iv Assessing the state of pollution caused by ships in particularly sensitive areas identified by IMO and taking action to implement applicable measures, where necessary, within such areas to ensure compliance with generally accepted international regulations;
v Taking action to ensure respect of areas designated by coastal States, within their exclusive economic zones, consistent with international law, in order to protect and preserve rare or fragile ecosystems, such as coral reefs and mangroves;
vi Considering the adoption of appropriate rules on ballast water discharge to prevent the spread of non-indigenous organisms;
vii Promoting navigational safety by adequate charting of coasts and ship-routing, as appropriate;
viii Assessing the need for stricter international regulations to further reduce the risk of accidents and pollution from cargo ships (including bulk carriers);
ix Encouraging IMO and IAEA to work together to complete consideration of a code on the carriage of irradiated nuclear fuel in flasks on board ships;
x Revising and updating the IMO Code of Safety for Nuclear Merchant Ships and considering how best to implement a revised code;
xi Supporting the ongoing activity within IMO regarding development of appropriate measures for reducing air pollution from ships;
xii Supporting the ongoing activity within IMO regarding the development of an international regime governing the transportation of hazardous and noxious substances carried by ships and further considering whether the compensation funds similar to the ones established under the Fund Convention would be appropriate in respect of pollution damage caused by substances other than oil;
b From dumping, by:
i Supporting wider ratification, implementation and participation in relevant Conventions on dumping at sea, including early conclusion of a future strategy for the London Dumping Convention;
ii Encouraging the London Dumping Convention parties to take appropriate steps to stop ocean dumping and incineration of hazardous substances;
c From offshore oil and gas platforms, by assessing existing regulatory measures to address discharges, emissions and safety and the need for additional measures;
d From ports, by facilitating establishment of port reception facilities for the collection of oily and chemical residues and garbage from ships, especially in MARPOL special areas, and promoting the establishment of smaller scale facilities in marinas and fishing harbours.

IMO and as appropriate, other competent United Nations organizations, when requested by the States concerned, should assess, where appropriate, the state of marine pollution in areas of congested shipping, such as heavily used international straits, with a view to ensuring compliance with generally accepted international regulations, particularly those related to illegal discharges from ships, in accordance with the provisions of Part III of the United Nations Convention on the Law of the Sea.

States should take measures to reduce water pollution caused by organotin compounds used in anti-fouling paints.

States should consider ratifying the Convention on Oil Pollution Preparedness, Response and Cooperation, which addresses, *inter alia*, the development of contingency plans on the national and international level, as appropriate, including provision of oil-spill response material and training of personnel, including its possible extension to chemical spill response.

States should intensify international cooperation to strengthen or establish, where necessary, regional oil/chemical-spill response centres and/or, as appropriate, mechanisms in cooperation with relevant subregional, regional or global intergovernmental organizations and, where appropriate, industry-based organizations.

Financing and cost evaluation $200 million from the international community on grant or concessional terms.

ELECTRIC POWER AND SOCIETY

It is not just a goal. It is not just a challenge. Environmental preservation has become a part of our daily behaviour as citizens and professionals. It has turned into a primary element in decision-making, in the planning and in the management of the Electric Power Service.

The Spanish Electricity Utilities have built nearly 1,000 hydroelectric power plants whose capacity exceeds 15,000 MW and whose construction has always taken into consideration the protection of the natural, cultural and historical heritage of the site.

The new technologies of gasification and clean combustion are being applied in the conventional thermoelectric power plants. The Spanish electrical companies develop new gas, cogeneration and combined cycle power plants which significantly improve energy efficiency and reduce environmental impact.

Spain also produces electricity through nine nuclear power plants whose operation records high safety levels.

Very significant efforts are being made in the development of the technologies that are necessary for the use of new forms of energy such as thermal solar, wind, photovoltaic, through facilities which rank among the most important of their kind in the world.

The efforts and the behavioural guidelines of the Spanish electric power utilities are orientated towards the harmonising and alliance of, on the one hand, science, technology and the preservation of nature and, on the other hand, of economic development and quality of life.

This effort and behaviour is inspired by a set of values and sensibilities, by the very nature of a company's culture.

UNCED offered us a unique opportunity: to act as catalysts for universal awareness of the links between environment and development, between environmental deterioration and poverty, factors that threaten the survival of our planet. This we can accomplish only if we work together to enhance national and international efforts through global partnership and cooperation. The process towards Rio mobilized countries and people, giving the world community a common cause. There is no turning back after Rio. Let us all work together, developed and developing countries, so as to secure the survival of humankind, within an environment conducive to human dignity.
H.E. Mr. George Vassiliou
President
Republic of Cyprus

C Sustainable use and conservation of marine living resources of the high seas

Basis for action Over the last decade, fisheries on the high seas have considerably expanded and currently represent approximately 5 per cent of total world landings. The provisions of the United Nations Convention on the Law of the Sea on the marine living resources of the high seas sets forth rights and obligations of States with respect to conservation and utilization of those resources.

However, management of high seas fisheries, including the adoption, monitoring and enforcement of effective conservation measures, is inadequate in many areas and some resources are overutilized. There are problems of unregulated fishing, overcapitalization, excessive fleet size, vessel reflagging to escape controls, insufficiently selective gear, unreliable databases and lack of sufficient cooperation between States. Action by States whose nationals and vessels fish on the high seas, as well as cooperation at the bilateral, subregional, regional and global levels, is essential particularly for highly migratory species and straddling stocks. Such action and cooperation should address inadequacies in fishing practices, as well as in biological knowledge, fisheries statistics and improvement of systems for handling data. Emphasis should also be on multi-species management and other approaches that take into account the relationships among species, especially in addressing depleted species, but also in identifying the potential of underutilized or unutilized populations.

Objectives States commit themselves to the conservation and sustainable use of marine living resources on the high seas. To this end, it is necessary to :

a Develop and increase the potential of marine living resources to meet human nutritional needs, as well as social, economic and development goals;
b Maintain or restore populations of marine species at levels that can produce the maximum sustainable yield as qualified by relevant environmental and economic factors, taking into consideration relationships among species;
c Promote the development and use of selective fishing gear and practices that minimize waste in the catch of target species and minimize by-catch of non-target species;
d Ensure effective monitoring and enforcement with respect to fishing activities;
e Protect and restore endangered marine species;
f Preserve habitats and other ecologically sensitive areas;
g Promote scientific research with respect to the marine living resources in the high seas;

Nothing in the above paragraph restricts the right of a State or the competence of an international organization, as appropriate, to prohibit, limit or regulate the exploitation of marine mammals on the high seas more strictly than provided for in that paragraph. States shall cooperate with a view to the conservation of marine mammals and, in the case of cetaceans, shall in particular work through the appropriate international organizations for their conservation, management and study.

The ability of developing countries to fulfil the above objectives is dependent upon their capabilities, including the financial, scientific and technological means at their disposal. Adequate financial, scientific and technological cooperation should be provided to support action by them to implement these objectives.

Management-related activities States should take effective action, including bilateral and multilateral cooperation, where appropriate at the subregional, regional and global levels, to ensure that high seas fisheries are managed in accordance with the provisions of the United Nations Convention on the Law of the Sea. In particular, they should:

a Give full effect to these provisions with regard to fisheries populations whose ranges lie both within and beyond exclusive economic zones (straddling stocks);
b Give full effect to these provisions with regard to highly migratory species;
c Negotiate, where appropriate, international agreements for the effective management and conservation of fishery stocks;
d Define and identify appropriate management units;

States, should convene, as soon as possible, an intergovernmental conference under United Nations auspices, taking into account relevant activities at the subregional, regional and global levels, with a view to promoting effective implementation of the provisions of the United Nations Convention on the Law of the Sea on straddling fish stocks and highly migratory fish stocks. The conference, drawing *inter alia* on scientific and technical studies by FAO, should identify and assess existing problems related to the conservation and management of such fish stocks, and consider means of improving cooperation on fisheries among States, and formulate appropriate recommendations. The work and the results of the conference should be fully consistent with the provisions of UNCLOS, in particular the rights and obligations of coastal states and states fishing on the high seas.

States should ensure that fishing activities by vessels flying their flags on the high seas take place in a manner so as to minimize incidental catch.

States should take effective action consistent with international law to monitor and control fishing activities by vessels flying their flags on the high seas to ensure compliance with applicable conservation and management rules, including full, detailed, accurate and timely reporting of catches and effort.

States should take effective action consistent with international law to deter reflagging of vessels by their nationals as a means of avoiding compliance with applicable conservation and management rules for fishing activities on the high seas.

States should prohibit dynamiting, poisoning and other comparable destructive fishing practices.

States should fully implement General Assembly resolution 46/215 on large-scale pelagic drift-net fishing.

States should take measures to increase the availability of marine living resources as human food by reducing wastage, post-harvest losses and discards, and improving techniques of processing, distribution and transportation.

Financing and cost evaluation $12 million from the international community on grant or concessional terms.

D Sustainable use and conservation of marine living resources under national jurisdiction

Basis for action Marine fisheries yield 80 to 90 million tons of fish and shellfish per year, 95 per cent of which is taken from waters under national jurisdiction. Yields have increased nearly fivefold over the past four decades. The provisions of the United Nations Convention on the Law of the Sea on marine living resources of the exclusive economic zone and other areas under national jurisdiction set forth rights and obligations of States with respect to conservation and utilization of those resources.

Marine living resources provide an important source of protein in many countries and their use is often of major importance to local communities and indigenous people. Such resources provide food and

Land activities including agriculture, forestry and human settlements cause marine environment degradation. Deforestation of the Mangrove forest on this part of the Haitian coastline has led to topsoil being washed into the sea.

livelihoods to millions of people and, if sustainably utilized, offer increased potential to meet nutritional and social needs, particularly in developing countries. To realize this potential requires improved knowledge and identification of marine living resource stocks, particularly of underutilized and unutilized stocks and species, use of new technologies, better handling and processing facilities to avoid wastage, and improved quality and training of skilled personnel to manage and conserve effectively the marine living resources of the exclusive economic zone and other areas under national jurisdiction. Emphasis should also be on multi-species management and other approaches that take into account the relationships among species.

Fisheries in many areas under national jurisdiction face mounting problems, including local overfishing, unauthorized incursions by foreign fleets, ecosystem degradation, overcapitalization and excessive fleet sizes, underevaluation of catch, insufficiently selective gear, unreliable databases, and increasing competition between artisanal and large-scale fishing, and between fishing and other types of activities.

Problems extend beyond fisheries. Coral reefs and other marine and coastal habitats, such as mangroves and estuaries, are among the most highly diverse, integrated and productive of the Earth's ecosystems. They often serve important ecological functions, provide coastal protection, and are critical resources for food, energy, tourism and economic development. In many parts of the world, such marine and coastal systems are under stress or are threatened from a variety of sources, both human and natural.

Objectives Coastal States, particularly developing countries and States whose economies are overwhelmingly dependent on the exploitation of the marine living resources of their exclusive economic zones, should obtain the full social and economic benefits from sustainable utilization of marine living resources within their exclusive economic zones and other areas under national jurisdiction.

States commit themselves to the conservation and sustainable use of marine living resources under national jurisdiction. To this end, it is necessary to:

There is no easy road for a solution to global environmental degradation. This is an international burden of responsibility from which there can be no escape for any nation, rich or poor, North or South. As a father, and as the leader of my people, I share their hope that the world can move beyond moral ambiguity on the question of the allocation of duties to ensure environmental protection, towards the recognition of the Earth's resources as our finite and irreplaceable resource base. A sustainable future is in our hands; our natural resources are in a shared account. The whole world stands to gain on the future road agreed upon in Rio.
King Hussein of Jordan

a Develop and increase the potential of marine living resources to meet human nutritional needs, as well as social, economic and development goals;
b Take into account traditional knowledge and interests of local communities, small-scale artisanal fisheries and indigenous people in development and management programmes;
c Maintain or restore populations of marine species at levels that can produce the maximum sustainable yield as qualified by relevant environmental and economic factors, taking into consideration relationships among species;
d Promote the development and use of selective fishing gear and practices that minimize waste in the catch of target species and minimize by-catch of non-target species;
e Protect and restore endangered marine species;
f Preserve rare or fragile ecosystems, as well as habitats and other ecologically sensitive areas.

Nothing in the above paragraph restricts the right of a coastal State or the competence of an international organization, as appropriate, to prohibit, limit or regulate the exploitation of marine mammals more strictly than provided for in that paragraph. States shall cooperate with a view to the conservation of marine mammals and in the case of cetaceans shall in particular work through the appropriate international organizations for their conservation, management and study.

The ability of developing countries to fulfil the above objectives is dependent upon their capabilities, including the financial, scientific and technological means at their disposal. Adequate financial, scientific and technological cooperation should be provided to support action by them to implement these objectives.

Management-related activities States should ensure that marine living resources of the exclusive economic zone and other areas under national jurisdiction are conserved and managed in accordance with the provisions of the United Nations Convention on the Law of the Sea.

Coastal States, individually or through bilateral and/or multilateral cooperation and with the support, as appropriate of international organizations, whether subregional, regional or global, should *inter alia*:
a Assess the potential of marine living resources, including underutilized or unutilized stocks and species, by developing inventories, where necessary, for their conservation and sustainable use;
b Implement strategies for the sustainable use of marine living resources, taking into account the special needs and interests of small-scale artisanal fisheries, local communities and indigenous people to meet human nutritional and other development needs;
c Implement, in particular in developing countries, mechanisms to develop mariculture, aquaculture and small-scale, deep-sea and oceanic fisheries within areas under national jurisdiction where assessments show that marine living resources are potentially available;
d Strengthen their legal and regulatory frameworks, where appropriate, including management, enforcement and surveillance capabilities, to regulate activities related to the above strategies;
e Take measures to increase the availability of marine living resources as human food by reducing wastage, post-harvest losses and discards, and improving techniques of processing, distribution and transportation;
f Develop and promote the use of environmentally sound technology under criteria compatible with the sustainable use of marine living resources, including assessment of the environmental impact of major new fishery practices;
g Enhance the productivity and utilization of their marine living resources for food and income.

States, in implementing the provisions of the United Nations Convention on the Law of the Sea, should address the issues of straddling stocks and highly migratory species, and taking fully into account the first paragraph of Objectives above, access to the surplus of allowable catches.

Coastal States should explore the scope for expanding recreational and tourist activities based on marine living resources, including those for providing alternative sources of income. Such activities should be compatible with conservation and sustainable development policies and plans.

Coastal States should support the sustainability of small-scale artisanal fisheries. To this end, they should, as appropriate:
a Integrate small-scale artisanal fisheries development in marine and coastal planning, taking into account the interests and, where appropriate, encouraging representation of fishermen, small-scale fisherworkers, women, local communities and indigenous people;
b Recognize the rights of small-scale fishworkers and the special situation of indigenous people and local communities, including their rights to utilization and protection of their habitats on a sustainable basis;
c Develop systems for the acquisition and recording of traditional knowledge concerning marine living resources and environment and promote the incorporation of such knowledge into management systems.

Coastal States should ensure that, in the negotiation and implementation of international agreements on the development or conservation of marine living resources, the interests of local communities and indigenous people are taken into account, in particular their right to subsistence.

Coastal States, with the support, as appropriate, of international organizations should conduct analyses of the potential for aquaculture in marine and coastal areas under national jurisdiction and apply appropriate safeguards as to the introduction of new species.

States should prohibit dynamiting, poisoning and other comparable destructive fishing practices.

States should identify marine ecosystems exhibiting high levels of biodiversity and productivity and other critical habitat areas and provide necessary limitations on use in these areas, through, *inter alia*, designation of protected areas. Priority should be accorded, as appropriate, to:
a Coral reef ecosystems;
b Estuaries;
c Temperate and tropical wetlands, including mangroves;
d Seagrass beds;
e Other spawning and nursery areas.

Financing and cost evaluation $6 billion including about $60 million from the international community on grant or concessional terms.

E Addressing critical uncertainties for the management of the marine environment and climate change

Basis for action The marine environment is vulnerable and sensitive to climate and atmospheric changes. Rational use and development of coastal areas, all seas and marine resources, as well as conservation of the marine environment, requires the ability to determine the present state of these systems and to predict future conditions. The high degree of uncertainty in present information inhibits effective management and limits the ability to make predictions and assess environmental change. Systematic collection of data on marine environmental parameters will be needed to apply integrated management approaches and to predict effects of global climate change and of atmospheric phenomena, such as ozone depletion, on living marine resources and the marine environment. In order to determine the role of the oceans and all seas in

Marine and coastal habitats are among some of the most highly diverse of the Earth's ecosystems. Above: the garabaldi feeds on the pelagic jellyfish. Below: Cancer growing on a fish caused by pollution.

NORBERT WU/STILL PICTURES

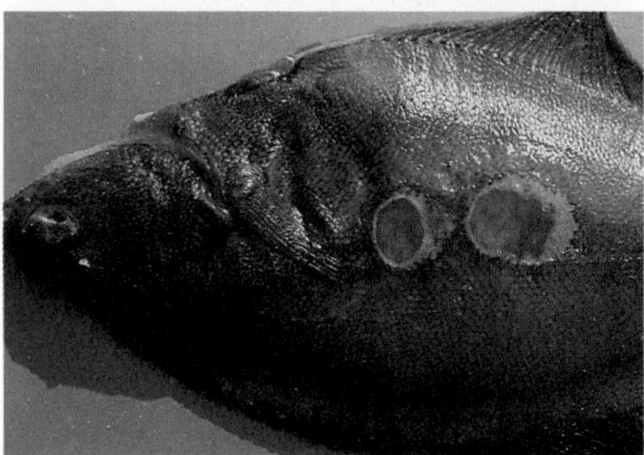

driving global systems and to predict natural and human-induced changes in marine and coastal environments, the mechanisms to collect, synthesize and disseminate information from research and systematic observation activities need to be restructured and reinforced considerably. There are many uncertainties about climate change and particularly about sealevel rise. Small increases in sealevel have the potential of causing significant damage to small islands and low-lying coasts. Response strategies should be based on sound data. A long-term cooperative research commitment is needed to provide the data required for global climate models and to reduce uncertainty. Meanwhile, precautionary measures should be undertaken to diminish the risks and effects, particularly on small islands and on low-lying and coastal areas of the world.

Increased ultraviolet radiation derived from ozone depletion has been reported in some areas of the world. An assessment of its effects in the marine environment is needed to reduce uncertainty and to provide a basis for action.

Objectives States, in accordance with provisions of the United Nations Convention on the Law of the Sea on marine scientific research, commit themselves to improve the understanding of the marine environment and its role on global processes. To this end, it is necessary to:

a Promote scientific research on and systematic observation of the marine environment within the limits of national jurisdiction and high seas, including interactions with atmospheric phenomena, such as ozone depletion;

b Promote exchange of data and information resulting from scientific research and systematic observation and from traditional ecological knowledge and ensure its availability to policy makers and the public at the national level;

c Cooperate with a view to the development of standard inter-calibrated procedures, measuring techniques, data storage and management capabilities for scientific research on and systematic observation of the marine environment.

Management-related activities States should consider, *inter alia*:

a Coordinating national and regional observation programmes for coastal and near-shore phenomena related to climate change and for research parameters essential for marine and coastal management in all regions;

b Providing improved forecasts of marine conditions for the safety of inhabitants of coastal areas and for the efficiency of maritime operations;

c Cooperating with a view to adopting special measures to cope with and adapt to potential climate change and sealevel rise, including the development of globally accepted methodologies for coastal vulnerability assessment, modelling and response strategies particularly for priority areas, such as small islands and low-lying and critical coastal areas;

d Identifying ongoing and planned programmes of systematic observation of the marine environment, with a view to integrating activities and establishing priorities to address critical uncertainties for oceans and all seas;

e Initiating a programme of research to determine the marine biological effects of increased levels of ultraviolet rays due to the depletion of the stratospheric ozone layer and to evaluate the possible effects.

Recognizing the important role that oceans and all seas play in attenuating potential climate change, IOC and other relevant competent United Nations agencies, with the support of countries having the resources and expertise, should carry out analysis, assessments and systematic observation of the role of oceans as a carbon sink.

Financing and cost evaluation $750 million including about $480 million from the international community on grant or concessional terms.

F Strengthening international, including regional, cooperation and coordination

Basis for action It is recognized that the role of international cooperation is to support and supplement national efforts. Implementation of strategies and activities under the programme areas relative to marine and coastal areas and seas requires effective institutional arrangements at national, subregional, regional and global levels, as appropriate. There are numerous national and international, including regional, institutions, both within and outside the United Nations system, with competence in marine issues, and there is a need to improve coordination and strengthen links among them. It is also important to ensure that an integrated and multisectoral approach to marine issues is pursued at all levels.

Objectives States commit themselves, in accordance with their policies, priorities and resources, to promote institutional arrangements necessary to support the implementation of the programme areas in this chapter. To this end, it is necessary, as appropriate, to:

a Integrate relevant sectoral activities addressing environment and development in marine and coastal areas at national, subregional, regional and global levels, as appropriate;

b Promote effective information exchange and, where appropriate, institutional linkages between bilateral and multilateral national, regional, subregional and interregional institutions dealing with environment and development in marine and coastal areas;

c Promote within the United Nations system, regular intergovernmental review and consideration of environment and development issues with respect to marine and coastal areas;

d Promote the effective operation of coordinating mechanisms for the components of the United Nations system dealing with issues of environment and development in marine and coastal areas, as well as links with relevant international development bodies.

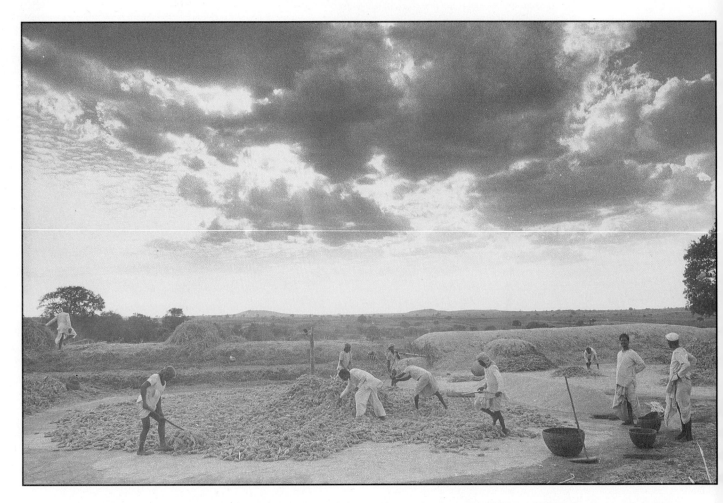

Management-related activities

Global

The General Assembly should provide for regular consideration, within the United Nations system, at the intergovernmental level of general marine and coastal issues, including environment and development matters, and should request the Secretary-General and executive heads of United Nations agencies and organizations to:

a Strengthen coordination and develop improved arrangements among the relevant United Nations organizations with major marine and coastal responsibilities, including their subregional and regional components;

b Strengthen coordination between those organizations and other United Nations organizations, institutions and specialized agencies dealing with development, trade and other related economic issues, as appropriate;

c Improve representation of United Nations agencies dealing with the marine environment in United Nations system-wide coordination efforts;

d Promote, where necessary, greater collaboration between the United Nations agencies and subregional and regional coastal and marine programmes;

e Develop a centralized system to provide for information on legislation and advice on implementation of legal agreements on marine environmental and development issues.

States recognize that environmental policies should deal with the root causes of environmental degradation, thus preventing environmental measures from resulting in unnecessary restrictions to trade. Trade policy measures for environmental purposes should not constitute a means of arbitrary or unjustifiable discrimination or a disguised restriction on international trade. Unilateral actions to deal with environmental challenges outside the jurisdiction of the importing country should be avoided. Environmental measures addressing international environmental problems should, as far as possible, be based on an international consensus. Domestic measures targeted to achieve certain environmental objectives may need trade measures to render them effective. Should trade policy measures be found necessary for the enforcement of environmental policies, certain principles and rules should apply. These could include, *inter alia*, the principle of non-discrimination; the principle that the trade measure chosen should be the least trade-restrictive necessary to achieve the objectives; an obligation to ensure transparency in the use of trade measures related to the environment and to provide adequate notification of national regulations; and the need to give consideration to the special conditions and development requirements of developing countries as they move towards internationally agreed environmental objectives.

Subregional and regional

States should consider, as appropriate:

a Strengthening, and extending where necessary, intergovernmental regional cooperation, the Regional Seas Programmes of UNEP, regional and subregional fisheries organizations and regional commissions;

b Introduce, where necessary, coordination among relevant United Nations and other multilateral organizations at the subregional and regional levels, including consideration of co-location of their staff;

c Arrange for periodic intraregional consultations;

d Facilitate access to and use of expertise and technology through relevant national bodies to subregional and regional centres and networks, such as the Regional Centres for Marine Technology.

Financing and cost evaluation $50 million from the international community on grant or concessional terms.

G Sustainable development of small islands

Basis for action Small island developing States, and islands supporting small communities are a special case both for environment and development. They are ecologically fragile and vulnerable. Their small size, limited resources, geographic dispersion and isolation from markets, place them at a disadvantage economically and prevent economies of scale. For small island developing States the ocean and coastal environment is of strategic importance and constitutes a valuable development resource.

Their geographic isolation has resulted in their habitation of a comparatively large number of unique species of flora and fauna, giving them a very high share of global biodiversity. They also have rich and diverse cultures with special adaptations to island environments and knowledge of the sound management of island resources.

Children play on a Danish beach which is closed because of pollution. The causes of degradation of the marine environment are numerous; there is currently no global scheme to address marine pollution from land based sources.

The Sewerage Revolution

Throwing slops out of the window with a shout of **"Garde l'eau!"**, was common practice in many European cities until the 19th century. Wary pedestrians used to carry umbrellas to protect themselves as much from the **"l'eau"** as from the rain. Once the sophisticated sewerage systems of so many ancient civilisations, from the Mediterranean to the Indus Valley, had fallen into oblivion, man did not discover sewers again for a couple of millenia.

Street lighting, mains, gas and electricity, and tramways are just some of the radical innovations city dwellers enjoyed from the mid-19th century onwards. Wonderful though this progress was, however, it was the first-time supply of pressurised mains water and sewerage which transformed people's lives. Water flowing from taps saved women endless hours of drudgery, while sewers saved countless lives from public health hazards.

With sewerage systems neatly underground, urban dwellers could conveniently ignore what happened to the wastewater which flowed out of sight and out of mind. Mere disposal is no longer enough if the environment on which we depend for our survival is to be preserved for future generations. Sophisticated treatment has become essential to prevent our sewage contaminating our rivers, lakes, seas and groundwater.

The Advanced Treatment Plants being established in İstanbul today provide the answer to this problem by removing the harmful pollutants from sewage. These plants represent the responsibility felt by us all towards the natural world in which we live.

Istanbul Water and Sewerage Administration İSKİ General Directorate 34410 Inkilap Caddesi, 34 Aksaray-İstanbul/TURKEY Phone: (901) 588 38 00 (60 lines) Fax: (901) 588 38 98

The debris from human settlements and tourism illustrated by the plastic garbage on an Italian beach.

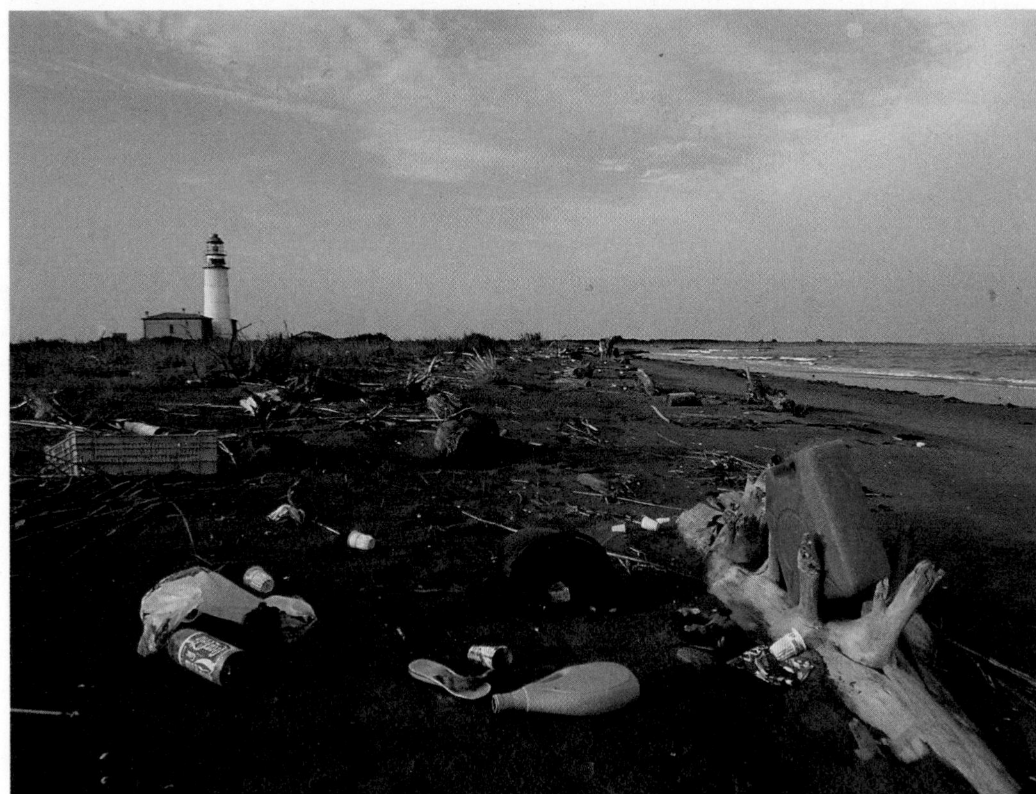

Small island developing States have all the environmental problems and challenges of the coastal zone concentrated in a limited land area. They are considered extremely vulnerable to global warming and sealevel rise, with certain small low-lying islands facing the increasing threat of the loss of their entire national territories. Most tropical islands are also now experiencing the more immediate impacts of increasing frequency of cyclones, storms and hurricanes associated with climate change. These are causing major set-backs to their socio-economic development.

Because small island development options are limited, there are special challenges to planning for and implementing sustainable development. Small island developing States will be constrained in meeting these challenges without the cooperation and assistance of the international community.

Objectives States commit themselves to addressing the problems of sustainable development of small island developing States. To this end, it is necessary:

a To adopt and implement plans and programmes to support the sustainable development and utilization of their marine and coastal resources, including meeting essential human needs, maintaining biodiversity and improving the quality of life for island people;

b To adopt measures which will enable small island developing States to cope effectively, creatively and sustainably with environmental change and to mitigate impacts and reduce the threats posed to marine and coastal resources.

Management-related activities Small island developing States, with the assistance as appropriate of the international community and on the basis of existing work of national and international organizations, should:

a Study the special environmental and developmental characteristics of small islands, producing an environmental profile and inventory of their natural resources, critical marine habitats and biodiversity;

b Develop techniques for determining and monitoring the carrying capacity of small islands under different development assumptions and resource constraints;

c Prepare medium- and long-term plans for sustainable development that emphasize multiple use of resources, integrate environmental considerations with economic and sectoral planning and policies, define measures for maintaining cultural and biological diversity and conserve endangered species and critical marine habitats;

d Adapt coastal area management techniques, such as planning, siting and environmental impact assessments, using Geographical Information Systems (GIS), suitable to the special characteristics of small islands, taking into account the traditional and cultural values of indigenous people of island countries;

e Review the existing institutional arrangements and identify and undertake appropriate institutional reforms essential to the effective implementation of sustainable development plans, including intersectoral coordination and community participation in the planning process;

f Implement sustainable development plans, including the review and modification of existing unsustainable policies and practices;

g Based on precautionary and anticipatory approaches, design and implement rational response strategies to address the environmental, social and economic impacts of climate change and sealevel rise, and prepare appropriate contingency plans;

h Promote environmentally sound technology for sustainable development within small island developing States and identify technologies that should be excluded because of their threats to essential island ecosystems.

Financing and cost evaluation $130 million including about $50 million from the international community on grant or concessional terms.

1 References to the United Nations Convention on the Law of the Sea in this chapter do not prejudice the position of any State with respect to signature, ratification of or accession to the Convention.

2 References to the United Nations Convention on the Law of the Sea in this chapter do not prejudice the position of States which view the Convention as having a unified character.

3 Nothing in the programme areas of this chapter should be interpreted as prejudicing the rights of the States involved in a dispute of sovereignty or in the delimitation of the maritime areas concerned.

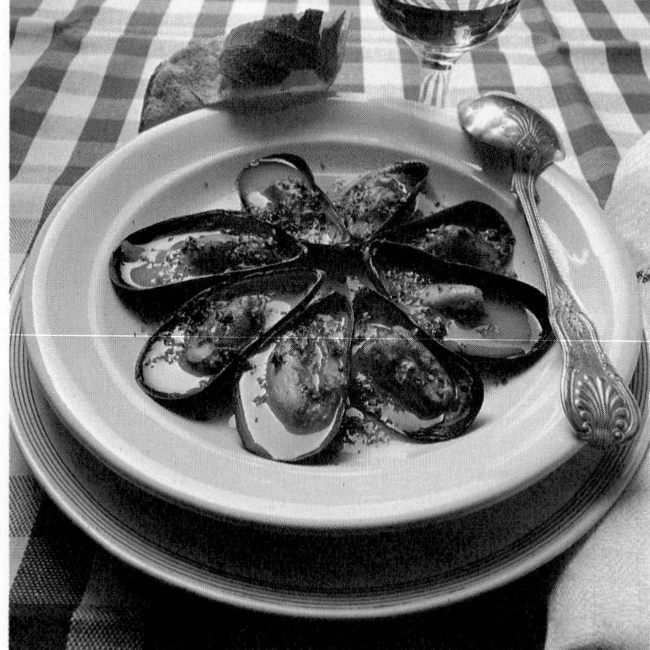

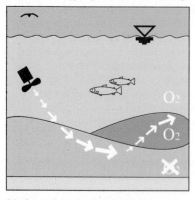

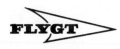

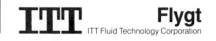

Chapter 18

Protection of the quality and supply of freshwater resources: application of integrated approaches to the development, management and use of water resources

Freshwater resources are an essential component of the earth's hydrosphere and an indispensable part of all terrestrial ecosystems. The freshwater environment is characterized by the hydrological cycle, including floods and droughts, which in some regions have become more extreme and dramatic in their consequences. Global climate change and atmospheric pollution could also have an impact on freshwater resources and their availability and, through sea-level rise, threaten low-lying coastal areas and small island ecosystems.

Water is needed in all aspects of life. The general objective is to make certain that adequate supplies of water of good quality are maintained for the entire population of this planet, while preserving the hydrological, biological and chemical functions of ecosystems, adapting human activities within the capacity limits of nature and combating vectors of water-related diseases. Innovative technologies, including the improvement of indigenous technologies, are needed to fully utilize limited water resources and to safeguard those resources against pollution.

The widespread scarcity, gradual destruction and aggravated pollution of freshwater resources in many world regions, along with the progressive encroachment of incompatible activities, demand integrated water resources planning and management. Such integration must cover all types of interrelated freshwater bodies, including both surface water and groundwater, and duly consider water quantity and quality aspects. The multisectoral nature of water resources development in the context of socio-economic development must be recognized, as well as the multi-interest utilization of water resources for water supply and sanitation, agriculture, industry, urban development, hydropower generation, inland fisheries, transportation, recreation, low and flat lands management and other activities. Rational water utilization schemes for the development of surface and underground water-supply sources and other potential sources have to be supported by concurrent water conservation and wastage minimization measures. Priority, however, must be accorded to flood prevention and control measures, as well as sedimentation control, where required.

Transboundary water resources and their use are of great importance to riparian States. In this connection, cooperation among those States may be desirable in conformity with existing agreements and/or other relevant arrangements, taking into account the interests of all riparian States concerned.

A Integrated water resources development and management

Basis for action The extent to which water resources development contributes to economic productivity and social well-being is not usually appreciated, although all social and economic activities rely heavily on the supply and quality of freshwater. As populations and economic activities grow, many countries are rapidly reaching conditions of water scarcity or facing limits to economic development. Water demands are increasing rapidly, with 70-80 per cent required for irrigation, less than 20 per cent for industry and a mere 6 per cent for domestic consumption. The holistic management of freshwater as a finite and vulnerable resource, and the integration of sectoral water plans and programmes within the framework of national economic and social policy, are of paramount importance for action in the 1990s and beyond. The fragmentation of responsibilities for water resources development among sectoral agencies is proving, however, to be an even greater impediment to promoting integrated water management than had been anticipated. Effective implementation and coordination mechanisms are required.

Objectives The overall objective is to satisfy the freshwater needs of all countries for their sustainable development.

Integrated water resources management is based on the perception of water as an integral part of the ecosystem, a natural resource and a social and economic good, whose quantity and quality determine the nature of its utilization. To this end, water resources have to be protected, taking into account the functioning of aquatic ecosystems and the perenniality of the resource, in order to satisfy and reconcile needs for water in human activities. In developing and using water resources, priority has to be given to the satisfaction of basic needs and the safeguarding of ecosystems. Beyond these requirements, however, water users should be charged appropriately.

Integrated water resources management, including the integration of land- and water-related aspects, should be carried out at the level of the catchment basin or sub-basin. Four principal objectives should be pursued:

a To promote a dynamic, interactive, iterative and multisectoral approach to water resources management, including the identification and protection of potential sources of freshwater supply, that integrates technological, socio-economic, environmental and human health considerations;

b To plan for the sustainable and rational utilization, protection, conservation and management of water resources based on community needs and priorities within the framework of national economic development policy;

c To design, implement and evaluate projects and programmes that are both economically efficient and socially appropriate within clearly defined strategies, based on an approach of full public participation, including that of women, youth, indigenous people, local communities, in water management policy-

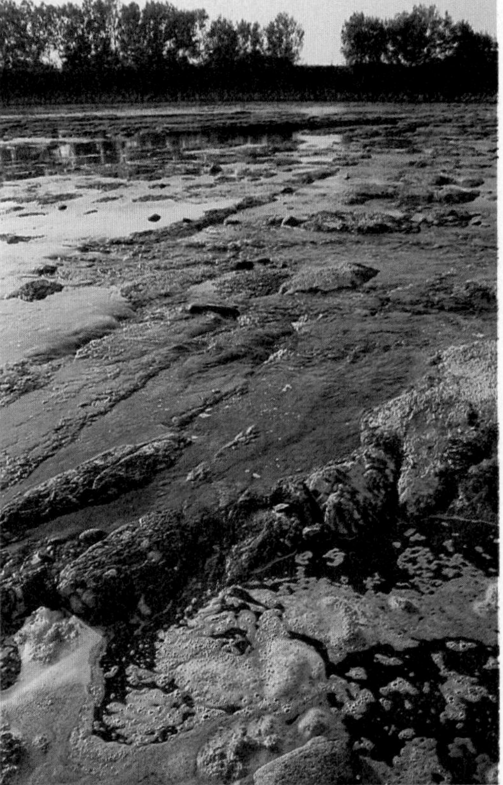

The River Po, near the Casale dam in Italy. Water taken from the Po for intensive farming averages 18 billion cubic metres each year. The result is that in many places the river is almost empty exposing the rocky river bed.

Section II

Africa is frequently a harsh and unforgiving continent which forces people to opt for short-term survival, often at the expense of long-term sustainability. Yet, as business leaders, it remains our task to meet the developmental aspirations of millions of people within the environmental constraints imposed upon us.

We have to accept this responsibility. While circumstances may want to force us along a different path, our commitment to a healthy and productive environment must remain unquestionable. Sustained development is just not possible without the protection and wise management of our resource base.

Dr. Ian McRae

Chief Executive of Eskom and member of the Executive Committee of the Industrial Environmental Forum of Southern Africa.

Purifying plant in Melbourne, Australia treating water contaminated with sewage. Social and economic activities rely on the supply and quality of freshwater. Water resources must be protected as well as recognised as a finite resource.

making and decision-making;

d To identify and strengthen or develop, as required, in particular in developing countries, the appropriate institutional, legal and financial mechanisms to ensure that water policy and its implementation are a catalyst for sustainable social progress and economic growth.

In the case of transboundary water resources, there is a need for riparian States to formulate water resources strategies, prepare water resources action programmes and consider, where appropriate, the harmonization of those strategies and action programmes.

All States, according to their capacity and available resources, and through bilateral or multilateral cooperation, including the United Nations and other relevant organizations as appropriate, could set the following targets:

a By the year 2000:

i To have designed and initiated costed and targeted national action programmes, and have put in place appropriate institutional structures and legal instruments;

ii To have established efficient water-use programmes to attain sustainable resource utilization patterns;

b By the year 2025:

i To have achieved subsectoral targets of all freshwater programme areas.

It is understood that the fulfilment of the targets quantified in (i) and (ii) above will depend upon new and additional financial resources that will be made available to developing countries in accordance with the relevant provisions of General Assembly resolution 44/228.

Activities All States, according to their capacity and available resources, and through bilateral or multilateral cooperation, including the United Nations and other relevant organizations as appropriate, could implement the following activities to improve integrated water resources management:

a Formulation of costed and targeted national action plans and investment programmes;

b Integration of measures for the protection and conservation of potential sources of freshwater supply, including the inventorying of water resources, with land-use planning, forest resource utilization, protection of mountain slopes and riverbanks and other relevant development and conservation activities;

c Development of interactive databases, forecasting models, economic planning models and methods for water management and planning, including environmental impact assessment methods;

d Optimization of water resources allocation under physical and socio-economic constraints;

e Implementation of allocation decisions through demand management, pricing mechanisms and regulatory measures;

f Flood and drought management, including risk analysis and environmental and social impact assessment;

g Promotion of schemes for rational water use through public awareness-raising, educational programmes and levying of water tariffs and other economic instruments;

h Mobilization of water resources, particularly in arid and semi-arid areas;

i Promotion of international scientific research cooperation on freshwater resources;

j Development of new and alternative sources of water-supply such as sea-water desalination, artificial groundwater recharge, use of marginal-quality water, waste-water reuse and water recycling;

k Integration of water (including surface and underground water resources) quantity and quality management;

l Promotion of water conservation through improved water-use efficiency and wastage minimization schemes for all users, including the development of water-saving devices;

m Support to water-users groups to optimize local water resources management;

n Development of public participatory techniques and their implementation in decision-making, particularly the enhancement of the role of women in water resources planning and management;

o Development and strengthening, as appropriate, of cooperation, including mechanisms where appropriate, at all levels concerned, namely:

i At the lowest appropriate level, delegation of water resources management, generally, to such a level, in accordance with national legislation, including decentralization of government services to local authorities, private enterprises and communities;

ii At the national level, integrated water resources planning and management in the framework of the national planning process and, where appropriate, establishment of independent regulation and monitoring of freshwater, based on national legislation and economic measures;

Much of the environmental destruction that has occurred to freshwater systems has been the result of a lack of public awareness and education. Preventative measures will prove less costly than rehabilitation.

iii At the regional level, consideration, where appropriate, of the harmonization of national strategies and action programmes;
iv At the global level, improved delineation of responsibilities, division of labour and coordination of international organizations and programmes, including facilitating discussions and sharing of experiences in areas related to water resources management;
p Dissemination of information, including operational guidelines, and promotion of education for water users, including the consideration by the United Nations of a World Water Day.

Financing and cost evaluation $115 million from the international community on grant or concessional terms.

B Water resources assessment

Basis for action Water resources assessment, including the identification of potential sources of freshwater supply, comprises the continuing determination of sources, extent, dependability and quality of water resources and of the human activities that affect those resources. Such assessment constitutes the practical basis for their sustainable management and a pre-requisite for evaluation of the possibilities for their development. There is, however, growing concern that at a time when more precise and reliable information is needed about water resources, hydrologic services and related bodies are less able than before to provide this information, especially information on groundwater and water quality. Major impediments are the lack of financial resources for water resources assessment, the fragmented nature of hydrologic services and the insufficient numbers of qualified staff. At the same time, the advancing technology for data capture and management is increasingly difficult to access for developing countries. Establishment of national databases is, however, vital to water resources assessment and to mitigation of the effects of floods, droughts, desertification and pollution.

Objectives Based upon the Mar del Plata Action Plan, this programme area has been extended into the 1990s and beyond with the overall objective of ensuring the assessment and forecasting of the quantity and quality of water resources, in order to estimate the total quantity of water resources available and their future supply potential, to determine their current quality status, to predict possible conflicts between supply and demand and to provide a scientific database for rational water resources utilization.

Five specific objectives have been set accordingly:
a To make available to all countries water resources assessment technology that is appropriate to their needs irrespective of their level of development, including methods for the impact assessment of climate change on freshwaters;
b To have all countries, according to their financial means, allocate to water resources assessment financial resources in line with the economic and social needs for water resources data;
c To ensure that the assessment information is fully utilized in the development of water management policies;
d To have all countries establish the institutional arrangements needed to ensure the efficient collection, processing, storage, retrieval and dissemination to users of information about the quality and quantity of available water resources at the level of catchments and groundwater aquifers in an integrated manner;
e To have sufficient numbers of appropriately qualified and capable staff recruited and retained by water resources assessment agencies and provided with the training and retraining they will need to carry out their responsibilities successfully.

All States, according to their capacity and available resources, and through bilateral or multilateral cooperation, including cooperation with the United Nations and other relevant organizations, as appropriate, could set the following targets:
a By the year 2000, to have studied in detail the feasibility of installing water resources assessment services;
b As a long-term target, to have fully operational services available based upon high-density hydrometric networks.

Activities All States, according to their capacity and available resources, and through bilateral or multilateral cooperation, including the United Nations and other relevant organizations as appropriate, could undertake the following activities:
a Institutional framework:
i Establish appropriate policy frameworks and national priorities;
ii Establish and strengthen the institutional capabilities of countries, including legislative and regulatory arrangements, that are required to ensure the adequate assessment of their water resources and the provision of flood and drought forecasting services;
iii Establish and maintain effective cooperation at the national level between the various agencies responsible for the collection, storage and analysis of hydrologic data;
iv Cooperate in the assessment of transboundary water resources, subject to the prior agreement of each riparian State concerned;
b Data systems:
i Review existing data-collection networks and assess their adequacy, including those that provide real-time data for flood and drought forecasting;
ii Improve networks to meet accepted guidelines for the provision of data on water quantity and quality for surface and groundwater, as well as relevant land-use data;
iii Apply standards and other means to ensure data compatibility;
iv Upgrade facilities and procedures used to store, process and analyse hydrologic data and make such data and the forecasts derived from them available to potential users;

As the twentieth century draws to a close, the dangers which threaten our planet are both obvious and serious. Economic development and technological progress have undoubtedly provided a great segment of humanity with a high standard of living but the price of this development has begun to be prohibitive. The dangers of underdevelopment are equally serious. The great challenge is to formulate a common environmental policy on a world scale which will reconcile development with protection of the environment. To formulate such a policy is not an easy task. It is, however, indispensable and the future of mankind will depend upon it.

Mr Constantine Karamanlis
President
Republic of Greece

v Establish databases on the availability of all types of hydrologic data at the national level;
vi Implement "data rescue" operations, for example, establishment of national archives of water resources;
vii Implement appropriate well-tried techniques for the processing of hydrologic data;
viii Derive area-related estimates from point hydrologic data;
ix Assimilate remotely sensed data and the use, where appropriate, of geographical information systems;
c Data dissemination:
i Identify the need for water resources data for various planning purposes;
ii Analyse and present data and information on water resources in the forms required for planning and management of countries' socio-economic development and for use in environmental protection strategies and in the design and operation of specific water-related projects;
iii Provide forecasts and warnings of flood and drought to the general public and civil defence;
d Research and development:
i Establish or strengthen research and development programmes at the national, subregional, regional and international levels in support of water resources assessment activities;
ii Monitor research and development activities to ensure that they make full use of local expertise and other local resources and that they are appropriate for the needs of the country or countries concerned.

Financing and cost evaluation $355 million, including about $145 million from the international community on grant or concessional terms.

C Protection of water resources, water quality and aquatic ecosystems

Basis for action Freshwater is a unitary resource. Long-term development of global freshwater requires holistic management of resources and a recognition of the interconnectedness of the elements related to freshwater and freshwater quality. There are few regions of the world that are still exempt from problems of loss of potential sources of freshwater supply, degraded water quality and pollution of surface and groundwater sources. Major problems affecting the water quality of rivers and lakes arise, in variable order of importance according to different situations, from inadequately treated domestic sewage, inadequate controls on the discharges of industrial waste waters, loss and destruction of catchment areas, ill-considered siting of industrial plants, deforestation, uncontrolled shifting cultivation and poor agricultural practices. This gives rise to the leaching of nutrients and pesticides. Aquatic ecosystems are disturbed and living freshwater resources are threatened. Under certain circumstances, aquatic ecosystems are also affected by agricultural water resource development projects such as dams, river diversions, water installations and irrigation schemes. Erosion, sedimentation, deforestation and desertification have led to increased land degradation, and the creation of reservoirs has, in some cases, resulted in adverse effects on ecosystems. Many of these problems have arisen from a development model that is environmentally destructive and from a lack of public awareness and education about surface and groundwater resource protection. Ecological and human health effects are the measurable consequences, although the means to monitor them are inadequate or non-existent in many countries. There is a widespread lack of perception of the linkages between the development, management, use and treatment of water resources and aquatic ecosystems. A preventive approach, where appropriate, is crucial to the avoiding of costly subsequent measures to rehabilitate, treat and develop new water supplies.

Objectives The complex interconnectedness of freshwater systems demands that freshwater management be holistic (taking a catchment management approach) and based on a balanced consideration of the needs of people and the environment. The Mar del Plata Action Plan has already recognized the intrinsic linkage between water resource development projects and their significant physical, chemical, biological, health and socio-economic repercussions. The overall environmental health objective was set as follows: "to evaluate the consequences which the various users of water have on the environment, to support measures aimed at controlling water-related diseases, and to protect ecosystems".[1]

The extent and severity of contamination of unsaturated zones and aquifers have long been underestimated owing to the relative inaccessibility of aquifers and the lack of reliable information on aquifer systems. The protection of groundwater is therefore an essential element of water resource management.

Three objectives will have to be pursued concurrently to integrate water-quality elements into water resource management:
a Maintenance of ecosystem integrity, according to a management principle of preserving aquatic ecosystems, including living resources, and of effectively protecting them from any form of degradation on a drainage basin basis;
b Public health protection, a task requiring not only the provision of safe drinking-water but also the control of disease vectors in the aquatic environment;
c Human resources development, a key to capacity-building and a prerequisite for implementing water-quality management.
All States, according to their capacity and available resources, through bilateral or multilateral cooperation, including the United Nations and other relevant organizations as appropriate, could set the following targets:
a To identify the surface and groundwater resources that could be developed for use on a sustainable basis and other major developable water-dependent resources and, simultaneously, to initiate programmes for the protection, conservation and rational use of these resources on a sustainable basis;
b To identify all potential sources of water-supply and prepared outlines for their protection, conservation and rational use;
c To initiate effective water pollution prevention and control programmes, based on an appropriate mixture of pollution reduction-at-source strategies, environmental impact assessments and enforceable standards for major point-source discharges and high-risk non-point sources, commensurate with their socio-economic development;
d To participate, as far as appropriate, in international water-quality monitoring and management programmes such as the Global Water Quality Monitoring Programme (GEMS/WATER), the UNEP Environmentally Sound Management of Inland Waters (EMINWA), the FAO regional inland fishery bodies, and the Convention on Wetlands of International Importance Especially as Waterfowl Habitat (Ramsar Convention);
e To reduce the prevalence of water-associated diseases, starting with the eradication of dracunculiasis (guinea worm disease) and onchocerciasis (river blindness) by the year 2000;
f To establish, according to capacities and needs, biological, health, physical and chemical quality criteria for all water bodies (surface and

groundwater), with a view to an ongoing improvement of water quality;

g To adopt an integrated approach to environmentally sustainable management of water resources, including the protection of aquatic ecosystems and freshwater living resources;

h To put in place strategies for the environmentally sound management of freshwaters and related coastal ecosystems, including consideration of fisheries, aquaculture, animal grazing, agricultural activities and biodiversity.

Activities All States, according to their capacity and available resources, and through bilateral or multilateral cooperation, including United Nations and other relevant organizations as appropriate, could implement the following activities:

a Water resources protection and conservation:

i Establishment and strengthening of technical and institutional capacities to identify and protect potential sources of water-supply within all sectors of society;

ii Identification of potential sources of water-supply and preparation of national profiles;

iii Preparation of national plans for water resources protection and conservation;

iv Rehabilitation of important, but degraded, catchment areas, particularly on small islands;

v Strengthening of administrative and legislative measures to prevent encroachment on existing and potentially usable catchment areas;

b Water pollution prevention and control:

i Application of the "polluter pays" principle, where appropriate, to all kinds of sources, including on-site and off-site sanitation;

ii Promotion of the construction of treatment facilities for domestic sewage and industrial effluents and the development of appropriate technologies, taking into account sound traditional and indigenous practices;

iii Establishment of standards for the discharge of effluents and for the receiving waters;

iv Introduction of the precautionary approach in water-quality management, where appropriate, with a focus on pollution minimization and prevention through use of new technologies, product and process change, pollution reduction at source and effluent re-use, recycling and recovery, treatment and environmentally safe disposal;

v Mandatory environmental impact assessment of all major water resource development projects potentially impairing water quality and aquatic ecosystems, combined with the delineation of appropriate remedial measures and a strengthened control of new industrial installations, solid waste landfills and infrastructure development projects;

vi Use of risk assessment and risk management in reaching decisions in this area and ensuring compliance with those decisions;

vii Identification and application of best environmental practices at reasonable cost to avoid diffuse pollution, namely, through a limited, rational and planned use of nitrogenous fertilizers and other agrochemicals (pesticides, herbicides) in agricultural practices;

viii Encouragement and promotion of the use of adequately treated and purified waste waters in agriculture, aquaculture, industry and other sectors;

c Development and application of clean technology:

i Control of industrial waste discharges, including low-waste production technologies and water recirculation, in an integrated manner and through application of precautionary measures derived from a broad-based life-cycle analysis;

ii Treatment of municipal waste water for safe reuse in agriculture and aquaculture;

iii Development of biotechnology, *inter alia*, for waste treatment, production of biofertilizers and other activities;

iv Development of appropriate methods for water pollution control, taking into account sound traditional and indigenous practices;

d Groundwater protection:

i Development of agricultural practices that do not degrade groundwaters;

ii Application of the necessary measures to mitigate saline intrusion into aquifers of small islands and coastal plains as a consequence of sea level rise or overexploitation of coastal aquifers;

iii Prevention of aquifer pollution through the regulation of toxic substances that permeate the ground and the establishment of protection zones in groundwater recharge and abstraction areas;

iv Design and management of landfills based upon sound hydrogeologic information and impact assessment, using the best practicable and best available technology;

v Promotion of measures to improve the safety and integrity of wells and well-head areas to reduce intrusion of biological pathogens and hazardous chemicals into aquifers at well sites;

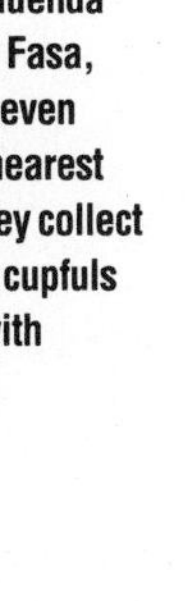

Women from the Guenda village in Burkima Fasa, West Africa walk seven kilometres to the nearest well. The water they collect allows them three cupfuls of water to wash with on alternate days.

The challenges to development, particularly in the developing countries, can only be successfully met by the resolve of all states to cooperate in democratic, multilateral enterprises. UNCED provided such an opportunity. The attainment of the goals of balanced development and the better utilization of the environment depend upon the extent to which diplomacy, international law, science, technology and basic economic prudence are embraced as valuable conduits to the development process. Grenada sees UNCED as the beginning of a process aimed at redirecting development priorities. Success will necessarily be incremental; but, within a sound policy framework, adequate resource allocation and a spirit of cooperation among all nations, we can all be better off.
Rt.Hon. Nicholas Brathwaite
Prime Minister
Grenada

vi Water-quality monitoring, as needed, of surface and groundwaters potentially affected by sites storing toxic and hazardous materials;
e Protection of aquatic ecosystems:
i Rehabilitation of polluted and degraded water bodies to restore aquatic habitats and ecosystems;
ii Rehabilitation programmes for agricultural lands and for other users, taking into account equivalent action for the protection and use of groundwater resources important for agricultural productivity and for the biodiversity of the tropics;
iii Conservation and protection of wetlands (owing to their ecological and habitat importance for many species), taking into account social and economic factors;
iv Control of noxious aquatic species that may destroy some other water species;
f Protection of freshwater living resources:
i Control and monitoring of water quality to allow for the sustainable development of inland fisheries;
ii Protection of ecosystems from pollution and degradation for the development of freshwater aquaculture projects;
g Monitoring and surveillance of water resources and waters receiving wastes:
i Establishment of networks for the monitoring and continuous surveillance of waters receiving wastes and of point and diffuse sources of pollution;
ii Promotion and extension of the application of environmental impact assessments of geographical information systems;
iii Surveillance of pollution sources to improve compliance with standards and regulations and to regulate the issue of discharge permits;
iv Monitoring of the utilization of chemicals in agriculture that may have an adverse environmental effect;
v Rational land use to prevent land degradation, erosion and siltation of lakes and other water bodies;
h Development of national and international legal instruments that may be required to protect the quality of water resources, as appropriate, particularly for:
i Monitoring and control of pollution and its effects in national and transboundary waters;
ii Control of long-range atmospheric transport of pollutants;
iii Control of accidental and/or deliberate spills in national and/or transboundary water bodies;
iv Environmental impact assessment.

Financing and cost evaluation $1 billion, including about $340 million from the international community on grant or concessional terms.

D Drinking-water supply and sanitation

Basis for action Safe water-supplies and environmental sanitation are vital for protecting the environment, improving health and alleviating poverty. Safe water is also crucial to many traditional and cultural activities. An estimated 80 per cent of all diseases and over one third of deaths in developing countries are caused by the consumption of contaminated water, and on average as much as one tenth of each person's productive time is sacrificed to water-related diseases. Concerted efforts during the 1980s brought water and sanitation services to hundreds of millions of the world's poorest people. The most outstanding of these efforts was the launching in 1981 of the International Drinking Water Supply and Sanitation Decade, which resulted from the Mar del Plata Action Plan adopted by the United Nations Water Conference in 1977. The commonly agreed premise was that "all peoples, whatever their stage of development and their social and economic conditions, have the right to have access to drinking water in quantities and of a quality equal to their basic needs".[2] The target of the Decade was to provide safe drinking-water and sanitation to underserved urban and rural areas by 1990, but even the unprecedented progress achieved during the Decade was not enough. One in three people in the developing world still lacks these two most basic requirements for health and dignity. It is also recognized that human excreta and sewage are important causes of the deterioration of water-quality in developing countries, and the introduction of available technologies, including appropriate technologies, and the construction of sewage treatment facilities could bring significant improvement.

Objectives The New Delhi Statement (adopted at the Global Consultation on Safe Water and Sanitation for the 1990s, which was held in New Delhi from 10 to 14 September 1990) formalized the need to provide, on a sustainable basis, access to safe water in sufficient quantities and proper sanitation for all, emphasizing the "some for all rather than more for some" approach. Four guiding principles provide for the programme objectives:
a Protection of the environment and safeguarding of health through the integrated management of water resources and liquid and solid wastes;
b Institutional reforms promoting an integrated approach and including changes in procedures, attitudes and behaviour, and the full participation of women at all levels in sector institutions;
c Community management of services, backed by measures to strengthen local institutions in implementing and sustaining water and sanitation programmes;
d Sound financial practices, achieved through better management of existing assets, and widespread use of appropriate technologies.

Past experience has shown that specific targets should be set by each individual country. At the World Summit for Children, in September 1990, heads of State or Government called for both universal access to water-supply and sanitation and the eradication of guinea worm disease by 1995. Even for the more realistic target of achieving full coverage in water-supply by 2025, it is estimated that annual investments must reach double the current levels. One realistic strategy to meet present and future needs, therefore, is to develop lower-cost but adequate services that can be implemented and sustained at the community level.

Activities All States, according to their capacity and available resources, and through bilateral or multilateral cooperation, including the United Nations and other relevant organizations as appropriate, could implement the following activities:
a Environment and health:
i Establishment of protected areas for sources of drinking-water supply;
ii Sanitary disposal of excreta and sewage, using appropriate systems to treat waste waters in urban and rural areas;
iii Expansion of urban and rural water-supply and development and expansion of rainwater catchment systems, particularly on small islands, in addition to the reticulated water-supply system;
iv Building and expansion, where appropriate, of sewage treatment facilities and drainage systems;
v Treatment and safe reuse of domestic and industrial waste waters in urban and rural areas;
vi Control of water-associated diseases;
b People and institutions:
i Strengthening of the functioning of Governments in water resources management and, at the same time, giving of full recognition to the role of local authorities;
ii Encouragement of water development and management based on a participatory approach,

Cranes and bulldozers, backhoes and power shovels–together they create the sound of thunder as they excavate and move the earth, while the other cranes carry on a lively conversation.

The earth is levelled, ready for the foundation columns to be placed. – The cranes move away to search for food.

As the cranes, bulldozers, and other earth–moving machinery clear the way for construction, the cranes here are busy too, with their everyday activities, like their ancestors when Bandar Kemayoran was used as an airfield for domestic and international aircraft. Now the former airport of Kemayoran is being readied to become a new city within the city of Jakarta, a future international business center, to welcome the Golden Age of the Pacific Rim, complete with infrastructure and business facilities of international standard. Among them are a 32–story International Trademart, an international business information center containing an exhibition hall; the Jakarta International Fairgrounds; offices; apartments with very reasonable rental rates; luxurious hotels and condominiums, malls, and a sports center.

Bandar Kemayoran will be surrounded by the beauty of parks and gardens and the tropical forest. A 30–meter–wide greenbelt on either side of the arterial highway is mandatory, and each building constructed must meet current environmental standards.

Bandar Kemayoran will be a modern tropical city, growing and developing in harmony. Rich and poor, national and international entrepreneurs, the people and their environment, flora and fauna, will together create a new Indonesian civilization, imbued with the wisdom of our forebears to preserve togetherness and harmony.

In line with the national policy of the Republic of Indonesia, Bandar Kemayoran values and fully supports the initiative of the United Nations to preserve the environment, realized through the 1992 Earth Summit.

BANDAR KEMAYORAN

An international commercial estate

Kemayoran Development Authority, Jalan Angkasa Kemayoran, Jakarta Indonesia. Phone : (26-021) 4217112, 4217117
Fax: (62-021) 4217421.

Government Regulation of the Republic of Indonesia number 29 year 1986 requires every medium and large–scale project to make an environmental impact analysis prior to ecquiring a permit to execute the project.

We in Hungary think of UNCED as a most significant multilateral international event. Integrating the development needs of world economy, world trade and the protection of the environment can put human history on a new track. One major achievement has been to make governments and the public fully aware of our interdependence and the need for efficient cooperation to preserve the quality of the environment. Adopting the attitudes and strategies conducive to sustainable development is a real challenge. I trust that the word will be understood, and we will be able to create that broad consensus so as to avert the global threats to the environment and thence mankind.
Arpad Goncz
President
Republic of Hungary

involving users, planners and policy makers at all levels;
iii Application of the principle that decisions are to be taken at the lowest appropriate level, with public consultation and involvement of users in the planning and implementation of water projects;
iv Human resource development at all levels, including special programmes for women;
v Broad-based education programmes, with particular emphasis on hygiene, local management and risk reduction;
vi International support mechanisms for programme funding, implementation and follow-up;
c National and community management:
i Support and assistance to communities in managing their own systems on a sustainable basis;
ii Encouragement of the local population, especially women, youth, indigenous people and local communities, in water management;
iii Linkages between national water plans and community management of local waters;
iv Integration of community management of water within the context of overall planning;
v Promotion of primary health and environmental care at the local level, including training for local communities in appropriate water management techniques and primary health care;
vi Assistance to service agencies in becoming more cost-effective and responsive to consumer needs;
vii Providing of more attention to underserved rural and low-income periurban areas;
viii Rehabilitation of defective systems, reduction of wastage and safe reuse of water and waste water;
ix Programmes for rational water use and ensured operation and maintenance;
x Research and development of appropriate technical solutions;
xi Substantially increase urban wastewater treatment capacity commensurate with increasing loads;
d Awareness creation and public information/participation:
i Strengthening of sector monitoring and information management at subnational and national levels;
ii Annual processing, analysis and publication of monitoring results at national and local levels as a sector management and advocacy/awareness creation tool;
iii Use of limited sector indicators at regional and global levels to promote the sector and raise funds;
iv Improvement of sector coordination, planning and implementation, with the assistance of improved monitoring and information management, to increase the sector's absorptive capacity, particularly in community-based self-help projects.

Financing and cost evaluation $20 billion, including about $7.4 billion from the international community on grant or concessional terms.

E Water and sustainable urban development

Basis for action Early in the next century, more than half of the world's population will be living in urban areas. By the year 2025, that proportion will have risen to 60 per cent, comprising some 5 billion people. Rapid urban population growth and industrialization are putting severe strains on the water resources and environmental protection capabilities of many cities. Special attention needs to be given to the growing effects of urbanization on water demands and usage and to the critical role played by local and municipal authorities in managing the supply, use and overall treatment of water, particularly in developing countries for which special support is needed. Scarcity of freshwater resources and the escalating costs of developing new resources have a considerable impact on national industrial, agricultural and human settlement development and economic growth. Better management of urban water resources, including the elimination of unsustainable consumption patterns, can make a substantial contribution to the alleviation of poverty and improvement of the health and quality of life of the urban and rural poor. A high proportion of large urban agglomerations are located around estuaries and in coastal zones. Such an arrangement leads to pollution from municipal and industrial discharges combined with overexploitation of available water resources and threatens the marine environment and the supply of freshwater resources.

Objectives The development objective of this programme is to support local and central Governments' efforts and capacities to sustain national development and productivity through environmentally sound management of water resources for urban use. Supporting this objective is the identification and implementation of strategies and actions to ensure the continued supply of affordable water for present and future needs and to reverse current trends of resource degradation and depletion.

All States, according to their capacity and available resources, and through bilateral or multilateral cooperation, including the United Nations and other relevant organizations as appropriate, could set the following targets:
a By the year 2000, to have ensured that all urban residents have access to at least 40 litres per capita per day of safe water and that 75 per cent of the urban population are provided with on-site or community facilities for sanitation;
b By the year 2000, to have established and applied quantitative and qualitative discharge standards for municipal and industrial effluents;
c By the year 2000, to have ensured that 75 per cent of solid waste generated in urban areas are collected and recycled or disposed of in an environmentally safe way.

Activities All States, according to their capacity and available resources, and through bilateral or multilateral cooperation, including the United Nations and other relevant organizations as appropriate, could implement the following activities:
a Protection of water resources from depletion, pollution and degradation:
i Introduction of sanitary waste disposal facilities based on environmentally sound low-cost and upgradable technologies;
ii Implementation of urban storm-water run-off and drainage programmes;
iii Promotion of recycling and reuse of waste water and solid wastes;
iv Control of industrial pollution sources to protect water resources;
iv Protection of watersheds with respect to depletion and degradation of their forest cover and from harmful upstream activities;
vi Promotion of research into the contribution of forests to sustainable water resources development;
vii Encouragement of the best management practices for the use of agrochemicals with a view to minimizing their impact on water resources;
b Efficient and equitable allocation of water resources:
i Reconciliation of city development planning with the availability and sustainability of water resources;
ii Satisfaction of the basic water needs of the urban population;
iii Introduction of water tariffs, taking into account the circumstances in each country and where affordable, that reflect the marginal and opportunity

A high proportion of large urban agglomerations are located around estuaries and in coastal zones. Such arrangements lead to pollution from municipal and industrial discharge with the concomitant risks to the urban population.

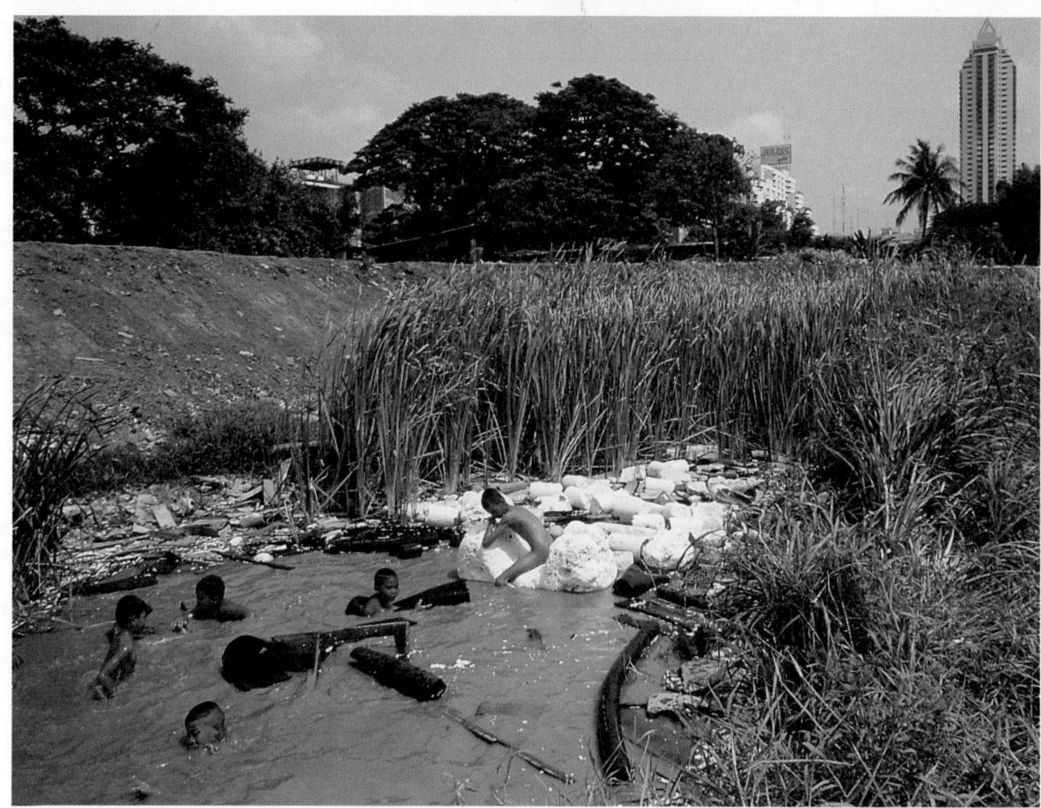

cost of water, especially for productive activities;

c Institutional/legal/management reforms:

i Adoption of a city-wide approach to the management of water resources;

ii Promotion at the national and local level of the elaboration of land-use plans that give due consideration to water resources development;

iii Utilization of the skills and potential of non-governmental organizations, the private sector and local people, taking into account the public's and strategic interests in water resources;

d Promotion of public participation:

i Initiation of public-awareness campaigns to encourage the public's move towards rational water utilization;

ii Sensitization of the public to the issue of protecting water quality within the urban environment;

iii Promotion of public participation in the collection, recycling and elimination of wastes;

e Support to local capacity-building:

i Development of legislation and policies to promote investments in urban water and waste management, reflecting the major contribution of cities to national economic development;

ii Provision of seed money and technical support to the local handling of materials supply and services;

iii Encouragement, to the extent possible, of autonomy and financial viability of city water, solid waste and sewerage utilities;

iv Creation and maintenance of a cadre of professionals and semi-professionals, for water, waste-water and solid waste management;

f Provision of enhanced access to sanitary services:

i Implementation of water, sanitation and waste management programmes focused on the urban poor;

ii Making available of low-cost water-supply and sanitation technology choices;

iii Basing of choice of technology and service levels on user preferences and willingness to pay;

iv Mobilization and facilitation of the active involvement of women in water management teams;

v Encouragement and equipment of local water associations and water committees to manage community water-supply systems and communal latrines, with technical back-up available when required;

vi Consideration of the merits and practicality of rehabilitating existing malfunctioning systems and of correcting operation and maintenance inadequacies.

Financing and cost evaluation $20 billion, including about $4.5 billion from the international community on grant or concessional terms.

F Water for sustainable food production and rural development

Basis for action Sustainability of food production increasingly depends on sound and efficient water use and conservation practices consisting primarily of irrigation development and management, including water management with respect to rain-fed areas, livestock water-supply, inland fisheries and agro-forestry. Achieving food security is a high priority in many countries, and agriculture must not only provide food for rising populations, but also save water for other uses. The challenge is to develop and apply water-saving technology and management methods and, through capacity-building, enable communities to introduce institutions and incentives for the rural population to adopt new approaches, for both rain-fed and irrigated agriculture. The rural population must also have better access to a potable water-supply and to sanitation services. It is an immense task but not an impossible one, provided appropriate policies and programmes are adopted at all levels – local, national and international. While significant expansion of the area under rain-fed agriculture has been achieved during the past decade, the productivity response and sustainability of irrigation systems have been constrained by problems of waterlogging and salinization. Financial and market constraints are also a common problem. Soil erosion, mismanagement and over-exploitation of natural resources and acute competition for water have all influenced the extent of poverty, hunger and famine in the developing countries. Soil erosion caused by overgrazing of livestock is also often responsible for the siltation of lakes. Most often, the development of irrigation schemes is supported neither by environmental impact assessments identifying hydrologic consequences within watersheds of inter-basin transfers, nor by the assessment of social impacts on peoples in river valleys. The non-availability of water-supplies of suitable quality is a significant limiting factor to livestock production in many

The Rio Conference while building on the foundations of Stockholm, has also added the dimension of development. This is indeed a necessary and timely correction. For it is obvious by now that we cannot effectively address the problem of environmental degradation without at the same time resolving the problems of development and in particular of human poverty. We see the Earth Summit as a vital first step towards the establishment of a new global partnership. We hope that the Rio Declaration, Agenda 21 and all the other agreements adopted will bring us closer to its realisation.
H.E. President Soeharto
Republic of Indonesia

countries, and improper disposal of animal wastes can in certain circumstances result in pollution of water-supplies for both humans and animals. The drinking-water requirements of livestock vary according to species and the environment in which they are kept. It is estimated that the current global livestock drinking-water requirement is about 60 billion litres per day and based on livestock population growth estimates, this daily requirement is predicted to increase by 0.4 billion litres per annum in the foreseeable future.

Freshwater fisheries in lakes and streams are an important source of food and protein. Fisheries of inland waters should be so managed as to maximize the yield of aquatic food organisms in an environmentally sound manner. This requires the conservation of water-quality and quantity, as well as of the functional morphology of the aquatic environment. On the other hand, fishing and aquaculture may themselves damage the aquatic ecosystem; hence their development should conform to guidelines for impact limitation. Present levels of production from inland fisheries, from both fresh and brackish water, are about 7 million tons per year and could increase to 16 million tons per year by the year 2000; however, any increase in environmental stress could jeopardize this rise.

Objectives The key strategic principles for holistic and integrated environmentally sound management of water resources in the rural context may be set forth as follows:

a Water should be regarded as a finite resource having an economic value with significant social and economic implications reflecting the importance of meeting basic needs;

b Local communities must participate in all phases of water management, ensuring the full involvement of women in view of their crucial role in the practical day-to-day supply, management and use of water;

c Water resource management must be developed within a comprehensive set of policies for (i) human health; (ii) food production, preservation and distribution; (iii) disaster mitigation plans; (iv) environmental protection and conservation of the natural resource base;

d It is necessary to recognize and actively support the role of rural populations, with particular emphasis on women.

An International Action Programme on Water and Sustainable Agricultural Development (IAP-WASAD) has been initiated by FAO in cooperation with other international organizations. The main objective of the Action Programme is to assist developing countries in planning, developing and managing water resources on an integrated basis to meet present and future needs for agricultural production, taking into account environmental considerations. The Action Programme has developed a framework for sustainable water use in the agricultural sector and identified priority areas for action at national, regional and global levels. Quantitative targets for new irrigation development, improvement of existing irrigation schemes and reclamation of waterlogged and salinized lands through drainage for 130 developing countries are estimated on the basis of food requirements, agro-climatic zones and availability of water and land.

FAO global projections for irrigation, drainage and small-scale water programmes by the year 2000 for 130 developing countries are as follows: (a) 15.2 million hectares of new irrigation development; (b) 12 million hectares of improvement/modernization of existing schemes; (c) 7 million hectares installed with drainage and water control facilities; and (d) 10 million hectares of small-scale water programmes and conservation.

The development of new irrigation areas at the above-mentioned level may give rise to environmental concerns in so far as it implies the destruction of wetlands, water pollution, increased sedimentation and a reduction in biodiversity. Therefore, new irrigation schemes should be accompanied by an environmental impact assessment, depending upon the scale of the scheme, in case significant negative environmental impacts are expected. When considering proposals for new irrigation schemes, consideration should also be given to a more rational exploitation, and an increase in the efficiency or productivity, of any existing schemes capable of serving the same localities. Technologies for new irrigation schemes should be thoroughly evaluated, including their potential conflicts with other land uses. The active involvement of water-users groups is a supporting objective.

It should be ensured that rural communities of all countries, according to their capacities and available resources and taking advantage of international co-operation as appropriate, will have access to safe water in sufficient quantities and adequate sanitation to meet their health needs and maintain the essential qualities of their local environments.

The objectives with regard to water management for inland fisheries and aquaculture include conservation of water-quality and water-quantity requirements for optimum production and prevention of water pollution by aquacultural activities. The Action Programme seeks to assist member countries in managing the fisheries of inland waters through the promotion of sustainable management of capture fisheries as well as the development of environmentally sound approaches to intensification of aquaculture.

The objectives with regard to water management for livestock supply are twofold: provision of adequate amounts of drinking-water and safeguarding of drinking-water quality in accordance with the specific needs of different animal species. This entails maximum salinity tolerance levels and the absence of pathogenic organisms. No global targets can be set owing to large regional and intra-country variations.

Activities All States, according to their capacity and available resources, and through bilateral or multilateral cooperation, including the United Nations and other relevant organizations as appropriate, could implement the following activities:

a Water-supply and sanitation for the unserved rural poor:

i Establish national policies and budget priorities with regard to increasing service coverage;

ii Promote appropriate technologies;

iii Introduce suitable cost-recovery mechanisms, taking into account efficiency and equity through demand management mechanisms;

iv Promote community ownership and rights to water-supply and sanitation facilities;

v Establish monitoring and evaluation systems;

vi Strengthen the rural water-supply and sanitation sector with emphasis on institutional development, efficient management and an appropriate framework for financing of services;

vii Increase hygiene education and eliminate disease transmission foci;

viii Adopt appropriate technologies for water treatment;

ix Adopt wide-scale environmental management measures to control disease vectors;

b Water-use efficiency:

i Increase of efficiency and productivity in agricultural water use for better utilization of limited water resources;

ii Strengthen water and soil management research under irrigation and rain-fed conditions;

iii Monitor and evaluate irrigation project

From Stockholm to Rio has been a journey of awakening. We now have the opportunity to forge a consensus and a working partnership in order to address the pressing problems of poverty and physical degradation of our planet. We have through Rio an opportunity to reaffirm that human development is the objective of our endeavour; without respect for the physical environment, human development is simply not sustainable. The inextricable link between environment and development must be the guiding principle for assured survival of the human race and a sustainable quality of life for all. The Rio Conference has demonstrated its unshakable will to succeed in this task.
Hon P. J. Patterson
Prime Minister
Jamaica

performance to ensure, *inter alia*, the optimal utilization and proper maintenance of the project;
iv Support water-users groups with a view to improving management performance at the local level;
v Support the appropriate use of relatively brackish water for irrigation;
c Waterlogging, salinity control and drainage:
i Introduce surface drainage in rain-fed agriculture to prevent temporary waterlogging and flooding of lowlands;
ii Introduce artificial drainage in irrigated and rain-fed agriculture;
iii Encourage conjunctive use of surface and groundwaters, including monitoring and water-balance studies;
iv Practise drainage in irrigated areas of arid and semi-arid regions;
d Water-quality management:
i Establish and operate cost-effective water-quality monitoring systems for agricultural water uses;
ii Prevent adverse effects of agricultural activities on water-quality for other social and economic activities and on wetlands, *inter alia*, through optimal use of on-farm input and the minimization of the use of external input in agricultural activities;
iii Establish biological, physical and chemical water-quality criteria for agricultural water-users and for marine and riverine ecosystems;
iv Minimize soil run-off and sedimentation;
v Dispose properly of sewage from human settlements and of manure produced by intensive livestock breeding;
vi Minimize adverse effects from agricultural chemicals by use of integrated pest management;
vii Educate communities about the pollution-related impacts of the use of fertilizers and chemicals on water-quality, food safety and human health;
e Water resources development programmes:
i Develop small-scale irrigation and water-supply for humans and livestock and for water and soil conservation;
ii Formulate large-scale and long-term irrigation development programmes, taking into account their effects on the local level, the economy and the environment;
iii Promote local initiatives for the integrated development and management of water resources;
iv Provide adequate technical advice and support and enhancement of institutional collaboration at the local community level;
v Promote a farming approach for land and water management that takes account of the level of education, the capacity to mobilize local communities and the ecosystem requirements of arid and semi-arid regions;
vi Plan and develop multi-purpose hydroelectric power schemes, making sure that environmental concerns are duly taken into account;
f Scarce water resources management:
i Develop long-term strategies and practical implementation programmes for agricultural water use under scarcity conditions with competing demands for water;
ii Recognize water as a social, economic and strategic good in irrigation planning and management;
iii Formulate specialized programmes focused on drought preparedness, with emphasis on food scarcity and environmental safeguards;
iv Promote and enhance waste-water reuse in agriculture;
g Water-supply for livestock:
i Improve quality of water available to livestock, taking into account their tolerance limits;
ii Increase the quantity of water sources available to livestock, in particular those in extensive grazing systems, in order to both reduce the distance needed to travel for water and to prevent overgrazing around water sources;
iii Prevent contamination of water sources with animal excrement in order to prevent the spread of diseases, in particular zoonosis;
iv Encourage multiple use of water-supplies through promotion of integrated agro-livestock-fishery systems;
v Encourage water spreading schemes for increasing water retention of extensive grasslands to stimulate forage production and prevent run-off;
h Inland fisheries:
i Develop the sustainable management of fisheries as part of national water resources planning;
ii Study specific aspects of the hydrobiology and environmental requirements of key inland fish species in relation to varying water regimes;
iii Prevent or mitigate modification of aquatic environments by other users or rehabilitate environments subjected to such modification on behalf of the sustainable use and conservation of biological diversity of living aquatic resources;
iv Develop and disseminate environmentally sound water resources development and management methodologies for the intensification of fish yield from inland waters;
v Establish and maintain adequate systems for the collection and interpretation of data on water quality and quantity and channel morphology related to the state and management of living aquatic resources, including fisheries;
i Aquaculture development:
i Develop environmentally sound aquaculture technologies that are compatible with local, regional and national water resources management plans and take into consideration social factors;
ii Introduce appropriate aquaculture techniques and related water development and management practices in countries not yet experienced in aquaculture;
iii Assess environmental impacts of aquaculture with specific reference to commercialized culture units and potential water pollution from processing centres;
iv Evaluate economic feasibility of aquaculture in relation to alternative use of water, taking into consideration the use of marginal-quality water and investment and operational requirements.

Financing and cost evaluation $13.2 billion, including about $4.5 billion from the international community on grant or concessional terms.

G Impacts of climate change on water resources

Basis for action There is uncertainty with respect to the prediction of climate change at the global level. Although the uncertainties increase greatly at the regional, national and local levels, it is at the national level that the most important decisions would need to be made. Higher temperatures and decreased precipitation would lead to decreased water-supplies and increased water demands; they might cause deterioration in the quality of freshwater bodies, putting strains on the already fragile balance between supply and demand in many countries. Even where precipitation might increase, there is no guarantee that it would occur at the time of year when it could be used; in addition, there might be a likelihood of increased flooding. Any rise in sealevel will often cause the intrusion of salt water into estuaries, small islands and coastal aquifers and the flooding of low-lying coastal areas; this puts low-lying countries at great risk.

The Ministerial Declaration of the Second World Climate Conference states that "the potential impact of such climate change could pose an environmental threat of an up to now unknown magnitude ... and

This sewage reed bed digestor is part of a cyclical chain. Sewage containing animal waste is fed into a pond and used to fertilise reeds. The reeds are then harvested and can be used to feed animals.

could even threaten survival in some small island States and in low-lying coastal, arid and semi-arid areas" The Conference recognized that among the most important impacts of climate change were its effects on the hydrologic cycle and on water management systems and, through these, on socio-economic systems. Increase in incidence of extremes, such as floods and droughts, would cause increased frequency and severity of disasters. The Conference therefore called for a strengthening of the necessary research and monitoring programmes and the exchange of relevant data and information, these actions to be undertaken at the national, regional and international levels.

Objectives The very nature of this topic calls first and foremost for more information about and greater understanding of the threat being faced. This topic may be translated into the following objectives, consistent with the United Nations Framework Convention on Climate Change:

a To understand and quantify the threat of the impact of climate change on freshwater resources;

b To facilitate the implementation of effective national countermeasures, as and when the threatening impact is seen as sufficiently confirmed to justify such action;

c To study the potential impacts of climate change on areas prone to droughts and floods.

Activities All States, according to their capacity and available resources, and through bilateral or multilateral cooperation, including the United Nations and other relevant organizations as appropriate, could implement the following activities:

a Monitor the hydrologic regime, including soil moisture, groundwater balance, penetration and transpiration of water-quality, and related climate factors, especially in the regions and countries most likely to suffer from the adverse effects of climate change and where the localities vulnerable to these effects should therefore be defined;

b Develop and apply techniques and methodologies for assessing the potential adverse effects of climate change, through changes in temperature, precipitation and sealevel rise, on freshwater resources and the flood risk;

c Initiate case-studies to establish whether there are linkages between climate changes and the current occurrences of droughts and floods in certain regions;

d Assess the resulting social, economic and environmental impacts;

e Develop and initiate response strategies to counter the adverse effects that are identified, including changing groundwater levels and to mitigate saline intrusion into aquifers;

f Develop agricultural activities based on brackish-water use;

g Contribute to the research activities under way within the framework of current international programmes.

Financing and cost evaluation $100 million, including about $40 million from the international community on grant or concessional terms.

1 Report of the United Nations Water Conference, Mar del Plata, 14-25 March 1977 (United Nations publication, Sales No. E.77.II.A.12), part one, chap. I, sect. C, para. 35.

2 Ibid., part one, chap. I, resolution II.

Chapter 19

Environmentally sound management of toxic chemicals including prevention of illegal international traffic in toxic and dangerous products

A substantial use of chemicals is essential to meet the social and economic goals of the world community and today's best practice demonstrates that they can be used widely in a cost-effective manner and with a high degree of safety. However, a great deal remains to be done to ensure the environmentally sound management of toxic chemicals, within the principles of sustainable development and improved quality of life for humankind. Two of the major problems, particularly in developing countries, are (a) lack of sufficient scientific information for the assessment of risks entailed by the use of a great number of chemicals, and (b) lack of resources for assessment of chemicals for which data are at hand.

Gross chemical contamination, with grave damage to human health, genetic structures and reproductive outcomes, and the environment, has in recent times been continuing within some of the world's most important industrial areas. Restoration will require major investment and development of new techniques. The long-range effects of pollution, extending even to the fundamental chemical and physical processes of the Earth's atmosphere and climate, are becoming understood only recently and the importance of those effects is becoming recognized only recently as well.

A considerable number of international bodies are involved in work on chemical safety. In many countries work programmes for the promotion of chemical safety are in place. Such work has international implications, as chemical risks do not respect national boundaries. However, a significant strengthening of both national and international efforts is needed to achieve an environmentally sound management of chemicals.

The six programme areas are together dependent for their successful implementation on intensive international work and improved coordination of current international activities, as well as on the identification and application of technical, scientific, educational and financial means, in particular for developing countries. To varying degrees, the programme areas involve hazard assessment (based on the intrinsic properties of chemicals), risk assessment (including assessment of exposure), risk acceptability and risk management.

Collaboration on chemical safety between the United Nations Environment Programme (UNEP), the International Labour Organisation (ILO) and the World Health Organization (WHO) in the International Programme on Chemical Safety (IPCS) should be the nucleus for international cooperation on environmentally sound management of toxic chemicals. All efforts should be made to strengthen this programme. Cooperation with other programmes, such as those of the Organisation for Economic Cooperation and

Development (OECD) and the European Communities (EC) and other regional and governmental chemical programmes, should be promoted.

Increased coordination of United Nations bodies and other international organizations involved in chemicals assessment and management should be further promoted. Within the framework of IPCS, an intergovernmental meeting, convened by the Executive Director of UNEP, was held in London in December 1991 to further explore this matter.

The broadest possible awareness of chemical risks is a prerequisite for achieving chemical safety. The principle of the right of the community and of workers to know those risks should be recognized. However, the right to know the identity of hazardous ingredients should be balanced with industry's right to protect confidential business information. (Industry, as referred to in this chapter, shall be taken to include large industrial enterprises and transnational corporations as well as domestic industries.) The industry initiative on responsible care and product stewardship should be developed and promoted. Industry should apply adequate standards of operation in all countries in order not to damage human health and the environment.

There is international concern that part of the international movement of toxic and dangerous products is being carried out in contravention of existing national legislation and international instruments, to the detriment of the environment and public health of all countries, particularly developing countries.

In resolution 44/226 of 22 December 1989, the General Assembly requested each regional commission, within existing resources, to contribute to the prevention of the illegal traffic in toxic and dangerous products and wastes by monitoring and making regional assessments of that illegal traffic and its environmental and health implications. The Assembly also requested the regional commissions to interact among themselves and to cooperate with the United Nations Environment Programme, with a view to maintaining efficient and coordinated monitoring and assessment of the illegal traffic in toxic and dangerous products and wastes.

A Expanding and accelerating international assessment of chemical risks

Assessing the risks to human health and the environment hazards that a chemical may cause is a prerequisite to planning for its safe and beneficial use. Among the approximately 100,000 chemical substances in commerce and the thousands of substances of natural origin with which human beings come into contact, many appear as pollutants and contaminants in food, commercial products and the various environmental media. Fortunately, exposure to most chemicals (some 1,500 cover over 95 per cent of total world production) is rather limited, as most are used in very small amounts. However, a serious problem is that even for a great number of chemicals characterized by high-volume production, crucial data for risk assessment are often lacking. Within the framework of the OECD chemicals programme such data are now being generated for a number of chemicals.

Risk assessment is resource-intensive. It could be made cost-effective by strengthening international cooperation and better coordination, thereby making the best use of available resources and avoiding unnecessary duplication of effort. However, each nation should have a critical mass of technical staff with experience in toxicity testing and exposure analysis, which are two important components of risk assessment.

Objectives

a To strengthen international risk assessment. Several hundred priority chemicals or groups of chemicals, including major pollutants and contaminants of global significance, should be assessed by the year 2000, using current selection and assessment criteria;

b To produce guidelines for acceptable exposure for a greater number of toxic chemicals, based on peer review and scientific consensus distinguishing between health- or environment-based exposure limits and those relating to socio-economic factors.

Management-related activities Governments, through the cooperation of relevant international organizations and industry, where appropriate, should:

a Strengthen and expand programmes on chemical risk assessment within the United Nations system IPCS (UNEP, ILO, WHO) and the Food and Agriculture Organization of the United Nations (FAO), together with other organizations, including the Organisation for Economic Cooperation and Development (OECD), based on an agreed approach to data-quality assurance, application of assessment criteria, peer review and linkages to risk management activities, taking into account the precautionary approach;

b Promote mechanisms to increase collaboration

RON GILING/STILL PICTURES

Workers in Zambia handle chemical waste packed into oil drums. The rights of the community and workers to be aware of chemical risks needs to be balanced with those of industry to protect confidential information.

Risks connected with toxic chemicals can be reduced by the use of non-chemical technology. Integrated pest management and biological control agents have proved to be viable alternatives in agricultural activities.

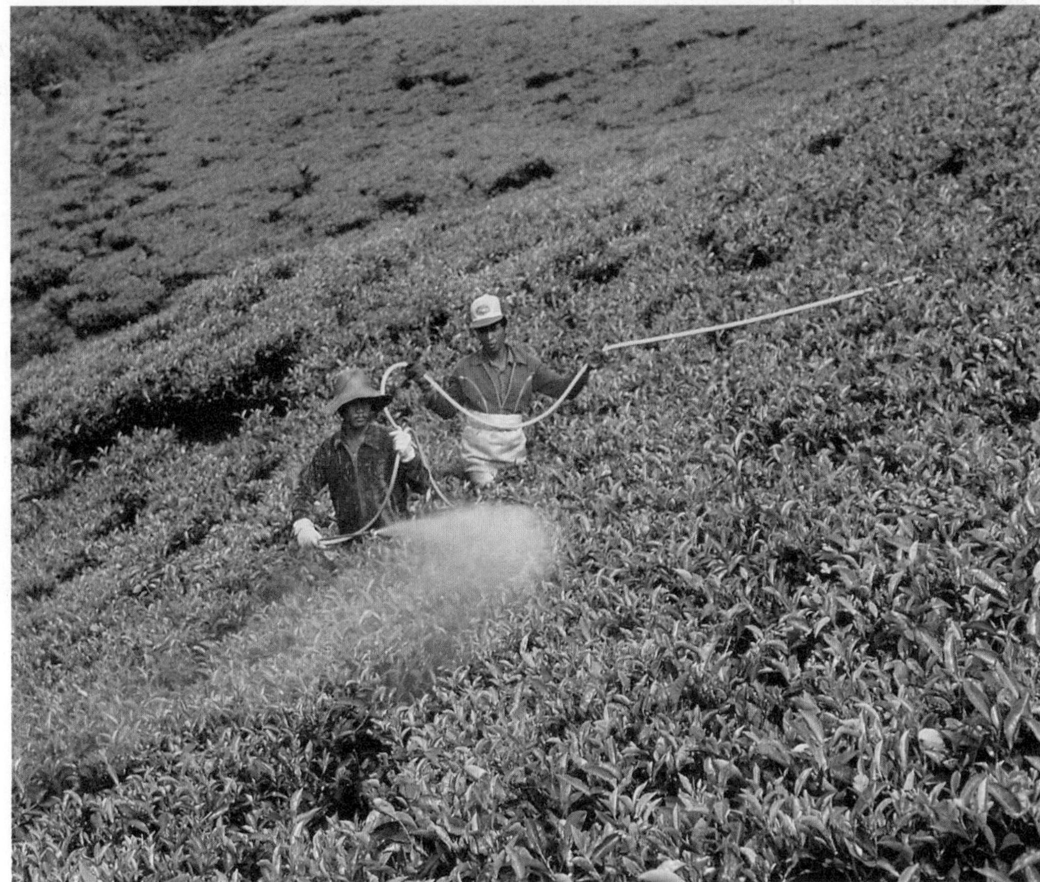

among Governments, industry, academia and relevant non-governmental organizations involved in the various aspects of risk assessment of chemicals and related processes, in particular the promoting and coordinating of research activities to improve understanding of the mechanisms of action of toxic chemicals;

c Encourage the development of procedures for the exchange by countries of their assessment reports on chemicals with other countries for use in national chemical assessment programmes.

Financial and cost evaluation Most of the data and methods for chemical risk assessment are generated in the developed countries and an expansion and acceleration of the assessment work will call for a considerable increase in research and safety testing by industry and research institutions. The cost projections address the needs to strengthen the capacities of relevant United Nations bodies and are based on current experience in IPCS. It should be noted that there are considerable costs, often not possible to quantify, that are not included. These comprise costs to industry and Governments of generating the safety data underlying the assessments and costs to Governments of providing background documents and draft assessment statements to IPCS, the International Register of Potentially Toxic Chemicals (IRPTC) and OECD. They also include the cost of accelerated work in non-United Nations bodies such as OECD and EC.

Average total cost about $30 million from the international community on grant or concessional terms.

B Harmonization of classification and labelling of chemicals

Basis for action Adequate labelling of chemicals and the dissemination of safety data sheets such as ICSCs (International Chemical Safety Cards) and similarly written materials, based on assessed hazards to health and environment, are the simplest and most efficient way of indicating how to handle and use chemicals safely.

For the safe transport of dangerous goods, including chemicals, a comprehensive scheme elaborated within the United Nations system is in current use. This scheme mainly takes into account the acute hazards of chemicals.

Globally harmonized hazard classification and labelling systems are not yet available to promote the safe use of chemicals, *inter alia*, at the workplace or in the home. Classification of chemicals can be made for different purposes and is a particularly important tool in establishing labelling systems. There is a need to develop harmonized hazard classification and labelling systems, building on ongoing work.

Objectives A globally harmonized hazard classification and compatible labelling system, including material safety data sheets and easily understandable symbols, should be available, if feasible, by the year 2000.

Management-related activities Governments, through the cooperation of relevant international organizations and industry, where appropriate, should launch a project with a view to establishing and elaborating a harmonized classification and compatible labelling system for chemicals for use in all United Nations official languages including adequate pictograms. Such a labelling system should not lead to the imposition of unjustified trade barriers. The new system should draw on current systems to the greatest extent possible; it should be developed in steps and should address the subject of compatibility with labels of various applications.

Financial and cost evaluation The Conference secretariat has included the technical assistance costs related to this programme in estimates provided in programme area E. They estimate the average total annual cost (1993-2000) for strengthening international organizations to be about $3 million from the international community on grant or concessional terms.

C Information exchange on toxic chemicals and chemical risks

Basis for action The following activities, related to information exchange on the benefits as well as the

The Chinese have a proverb: if a man cheats the Earth, the Earth will cheat man. We must leave this Earth in better condition than we found it. Some find the challenges ahead overwhelming. I believe that their pessimism is unfounded. It has been said that we don't inherit the Earth from our ancestors, we borrow it from our children. When our children look back on this time and this place, they will be grateful that we met at Rio, and they will certainly be pleased wuth the intentions stated and the commitments made. But they will judge us by the actions we take from this day forward. Let us not disappoint them.
George Bush
President
United States of America

risks associated with the use of chemicals, are aimed at enhancing the sound management of toxic chemicals through the exchange of scientific, technical, economic and legal information.

The London Guidelines for the Exchange of Information on Chemicals in International Trade are a set of guidelines adopted by Governments with a view to increasing chemical safety through the exchange of information on chemicals. Special provisions have been included in the guidelines with regard to the exchange of information on banned and severely restricted chemicals.

The export to developing countries of chemicals that have been banned in producing countries or whose use has been severely restricted in some industrialized countries has been the subject of concern, as some importing countries lack the ability to ensure safe use, owing to inadequate infrastructure for controlling the importation, distribution, storage, formulation and disposal of chemicals.

In order to address this issue, provisions for Prior Informed Consent (PIC) procedures were introduced in 1989 in the London Guidelines (UNEP) and in the International Code of Conduct on the Distribution and Use of Pesticides (FAO). In addition a joint FAO/UNEP programme has been launched for the operation of the PIC procedures for chemicals, including the selection of chemicals to be included in the PIC procedure and preparation of PIC decision guidance documents. The ILO chemicals convention calls for communication between exporting and importing countries when hazardous chemicals have been prohibited for reasons of safety and health at work. Within the General Agreement on Tariffs and Trade (GATT) framework, negotiations have been pursued with a view to creating a binding instrument on products banned or severely restricted in the domestic market. Further, the GATT Council has agreed, as stated in its decision contained in C/M/251, to extend the mandate of the working group for a period of three months, to begin from the date of the group's next meeting, and has authorized the Chairman to hold consultations on timing with respect to convening this meeting.

Notwithstanding the importance of the PIC procedure, information exchange on all chemicals is necessary.

Objectives

a To promote intensified exchange of information on chemical safety, use and emissions among all involved parties;

b To achieve by the year 2000, as feasible, full participation in and implementation of the PIC procedure, including possible mandatory applications through legally binding instruments contained in the Amended London Guidelines and in the FAO International Code of Conduct, taking into account the experience gained within the PIC procedure.

Management-related activities Governments and relevant international organizations with the cooperation of industry should:

a Strengthen national institutions responsible for information exchange on toxic chemicals and promote the creation of national centres where these centres do not exist;

b Strengthen international institutions and networks, such as IRPTC, responsible for information exchange on toxic chemicals;

c Establish technical cooperation with, and provide information to, other countries, especially those with shortages of technical expertise, including training in the interpretation of relevant technical data, such as Environmental Health Criteria Documents, Health and Safety Guides and International Chemical Safety Cards (published by IPCS); monographs on the Evaluation of Carcinogenic Risks of Chemicals to Humans (published by the International Agency for Research on Cancer (IARC)); and decision guidance documents (provided through the FAO/UNEP joint programme on PIC), as well as those submitted by industry and other sources;

d Implement the PIC procedures as soon as possible and, in the light of experience gained, invite relevant international organizations, such as UNEP, GATT, FAO, WHO and others, in their respective area of competence to consider working expeditiously towards the conclusion of legally binding instruments.

Financing and cost evaluation $10 million from the international community on grant or concessional terms.

D Establishment of risk reduction programmes

Basis for action There are often alternatives to toxic chemicals currently in use. Thus, risk reduction can sometimes be achieved by using other chemicals or even non-chemical technologies. The classic example of risk reduction is the substitution of harmless or less harmful substances for harmful ones. Establishment of pollution prevention procedures and setting standards for chemicals in each environmental medium, including food and water, and in consumer goods, constitute another example of risk reduction. In a wider context, risk reduction involves broad-based approaches to reducing the risks of toxic chemicals, taking into account the entire life cycle of the chemicals. Such approaches could encompass both regulatory and non-regulatory measures, such as promotion of the use of cleaner products and technologies, pollution prevention procedures and programmes, emission inventories, product labelling, use limitations, economic incentives, procedures for safe handling and exposure regulations, and the phasing out or banning of chemicals that pose unreasonable and otherwise unmanageable risks to human health and the environment and of those that are toxic, persistent and bio-accumulative and whose use cannot be adequately controlled.

In the agricultural area, integrated pest management, including the use of biological control agents as alternatives to toxic pesticides, is one approach to risk reduction.

Other areas of risk reduction encompass the prevention of chemical accidents, prevention of poisoning by chemicals and the undertaking of toxicovigilance and coordination of clean-up and rehabilitation of areas damaged by toxic chemicals.

The OECD Council has decided that OECD member countries should establish or strengthen national risk reduction programmes. The International Council of Chemical Associations (ICCA) has introduced initiatives regarding responsible care and product stewardship aimed at reduction of chemical risks. The Awareness and Preparedness for Emergencies at Local Level (APELL) programme of UNEP is designed to assist decision makers and technical personnel in improving community awareness of hazardous installations and in preparing response plans. ILO has published a Code of Practice on the prevention of major industrial accidents and is preparing an international instrument on the prevention of industrial disasters for eventual adoption in 1993.

Objectives The objective of the programme area is to eliminate unacceptable or unreasonable risks and, to the extent economically feasible, to reduce risks posed by toxic chemicals, by employing a broad-based approach involving a wide range of risk reduction options and by taking precautionary measures derived from a broad-based life-cycle analysis.

Management-related activities Governments, through the cooperation of relevant international organizations and industry, where appropriate, should:

a Consider adopting policies based on accepted producer liability principles, where appropriate, as well as precautionary, anticipatory and life-cycle approaches to chemical management, covering manufacturing, trade, transport, use and disposal;

b Undertake concerted activities to reduce risks for toxic chemicals, taking into account the entire life cycle of the chemicals. These activities could encompass both regulatory and non-regulatory measures, such as promotion of the use of cleaner products and technologies; emission inventories; product labelling; use limitations; economic incentives; and the phasing out or banning of toxic chemicals that pose an unreasonable and otherwise unmanageable risk to the environment or human health and those that are toxic, persistent and bio-accumulative and whose use cannot be adequately controlled;

c Adopt policies and regulatory and non-regulatory measures to identify, and minimize exposure to, toxic chemicals by replacing them with less toxic substitutes and ultimately phasing out the chemicals that pose unreasonable and otherwise unmanageable risk to human health and the environment and those that are toxic, persistent and bio-accumulative and whose use cannot be adequately controlled;

d Increase efforts to identify national needs for standard setting and implementation in the context of the FAO/WHO Codex Alimentarius in order to minimize adverse effects of chemicals in food;

e Develop national policies and adopt the necessary regulatory framework for prevention of accidents, preparedness and response, *inter alia*, through land-use planning, permit systems and reporting requirements on accidents, and work with the OECD/UNEP international directory of regional response centres and the APELL programme;

f Promote establishment and strengthening, as appropriate, of national poison control centres to ensure prompt and adequate diagnosis and treatment of poisonings;

g Reduce overdependence on the use of agricultural chemicals through alternative farming practices, integrated pest management and other appropriate means;

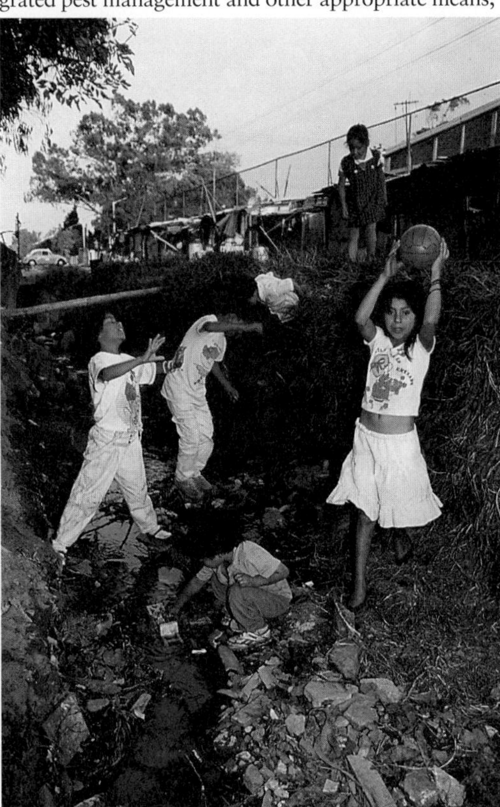

Children play in a factory outflow polluted by chemicals. The introduction of cleaner products and technologies as well as the phasing out or banning of chemicals that pose risks to human health would reduce the hazards involved.

h Require manufacturers, importers and others handling toxic chemicals to develop, with the cooperation of producers of such chemicals, where applicable, emergency response procedures and preparation of on-site and off-site emergency response plans;

i Identify, assess, reduce and minimize, or eliminate as far as feasible by environmentally sound disposal practices, risks from storage of outdated chemicals.

Industry should be encouraged to:

a Develop an internationally agreed upon code of principles for the management of trade in chemicals, recognizing in particular the responsibility for making available information on potential risks and environmentally sound disposal practices if those chemicals become wastes, in cooperation with Governments and relevant international organizations and appropriate agencies of the United Nations system;

b Develop application of a "responsible care" approach by producers and manufacturers towards chemical products, taking into account the total life cycle of such products;

c Adopt, on a voluntary basis, community right-to-know programmes based on international guidelines, including sharing of information on causes of accidental and potential releases and means of preventing them, and reporting on annual routine emissions of toxic chemicals to the environment in the absence of host country requirements.

Financial and cost evaluation The Conference secretariat has included most costs related to this programme in estimates provided for programme areas A and E. They estimate other requirements for training and strengthening the emergency and poison control centres to be about $4 million annually from the international community on grant or concessional terms.

E Strengthening of national capabilities and capacities for management of chemicals

Basis for action Many countries lack national systems to cope with chemical risks. Most countries lack scientific means of collecting evidence of misuse and of judging the impact of toxic chemicals on the environment, because of the difficulties involved in the detection of many problematic chemicals and systematically tracking their flow. Significant new uses are among the potential hazards to human health and the environment in developing countries. In several countries with systems in place there is an urgent need to make those systems more efficient.

Basic elements for sound management of chemicals are: (a) adequate legislation, (b) information gathering and dissemination, (c) capacity for risk assessment and interpretation, (d) establishment of risk management policy, (e) capacity for implementation and enforcement, (f) capacity for rehabilitation of contaminated sites and poisoned persons, (g) effective education programmes and (h) capacity to respond to emergencies.

As management of chemicals takes place within a number of sectors related to various national ministries, experience suggests that a coordinating mechanism is essential.

Objective By the year 2000, national systems for environmentally sound management of chemicals, including legislation and provisions for implementation and enforcement, should be in place in all countries to the extent possible.

Management-related activities Governments, where appropriate and with the collaboration of relevant intergovernmental organizations, agencies and

GUJARAT NARMADA VALLEY FERTILIZERS COMPANY LIMITED

K.G. RAMANATHAN, I.A.S.
Managing Director

DEVELOPMENT IN HARMONY WITH NATURE

Gujarat Narmada Valley Fertilizers Company Limited (GNFC) is a leader in the field of chemical fertilizers, producing the much needed input for increasing food production in India, to feed its large population. Starting its commercial production in 1982, GNFC operates at more than 100% capacity, fulfilling its commitments to the nation.

We in GNFC believe that high levels of production can be achieved in harmony with environmental preservation. In fact, we believe that both these goals are complementary to each other. It is this philosophy which guides GNFC in its endeavours. In fact, our efforts are to enrich the environment in which we are placed. Plantation of over 750,000 trees and treating of liquid effluent to irrigation standards are some of the enrichment measures.

GNFC has also found applications for most of the solid wastes - such as making building bricks out of fly ash. Recycling and re-using 71% of liquid effluent is another of GNFC's achievements. Finding applications for waste gases to produce useful chemicals like formic acid and sulfur is yet further proof of GNFC's awareness in environment enrichment.

A large number of awards in the field of pollution control, from the Fertilizers Association of India (FAI), the Federation of Indian Chambers of Commerce and Industry (FICCI) and the Indian Chemical Manufacturers Association (ICMA) has only increased GNFC's enthusiasm and commitment.

Environment is an everyday concern at GNFC - pollution control is an ON-GOING process.

Development is a must - but in harmony with nature.

K.G.Ramanathan
Managing Director

REGD. OFFICE : P.O. Narmadanagar 392 015, Dist. Bharuch, Gujarat, India. Cable : GNFC. Telex : 01813-201/202/214/215. Phones-Office : 34600 Res.: 33303. FAX : 02642-31595.

DELHI OFFICE : Phone : 4623951. Cable : KALPATARU. Telex : ND 031-63265/74143. BOMBAY OFFICE : Phone : 2040052. Telex : 011-83270.

programmes of the United Nations system, should:
a Promote and support multidisciplinary approaches to chemical safety problems;
b Consider the need to establish and strengthen, where appropriate, a national coordinating mechanism to provide a liaison for all parties involved in chemical safety activities (for example, agriculture, environment, education, industry, labour, health, transportation, police, civil defence, economic affairs, research institutions, and poison control centres);
c Develop institutional mechanisms for the management of chemicals, including effective means of enforcement;
d Establish and develop or strengthen, where appropriate, networks of emergency response centres, including poison control centres;
e Develop national and local capabilities to prepare for and respond to accidents by taking into account the UNEP APELL programme and similar programmes on accident prevention, preparedness and response, where appropriate, including regularly tested and updated emergency plans;
f Develop, in cooperation with industry, emergency response procedures, identifying means and equipment in industries and plants necessary to reduce impacts of accidents.

Financing and cost evaluation In developing countries about $600 million, including $150 million from the international community on grant or concessional terms.

F Prevention of illegal international traffic in toxic and dangerous products

There is currently no global international agreement on traffic in toxic and dangerous products (toxic and dangerous products are those that are banned, severely restricted, withdrawn or not approved for use or sale by Governments in order to protect public health and the environment). However, there is international concern that illegal international traffic in these products is detrimental to public health and the environment, particularly in developing countries, as acknowledged by the General Assembly in resolutions 42/183 and 44/226. Illegal traffic refers to traffic that is carried out in contravention of a country's laws or relevant international legal instruments. The concern also relates to transboundary movements of those products that are not carried out in accordance with applicable internationally adopted guidelines and principles. Activities under this programme area are intended to improve detection and prevention of the traffic concerned.

Further strengthening of international and regional cooperation is needed to prevent illegal transboundary movement of toxic and dangerous products. Furthermore, capacity-building at the national level is needed to improve monitoring and enforcement capabilities involving recognition of the fact that appropriate penalties may need to be imposed under an effective enforcement programme. Other activities envisaged in the present chapter will also contribute to achieving these objectives.

Objectives
a To reinforce national capacities to detect and halt any illegal attempt to introduce toxic and dangerous products into the territory of any State, in contravention of national legislation and relevant international legal instruments;
b To assist all countries, particularly developing countries, in obtaining all appropriate information concerning illegal traffic in toxic and dangerous products.

Management-related activities Governments, according to their capacities and available resources and with the cooperation of the United Nations and other relevant organizations, as appropriate, should:
a Adopt, where necessary, and implement legislation to prevent the illegal import and export of toxic and dangerous products;
b Develop appropriate national enforcement programmes to monitor compliance with such legislation, and detect and deter violations through appropriate penalties.

G Enhancement of international cooperation relating to several of the programme areas

A meeting of government-designated experts, held in London in December 1991, made recommendations for increased coordination among United Nations bodies and other international organizations involved in chemical risk assessment and management. That meeting called for the taking of appropriate measures to enhance the role of IPCS and establish an intergovernmental forum on chemical risk assessment and management.

To further consider the recommendations of the London meeting and initiate action on them, as appropriate, the Executive Heads of WHO, ILO and UNEP are invited to convene an intergovernmental meeting within one year, which could constitute the first meeting of the intergovernmental forum.

Chapter 20 Environmentally sound management of hazardous wastes including prevention of illegal international traffic in hazardous wastes

Effective control of the generation, storage, treatment, recycling and reuse, transport, recovery and disposal of hazardous wastes is of paramount importance for proper health, environmental protection and natural resource management, and sustainable development. This will require the active cooperation and participation of the international community, Governments and industry. Industry, as referred to in this paper, shall include large industrial enterprises, including transnational corporations and domestic industry.

Prevention of the generation of hazardous wastes and the rehabilitation of contaminated sites are the key elements, and both require knowledge, experienced people, facilities, financial resources and technical and scientific capacities.

The activities outlined in the present chapter are very closely related to, and have implications for, many of the programme areas described in other chapters, so that an overall integrated approach to hazardous waste management is necessary.

There is international concern that part of the international movement of hazardous wastes is being carried out in contravention of existing national legislation and international instruments to the detriment of the environment and public health of all countries, particularly developing countries.

In section I of resolution 44/226 of 22 December 1989, the General Assembly requested each regional commission, within existing resources, to contribute to the prevention of the illegal traffic in toxic and dangerous products and wastes by monitoring and making regional assessments of that illegal traffic and its environmental and health implications. The Assembly also requested the regional commissions to

The human race has reached a critical stage in its development. Our environment is being polluted at an escalating pace and is threatened by climate change and habitat destruction. Development is essential but it must take into account the finite resources that we have at our disposal. To achieve this aim involves changing from consumptive development in which large environmental debts are incurred to sustainable development with no environmental debts; it involves global planning, understanding, cooperation and mutual support. It is my sincere hope that UNCED will prove to be the springboard for a new global outlook to responsible environmental management and sustainable development.
Sam Nujoma
President
Republic of Namibia

interact among themselves and cooperate with the United Nations Environment Programme (UNEP), with a view to maintaining efficient and coordinated monitoring and assessment of the illegal traffic in toxic and dangerous products and wastes.

Overall objective Within the framework of integrated life-cycle management, the overall objective is to prevent to the extent possible, and minimize, the generation of hazardous wastes, as well as to manage those wastes in such a way that they do not cause harm to health and the environment.

Overall targets The overall targets are:
a Preventing or minimizing the generation of hazardous wastes as part of an overall integrated cleaner production approach; eliminating or reducing to a minimum transboundary movements of hazardous wastes, consistent with the environmentally sound and efficient management of those wastes; and ensuring that environmentally sound hazardous waste management options are pursued to the maximum extent possible within the country of origin (the self-sufficiency principle). The transboundary movements that take place should be on environmental and economic grounds and based upon agreements between the States concerned;
b Ratification of the Basel Convention on the Control of Transboundary Movements of Hazardous Wastes and their Disposal and the expeditious elaboration of related protocols, such as the protocol on liability and compensation, mechanisms and guidelines to facilitate the implementation of the Basel Convention;
c Ratification and full implementation by the countries concerned of the Bamako Convention on the Ban on the Import into Africa and the Control of Transboundary Movement of Hazardous Wastes within Africa and the expeditious elaboration of a protocol on liability and compensation;
d Elimination of the export of hazardous wastes to countries that, individually or through international agreements, prohibits the import of such wastes, such as, the contracting parties to the Bamako Convention, the fourth Lomé Convention or other relevant conventions, where such prohibition is provided for.

A Promoting the prevention and minimization of hazardous waste

Basis for action Human health and environmental quality are undergoing continuous degradation by the increasing amount of hazardous wastes being produced. There are increasing direct and indirect costs to society and to individual citizens in connection with the generation, handling and disposal of such wastes. It is therefore crucial to enhance knowledge and information on the economics of prevention and management of hazardous wastes, including the impact in relation to the employment and environmental benefits, in order to ensure that the necessary capital investment is made available in development programmes through economic incentives. One of the first priorities in hazardous waste management is minimization, as part of a broader approach to changing industrial processes and consumer patterns through pollution prevention and cleaner production strategies.

Among the most important factors in these strategies is the recovery of hazardous wastes and their tranformation into useful material. Technology application, modification and development of new low-waste technologies are therefore currently a central focus of hazardous waste minimization.

Objectives
a To reduce the generation of hazardous wastes, to the extent feasible, as part of an integrated cleaner production approach;
b To optimize the use of materials by utilizing, where practicable and environmentally sound, the residues from production processes;
c To enhance knowledge and information on the economics of prevention and management of hazardous wastes.

To achieve those objectives, and thereby reduce the impact and cost of industrial development, countries that can afford to adopt the requisite technologies without detriment to their development should establish policies that include:
a Integration of cleaner production approaches and hazardous waste minimization in all planning, and the adoption of specific goals;
b Promotion of the use of regulatory and market mechanisms;
c Establishment of an intermediate goal for the stabilization of the quantity of hazardous waste generated;
d Establishment of long-term programmes and policies including targets where appropriate for reducing the amount of hazardous waste produced per unit of manufacture;
e Achievement of a qualitative improvement of waste streams, mainly through activities aimed at reducing their hazardous characteristics;
f Facilitation of the establishment of cost-effective policies and approaches to hazardous waste prevention and management, taking into consideration the state of development of each country.

Management-related activites
a Governments should establish or modify standards or purchasing specifications to avoid discrimination against recycled materials, provided that those materials are environmentally sound;
b Governments, according to their possibilities and with the help of multilateral cooperation, should provide economic or regulatory incentives, where appropriate, to stimulate industrial innovation towards cleaner production methods, to encourage industry to invest in preventive and/or recycling technologies so as to ensure environmentally sound management of all hazardous wastes, including recyclable wastes, and to encourage waste minimization investments;
c Governments should intensify research and development activities on cost-effective alternatives for processes and substances that currently result in the generation of hazardous wastes that pose particular problems for environmentally sound disposal or treatment, the possibility of ultimate phase-out of those substances that present an unreasonable or otherwise unmanageable risk and are toxic, persistent and bio-accumulative to be considered as soon as practicable. Emphasis should be given to alternatives that could be economically accessible to developing countries;
d Governments, according to their capacities and available resources and with the cooperation of the United Nations and other relevant organizations and industries, as appropriate, should support the establishment of domestic facilities to handle hazardous wastes of domestic origin;
e Governments of developed countries should promote the transfer of environmentally sound technologies and know-how on clean technologies and low-waste production to developing countries in conformity with chapter 34, which will bring about changes to sustain innovation. Governments should cooperate with industry to develop guidelines and codes of conduct, where appropriate, leading to cleaner production through sectoral trade industry associations.

Minimization is the first priority in hazardous waste management. Where its use is found to be necessary careful management of its disposal is essential. Ideally it should be transformed into re-usable material.

f Governments should encourage industry to treat, recycle, reuse and dispose of wastes at the source of generation, or as close as possible thereto, whenever hazardous waste generation is unavoidable and when it is both economically and environmentally efficient for industry to do so;
g Governments should encourage technology assessments, for example through the use of technology assessment centres;
h Governments should promote cleaner production through the establishment of centres providing training and information on environmentally sound technologies;
i Industry should establish environmental management systems, including environmental auditing of its production or distribution sites, in order to identify where the installation of cleaner production methods is needed;
j A relevant and competent United Nations organization should take the lead, in cooperation with other organizations, to develop guidelines for estimating the costs and benefits of various approaches to the adoption of cleaner production and waste minimization and environmentally sound management of hazardous wastes, including rehabilitation of contaminated sites, taking into account, where appropriate, the report of the 1991 Nairobi meeting of government-designated experts on an international strategy and an action programme, including technical guidelines for the environmentally sound management of hazardous wastes; in particular in the context of the work of the Basel Convention, being developed under the UNEP secretariat;
k Governments should establish regulations that lay down the ultimate responsibility of industries for environmentally sound disposal of the hazardous wastes their activities generate.

Financing and cost evaluation $750 million from the international community on grant or concessional terms.

B Promoting and strengthening institutional capacities in hazardous waste management

Basis for action Many countries lack the national capacity to handle and manage hazardous wastes. This is primarily due to inadequate infrastructure, deficiencies in regulatory frameworks, insufficient education and training programmes and lack of coordination between the different ministries and institutions involved in various aspects of waste management. In addition, there is a lack of knowledge about environmental contamination and pollution and the associated health risk from the exposure of populations, especially women and children, and ecosystems to hazardous wastes; assessment of risks; and the characteristics of wastes. Steps need to be taken immediately to identify populations at high risk and to take remedial measures, where necessary. One of the main priorities in ensuring environmentally sound management of hazardous wastes is to provide awareness, education and training programmes covering all levels of society. There is also a need to undertake research programmes to understand the nature of hazardous wastes, to identify their potential environmental effects and to develop technologies to safely handle those wastes. Finally, there is a need to strengthen the capacities of institutions that are responsible for the management of hazardous wastes.

Objectives
a To adopt appropriate coordinating, legislative and regulatory measures at the national level for the environmentally sound management of hazardous wastes, including the implementation of international and regional conventions;
b To establish public awareness and information programmes on hazardous waste issues and to ensure that basic education and training programmes are provided for industry and government workers in all countries;
c To establish comprehensive research programmes on hazardous wastes in countries;
d To strengthen service industries to enable them to handle hazardous wastes, and to build up international networking;
e To develop endogenous capacities in all developing countries to educate and train staff at all levels in environmentally sound hazardous waste handling and monitoring and in environmentally sound management;
f To promote human exposure assessment with

An intricate web of interdependence unites the global habitat and plant and animal species in a relationship that guarantees the continuity of all. However, human development has launched us on a perilous course. UNCED is tangible proof that the world has awoken to the dark clouds of environmental degradation gathering overhead. What has been done can yet be undone. We all know that the flame of the world's environment has grown dim in recent years. We now have a golden opportunity to fan it back to brightness, thus restoring the splendour of God's greatest legacy to man. Let us not, for the Earth's sake, squander it.
Alhaji Sir Dawda Kairaba Jawara
President
Republic of the Gambia

respect to hazardous waste sites and identify the remedial measures required;
g To facilitate the assessment of impacts and risks of hazardous wastes on human health and the environment by establishing appropriate procedures, methodologies, criteria and/or effluent-related guidelines and standards;
h To improve knowledge regarding the effects of hazardous wastes on human health and the environment;
i To make information available to Governments and to the general public on the effects of hazardous wastes, including infectious wastes, on human health and the environment.

Management-related activities
a Governments should establish and maintain inventories, including computerized inventories, of hazardous wastes and their treatment/disposal sites, as well as of contaminated sites that require rehabilitation, and assess exposure and risk to human health and the environment; they should also identify the measures required to clean up the disposal sites. Industry should make the necessary information available;
b Governments, industry and international organizations should collaborate in developing guidelines and easy-to-implement methods for the characterization and classification of hazardous wastes;
c Governments should carry out exposure and health assessments of populations residing near uncontrolled hazardous waste sites and initiate remedial measures;
d International organizations should develop improved health-based criteria, taking into account national decision-making processes, and assist in the preparation of practical technical guidelines for the prevention, minimization and safe handling and disposal of hazardous wastes;
e Governments of developing countries should encourage interdisciplinary and intersectoral groups, in cooperation with international organizations and agencies, to implement training and research activities related to evaluation, prevention and control of hazardous waste health risks. Such groups should serve as models to develop similar regional programmes;
f Governments, according to their capacities and available resources and with the cooperation of the United Nations and other relevant organizations as appropriate, should encourage as far as possible the establishment of combined treatment/disposal facilities for hazardous wastes in small- and medium-sized industries;
g Governments should promote identification and clean-up of sites of hazardous wastes in collaboration with industry and international organizations. Technologies, expertise and financing should be available for this purpose, as far as possible and when appropriate with the application of the "polluter pays" principle;
h Governments should ascertain that their military establishments conform to their nationally applicable environmental norms in the treatment and disposal of hazardous wastes.

Financing and cost evaluation $18.5 billion on a global basis with about $3.5 billion related to developing countries, including about $500 million from the international community on grant or concessional terms.

C Promoting and strengthening international cooperation in the management of transboundary movements of hazardous wastes

Basis for action In order to promote and strengthen international cooperation in the management, including control and monitoring, of transboundary movements of hazardous wastes, a precautionary approach should be applied. There is a need to harmonize the procedures and criteria used in various international and legal instruments. There is also a need to develop or harmonize existing criteria for identifying wastes dangerous to the environment and to build monitoring capacities.

Objectives
a To facilitate and strengthen international cooperation in the environmentally sound management of hazardous wastes, including control and monitoring of transboundary movements of such wastes, including wastes for recovery, by using internationally adopted criteria to identify and classify hazardous wastes and to harmonize relevant international legal instruments;
b To adopt a ban on or prohibit, as appropriate, the export of hazardous wastes to countries that do not have the capacity to deal with those wastes in an environmentally sound way or that have banned the import of such wastes;
c To promote the development of control procedures for the transboundary movement of hazardous wastes destined for recovery operations under the Basel Convention that encourage environmentally and economically sound recycling options.

Management-related activities Strengthening and harmonizing criteria and regulations
Governments, according to their capacities and available resources and with the cooperation of United Nations and other relevant organizations, as appropriate, should:
a Incorporate the notification procedure called for in the Basel Convention and relevant regional conventions, as well as in their annexes, into national legislation;
b Formulate, where appropriate, regional agreements such as the Bamako Convention regulating the transboundary movement of hazardous wastes;
c Help promote the compatibility and complementarity of such regional agreements with international conventions and protocols;
d Strengthen national and regional capacities and capabilities to monitor and control the transboundary movement of hazardous wastes;
e Promote the development of clear criteria and guidelines, within the framework of the Basel Convention and regional conventions, as appropriate, for environmentally and economically sound operation in resource recovery, recycling reclamation, direct use or alternative uses and for determination of acceptable recovery practices, including recovery levels where feasible and appropriate, with a view to preventing abuses and false presentation in the above operations;
f Consider setting up, at national and regional levels, as appropriate, systems for monitoring and surveillance of the transboundary movements of hazardous wastes;
g Develop guidelines for the assessment of environmentally sound treatment of hazardous wastes;
h Develop guidelines for the identification of hazardous wastes at the national level, taking into account existing internationally – and, where appropriate, regionally – agreed criteria and prepare a list of hazard profiles for the hazardous wastes listed in national legislation;
i Develop and use appropriate methods for testing, characterizing and classifying hazardous wastes and adopt or adapt safety standards and principles for managing hazardous wastes in an environmentally sound way.

Implementing existing agreements Governments are urged to ratify the Basel Convention and the Bamako Convention, as applicable, and to pursue the

A leisurely canoeing trip on the river is marred by the debris and rubbish. The water is also heavily contaminated with phosphates which results in eutrophication.

expeditious elaboration of related protocols, such as protocols on liability and compensation, and of mechanisms and guidelines to facilitate the implementation of the Conventions.

Financing and cost evaluation Because this programme area covers a relatively new field of operation and because of the lack so far of adequate studies on costing of activities under this programme, no cost estimate is available at present. However, the costs for some of the activities related to capacity-building that are presented under this programme could be considered to have been covered under the costing of programme area B above.

The interim secretariat for the Basel Convention should undertake studies in order to arrive at a reasonable cost estimate for activities to be undertaken initially until the year 2000.

D Preventing illegal international traffic in hazardous wastes

Basis for action The prevention of illegal traffic in hazardous wastes will benefit the environment and public health in all countries, particularly developing countries. It will also help to make the Basel Convention and regional international instruments, such as the Bamako Convention and the fourth Lomé Convention, more effective by promoting compliance with the controls established in those agreements. Article IX of the Basel Convention specifically addresses the issue of illegal shipments of hazardous wastes. Illegal traffic of hazardous wastes may cause serious threats to human health and the environment and impose a special and abnormal burden on the countries that receive such shipments.

Effective prevention requires action through effective monitoring and the enforcement and imposition of appropriate penalties.

Objectives

a To reinforce national capacities to detect and halt any illegal attempt to introduce hazardous wastes into the territory of any State in contravention of national legislation and relevant international legal instruments;
b To assist all countries, particularly developing countries, in obtaining all appropriate information concerning illegal traffic in hazardous wastes;

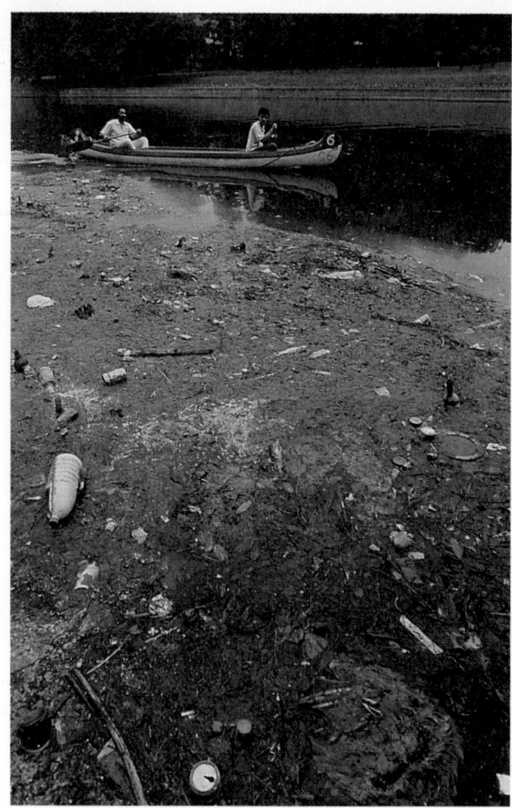

c To cooperate, within the framework of the Basel Convention, in assisting countries that suffer the consequences of illegal traffic.

Management-related activities Governments, according to their capacities and available resources and with the cooperation of the United Nations and other relevant organizations, as appropriate, should:
a Adopt, where necessary, and implement legislation to prevent the illegal import and export of hazardous wastes;
b Develop appropriate national enforcement programmes to monitor compliance with such legislation, detect and deter violations through appropriate penalties and give special attention to those who are known to have conducted illegal traffic in hazardous wastes and to hazardous wastes that are particularly susceptible to illegal traffic.

Chapter 21

Environmentally sound management of solid waste and sewage-related issues

The incorporation of the chapter on environmentally sound management of solid wastes within Agenda 21 is in response to General Assembly resolution 44/228, section I, paragraph 3, in which the Assembly affirmed that the Conference should elaborate strategies and measures to halt and reverse the effects of environmental degradation in the context of increased national and international efforts to promote sustainable and environmentally sound development in all countries, and to section I, paragraph 12 (g), of the same resolution, in which the Assembly affirmed that environmentally sound management of wastes was among the environmental issues of major concern in maintaining the quality of the Earth's environment and especially in achieving environmentally sound and sustainable development in all countries. Programme areas included under the present chapter are closely related to the following programme areas of other chapters of Agenda 21:
a Protection of the quality and supply of fresh water resources (chapter 18);
b Promoting sustainable human settlement development (chapter 7);
c Protecting and promoting human health conditions (chapter 6);
d Changing consumption patterns (chapter 4).

Solid wastes, as defined in this chapter, include all domestic refuse and non-hazardous wastes such as commercial and institutional wastes, street sweepings and construction debris. In some countries, the solid wastes management system also handles human wastes such as night-soil, ashes from incinerators, septic tank sludge and sludge from sewage treatment plants. If these wastes manifest hazardous characteristics they should be treated as hazardous wastes.

Environmentally sound waste management must go beyond the mere safe disposal or recovery of wastes that are generated and seek to address the root cause of the problem by attempting to change unsustainable patterns of production and consumption. This implies the application of the integrated life cycle management concept, which presents a unique opportunity to reconcile development with environmental protection.

Accordingly, the framework for requisite action should be founded on a hierarchy of objectives and focused on the four major waste-related programme areas which are interrelated and mutually supportive and must therefore be integrated in order to provide a comprehensive and environmentally responsive framework for managing municipal solid wastes. The mix and emphasis given to each of the four programme areas will vary according to the local socio-economic and physical conditions, rates of waste generation and waste composition. All sectors of society should participate in all the programme areas.

A Minimizing wastes

Basis for action Unsustainable patterns of production and consumption are increasing the quantities and variety of environmentally persistent wastes at unprecedented rates. The trend could significantly increase the quantities of wastes produced by the end of the century and increase quantities four to fivefold by the year 2025. A preventive waste management approach focused on changes in lifestyles and in production and consumption patterns offers the best chance for reversing current trends.

Objectives

a To stabilize or reduce the production of wastes destined for final disposal, over an agreed time-frame, by formulating goals based on waste weight, volume and composition and to induce separation to facilitate waste recycling and reuse;

b To strengthen procedures for assessing waste quantity and composition changes for the purpose of formulating operational waste minimization policies utilizing economic or other instruments to induce beneficial modifications of production and consumption patterns.

Governments, according to their capacities and available resources and with the cooperation of the United Nations and other relevant organizations, as appropriate, should:

a By the year 2000, ensure sufficient national, regional and international capacity to access, process and monitor waste trend information and implement waste minimization policies;

b By the year 2000, have in place in all industrialized countries programmes to stabilize or reduce, if practicable, production of wastes destined for final disposal, including per capita wastes (where this concept applies), at the level prevailing at that date; developing countries as well should work towards that goal without jeopardizing their development prospects;

c Apply by the year 2000, in all countries, in particular in industrialized countries, programmes to reduce the production of agrochemical wastes, containers and packaging materials, which do not meet hazardous characteristics.

Management-related activities Governments should initiate programmes to achieve sustained minimization of waste generation. Non-governmental organizations and consumer groups should be encouraged to participate in such programmes, which could be drawn up with the cooperation of international organizations, where necessary. These programmes should, wherever possible, build upon existing or planned activities and should:

a Develop and strengthen national capacities in research and design of environmentally sound technologies, as well as adopt measures to reduce wastes to a minimum;

b Provide for incentives to reduce unsustainable patterns of production and consumption;

c Develop, where necessary, national plans to minimize waste generation as part of overall national development plans;

d Emphasize waste minimization considerations in procurement within the United Nations system.

Financial and cost evaluation The Conference secretariat suggests that industrialized countries should consider investing in waste minimization the equivalent of about 1 per cent of the expenditures on solid wastes and sewage disposal. At current levels, this would amount to about $6.5 billion annually, including about $1.8 billion related to minimizing municipal solid wastes. Actual amounts would be determined by relevant municipal, provincial and national budget authorities based on local circumstances.

B Maximizing environmentally sound waste reuse and recycling

Basis for action The exhaustion of traditional disposal sites, stricter environmental controls governing waste disposal and increasing quantities of more persistent wastes, particularly in industrialized countries, have all contributed to a rapid increase in the cost of waste disposal services. Costs could double or triple by the end of the decade. Some current disposal practices pose a threat to the environment. As the economics of waste disposal services change, waste recycling and resource recovery are becoming increasingly cost-effective. Future waste management programmes should take maximum advantage of resource-efficient approaches

Working the Sante Fe refuse dump in Mexico City sifting rubbish for items to sell and food to eat. As the cost of waste disposal increases recycling becomes a more attractive and viable alternative - but not at the cost of human health.

Section II

Above: Fresh Kills Landfill in New York City, the world's largest landfill site, covers an area of 3,000 acres.

to the control of wastes. These activities should be carried out in conjunction with public education programmes. It is important that markets for products from reclaimed materials be identified in the development of reuse and recycling programmes.

Objectives
a To strengthen and increase national waste reuse and recycling systems;
b To create a model internal waste reuse and recycling programme for waste streams, including paper, within the United Nations system;
c To make available information, techniques and appropriate policy instruments to encourage and make operational waste reuse and recycling schemes.

Governments, according to their capacities and available resources and with the cooperation of the United Nations and other relevant organizations, as appropriate, should:
a By the year 2000, promote sufficient financial and technological capacities at the regional, national and local levels, as appropriate, to implement waste reuse and recycling policies and actions;
b By the year 2000, in all industrialized countries, and by the year 2010, in all developing countries, have a national programme, including, to the extent possible, targets for efficient waste reuse and recycling.

Management-related activities Governments and institutions and non-governmental organizations, including consumer, women's and youth groups, in collaboration with appropriate organizations of the United Nations system, should launch programmes to demonstrate and make operational enhanced waste reuse and recycling. These programmes should, wherever possible, build upon existing or planned activities and should:
a Develop and strengthen national capacity to reuse and recycle an increasing proportion of wastes;
b Review and reform national waste policies to provide incentives for waste reuse and recycling;
c Develop and implement national plans for waste management that take advantage of, and give priority to, waste reuse and recycling;
d Modify existing standards or purchase specifications to avoid discrimination against recycled materials, taking into account the saving in energy and raw materials;
e Develop public education and awareness programmes to promote the use of recycled products.
Financial and cost evaluation The Conference secretariat has estimated that if the equivalent of 1 per cent of waste-related municipal expenditures was devoted to safe waste reuse schemes, world-wide expenditures for this purpose would amount to $8 billion. The secretariat estimates the total annual cost (1993-2000) of implementing the activities of this programme area in developing countries to be about $850 million on grant or concessional terms. These are indicative and order of magnitude estimates only and have not been reviewed by Governments. Actual costs and financial terms, including any that are non-concessional, will depend upon, *inter alia*, the specific programmes proposed by international institutions and approved by their governing bodies.

C Promoting environmentally sound waste disposal and treatment

Basis for action Even when wastes are minimized, some wastes will still remain. Even after treatment, all discharges of wastes have some residual impact on the receiving environment. Consequently, there is scope for improving waste treatment and disposal practices such as, for example, avoiding the discharge of sludges at

sea. In developing countries, the problem is of a more fundamental nature: less than 10 per cent of urban wastes receive some form of treatment and only a small proportion of treatment is in compliance with any acceptable quality standard. Faecal matter treatment and disposal should be accorded due priority given the potential threat of faeces to human health.

Objectives The objective in this area is to treat and safely dispose of a progressively increasing proportion of the generated wastes.

Governments, according to their capacities and available resources and with the cooperation of the United Nations and other relevant organizations, as appropriate, should:
a By the year 2000, establish waste treatment and disposal quality criteria, objectives and standards based on the nature and assimilative capacity of the receiving environment;
b By the year 2000, establish sufficient capacity to undertake waste-related pollution impact monitoring and conduct regular surveillance, including epidemiological surveillance, where appropriate;
c By the year 1995, in industrialized countries, and by the year 2005, in developing countries, ensure that at least 50 per cent of all sewage, waste waters and solid wastes are treated or disposed of in conformity with national or international environmental and health quality guidelines;
d By the year 2025, dispose of all sewage, waste waters and solid wastes in conformity with national or international environmental quality guidelines.

Management-related activities Governments, institutions and non-governmental organizations, together with industries, in collaboration with appropriate organizations of the United Nations system, should launch programmes to improve the control and management of waste-related pollution. These programmes should, wherever possible, build upon existing or planned activities and should:
a Develop and strengthen national capacity to treat and safely dispose of wastes;
b Review and reform national waste management policies to gain control over waste-related pollution;
c Encourage countries to seek waste disposal solutions within their sovereign territory and as close as possible to the sources of origin that are compatible with environmentally sound and efficient management. In a number of countries, transboundary movements take place to ensure that wastes are managed in an environmentally sound and efficient way. Such movements observe the relevant conventions, including those that apply to areas that are not under national jurisdiction;
d Develop human wastes management plans, giving due attention to the development and application of appropriate technologies and the availability of resources for implementation.

Financial and cost evaluation Safe waste disposal programmes are relevant to both developed and developing countries. In developed countries the focus is on improving facilities to meet higher environmental quality criteria, while in developing countries considerable investment is required to build new treatment facilities.

Estimated average total annual cost about \$15 billion, including about \$3.4 billion from the international community on grant or concessional terms.

D Extending waste service coverage

Basis for action By the end of the century, over 2 billion people will be without access to basic sanitation, and an estimated half of the urban population in developing countries will be without adequate solid waste disposal services. As many as 5.2 million people, including 4 million children under five years of age, die each year from waste-related diseases. The health impacts are particularly severe for the urban poor. The health and environmental impacts of inadequate waste management, however, go beyond the unserved settlements themselves and result in water, land and air contamination and pollution over a wider area. Extending and improving waste collection and safe disposal services are crucial to gaining control over this form of pollution.

Objectives The overall objective of this programme is to provide health-protecting, environmentally safe waste collection and disposal services to all people. Governments, according to their capacities and available resources and with the cooperation of the United Nations and other relevant organizations, as appropriate, should:

a By the year 2000, have the necessary technical, financial and human resource capacity to provide waste collection services commensurate with needs;
b By the year 2025, provide all urban populations with adequate waste services;
c By the year 2025, ensure that full urban waste service coverage is maintained and sanitation coverage achieved in all rural areas.

Management-related activities Governments, according to their capacities and available resources and with the cooperation of the United Nations and other relevant organizations, as appropriate, should:

a Establish financing mechanisms for waste management service development in deprived areas, including appropriate modes of revenue generation;
b Apply the "polluter pays" principle, where appropriate, by setting waste management charges at rates that reflect the costs of providing the service and ensure that those who generate the wastes pay the full cost of disposal in an environmentally safe way;
c Encourage institutionalization of communities' participation in planning and implementation procedures for solid waste management.

Financial and cost evaluation \$7.5 billion, including about \$2.6 billion from the international community on grant or concessional terms.

Chapter 22 Safe and environmentally sound management of radioactive wastes

Basis for action Radioactive wastes are generated in the nuclear fuel cycle as well as in nuclear applications (the use of radionuclides in medicine, research and industry). The radiological and safety risk from radioactive wastes varies from very low in short-lived, low-level wastes up to very large for high-level wastes. Annually about 200,000 m^3 of low-level and intermediate-level waste and 10,000 m^3 of high-level waste (as well as spent nuclear fuel destined for final disposal) is generated world wide from nuclear power production. These volumes are increasing as more nuclear power units are taken into operation, nuclear facilities are decommissioned and the use of radionuclides increases. The high-level waste contains about 99 per cent of the radionuclides and thus represents the largest radiological risk. The waste volumes from nuclear applications are generally much smaller, typically some tens of cubic metres or less per year and country. However, the activity concentration, especially in sealed radiation sources, might be high, thus justifying very stringent radiological protection measures. The growth of waste volumes should continue to be kept under close review.

The safe and environmentally sound management of radioactive wastes, including their minimization, transportation and disposal, is important, given their characteristics. In most countries with a substantial nuclear power programme, technical and administrative measures have been taken to implement a waste management system. In many other countries still only in preparation for a national nuclear programme or having only nuclear applications, such systems are still needed.

Objective The objective of this programme area is to ensure that radioactive wastes are safely managed, transported, stored and disposed of, with a view to protecting human health and the environment, within a wider framework of an interactive and integrated approach to radioactive waste management and safety.

Management-related activities States, in cooperation with relevant international organizations, where appropriate, should:

a Promote policies and practical measures to minimize and limit, where appropriate, the generation of radioactive wastes and provide for their safe processing, conditioning, transportation and disposal;
b Support efforts within IAEA to develop and promulgate radioactive waste safety standards or guidelines and codes of practice as an internationally accepted basis for the safe and environmentally sound management and disposal of radioactive wastes;
c Promote safe storage, transportation and disposal of radioactive wastes, as well as spent radiation sources and spent fuel from nuclear reactors destined for final disposal, in all countries, in particular in developing countries, by facilitating the transfer of relevant technologies to those countries and/or the return to the supplier of radiation sources after their use, in accordance with relevant international regulations or guidelines;
d Promote proper planning, including environmental impact assessment where appropriate, of safe and environmentally sound management of radioactive waste, including emergency procedures, storage, transportation and disposal, prior to and after activities that generate such waste.

Financial and cost evaluation The costs at the national level of managing and disposing of radioactive wastes are considerable and will vary, depending on the technology used for disposal.

Estimated average total annual cost to international organizations about \$8 million.

SOMETIMES, BNP INVESTS IN FIELDS
THAT BEAR NO FRUIT. AND YET,
WE'RE WILLING TO CONTINUE.

Working Natural Wonders in the Energy World.
We at Enron Corp., America's largest natural gas company, are committed to providing clean energy worldwide for a better environment. Abundant, clean-burning natural gas serves a host of needs, from heating our homes to fueling our automobiles. Using clean natural gas to generate low cost electricity is just one example of its many environmentally safe applications.
Enron is one of the largest independent developers and producers of electricity in the United States and the United Kingdom with extensive experience in combined heat and power installations. Pollution prevention is obviously the key to achieving the twin goals of environmental protection and economic growth. Natural gas power generation is significantly cleaner and cheaper than other fossil fuel alternatives.
Compared with a best technology coal-fired facility, a new natural gas power plant:
•eliminates 60 percent of the carbon dioxide (CO_2) emissions, the primary global warming gas;
•eliminates 100 percent of the sulphur dioxide (SO_2) emissions, the main cause of acid rain; and
•eliminates 80 percent of the nitrogen oxides (NOx) emissions, the major contributor to smog.
Enron Corp. is working to deliver the environmental benefits of clean-burning natural gas around the world.
Ken Lay
Kenneth L. Lay
Chairman of the Board and Chief Executive Officer
ENRON CORP.
Houston, Texas

Strengthening the role of major groups

Chapter 23 Preamble

Critical to the effective implementation of the objectives, policies and mechanisms agreed to by Governments in all programme areas of Agenda 21 will be the commitment and genuine involvement of all social groups.

One of the fundamental prerequisites for the achievement of sustainable development is broad public participation in decision-making. Furthermore, in the more specific context of environment and development, the need for new forms of participation has emerged. This includes the need of individuals, groups and organizations to participate in environmental impact assessment procedures and to know about and participate in decisions, particularly those which potentially affect the communities in which they live and work. Individuals, groups and organizations should have access to information relevant to environment and development held by national authorities, including information on products and activities that have or are likely to have a significant impact on the environment, and information on environmental protection measures.

Any policies, definitions or rules affecting access to and participation by non-governmental organizations in the work of United Nations institutions or agencies associated with the implementation of Agenda 21 must apply equally to all major groups.

The programme areas set out below address the means for moving towards real social partnership in support of common efforts for sustainable development.

Chapter 24 Global action for women towards sustainable and equitable development

Basis for action The international community has endorsed several plans of action and conventions for the full, equal and beneficial integration of women in all development activities, in particular the Nairobi Forward-looking Strategies for the Advancement of Women,[1] which emphasize women's participation in national and international ecosystem management and control of environment degradation. Several conventions, including the Convention on the Elimination of All Forms of Discrimination against Women (General Assembly resolution 34/180, annex) and conventions of ILO and UNESCO have also been adopted to end gender-based discrimination and ensure women access to land and other resources, education and safe and equal employment. Also relevant are the 1990 World Declaration on the Survival, Protection and Development of Children and its Plan of Action (A/45/625, annex). Effective implementation of these programmes will depend on the active involvement of women in economic and political decision-making and will be critical to the successful implementation of Agenda 21.

Objectives The following objectives are proposed for national Governments:

a To implement the Nairobi Forward-looking Strategies for the Advancement of Women, particularly with regard to women's participation in national ecosystem management and control of environment degradation;

b To increase the proportion of women decision makers, planners, technical advisers, managers and extension workers in environment and development fields;

c To consider developing and issuing by the year 2000 a strategy of changes necessary to eliminate constitutional, legal, administrative, cultural, behavioural, social and economic obstacles to women's full participation in sustainable development and in public life;

d To establish by the year 1995 mechanisms at the national, regional and international levels to assess the implementation and impact of development and environment policies and programmes on women and to ensure their contributions and benefits;

e To assess, review, revise and implement, where appropriate, curricula and other educational material, with a view to promoting the dissemination to both men and women of gender-relevant knowledge and valuation of women's roles through formal and non-formal education, as well as through training institutions, in collaboration with non-governmental organizations;

f To formulate and implement clear governmental policies and national guidelines, strategies and plans for the achievement of equality in all aspects of society, including the promotion of women's literacy, education, training, nutrition and health and their participation in key decision-making positions and in management of the environment, particularly as

A mother breastfeeds her twins whilst working in a tree nursery in the Paro Valley, Bhutan. Suggested programmes should focus on the establishment of nurseries and kindergartens for working mothers.

it pertains to their access to resources, by facilitating better access to all forms of credit, particularly in the informal sector, taking measures towards ensuring women's access to property rights as well as agricultural inputs and implements;

g To implement, as a matter of urgency, in accordance with country-specific conditions, measures to ensure that women and men have the same right to decide freely and responsibly the number and spacing of their children and have access to information, education and means, as appropriate, to enable them to exercise this right in keeping with their freedom, dignity and personally held values;

h To consider adopting, strengthening and enforcing legislation prohibiting violence against women and to take all necessary administrative, social and educational measures to eliminate violence against women in all its forms.

Activities Governments should take active steps to implement the following:

a Measures to review policies and establish plans to increase the proportion of women involved as decision makers, planners, managers, scientists and technical advisers in the design, development and implementation of policies and programmes for sustainable development;

b Measures to strengthen and empower women's bureaux, women's non-governmental organizations and women's groups in enhancing capacity-building for sustainable development;

c Measures to eliminate illiteracy among females and to expand the enrolment of women and girls in educational institutions, to promote the goal of universal access to primary and secondary education for girl children and for women, and to increase educational and training opportunities for women and girls in sciences and technology, particularly at the post-secondary level;

d Programmes to promote the reduction of the heavy workload of women and girl children at home and outside through the establishment of more and affordable nurseries and kindergartens by Governments, local authorities, employers and other relevant organizations and the sharing of household tasks by men and women on an equal basis, and to promote the provision of environmentally sound technologies which have been designed, developed and improved in consultation with women, accessible and clean water, an efficient fuel supply and adequate sanitation facilities;

e Programmes to establish and strengthen preventive and curative health facilities, which include women-centred, women-managed, safe and effective reproductive health care and affordable, accessible, responsible planning of family size and services, as appropriate, in keeping with freedom, dignity and personally held values. Programmes should focus on providing comprehensive health care, including pre-natal care, education and information on health and responsible parenthood, and should provide the opportunity for all women to fully breastfeed at least during the first four months post-partum. Programmes should fully support women's productive and reproductive roles and well-being and should pay special attention to the need to provide equal and improved health care for all children and to reduce the risk of maternal and child mortality and sickness;

f Programmes to support and strengthen equal employment opportunities and equitable remuneration for women in the formal and informal sectors with adequate economic, political and social support systems and services, including child care, particularly day-care facilities and parental leave, and equal access to credit, land and other natural resources;

g Programmes to establish rural banking systems with a view to facilitating and increasing rural women's access to credit and to agricultural inputs and implements;

h Programmes to develop consumer awareness and the active participation of women, emphasizing their crucial role in achieving changes necessary to reduce or eliminate unsustainable patterns of consumption and production, particularly in industrialized countries, in order to encourage investment in environmentally sound productive activities and induce environmentally and socially friendly industrial development;

i Programmes to eliminate persistent negative images, stereotypes, attitudes and prejudices against women through changes in socialization patterns, the media, advertising, and formal and non-formal education;

j Measures to review progress made in these areas, including the preparation of a review and appraisal report which includes recommendations to be submitted to the 1995 world conference on women.

Governments are urged to ratify all relevant

conventions pertaining to women if they have not already done so. Those that have ratified conventions should enforce and establish legal, constitutional and administrative procedures to transform agreed rights into domestic legislation and should adopt measures to implement them in order to strengthen the legal capacity of women for full and equal participation in issues and decisions on sustainable development.

States parties to the Convention on the Elimination of All Forms of Discrimination against Women should review and suggest amendments to it by the year 2000, with a view to strengthening those elements of the Convention related to environment and development, giving special attention to the issue of access and entitlements to natural resources, technology, creative banking facilities and low-cost housing, and the control of pollution and toxicity in the home and workplace. States parties should also clarify the extent of the Convention's scope with respect to the issues of environment and development and request the Committee on the Elimination of Discrimination against Women to develop guidelines regarding the nature of reporting such issues, required under particular articles of the Convention.

A *Areas requiring urgent action*

Countries should take urgent measures to avert the ongoing rapid environmental and economic degradation in developing countries that generally affects the lives of women and children in rural areas suffering drought, desertification and deforestation, armed hostilities, natural disasters, toxic waste and the aftermath of the use of unsuitable agro-chemical products.

In order to reach these goals, women should be fully involved in decision-making and in the implementation of sustainable development activities.

B *Research, data collection and dissemination of information*

Countries should develop gender-sensitive databases, information systems and participatory action-oriented research and policy analyses with the collaboration of academic institutions and local women researchers on the following:

a Knowledge and experience on the part of women of the management and conservation of natural resources for incorporation in the databases and information systems for sustainable development;

b The impact of structural adjustment programmes on women. In research done on structural adjustment programmes, special attention should be given to the differential impact of those programmes on women, especially in terms of cut-backs in social services, education and health and in the removal of subsidies on food and fuel;

c The impact on women of environmental degradation, particularly drought, desertification, toxic chemicals and armed hostilities;

d Analysis of the structural linkages between gender relations, environment and development;

e The integration of the value of unpaid work, including work that is currently designated "domestic", in resource accounting mechanisms in order better to represent the true value of the contribution of women to the economy, using revised guidelines for the United Nations System of National Accounts, to be issued in 1993;

f Measures to develop and include environmental, social and gender impact analyses as an essential step in the development and monitoring of programmes and policies;

g Programmes to create rural and urban training, research and resource centres in developing and developed countries that will serve to disseminate environmentally sound technologies to women.

Finance and cost evaluation $40 million from the international community on grant and concessional terms.

1 Report of the World Conference to Review and Appraise the Achievements of the United Nations Decade for Women: Equality, Development and Peace, Nairobi, 15-26 July 1985 (United Nations publication, Sales No. E.85.IV.10), chap. I, sect. A.

Chapter 25 Children and youth in sustainable development

Youth comprise nearly 30 per cent of the world's population. The involvement of today's youth in environment and development decision-making and in the implementation of programmes is critical to the long-term success of Agenda 21.

A Advancing the role of youth and actively involving them in the protection of the environment and the promotion of economic and social development

Basis for action It is imperative that youth from all parts of the world participate actively in all relevant levels of decision-making processes because it affects their lives today and has implications for their futures. In addition to their intellectual contribution and their ability to mobilize support, they bring unique perspectives that need to be taken into account.

Numerous actions and recommendations within the international community have been proposed to ensure that youth are provided a secure and healthy future, including an environment of quality, improved standards of living and access to education and employment. These issues need to be addressed in development planning.

Objectives Each country should, in consultation with its youth communities, establish a process to promote dialogue between the youth community and Government at all levels and to establish mechanisms that permit youth access to information and provide them with the opportunity to present their perspectives on government decisions, including the implementation of Agenda 21.

Each country, by the year 2000, should ensure that more than 50 per cent of its youth, gender balanced, are enrolled in or have access to appropriate secondary education or equivalent educational or vocational training programmes by increasing participation and access rates on an annual basis.

Each country should undertake initiatives aimed at reducing current levels of youth unemployment, particularly where they are disproportionately high in comparison to the overall unemployment rate.

Each country and the United Nations should support the promotion and creation of mechanisms to involve youth representation in all United Nations processes in order to influence those processes.

Each country should combat human rights abuses against young people, particularly young women and girls, and should consider providing all youth with legal protection, skills, opportunities and the support necessary for them to fulfil their personal, economic and social aspirations and potentials.

Activities Governments, according to their strategies, should take measures to:

a Establish procedures allowing for consultation and possible participation of youth of both genders, by

Children worldwide are highly aware supporters of environmental thinking.
Top left: children in Mexico City plant tree seedlings in an attempt to alleviate environmental problems.
Top right: Australian children in Melbourne monitor the salt content of ground water.
Bottom left: Schoolchildren in England examine creatures in a pond they designed themselves.
Bottom right: English students plant tree seedlings bought with funds raised from a recycling project.

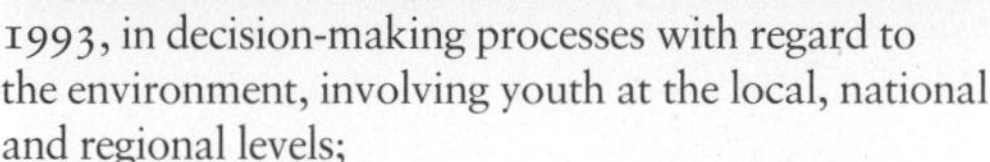

1993, in decision-making processes with regard to the environment, involving youth at the local, national and regional levels;

b Promote dialogue with youth organizations regarding the drafting and evaluation of environment plans and programmes or questions on development;

c Consider for incorporation into relevant policies the recommendations of international, regional and local youth conferences and other forums that offer youth perspectives on social and economic development and resource management;

d Ensure access for all youth to all types of education, wherever appropriate, providing alternative learning structures, ensure that education reflects the economic and social needs of youth and incorporates the concepts of environmental awareness and sustainable development throughout the curricula; and expand vocational training, implementing innovative methods aimed at increasing practical skills, such as environmental scouting;

e In cooperation with relevant ministries and organizations, including representatives of youth, develop and implement strategies for creating alternative employment opportunities and provide required training to young men and women;

f Establish task forces that include youth and youth non-governmental organizations to develop educational and awareness programmes specifically targeted to the youth population on critical issues pertaining to youth. These task forces should use formal and non-formal educational methods to reach a maximum audience. National and local media, non-governmental organizations, businesses and other organizations should assist in these task forces;

g Give support to programmes, projects, networks, national organizations and youth non-governmental organizations to examine the integration of programmes in relation to their project requirements, encouraging the involvement of youth in project identification, design, implementation and follow-up;

h Include youth representatives in their delegations to international meetings, in accordance with the relevant General Assembly resolutions adopted in 1968, 1977, 1985 and 1989.

The United Nations and international organizations with youth programmes should take measures to:

a Review their youth programmes and consider how coordination between them can be enhanced;

b Improve the dissemination of relevant information to governments, youth organizations and other non-governmental organizations on current youth positions and activities, and monitor and evaluate the application of Agenda 21;

c Promote the United Nations Trust Fund for the International Youth Year and collaborate with youth representatives in the administration of it, focusing particularly on the needs of youth from developing countries.

Financing and cost evaluation $1.5 million from the international community on grant or concessional terms.

B Children in sustainable development

Basis for action Children not only will inherit the responsibility of looking after the Earth, but in many developing countries they comprise nearly half the population. Furthermore, children in both developing and industrialized countries are highly vulnerable to the effects of environmental degradation. They are also highly aware supporters of environmental thinking. The specific interests of children need to be taken fully into account in the participatory process on environment and development in order to safeguard the future sustainability of any actions taken to improve the environment.

Objectives Governments, according to their policies, should take measures to:

a Ensure the survival, protection and development of children, in accordance with the goals endorsed by the 1990 World Summit for Children;

b Ensure that the interests of children are taken fully into account in the participatory process for sustainable development and environmental improvement.

Activities Governments should take active steps to:

a Implement programmes for children designed to reach the child-related goals of the 1990s in the areas of environment and development, especially health, nutrition, education, literacy and poverty alleviation;

b Ratify the Convention on the Rights of the Child (General Assembly resolution 44/25 of 20 November

1989, annex), at the earliest moment and implement it by addressing the basic needs of youth and children;
c Promote primary environmental care activities that address the basic needs of communities, improve the environment for children at the household and community level and encourage the participation and empowerment of local populations, including women, youth, children and indigenous people, towards the objective of integrated community management of resources, especially in developing countries;
d Expand educational opportunities for children and youth, including education for environmental and developmental responsibility, with overriding attention to the education of the girl child;
e Mobilize communities through schools and local health centres so that children and their parents become effective focal points for sensitization of communities to environmental issues;
f Establish procedures to incorporate children's concerns into all relevant policies and strategies for environment and development at the local, regional and national levels, including those concerning allocation of and entitlement to natural resources, housing and recreation needs, and control of pollution and toxicity in both rural and urban areas.

International and regional organizations should cooperate and coordinate in the proposed areas. UNICEF should maintain cooperation and collaboration with other organizations of the United Nations, Governments and non-governmental organizations to develop programmes for children and programmes to mobilize children in the activities outlined above.

Finance and cost evaluation Financing requirements for most of the activities are included in estimates for other programmes.

Chapter 26 Recognizing and strengthening the role of indigenous people and their communities

Basis for action Indigenous people and their communities have an historical relationship with their lands and are generally descendants of the original inhabitants of such lands. In the context of this chapter the term "lands" is understood to include the environment of the areas which the people concerned traditionally occupy. Indigenous people and their communities represent a significant percentage of the global population. They have developed over many generations a holistic traditional scientific knowledge of their lands, natural resources and environment. Indigenous people and their communities shall enjoy the full measure of human rights and fundamental freedoms without hindrance or discrimination. Their ability to participate fully in sustainable development practices on their lands has tended to be limited as a result of factors of an economic, social and historical nature. In view of the interrelationship between the natural environment and its sustainable development and the cultural, social, economic and physical well-being of indigenous people, national and international efforts to implement environmentally sound and sustainable development should recognize, accommodate, promote and strengthen the role of indigenous people and their communities.

Some of the goals inherent in the objectives and activities of this programme area are already contained in such international legal instruments as the ILO Indigenous and Tribal Peoples Convention (No. 169) and are being incorporated into the draft universal declaration on indigenous rights, being prepared by the United Nations working group on indigenous populations. The International Year for the World's Indigenous People (1993), proclaimed by the General Assembly in its resolution 45/164 of 18 December 1990, presents a timely opportunity to mobilize further international technical and financial cooperation.

Objectives In full partnership with indigenous people and their communities, Governments and, where appropriate, intergovernmental organizations should aim at fulfilling the following objectives:
a Establishment of a process to empower indigenous people and their communities through measures that include:
i Adoption or strengthening of appropriate policies and/or legal instruments at the national level;
ii Recognition that the lands of indigenous people and their communities should be protected from activities that are environmentally unsound or that the indigenous people concerned consider to be socially and culturally inappropriate;
iii Recognition of their values, traditional knowledge and resource management practices with a view to promoting environmentally sound and sustainable development;
iv Recognition that traditional and direct dependence on renewable resources and ecosystems, including sustainable harvesting, continues to be essential to the cultural, economic and physical well-being of indigenous people and their communities;
v Development and strengthening of national dispute-resolution arrangements in relation to settlement of land and resource-management concerns;
vi Support for alternative environmentally sound means of production to ensure a range of choices on how to improve their quality of life so that they effectively participate in sustainable development;
vii Enhancement of capacity-building for indigenous communities, based on the adaptation and exchange of traditional experience, knowledge and resource-management practices, to ensure their sustainable development;
b Establishment, where appropriate, of arrangements to strengthen the active participation of indigenous people and their communities in the national formulation of policies, laws and programmes relating to resource management and other development processes that may affect them, and their initiation of proposals for such policies and programmes;
c Involvement of indigenous people and their communities at the national and local levels in resource management and conservation strategies and other relevant programmes established to support and review sustainable development strategies, such as those suggested in other programme areas of Agenda 21.

Activities Some indigenous people and their communities may require, in accordance with national legislation, greater control over their lands, self-management of their resources, participation in development decisions affecting them, including, where appropriate, participation in the establishment or management of protected areas. The following are some of the specific measures which Governments could take:
a Consider the ratification and application of existing international conventions relevant to indigenous people and their communities (where not yet done) and provide support for the adoption by the General Assembly of a declaration on indigenous rights;
b Adopt or strengthen appropriate policies and/or legal instruments that will protect indigenous intellectual and cultural property and the right to preserve customary and administrative systems and practices.

United Nations organizations and other international development and finance organizations and

Amazon. A Yanamami mother breastfeeds her child and a baby monkey. The ability of indigenous people and their communities to participate fully in sustainable development practices on their lands has tended to be restricted by economic, social and historical factors.

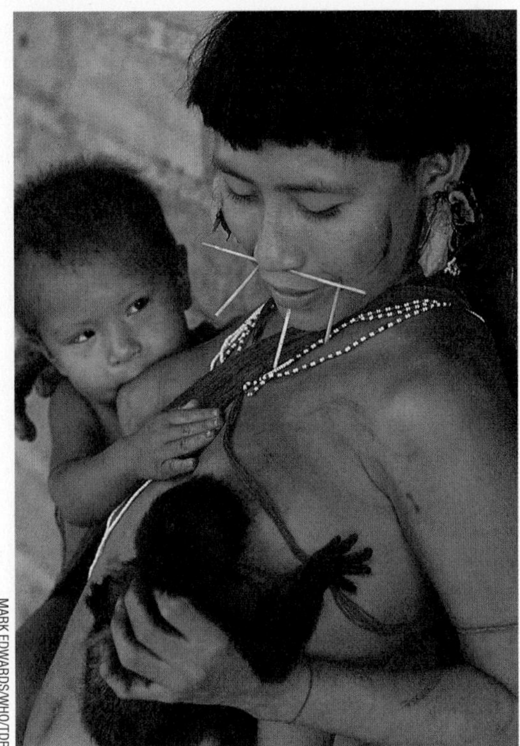

MARK EDWARDS/WHO/TDR

Governments should, drawing on the active participation of indigenous people and their communities, as appropriate, take the following measures, *inter alia*, to incorporate their values, views and knowledge, including the unique contribution of indigenous women, in resource management and other policies and programmes that may affect them:

a Appoint a special focal point within each international organization, and organize annual interorganizational coordination meetings in consultation with Governments and indigenous organizations, as appropriate, and develop a procedure within and between operational agencies for assisting Governments in ensuring the coherent and coordinated incorporation of the views of indigenous people in the design and implementation of policies and programmes. Under this procedure, indigenous people and their communities should be informed and consulted and allowed to participate in national decision-making, in particular regarding regional and international cooperative efforts. In addition, these policies and programmes should take fully into account strategies based on local indigenous initiatives;

b Provide technical and financial assistance for capacity-building programmes to support the sustainable self-development of indigenous people and their communities;

c Strengthen research and education programmes aimed at:

i Achieving a better understanding of indigenous people's knowledge and management experience related to the environment, and applying this to contemporary development challenges;

ii Increasing the efficiency of indigenous people's resource management systems, for example, by promoting the adaptation and dissemination of suitable technological innovations;

d Contribute to the endeavours of indigenous people and their communities in resource management and conservation strategies (such as those that may be developed under appropriate projects funded through the Global Environmental Facility and Tropical Forestry Action Plan) and other programme areas of Agenda 21, including programmes to collect, analyse and use data and other information in support of sustainable development projects.

Governments, in full partnership with indigenous people and their communities should, where appropriate:

a Develop or strengthen national arrangements to consult with indigenous people and their communities with a view to reflecting their needs and incorporating their values and traditional and other knowledge and practices in national policies and programmes in the field of natural resource management and conservation and other development programmes affecting them;

b Cooperate at the regional level, where appropriate, to address common indigenous issues with a view to recognizing and strengthening their participation in sustainable development.

Financing and cost evaluation $3 million from the international community on grant or concessional terms.

Chapter 27

Strengthening the role of non-governmental organisations: partners for sustainable development

Basis for action Non-governmental organizations play a vital role in the shaping and implementation of participatory democracy. Their credibility lies in the responsible and constructive role they play in society. Formal and informal organizations, as well as grassroots movements, should be recognized as partners in the implementation of Agenda 21. The nature of the independent role played by non-governmental organizations within a society calls for real participation; therefore, independence is a major attribute of non-governmental organizations and is the precondition of real participation.

One of the major challenges facing the world community as it seeks to replace unsustainable development patterns with environmentally sound and sustainable development is the need to activate a sense of common purpose on behalf of all sectors of society. The chances of forging such a sense of purpose will depend on the willingness of all sectors to participate in genuine social partnership and dialogue, while recognizing the independent roles, responsibilities and special capacities of each.

Non-governmental organizations, including those non-profit organizations representing groups addressed in the present section of Agenda 21, possess well-established and diverse experience, expertise and capacity in fields which will be of particular importance to the implementation and review of environmentally sound and socially responsible sustainable development, as envisaged throughout Agenda 21. The community of non-governmental organizations, therefore, offers a global network that should be tapped, enabled and strengthened in support of efforts to achieve these common goals.

To ensure that the full potential contribution of non-governmental organizations is realized, the fullest possible communication and cooperation between international organizations, national and local governments and non-governmental organizations should be promoted in institutions mandated, and programmes designed to carry out Agenda 21. Non-governmental organizations will also need to foster cooperation and communication among themselves to reinforce their effectiveness as actors in the implementation of sustainable development.

Objectives Society, Governments and international bodies should develop mechanisms to allow non-governmental organizations to play their partnership role responsibly and effectively in the process of

environmentally sound and sustainable development.

With a view to strengthening the role of non-governmental organizations as social partners, the United Nations system and Governments should initiate a process, in consultation with non-governmental organizations, to review formal procedures and mechanisms for the involvement of these organizations at all levels from policy-making and decision-making to implementation.

By 1995, a mutually productive dialogue should be established at the national level between all Governments and non-governmental organizations and their self-organized networks to recognize and strengthen their respective roles in implementing environmentally sound and sustainable development.

Governments and international bodies should promote and allow the participation of non-governmental organizations in the conception, establishment and evaluation of official mechanisms and formal procedures designed to review the implementation of Agenda 21 at all levels.

Activities The United Nations system, including international finance and development agencies, and all intergovernmental organizations and forums should, in consultation with non-governmental organizations, take measures to:

a Review and report on ways of enhancing existing procedures and mechanisms by which non-governmental organizations contribute to policy design, decision-making, implementation and evaluation at the individual agency level, in inter-agency discussions and in United Nations conferences;

b On the basis of subparagraph (a) above, enhance existing or, where they do not exist, establish, mechanisms and procedures within each agency to draw on the expertise and views of non-governmental organizations in policy and programme design, implementation and evaluation;

c Review levels of financial and administrative support for non-governmental organizations and the extent and effectiveness of their involvement in project and programme implementation, with a view to augmenting their role as social partners;

d Design open and effective means of achieving theparticipation of non-governmental organizations in the processes established to review and evaluate the implementation of Agenda 21 at all levels;

e Promote and allow non-governmental organizations and their self-organized networks to contribute to the review and evaluation of policies and programmes designed to implement Agenda 21, including support for developing country non-governmental organizations and their self-organized networks;

f Take into account the findings of non-governmental review systems and evaluation processes in relevant reports of the Secretary-General to the General Assembly, and of all pertinent United Nations organizations and other intergovernmental organizations and forums concerning implementation of Agenda 21, in accordance with the review process for Agenda 21;

g Provide access for non-governmental organizations to accurate and timely data and information to promote the effectiveness of their programmes and activities and their roles in support of sustainable development.

Governments should take measures to:

a Establish or enhance an existing dialogue with non-governmental organizations and their self-organized networks representing various sectors, which could serve to: (i) consider the rights and responsibilities of these organizations; (ii) efficiently channel integrated non-governmental inputs to the governmental policy development process; and (iii) facilitate non-governmental coordination in implementing national policies at the programme level;

b Encourage and enable partnership and dialogue between local non-governmental organizations and local authorities in activities aimed at sustainable development;

c Involve non-governmental organizations in national mechanisms or procedures established to carry out Agenda 21, making the best use of their particular capacities, especially in the fields of education, poverty alleviation and environmental protection and rehabilitation;

d Take into account the findings of non-governmental monitoring and review mechanisms in the design and evaluation of policies concerning the implementation of Agenda 21 at all levels;

e Review government education systems to identify ways to include and expand the involvement of non-governmental organizations in the field of formal and informal education and of public awareness;

f Make available and accessible to non-governmental organizations the data and information necessary for their effective contribution to research and to the design, implementation and evaluation of programmes.

Financing and cost evaluation Depending on the outcome of review processes and the evolution of views as to how best to build partnership and dialogue between official organizations and groups of non-governmental organizations, relatively limited but unpredictable, costs will be involved at the international and national levels in enhancing consultative procedures and mechanisms. Non-governmental organizations will also require additional funding in support of their establishment of, improvement of or contributions to Agenda 21 monitoring systems. These costs will be significant but cannot be reliably estimated on the basis of existing information.

The Global Forum, organised alongside the Earth Summit in Rio, featured thousands of non-governmental organisations. Their contribution to the awareness of environmental and development issues has been immense.

Chapter 28

Local authorities' initiatives in support of Agenda 21

Basis for action Because so many of the problems and solutions being addressed by Agenda 21 have their roots in local activities, the participation and cooperation of local authorities will be a determining factor in fulfilling its objectives. Local authorities construct, operate and maintain economic,social and environmental infrastructure, oversee planning processes, establish local environmental policies and regulations, and assist in implementing national and subnational environmental policies. As the level of governance closest to the people, they play a vital role in educating, mobilizing and responding to the public to promote sustainable development.

Objectives

a By 1996, most local authorities in each country should have undertaken a consultative process with their populations and achieved a consensus on "a local Agenda 21" for the community;
b By 1993, the international community should have initiated a consultative process aimed at increasing cooperation between local authorities;
c By 1994, representatives of associations of cities and other local authorities should have increased levels of cooperation and coordination with the goal of enhancing the exchange of information and experience among local authorities;
d All local authorities in each country should be encouraged to implement and monitor programmes which aim at ensuring that women and youth are represented in decision-making, planning and implementation processes.

Activities Each local authority should enter into a dialogue with its citizens, local organizations and private enterprises and adopt "a local Agenda 21". Through consultation and consensus-building, local authorities would learn from citizens and from local, civic, community, business and industrial organizations and acquire the information needed for formulating the best strategies. The process of consultation would increase household awareness of sustainable development issues. Local authority programmes, policies, laws and regulations to achieve Agenda 21 objectives would be assessed and modified, based on local programmes adopted. Strategies could also be used in supporting proposals for local, national, regional and international funding.

Partnerships should be fostered among relevant organs and organizations such as UNDP, the United Nations Centre for Human Settlements (Habitat) and UNEP, the World Bank, regional banks, the International Union of Local Authorities, the World Association of the Major Metropolises, Summit of Great Cities of the World, the United Towns Organization and other relevant partners, with a view to mobilizing increased international support for local authority programmes. An important goal would be to support, extend and improve existing institutions working in the field of local authority capacity-building and local environment management. For this purpose:
a Habitat and other relevant organs and organizations of the United Nations system are called upon to strengthen services in collecting information on strategies of local authorities, in particular for those that need international support;
b Periodic consultations involving both international partners and developing countries could review strategies and consider how such international support could best be mobilized. Such a sectoral consultation would complement concurrent country-focused consultations, such as those taking place in consultative groups and round tables.

Representatives of associations of local authorities are encouraged to establish processes to increase the exchange of information, experience and mutual technical assistance among local authorities.

Financing and cost evaluation It is recommended that all parties reassess funding needs in this area. Estimated average total annual cost about $1 million on grant or concessional terms.

Chapter 29

Strengthening the role of workers and their trade unions

Basis for action Efforts to implement sustainable development will involve adjustments and opportunities at the national and enterprise levels, with workers foremost among those concerned. As their representatives, trade unions are vital actors in facilitating the achievement of sustainable development in view of their experience in addressing industrial change, the extremely high priority they give to protection of the working environment and the related natural environment, and their promotion of socially responsible and economic development. The existing network of collaboration among trade unions and their extensive membership provide important channels through which the concepts and practices of sustainable development can be supported. The established principles of tripartism provide a basis for strengthened collaboration between workers and their representatives, Governments and employers in the implementation of sustainable development.

Objectives The overall objective is poverty alleviation and full and sustainable employment, which contribute to safe, clean and healthy environments – the working environment, the community and the physical environment. Workers should be full participants in the implementation and evaluation of activities related to Agenda 21.

To that end the following objectives are proposed for accomplishment by the year 2000:
a To promote ratification of relevant conventions of ILO and the enactment of legislation in support of those conventions;
b To establish bipartite and tripartite mechanisms on safety, health and sustainable development;
c To increase the number of environmental collective agreements aimed at achieving sustainable development;
d To reduce occupational accidents, injuries and diseases according to recognized statistical reporting procedures;
e To increase the provision of workers' education, training and retraining, particularly in the area of occupational health and safety and environment.

Activities

A *Promoting freedom of association*
For workers and their trade unions to play a full and informed role in support of sustainable development, Governments and employers should promote the rights of individual workers to freedom of association and the protection of the right to organize as laid down in ILO conventions. Governments should consider

Amazon. Rubber Tapper Union members vote in a new president. In view of their experience in addressing industrial change, trade unions are vital actors in facilitating the achievement of sustainable development.

ratifying and implementing those conventions, if they have not already done so.

B *Strengthening participation and consultation*
Governments, business and industry should promote the active participation of workers and their trade unions in decisions on the design, implementation and evaluation of national and international policies and programmes on environment and development, including employment policies, industrial strategies, labour adjustment programmes and technology transfers.

Trade unions, employers and Governments should cooperate to ensure that the concept of sustainable development is equitably implemented.

Joint (employer/worker) or tripartite (employer/worker/Government) collaborative mechanisms at the workplace, community and national levels should be established to deal with safety, health and environment, including special reference to the rights and status of women in the workplace.

Governments and employers should ensure that workers and their representatives are provided with all relevant information to enable effective participation in these decision-making processes.

Trade unions should continue to define, develop and promote policies on all aspects of sustainable development.

Trade unions and employers should establish the framework for a joint environmental policy, and set priorities to improve the working environment and the overall environmental performance of enterprise.

Trade unions should:

a Seek to ensure that workers are able to participate in environmental audits at the workplace and in environmental impact assessments;

b Participate in environment and development activities within the local community and promote joint action on potential problems of common concern;

c Play an active role in the sustainable development activities of international and regional organizations, particularly within the United Nations system.

C *Provide adequate training*
Workers and their representatives should have access to adequate training to augment environmental awareness, ensure their safety and health, and improve their economic and social welfare. Such training should ensure that the necessary skills are available to promote sustainable livelihoods and improve the working environment. Trade unions, employers, Governments and international agencies should cooperate in assessing training needs within their respective spheres of activity. Workers and their representatives should be involved in the design and implementation of worker training programmes conducted by employers and Governments.

Financial and cost evaluation $300 million from the international community on grant or concessional terms.

Chapter 30 Strengthening the role of business and industry

Business and industry, including transnational corporations, play a crucial role in the social and economic development of a country. A stable policy regime enables and encourages business and industry to operate responsibly and efficiently and to implement longer-term policies. Increasing prosperity, a major goal of the development process, is contributed primarily by the activities of business and industry. Business enterprises, large and small, formal and informal, provide major trading, employment and livelihood opportunities. Business opportunities available to women are contributing towards their professional development, strengthening their economic role and transforming social systems. Business and industry, including transnational corporations, and their representative organizations should be full participants in the implementation and evaluation of activities related to Agenda 21.

Through more efficient production processes, preventive strategies, cleaner production technologies and procedures throughout the product life cycle, hence minimizing or avoiding wastes, the policies and operations of business and industry, including transnational corporations, can play a major role in reducing impacts on resource use and the environment. Technological innovations, development, applications, transfer and the more comprehensive aspects of partnership and cooperation are to a very large extent within the province of business and industry.

Business and industry, including transnational corporations, should recognize environmental management as among the highest corporate priorities and as a key determinant to sustainable development. Some enlightened leaders of enterprises are already

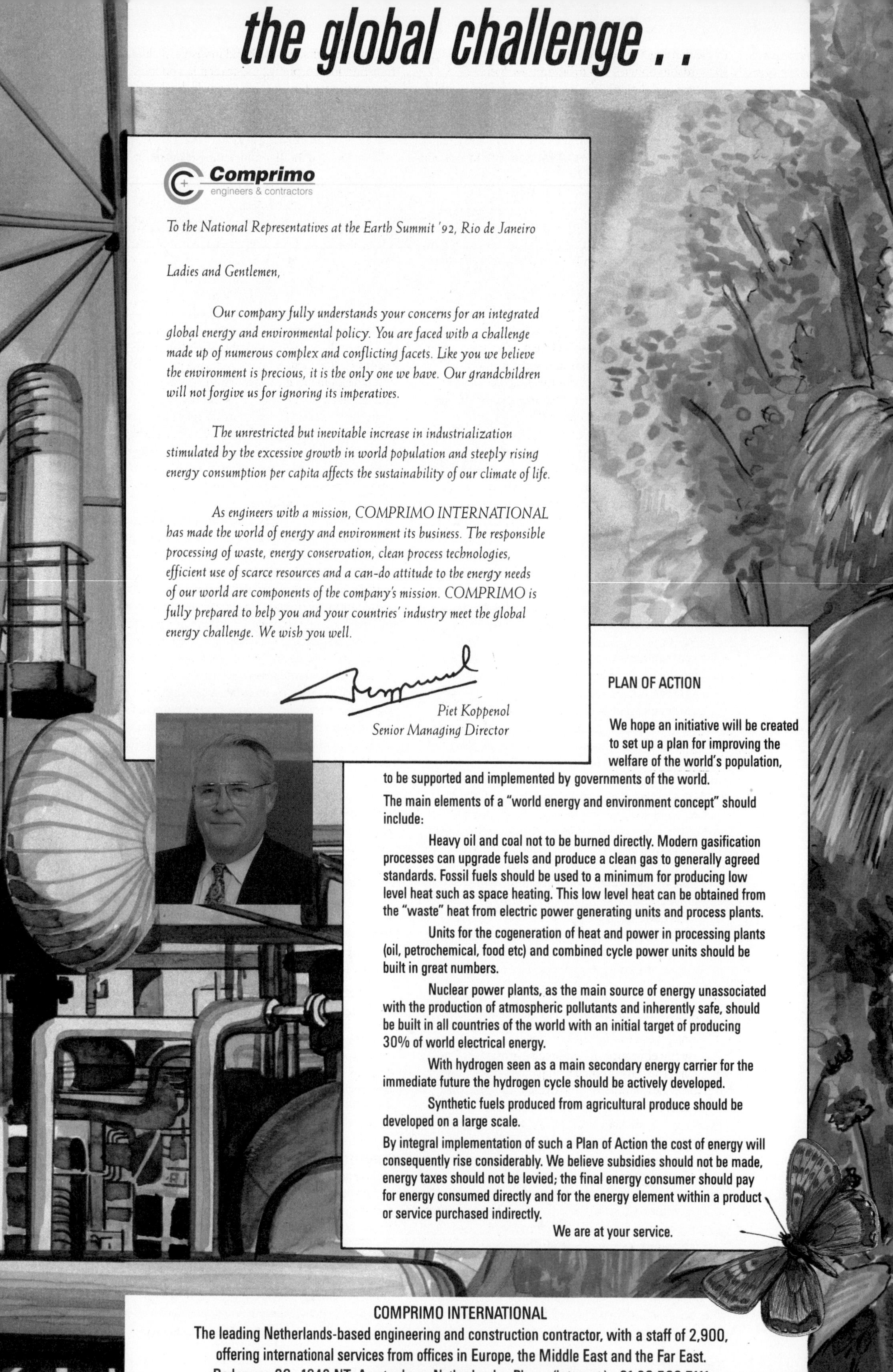
the global challenge . .
Comprimo
engineers & contractors
To the National Representatives at the Earth Summit '92, Rio de Janeiro
Ladies and Gentlemen,
Our company fully understands your concerns for an integrated global energy and environmental policy. You are faced with a challenge made up of numerous complex and conflicting facets. Like you we believe the environment is precious, it is the only one we have. Our grandchildren will not forgive us for ignoring its imperatives.
The unrestricted but inevitable increase in industrialization stimulated by the excessive growth in world population and steeply rising energy consumption per capita affects the sustainability of our climate of life.
As engineers with a mission, COMPRIMO INTERNATIONAL has made the world of energy and environment its business. The responsible processing of waste, energy conservation, clean process technologies, efficient use of scarce resources and a can-do attitude to the energy needs of our world are components of the company's mission. COMPRIMO is fully prepared to help you and your countries' industry meet the global energy challenge. We wish you well.
Piet Koppenol
Senior Managing Director
PLAN OF ACTION
We hope an initiative will be created to set up a plan for improving the welfare of the world's population, to be supported and implemented by governments of the world.
The main elements of a "world energy and environment concept" should include:
Heavy oil and coal not to be burned directly. Modern gasification processes can upgrade fuels and produce a clean gas to generally agreed standards. Fossil fuels should be used to a minimum for producing low level heat such as space heating. This low level heat can be obtained from the "waste" heat from electric power generating units and process plants.
Units for the cogeneration of heat and power in processing plants (oil, petrochemical, food etc) and combined cycle power units should be built in great numbers.
Nuclear power plants, as the main source of energy unassociated with the production of atmospheric pollutants and inherently safe, should be built in all countries of the world with an initial target of producing 30% of world electrical energy.
With hydrogen seen as a main secondary energy carrier for the immediate future the hydrogen cycle should be actively developed.
Synthetic fuels produced from agricultural produce should be developed on a large scale.
By integral implementation of such a Plan of Action the cost of energy will consequently rise considerably. We believe subsidies should not be made, energy taxes should not be levied; the final energy consumer should pay for energy consumed directly and for the energy element within a product or service purchased indirectly.
We are at your service.
COMPRIMO INTERNATIONAL
The leading Netherlands-based engineering and construction contractor, with a staff of 2,900, offering international services from offices in Europe, the Middle East and the Far East.
Radarweg 60 1043 NT Amsterdam Netherlands Phone (internat.) +31 20 580 7111

The Rio Conference was a milestone in human history. The declaration on environment and development expresses the responsiblity of all countries to take their share in achieving a sustainable world. The preparation of the declaration, Agenda 21, the conventions on climate change and biological diversity made clear that the problems to be solved will have a significant impact on patterns of production and consumption of the industrialized countries. Opportunities should be created; possibilities for the developing countries to reach a better quality of life for their inhabitants in a sustainable world. No time should be lost after Rio in implenting Agenda 21 and securing a prompt start to the two conventions.
Mr Ruud Lubbers
Prime Minister
The Netherlands

implementing "responsible care" and product stewardship policies and programmes, fostering openness and dialogue with employees and the public and carrying out environmental audits and assessments of compliance. These leaders in business and industry, including transnational corporations, are increasingly taking voluntary initiatives, promoting and implementing self-regulations and greater responsibilities in ensuring their activities have minimal impacts on human health and the environment. The regulatory regimes introduced in many countries and the growing consciousness of consumers and the general public and enlightened leaders of business and industry, including transnational corporations, have all contributed to this. A positive contribution of business and industry, including transnational corporations, to sustainable development can increasingly be achieved by using economic instruments such as free market mechanisms in which the prices of goods and services should increasingly reflect the environmental costs of their input, production, use, recycling and disposal subject to country-specific conditions.

The improvement of production systems through technologies and processes that utilize resources more efficiently and at the same time produce less wastes – achieving more with less – is an important pathway towards sustainability for business and industry. Similarly, facilitating and encouraging inventiveness, competitiveness and voluntary initiatives are necessary for stimulating more varied, efficient and effective options. To address these major requirements and strengthen further the role of business and industry, including transnational corporations, the following two programmes are proposed.

A Promoting cleaner production

Basis for action There is increasing recognition that production, technology and management that use resources inefficiently form residues that are not reused, discharge wastes that have adverse impacts on human health and the environment and manufacture products that when used have further impacts and are difficult to recycle, need to be replaced with technologies, good engineering and management practices and know-how that would minimize waste throughout the product life cycle. The concept of cleaner production implies striving for optimal efficiencies at every stage of the product life cycle. A result would be the improvement of the overall competitiveness of the enterprise. The need for a transition towards cleaner production policies was recognized at the UNIDO-organized Ministerial-level Conference on Ecologically Sustainable Industrial Development, held at Copenhagen in October 1991.

Objectives Governments, business and industry, including transnational corporations, should aim to increase the efficiency of resource utilization, including increasing the reuse and recycling of residues, and to reduce the quantity of waste discharge per unit of economic output.

Activities Governments, business and industry, including transnational corporations, should strengthen partnerships to implement the principles and criteria for sustainable development.

Governments should identify and implement an appropriate mix of economic instruments and normative measures such as laws, legislations and standards, in consultation with business and industry, including transnational corporations, that will promote the use of cleaner production, with special consideration for small and medium-sized enterprises. Voluntary private initiatives should also be encouraged.

Governments, business and industry, including transnational corporations, academia and international organizations, should work towards the development and implementation of concepts and methodologies for the internalization of environmental costs into accounting and pricing mechanisms.

Business and industry, including transnational corporations, should be encouraged:

a To report annually on their environmental records, as well as on their use of energy and natural resources;

b To adopt and report on the implementation of codes of conduct promoting best environmental practice, such as the International Chamber of Commerce's Business Charter on Sustainable Development and the chemical industry's responsible care initiative.

Governments should promote technological and know-how cooperation between enterprises, encompassing identification, assessment, research and development, management marketing and application of cleaner production.

Industry should incorporate cleaner production policies in its operations and investments, taking also into account its influence on suppliers and consumers.

Industry and business associations should cooperate with workers and trade unions to continuously improve the knowledge and skills for implementing sustainable development operations.

Industry and business associations should encourage individual companies to undertake programmes for improved environmental awareness and responsibility at all levels to make these enterprises dedicated to the task of improving environmental performance based on internationally accepted management practices.

International organizations should increase education, training and awareness activities relating to cleaner production, in collaboration with industry, academia and relevant national and local authorities.

International and non-governmental organizations, including trade and scientific associations, should strengthen cleaner production information dissemination by expanding existing databases such as the UNEP, International Cleaner Production Clearing House (ICPIC), the UNIDO Industrial and Technological Information Bank (INTIB) and the ICC/IEB, as well as forge networking of national and international information systems.

B Promoting responsible entrepreneurship

Basis for action Entrepreneurship is one of the most important driving forces for innovations, increasing market efficiencies and responding to challenges and opportunities. Small and medium-sized entrepreneurs, in particular, play a very important role in the social and economic development of a country. Often, they are the major means for rural development, increasing off-farm employment and providing the transitional means for improving the livelihoods of women. Responsible entrepreneurship can play a major role in improving the efficiency of resource use, reducing risks and hazards, minimizing wastes and safeguarding environmental qualities.

Objectives

a To encourage the concept of stewardship in the management and utilization of natural resources by entrepreneurs;

b To increase the number of entrepreneurs engaged in enterprises that subscribe to and implement sustainable development policies.

Activities Governments should encourage the establishment and operations of sustainably managed enterprises. The mix would include regulatory

Alcoa of Australia mining operation. Once bauxite has been extracted land is reshaped to blend in with surrounding forest. Contour banks, dykes and waterways are built to control run-off and soil erosion. Soil is prepared and seeded. The final result is carefully integrated forest with no scars from mining.

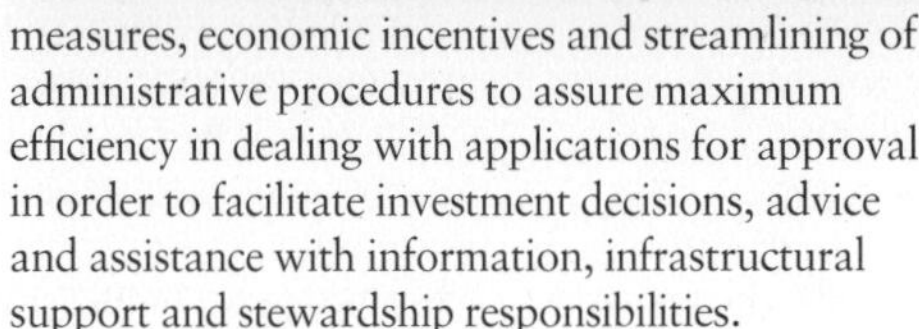

measures, economic incentives and streamlining of administrative procedures to assure maximum efficiency in dealing with applications for approval in order to facilitate investment decisions, advice and assistance with information, infrastructural support and stewardship responsibilities.

Governments should encourage, in cooperation with the private sector, the establishment of venture capital funds for sustainable development projects and programmes.

In collaboration with business, industry, academia and international organizations, Governments should support training in the environmental aspects of enterprise management. Attention should also be directed towards apprenticeship schemes for youth.

Business and industry, including transnational corporations, should be encouraged to establish world-wide corporate policies on sustainable development, arrange for environmentally sound technologies to be available to affiliates owned substantially by their parent company in developing countries without extra external charges, encourage overseas affiliates to modify procedures in order to reflect local ecological conditions and share experiences with local authorities, Governments and international organizations.

Large business and industry, including transnational corporations, should consider establishing partnership schemes with small and medium-sized enterprises to help facilitate the exchange of experience in managerial skills, market development and technological know-how, where appropriate, with the assistance of international organizations.

Business and industry should establish national councils for sustainable development and help promote entrepreneurship in the formal and informal sectors. The inclusion of women entrepreneurs should be facilitated.

Business and industry, including transnational corporations, should increase research and development of environmentally sound technologies and environmental management systems, in collaboration with academia and the scientific/engineering establishments, drawing upon indigenous knowledge, where appropriate.

Business and industry, including transnational corporations, should ensure responsible and ethical management of products and processes from the point of view of health, safety and environmental aspects. Towards this end, business and industry should increase self-regulation, guided by appropriate codes, charters and initiatives integrated into all elements of business planning and decision-making, and fostering openness and dialogue with employees and the public.

Multilateral and bilateral financial aid institutions should continue to encourage and support small- and medium-scale entrepreneurs engaged in sustainable development activities.

United Nations organizations and agencies should improve mechanisms for business and industry inputs, policy and strategy formulation processes, to ensure that environmental aspects are strengthened in foreign investment.

International organizations should increase support for research and development on improving the technological and managerial requirements for sustainable development, in particular for small and medium-sized enterprises in developing countries.

Financing and cost evaluation The activities included under this programme area are mostly changes in the orientation of existing activities and additional costs are not expected to be significant. The cost of activities by Governments and international organizations are already included in other programmes.

Chapter 31

Scientific and technological community

The present chapter focuses on how to enable the scientific and technological community, which includes, among others, engineers, architects, industrial designers, urban planners and other professionals and policy makers, to make a more open and effective contribution to the decision-making processes concerning environment and development. It is important that the role of science and technology in human affairs be more widely known and better understood, both by decision makers who help determine public policy and by the general public. The cooperative relationship existing between the scientific and technological community and the general public should be extended and deepened into a full partnership. Improved communication and cooperation between the scientific and technological community and decision makers will facilitate greater use of scientific and technical information and knowledge in policies and programme implementation. Decision makers should create more favourable conditions for improving training and independent research in sustainable development. Existing multidisciplinary approaches will have to be strengthened and more interdisciplinary studies developed between the scientific and technological community and policy makers and with the general public to provide leadership and practical know-how to the concept of sustainable development. The public should be assisted in communicating their sentiments to the scientific and technological community concerning how science and technology might be better managed to affect their lives in a beneficial way. By the same token, the independence of the scientific and technological community to investigate and publish without restriction and to exchange their findings freely must be assured. The adoption and implementation of ethical principles and codes of practice for the scientific and technological community that are internationally accepted could enhance professionalism and may improve and hasten recognition of the value of its contributions to environment and development, recognizing the continuing evolution and uncertainty of scientific knowledge.

A Improving communication and cooperation among the scientific and technological community and decision makers and the public

Basis for action The scientific and technological community and policy makers should increase their interaction in order to implement strategies for sustainable development on the basis of the best available knowledge. This implies that decision makers should provide the necessary framework for rigorous research and for full and open communication of the findings of the scientific and technological community, and develop with it ways in which research results and the concerns stemming from the findings can be communicated to decision-making bodies so as to better link scientific and technical knowledge with strategic policy and programme formulation. At the same time, this dialogue would assist the scientific and technological community in developing priorities for research and proposing actions for constructive solutions.

Objectives

a To extend and open up the decision-making process and broaden the range of developmental and environmental issues where cooperation at all levels between the scientific and technological community and decision makers can take place;

b To improve the exchange of knowledge and concerns between the scientific and technological community and the general public in order to enable policies and programmes to be better formulated, understood and supported.

Activities Governments should undertake the following activities:

a Review how national scientific and technological activities could be more responsive to sustainable development needs as part of an overall effort to strengthen national research and development systems, including through strengthening and widening the membership of national scientific and technological advisory councils, organizations and committees to assure that:

i The full range of national needs for scientific and technological programmes are communicated to Governments and the public;

ii The various strands of public opinion are represented;

b Promote regional cooperative mechanisms to address regional needs for sustainable development. Such regional cooperative mechanisms could be facilitated through public/private partnerships and provide support to Governments, industry, non-governmental educational institutions and other domestic and international organizations, and by strengthening global professional networks;

c Improve and expand scientific and technical inputs through appropriate mechanisms to intergovernmental consultative, cooperative and negotiating processes towards international and regional agreements;

d Strengthen science and technology advice to the highest levels of the United Nations, and other international institutions, in order to ensure the inclusion of science and technology know-how in sustainable development policies and strategies;

e Improve and strengthen programmes for disseminating research results of universities and research institutions. This requires recognition of and greater support to the scientists, technologists and teachers who are engaged in communicating and interpreting scientific and technological information to policy makers, professionals in other fields and the general public. Such support should focus on the transfer of skills and the transfer and adaptation of planning techniques. This requires full and open sharing of data and information among scientists and decision makers. The publication of national scientific research reports and technical reports that are understandable and relevant to local sustainable development needs would also improve the interface between science and decision-making, as well as the implementation of scientific results;

f Improve links between the official and independent research sector and industry so that research may become an important element of industrial strategy;

g Promote and strengthen the role of women as full partners in the science and technology disciplines;

h Develop and implement information technologies to enhance the dissemination of information for sustainable development.

Financing and cost evaluation \$15 million from the international community on grant or concessional terms.

B Promoting codes of practice and guidelines related to science and technology

Basis for action Scientists and technologists have a special set of responsibilities which belong to them both as inheritors of a tradition and as professionals and members of disciplines devoted to the search for

A research scientist studies eucalyptus clones. National research and development systems need to be reviewed and strengthened to provide a more positive contribution to sustainable development.

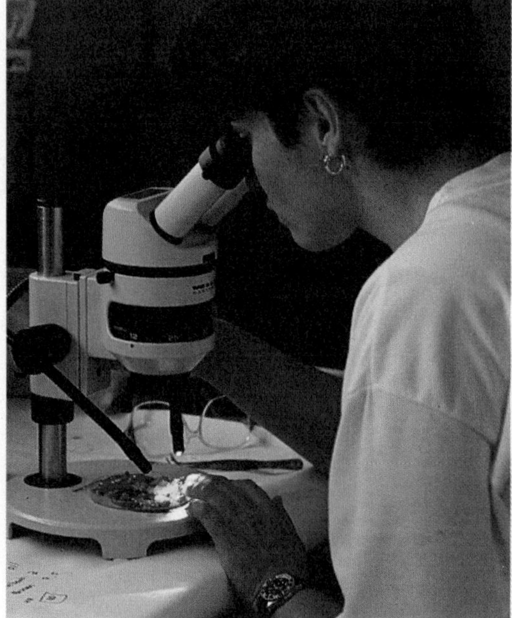

knowledge and to the need to protect the biosphere in the context of sustainable development.

Increased ethical awareness in environmental and developmental decision-making should help to place appropriate priorities for the maintenance and enhancement of life-support systems for their own sake, and in so doing ensure that the functioning of viable natural processes is properly valued by present and future societies. Therefore, a strengthening of the codes of practice and guidelines for the scientific and technological community would increase environmental awareness and contribute to sustainable development. It would build up the level of esteem and regard for the scientific and technological community and facilitate the "accountability" of science and technology.

Objectives The objective should be to develop, improve and promote international acceptance of codes of practice and guidelines relating to science and technology in which the integrity of life-support systems is comprehensively accounted for and where the important role of science and technology in reconciling the needs of environment and development is accepted. To be effective in the decision-making process, such principles, codes of practice and guidelines must not only be agreed upon by the scientific and technological community, but also recognized by the society as a whole.

Activities

a Strengthening national and international cooperation, including the non-governmental sector, to develop codes of practice and guidelines regarding environmentally sound and sustainable development, taking into account the Rio Declaration and existing codes of practice and guidelines;

b Strengthening and establishing national advisory groups on environmental and developmental ethics, in order to develop a common value framework between the scientific and technological community and society as a whole, and promote continuous dialogue;

c Extending education and training in developmental and environmental ethical issues to integrate such objectives into education curricula and research priorities;

d Reviewing and amending relevant national and international environment and development legal instruments to ensure appropriate codes of practice and guidelines are incorporated into such regulatory machinery.

Financing and cost evaluation $5 million from the international community on grant or concessional terms.

Section III

Chapter 32

Strengthening the role of farmers

All references in this chapter to "farmers" and "farming" include all rural people who derive their livelihood from activities such as farming, fishing and forest harvesting.

Basis for action Agriculture occupies one third of the land surface of the Earth, and is the central activity for much of the world's population. Rural activities take place in close contact with nature, adding value to it by producing renewable resources, while at the same time becoming vulnerable to overexploitation and improper management.

The rural household, indigenous people and their communities, and the family farmer, a substantial number of whom are women, have been the stewards of much of the Earth's resources. Farmers must conserve their physical environment as they depend on it for their sustenance. Over the past 20 years there has been impressive increase in aggregate agricultural production. Yet, in some regions, this increase has been outstripped by population growth or international debt or falling commodity prices. Further, the natural resources that sustain farming activity need proper care, and there is a growing concern about the sustainability of agricultural production systems.

A farmer-centred approach is the key to the attainment of sustainability in both developed and developing countries and many of the programme areas in Agenda 21 address this objective. A significant number of the rural population in developing countries depend primarily upon small-scale, subsistence-oriented agriculture based on family labour. However, they have limited access to resources, technology, alternative livelihood and means of production. As a result, they are engaged in the overexploitation of natural resources, including marginal lands.

The sustainable development of people in marginal and fragile ecosystems is also addressed in Agenda 21. The key to the successful implementation of these programmes lies in the motivation and attitudes of individual farmers and government policies that would provide incentives to farmers to manage their natural resources efficiently and in a sustainable way. Farmers, particularly women, face a high degree of economic, legal and institutional uncertainties when investing in their land and other resources. The decentralization of decision-making towards local and community organizations is the key in changing people's behaviour and implementing sustainable farming strategies. This programme area deals with activities which can contribute to this end.

Objectives

a To encourage a decentralized decision-making process through the creation and strengthening of local and village organizations that would delegate power and responsibility to primary users of natural resources;

b To support and enhance the legal capacity of women and vulnerable groups with regard to access, use and tenure of land;

c To promote and encourage sustainable farming practices and technologies;

d To introduce or strengthen policies that would encourage self-sufficiency in low-input and low-energy technologies, including indigenous practices, and pricing mechanisms that internalize environmental costs;

Small scale and traditional farming in Bangladesh and Indonesia. Agriculture occupies one third of the land surface of the Earth and is the central activity for much of the world's population.

e To develop a policy framework that provides incentives and motivation among farmers for sustainable and efficient farming practices;
f To enhance the participation of farmers, men and women, in the design and implementation of policies directed towards these ends, through their representative organizations.

Management-related activities Governments should:
a Ensure the implementation of the programmes on sustainable livelihoods, agriculture and rural development, managing fragile ecosystems, water use in agriculture, and integrated management of natural resources;
b Promote pricing mechanisms, trade policies, fiscal incentives and other policy instruments that positively affect individual farmer's decisions about an efficient and sustainable use of natural resources, and take full account of the impact of these decisions on household food security, farm incomes, employment and the environment;
c Involve farmers and their representative organizations in the formulation of policy;
d Protect, recognize and formalize women's access to tenure and use of land, as well as rights to land, access to credit, technology, inputs and training;
e Support the formation of farmers' organizations by providing adequate legal and social conditions.

Support for farmers' organizations could be arranged as follows:
a National and international research centres should cooperate with farmers' organizations in developing location-specific environment-friendly farming techniques;
b Governments, multilateral and bilateral development agencies and non-governmental organizations should collaborate with farmers' organizations in formulating agricultural development projects to specific agro-ecological zones.

Financing and cost evaluation The financing needed for this programme area is estimated in chapter 14 "Promoting sustainable agriculture and rural development", particularly in the programme area "Ensuring people's participation and promoting human resource development". The costs shown under chapters 3, 12 and 13 on combating poverty, combating desertification and drought, and sustainable mountain development are also relevant for this programme area.

Means of Implementation

Section IV

Chapter 33

Financial resources and mechanisms

The General Assembly, in resolution 44/228 of 22 December 1989, *inter alia*, decided that the Conference on Environment and Development should:

a Identify ways and means of providing new and additional financial resources, particularly to developing countries, for environmentally sound development programmes and projects in accordance with national development objectives, priorities and plans and to consider ways of effectively monitoring the provision of such new and additional financial resources, particularly to developing countries, so as to enable the international community to take further appropriate action on the basis of accurate and reliable data;

b Identify ways and means of providing additional financial resources for measures directed towards solving major environmental problems of global concern and especially of supporting those countries, in particular developing countries, for which the implementation of such measures would entail a special or abnormal burden, owing, in particular, to their lack of financial resources, expertise or technical capacity;

c Consider various funding mechanisms, including voluntary ones, and to examine the possibility of a special international fund and other innovative approaches, with a view to ensuring, on a favourable basis, the most effective and expeditious transfer of environmentally sound technologies to developing countries;

d Quantify the financial requirements for the successful implementation of Conference decisions and recommendations and identify possible sources, including innovative ones, of additional resources.

This chapter deals with the financing of the implementation of Agenda 21, which reflects a global consensus integrating environmental considerations into an accelerated development process. For each of the other chapters, the secretariat of the Conference has provided indicative estimates of the total costs of implementation for developing countries and the requirements for grant or other concessional financing needed from the international community. These describe the need for a substantially increased effort both by countries themselves and by the international community.

Basis for action Economic growth, social development and poverty eradication are the first and overriding priorities in developing countries and are themselves essential to meeting national and global sustainability objectives. In light of the global benefits to be realized by the implementation of Agenda 21 as a whole, the provision to developing countries of effective means, *inter alia*, financial resources and technology, without which it will be difficult for them to fully implement their commitments, will serve the common interests of developed and developing countries and of humankind in general, including future generations.

The cost of inaction could outweigh the financial costs of implementing Agenda 21. Inaction will narrow the choices of future generations.

For dealing with environmental issues special efforts will be required. Global and local environmental issues are interrelated. The United Nations Framework Convention on Climate Change and the Convention on Biological Diversity address two of the most important global issues.

Economic conditions, both domestic and international, that encourage free trade and access to markets will help make economic growth and environmental protection mutually supportive for all countries, particularly for developing countries and countries undergoing the process of transition to a market economy (see chapter 2 for a fuller discussion of these issues).

International cooperation for sustainable development should also be strengthened in order to support and complement the efforts of developing countries, particularly the least developed countries.

All countries should assess how to translate Agenda 21 into national policies and programmes through a process that will integrate environment and development considerations. National and local priorities should be established by means that include public participation and community involvement, promoting equal opportunity for men and women.

For an evolving partnership among all countries of the world, including, in particular, between developed and developing countries, sustainable development strategies and enhanced and predictable levels of funding in support of longer term objectives are required. For that purpose, developing countries should articulate their own priority actions and needs for support and developed countries should commit themselves to addressing these priorities. In this respect, consultative groups and roundtables and other nationally based mechanisms can play a facilitative role.

The implementation of the huge sustainable development programmes of Agenda 21 will require the provision to developing countries of substantial

GRUPO MEXICO
NON FERROUS METALS
" Preservar el medio ambiente sin detener el progreso "
Design: ALFREDO TELLO T.
Photo: ©1991 MARIO MUTSCHLECHNER

Climate change, biodiversity, water scarcity and pollutants no longer recognise borders. International cooperation, access to financial resources and technology, to markets and to clean production technologies are key aspects of change. Mexico allocates about one per cent of its annual national product to environmental restoration and has created several ecological reserves to protect Mexico's biodiversity, one of the four richest on the planet. We recognise our serious environmental problems, but we are committed to a future of clean growth. We must build a new future conciliating justice and the environment as conceived by the ancient indigenous peoples of our country. We will make it reality, for our children and the children of our children.
Carlos Salinas de Cortari
President
Mexico

new and additional financial resources. Grant or concessional financing should be provided according to sound and equitable criteria and indicators. The progressive implementation of Agenda 21 should be matched by the provision of such necessary financial resources. The initial phase will be accelerated by substantial early commitments of concessional funding.

Objectives
a To establish measures concerning financial resources and mechanisms for implementation of Agenda 21.
b Provision of new and additional financial resources should be both adequate and predictable.
c Full use and continuing qualitative improvement of funding mechanisms to be utilized for the implementation of Agenda 21 should be sought.

Activities Fundamentally, the activities of this chapter are related to the implementation of all the other chapters of Agenda 21.

Means of implementation In general, the financing for the implementation of Agenda 21 will come from a country's own public and private sectors. For developing countries, particularly the least developed countries, ODA is a main source of external funding, and substantial new and additional funding for sustainable development and implementation of Agenda 21 will be required. Developed countries reaffirm their commitments to reach the accepted United Nations target of 0.7 per cent of GNP for ODA and, to the extent that they have not yet achieved that target, agree to augment their aid programmes in order to reach that target as soon as possible and to ensure a prompt and effective implementation of Agenda 21. Some countries agree or have agreed to reach the target by the year 2000. It was decided that the Commission on Sustainable Development would regularly review and monitor progress towards this target. This review process should systematically combine the monitoring of the implementation of Agenda 21 with a review of the financial resources available. Those countries which have already reached the target are to be commended and encouraged to continue to contribute to the common effort to make available the substantial additional resources that have to be mobilized. Other developed countries, in line with their support for reform efforts in developing countries, agree to make their best efforts to increase their level of ODA. In this context, the importance of equitable burden-sharing among developed countries is recognized. Other countries, including those undergoing the process of transition to a market economy, may voluntarily augment the contributions of the developed countries.

Funding for Agenda 21 and other outcomes of the Conference should be provided in a way which maximizes the availability of new and additional resources and which uses all available funding sources and mechanisms. These include, among others:
A *The multilateral development banks and funds:*
a International Development Association (IDA). Among various issues and options that IDA Deputies will examine in the forthcoming 10th Replenishment, special consideration should be given to the statement made by the President of the International Bank for Reconstruction and Development at the Conference in plenary meeting in order to help the poorest countries meet their sustainable development objectives as contained in Agenda 21.
b Regional and subregional development banks. The regional and subregional development banks and funds should play an increased and more effective role in providing resources on concessional or other favourable terms needed to implement Agenda 21.
c The Global Environment Facility, managed jointly by the World Bank, UNDP and UNEP, whose additional grant and concessional funding is designed to achieve global environmental benefits should cover the agreed incremental costs of relevant activities under Agenda 21, in particular for developing countries. Therefore, it should be restructured so as to *inter alia*:
i Encourage universal participation;
ii Have sufficient flexibility to expand its scope and coverage to relevant programme areas of Agenda 21, with global environmental benefits, as agreed;
iii Ensure a governance that is transparent and democratic in nature, including in terms of decision-making and operations, by guaranteeing a balanced and equitable representation of the interests of developing countries, as well as giving due weight to the funding efforts of donor countries;
iv Ensure new and additional financial resources on grant and concessional terms, in particular to developing countries;
v Ensure predictability in the flow of funds by contributions from developed countries, taking into account the importance of equitable burden-sharing;
vi Ensure access to and disbursement of the funds under mutually agreed criteria without introducing new forms of conditionality;
B *The relevant specialized agencies, other United Nations bodies and other international organizations*, which have designated roles to play in supporting national Governments in implementing Agenda 21;
C *Multilateral institutions for capacity-building and technical cooperation.* Necessary financial resources should be provided to UNDP to use its network of field offices and its broad mandate and experience in the field of technical cooperation for facilitating capacity-building at the country level, making full use of the expertise of the specialized agencies and other United Nations bodies within their respective areas of competence, in particular UNEP and including the multilateral and regional development banks;
D *Bilateral assistance programmes.* These will need to be strengthened in order to promote sustainable development;
E *Debt relief.* It is important to achieve durable solutions to the debt problems of low- and middle-income developing countries in order to provide them with the needed means for sustainable development. Measures to address the continuing debt problems of low- and middle-income countries should be kept under review. All creditors in the Paris Club should promptly implement the agreement of December 1991 to provide debt relief for the poorest heavily indebted countries pursuing structural adjustment; debt relief measures should be kept under review so as to address the continuing difficulties of those countries;
F *Private funding.* Voluntary contributions through non-governmental channels, which have been running at about 10 per cent of ODA, might be increased.
G *Investment.* Mobilization of higher levels of foreign direct investment and technology transfers should be encouraged through national policies that promote investment and through joint ventures and other modalities.
H *Innovative financing.* New ways of generating new public and private financial resources should be explored, in particular:
a Various forms of debt relief, apart from official or Paris Club debt, including greater use of debt swaps;
b The use of economic and fiscal incentives and mechanisms;
c The feasibility of tradeable permits;
d New schemes for fund-raising and voluntary contributions through private channels, including non-governmental organizations;
e The reallocation of resources presently committed to military purposes.

A supportive international and domestic economic climate conducive to sustained economic growth and development is important, particularly for developing countries, in order to achieve sustainability.

The secretariat of the Conference has estimated the average annual costs (1993-2000) of implementing in developing countries the activities in Agenda 21 to be over $600 billion, including about $125 billion on grant or concessional terms from the international community. These are indicative and order of magnitude estimates only, and have not been reviewed by Governments. Actual costs will depend upon, *inter alia*, the specific strategies and programmes Governments decide upon for implementation.

Developed countries and others in a position to do so should make initial financial commitments to give effect to the decisions of the Conference. They should report on such plans and commitments to the United Nations General Assembly in the Fall of 1992 at its forty-seventh session.

Developing countries should also begin to draw up national plans for sustainable development to give effect to the decisions of the Conference.

Review and monitoring of the financing of Agenda 21 is essential. Questions related to the effective follow-up of the Conference are discussed in chapter 38. It will be important to review on a regular basis the adequacy of funding and mechanisms, including efforts to reach agreed objectives of this chapter, including targets where applicable.

Chapter 34

Transfer of environmentally sound technology, cooperation and capacity-building

Environmentally sound technologies protect the environment, are less polluting, use all resources in a more sustainable manner, recycle more of their wastes and products, and handle residual wastes in a more acceptable manner than the technologies for which they were substitutes.

Environmentally sound technologies in the context of pollution are "process and product technologies" that generate low or no waste, for the prevention of pollution. They also cover "end of the pipe" technologies for treatment of pollution after it has been generated.

Environmentally sound technologies are not just individual technologies, but total systems which include know-how, procedures, goods and services, and equipment as well as organizational and managerial procedures. This implies that when discussing transfer of technologies, the human resource development and local capacity-building aspects of technology choices, including gender-relevant aspects, should also be addressed. Environmentally sound technologies should be compatible with nationally determined socio-economic, cultural, and environmental priorities.

There is a need for favourable access to and transfer of environmentally sound technologies, in particular to developing countries, through supportive measures that promote technology cooperation and that should enable transfer of necessary technological know-how as well as building up of economic, technical, and managerial capabilities for the efficient use and further development of transferred technology. Technology cooperation involves joint efforts by enterprises and Governments, both suppliers of technology and its recipients. Therefore, such cooperation entails an iterative process involving government, the private sector, and research and development facilities to ensure the best possible results from transfer of technology. Successful long-term partnerships in technology cooperation necessarily require continuing systematic training and capacity-building at all levels over an extended period of time.

The activities proposed in this chapter aim at improving conditions and processes on information, access to and transfer of technology (including the state-of-the-art technology and related know-how), in particular to developing countries, as well as on capacity-building and cooperative arrangements and partnerships in the field of technology, in order to promote sustainable development. New and efficient technologies will be essential to increase the capabilities, in particular of developing countries, to achieve sustainable development, sustain the world's economy, protect the environment, and alleviate poverty and human suffering. Inherent in these activities is the need to address the improvement of technology currently used and its replacement, when appropriate, with more accessible and more environmentally sound technology.

Basis for action This chapter of Agenda 21 is without prejudice to specific commitments and arrangements on transfer of technology to be adopted in specific international instruments.

The availability of scientific and technological information and access to and transfer of environmentally sound technology are essential requirements for sustainable development. Providing adequate information on the environmental aspects of present technologies consists of two interrelated components: upgrading information on present and state-of-the-art technologies, including their environmental risks, and improving access to environmentally sound technologies.

The primary goal of improved access to technology information is to enable informed choices, leading to access to and transfer of such technologies and the strengthening of countries' own technological capabilities.

A large body of useful technological knowledge lies in the public domain. There is a need for the access of developing countries to such technologies as are not covered by patents or lie in the public domain. Developing countries would also need to have access to the know-how and expertise required for the effective utilization of the aforesaid technologies.

Consideration must be given to the role of patent protection and intellectual property rights along with an examination of their impact on the access to and transfer of environmentally sound technology, in particular to developing countries, as well as to further exploring efficiently the concept of assured access for developing countries to environmentally sound technology in its relation to proprietary rights with a view to developing effective responses to the needs of developing countries in this area.

Proprietary technology is available through commercial channels, and international business is an important vehicle for technology transfer. Tapping this pool of knowledge and recombining it with local innovations to generate alternative technologies should be pursued. At the same time that concepts and modalities for assured access to environmentally sound technologies, including state-of-the-art technologies, in particular by developing countries, continued to be explored, enhanced access to environmentally sound technologies should be promoted, facilitated and financed as appropriate, while providing fair incentives to innovators that promote research and development of new environmentally sound technologies.

Recipient countries require technology and strengthened support to help further develop their scientific, technological, professional and related capacities, taking into account existing technologies and capacities. This support would enable countries, in particular developing countries, to make more rational technology choices. These countries could then better assess environmentally sound technologies prior to their transfer and properly apply and manage them, as well as improve upon already existing technologies and adapt them to suit their specific development needs and priorities.

A critical mass of research and development capacity is crucial to the effective dissemination and use of environmentally sound technologies and their generation locally. Education and training programmes should reflect the needs of specific goal-oriented research activities and should work to produce specialists literate in environmentally sound technology and with an interdisciplinary outlook. Achieving this critical mass involves building the capabilities of craftspersons, technicians and middle-level managers, scientists, engineers and educators, as well as developing their corresponding social or managerial support systems. Transferring environmentally sound technologies also involves innovatively adapting and incorporating them into the local or national culture.

Objectives

a To help to ensure the access, in particular of developing countries, to scientific and technological information, including information on state-of-the-art technologies;

b To promote, facilitate, and finance, as appropriate, the access to and the transfer of environmentally sound technologies and corresponding know-how, in particular to developing countries, on favourable terms, including on concessional and preferential terms, as mutually agreed, taking into account the need to protect intellectual property rights as well as the special needs of developing countries for the implementation of Agenda 21;

c To facilitate the maintenance and promotion of environmentally sound indigenous technologies that may have been neglected or displaced, in particular in developing countries, paying particular attention to their priority needs and taking into account the complementary roles of men and women;

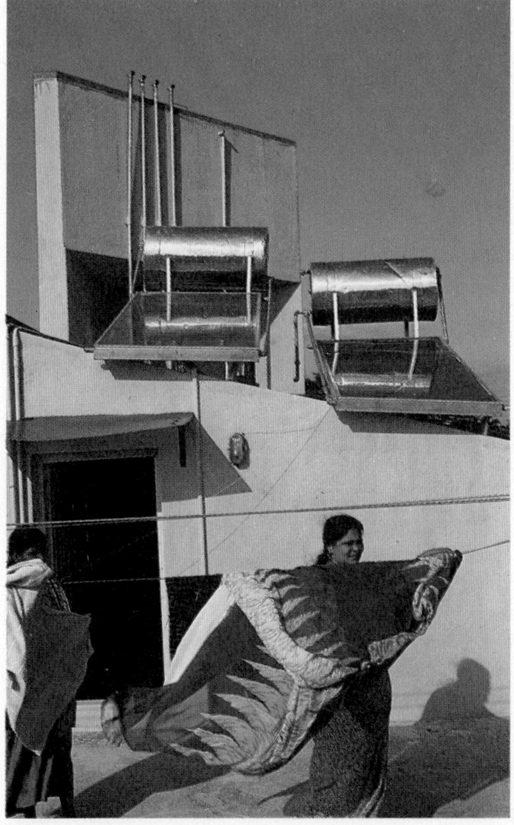

Technology developed by the Karnataka State Council for Science and Tecnology has provided solar heating for houses in the village of Melamangala, India.

d To support endogenous capacity-building, in particular in developing countries, so they can assess, adopt, manage and apply environmentally sound technologies. This could be achieved through *inter alia*:

i Human resource development;

ii Strengthening of institutional capacities for research and development and programme implementation;

iii Integrated sector assessments of technology needs, in accordance with countries' plans, objectives and priorities as foreseen in the implementation of Agenda 21 at the national level;

e To promote long-term technological partnerships between holders of environmentally sound technologies and potential users.

Activities

A *Development of international information networks which link national, subregional, regional and international systems*

Existing national, subregional, regional and international information systems should be developed and linked through regional clearing-houses covering broad-based sectors of the economy such as agriculture, industry and energy. Such a network might, *inter alia*, include national, subregional and regional patent offices that are equipped to produce reports on state-of-the-art technology. The clearing-house networks would disseminate information on available technologies, their sources, their environmental risks, and the broad terms under which they may be acquired. They would operate on an information-demand basis and focus on the information needs of the end-users. They would take into account the positive roles and contributions of international, regional and subregional organizations, business communities, trade associations, non-governmental organizations, national Governments, and newly established or strengthened national networks.

The international and regional clearing-houses would take the initiative, where necessary, in helping users to identify their needs and in disseminating information that meets those needs, including the use of existing news, public information, and communication systems. The disseminated information would highlight and detail concrete cases where environmentally sound technologies were successfully developed and implemented. In order to be effective, the clearing-houses need to provide not only information, but also referrals to other services, including sources of advice, training, technologies and technology assessment. The clearing-houses would thus facilitate the establishment of joint ventures and partnerships of various kinds.

An inventory of existing and international or regional clearing-houses or information exchange systems should be undertaken by the relevant United Nations bodies. The existing structure should be strengthened and improved when necessary. Additional information systems should be developed, if necessary, in order to fill identified gaps in this international network.

B *Support of and promotion of access to transfer of technology*

Governments and international organizations should promote, and encourage the private sector to promote, effective modalities for the access and transfer in particular to developing countries of environmentally sound technologies by activities, including the following:

a Formulation of policies and programmes for the effective transfer of environmentally sound technologies that are publicly owned or in the public domain;

b Creation of favourable conditions to encourage the private and public sectors to innovate, market and use environmentally sound technologies;

c Examination by Governments and, where

UNCED dealt with a range of issues important for sustainable development, but did not deal seriously enough with the debt crisis, the stagnating flows of foreign aid, the need for more open trade and its environmental and developmental impacts. It did not take forward-looking decisions on population growth. The future will not be secured and everybody will ultimately lose unless the environment and development crisis is dealt with in a comparably responsible manner where all countries pool their interest. Much stronger international decision-making procedures must be developed. We cannot proceed at the snail's-pace decided by the most reluctant movers. We cannot afford to cover the cost of less determined actions.
Gro Harlem Brundtland
Prime Minister
Norway

appropriate, by relevant organizations of existing policies, including subsidies and tax policies, and regulations to determine whether they encourage or impede the access to, transfer of and introduction of environmentally sound technologies;

d Addressing, in a framework which fully integrates environment and development, barriers to the transfer of privately owned environmentally sound technologies and adoption of appropriate general measures to reduce such barriers while creating specific incentives, fiscal or otherwise, for the transfer of such technologies;

e In the case of privately owned technologies the following measures could be adopted, in particular for developing countries:

i Creation and enhancement by developed countries, as well as other countries which might be in a position to do so, of appropriate incentives, fiscal or otherwise, to stimulate the transfer of environmentally sound technology by companies, in particular to developing countries, as integral to sustainable development;

ii Enhance the access to and transfer of patent protected environmentally sound technologies, in particular to developing countries;

iii Purchase of patents and licenses on commercial terms for their transfer to developing countries on non-commercial terms as part of development cooperation for sustainable development, taking into account the need to protect intellectual property rights;

iv In compliance with and under the specific circumstances recognized by the relevant international conventions adhered to by States, undertaking measures to prevent the abuse of intellectual property rights, including rules with respect to their acquisition through compulsory licensing, with the provision of equitable and adequate compensation;

v Provision of financial resources to acquire environmentally sound technologies in order to enable in particular developing countries to implement measures to promote sustainable development that would entail a special or abnormal burden to them;

f Develop mechanisms for the access to and transfer of environmentally sound technologies, in particular to developing countries, while taking into account development in the process of negotiating an international code of conduct on transfer of technology, as decided by UNCTAD at its eighth session in Cartagena.

C *Improvement of the capacity to develop and manage environmentally sound technologies*

Frameworks at subregional, regional and international levels should be established and/or strengthened for the development, transfer and application of environmentally sound technologies and corresponding technical know-how with a special focus on developing countries' needs, by adding such functions to already existing bodies. Such frameworks would facilitate initiatives from both developing and developed countries to stimulate the research, development and transfer of environmentally sound technologies, often through partnerships within and among countries and between the scientific and technological community, industry and Governments.

National capacities to assess, develop, manage and apply new technologies should be developed. This will require strengthening existing institutions, training of personnel at all levels, and education of the end-user of the technology.

D *Establishment of a collaborative network of research centres*

A collaborative network of national, subregional, regional and international research centres on environmentally sound technology should be established to enhance the access to and development, management and transfer of environmentally sound technologies, including transfer and cooperation among developing countries and between developed and developing countries, primarily based on existing subregional or regional research, development and demonstration centres which are linked with the national institutions, in close cooperation with the private sector.

E *Support for programmes of cooperation and assistance*

Support should be provided for programmes of cooperation and assistance, including those provided by United Nations agencies, international organizations, and other appropriate public and private organizations, in particular to developing countries, in the areas of research and development, technological and human resources capacity-building in the fields of training, maintenance, national technology needs assessments, environmental impact assessments, and sustainable development planning.

Support should also be provided for national, subregional, regional, multilateral and bilateral programmes of scientific research, dissemination of information and technology development among developing countries, including through the involvement of both public and private enterprises and research facilities, as well as funding for technical cooperation among developing countries' programmes in this area. This should include developing links among these facilities to maximize their efficiency in understanding, disseminating and implementing technologies for sustainable development.

The development of global, regional and subregional programmes should include identification and evaluation of regional, subregional and national need-based priorities. Plans and studies supporting these programmes should provide the basis for potential financing by multilateral development banks, bilateral organizations, private sector interests and non-governmental organizations.

Visits should be sponsored and, on a voluntary basis, the return of qualified experts from developing countries in the field of environmentally sound technologies who are currently working in developed country institutions should be facilitated.

F *Technology assessment in support of the management of environmentally sound technology*

The international community, in particular United Nations agencies, international organizations, and other appropriate and private organizations should help exchange experiences and develop capacity for technology needs assessment, in particular in developing countries, to enable them to make choices based on environmentally sound technologies. They should:

a Build up technology assessment capacity for the management of environmentally sound technology, including environmental impact and risk assessment, with due regard to appropriate safeguards on the transfer of technologies subject to prohibition on environmental or health grounds;

b Strengthen the international network of regional, subregional or national environmentally sound technology assessment centres, coupled with clearing-houses, to tap the technology assessment sources mentioned above for the benefit of all nations. These centres could, in principle, provide advice and training for specific national situations and promote the building up of national capacity in environmentally sound technology assessment. The possibility of assigning this activity to already existing regional organizations should be fully explored before creating entirely new institutions, and funding of this activity through public-private partnerships should also be explored, as appropriate.

G *Collaborative arrangements and partnerships*

Long-term collaborative arrangements should be promoted between enterprises of developed and developing countries for the development of environmentally sound technologies. Multinational companies, as repositories of scarce technical skills needed for the protection and enhancement of the environment, have a special role and interest in promoting cooperation in and related to technology transfer, as they are important channels for such transfer, and for building a trained human resource pool and infrastructure.

Joint ventures should be promoted between suppliers and recipients of technologies, taking into account developing countries' policy priorities and objectives. Together with direct foreign investment, these ventures could constitute important channels of transferring environmentally sound technologies. Through such joint ventures and direct investment, sound environmental management practices could be transferred and maintained.

Finance and Costs Between $450 million and $600 million from the international community on grant or concessional terms.

Chapter 35 Science for sustainable development

This chapter focuses on the role and the use of the sciences in supporting the prudent management of the environment and development for the daily survival and future development of humanity. The programme areas proposed herein are intended to be over-arching, in order to support the specific scientific requirements identified in the other Agenda 21 chapters. One role of the sciences should be to provide information to better enable formulation and selection of environment and development policies in the decision-making process. In order to fulfil this requirement, it will be essential to enhance scientific understanding, improve long-term scientific assessments, strengthen scientific capacities in all countries and ensure that the sciences are responsive to emerging needs.

Scientists are improving their understanding in areas such as climatic change, growth in rates of resource consumption, demographic trends, and environmental degradation. Changes in those and other areas need to be taken into account in working out long-term strategies for development. A first step towards improving the scientific basis for these strategies is a better understanding of land, oceans, atmosphere and their interlocking water, nutrient and biogeochemical cycles and energy flows which all form part of the Earth system. This is essential if a more accurate estimate is to be provided of the carrying capacity of the planet Earth and of its resilience under the many stresses placed upon it by human activities. The sciences can provide this understanding through increased research into the underlying ecological processes and through the application of modern, effective and efficient tools that are now available, such as remote-sensing devices, robotic monitoring instruments and computing and modelling capabilities. The sciences are playing an important role in linking the fundamental significance of the Earth system as life support to appropriate strategies for development which build on its continued functioning. The sciences should continue to play an increasing role in providing for an improvement in the efficiency of resource utilization and in finding new development practices, resources, and alternatives. There is a need for the sciences constantly to reassess and promote less intensive trends in resource utilization, including less intensive utilization of energy in industry, agriculture, and transportation. Thus, the sciences are increasingly being understood as an essential component in the search for feasible pathways towards sustainable development.

Scientific knowledge should be applied to articulate and support the goals of sustainable development, through scientific assessments of current conditions and future prospects for the Earth system. Such assessments, based on existing and emerging innovations within the sciences, should be used in the decision-making process and in the interactive processes between the sciences and policy-making. There needs to be an increased output from the sciences in order to enhance understanding and facilitate interaction between science and society. An increase in the scientific capacity and capability to achieve these goals will also be required, particularly in developing countries. Of crucial importance is the need for scientists in developing countries to participate fully in international scientific research programmes dealing with the global problems of environment and development so as to allow all countries to participate on equal footing in negotiations on global environmental and developmental issues. In the face of threats of irreversible environmental damage, lack of full scientific understanding should not be an excuse for postponing actions which are justified in their own right. The precautionary approach could provide a basis for policies relating to complex systems that are not yet fully understood and whose consequences of disturbances cannot yet be predicted.

The programme areas are in harmony with the conclusions and recommendations of the International Conference on an Agenda of Science for Environment and Development into the 21st Century (ASCEND/21)

A Strengthening the scientific basis for sustainable management

Basis for action Sustainable development requires taking longer-term perspectives, integrating local and regional effects of global change into the development process, and using the best scientific and traditional knowledge available. The development process should be constantly re-evaluated, in light of the findings of scientific research, to ensure that resource utilization has reduced impacts on the Earth system. Even so, the future is uncertain, and there will be surprises. Good environmental and developmental management policies must therefore be scientifically robust, seeking to keep open a range of options to ensure flexibility of response. The precautionary approach is important. Often, there is a communication gap among scientists, policy makers, and the public at large, whose interests are articulated by both governmental and non-governmental organizations. Better communication is required among scientists, decision makers, and the general public.

Objectives The primary objective is for each country with the support of international organizations, as requested, to identify the state of its scientific knowledge and its research needs and priorities in order to achieve, as soon as possible, substantial improvements in:

a Large-scale widening of the scientific base and strengthening of scientific and research capacities and capabilities – in particular, those of developing countries – in areas relevant to environment and development;

b Environmental and developmental policy formulation, building upon the best scientific knowledge and assessments, and taking into account the need to enhance international cooperation and the relative uncertainties of the various processes and options involved;

c The interaction between the sciences and decision-

The development of satellite systems has resulted in accurate meterological prediction and monitoring. This satellite picture shows Hurricane Andrew as it moved across Florida.

making, using the precautionary approach, where appropriate, to change the existing patterns of production and consumption and to gain time for reducing uncertainty with respect to the selection of policy options;

d The generation and application of knowledge, especially indigenous and local knowledge, to the capacities of different environments and cultures, to achieve sustained levels of development, taking into account interrelations at the national, regional and international levels;

e Improving cooperation between scientists by promoting interdisciplinary research programmes and activities;

f Participation of people in setting priorities and in decision-making relating to sustainable development.

Activities Countries, with the assistance of international organizations, where required, should:

a Prepare an inventory of their natural and social science data holdings relevant to the promotion of sustainable development;

b Identify their research needs and priorities in the context of international research efforts;

c Strengthen and design appropriate institutional mechanisms at the highest appropriate local, national, subregional and regional levels and within the United Nations system for developing a stronger scientific basis for the improvement of environmental and developmental policy formulation consistent with long-term goals of sustainable development. Current research in this area should be broadened to include more involvement of the public in establishing long-term societal goals for formulating the sustainable development scenarios;

d Develop, apply and institute the necessary tools for sustainable development, with regard to:

i Quality-of-life indicators covering, for example, health, education, social welfare, state of the environment, and the economy;

ii Economic approaches to environmentally sound development and new and improved incentive structures for better resource management;

iii Long-term environmental policy formulation, risk management and environmentally sound technology assessment;

e Collect, analyse and integrate data on the linkages between the state of ecosystems and the health of human communities in order to improve knowledge of the cost and benefit of different development policies and strategies in relation to health and the environment, particularly in developing countries;

f Conduct scientific studies of national and regional pathways to sustainable development, using comparable and complementary methodologies. Such studies, coordinated by an international science effort, should to a large extent involve local expertise and be conducted by multidisciplinary teams from regional networks and/or research centres, as appropriate and according to national capacities and the available resources;

g Improve capabilities for determining scientific research priorities at the national, regional and global levels to meet the needs of sustainable development. This is a process that involves scientific judgements regarding short-term and long-term benefits and possible long-term costs and risks. It should be adaptive and responsive to perceived needs and be carried out via transparent, "user-friendly", risk-evaluation methodologies;

h Develop methods to link the findings of the established sciences with the indigenous knowledge of different cultures. The methods should be tested using pilot studies. They should be developed at the local level and should concentrate on the links between the traditional knowledge of indigenous groups and corresponding, current "advanced science", with particular focus on disseminating and applying the results to environmental protection and sustainable development.

Financing and cost evaluation $150 million, including about $30 million from the international community on grant or concessional terms.

B Enhancing scientific understanding

Basis for action In order to promote sustainable development, more extensive knowledge is required of the Earth's carrying capacity, including the processes that could either impair or enhance its ability to support life. The global environment is changing more rapidly than at any time in recent centuries; as a result, sur-

A Fifty-year Dedication to Conservation of Resources

The Topsøe company was founded in 1940 by Dr. Haldor Topsøe and has ever since been devoted to the development of catalysts and their use in commercial processes. The humble beginning has now become a worldwide enterprise with important consequences to improvement of life on the planet.

The activities of the company within catalysis, fertilizers and energy-derived industries has led to transfer technology projects to numerous countries: Turkey, Pakistan, India, Bangladesh, China, to the Middle East and Kuwait in particular, to North Africa and to Eastern Europe. In direct continuation of these industrial and advisory collaborations Haldor Topsøe has taken up – with leaders all over the world – the problems of population, of resources, of environmental protection, and of capital transfer, four problems which to him are of equal importance.

In the 1960's the "Green Revolution" in agriculture was underway. The essential elements of this "revolution" which greatly increased grain yields per acre and laid the basis for the food self-sufficiency of the Sub-Continent, were new, fertilizer responsive varieties of wheat and rice – developed in Mexico and the Philippines – and large applications of plant nutrient, especially nitrogen. Abundant supplies of fertilizer were critical if these new strains of wheat and rice were to yield their full potential.

In the mid-1970's, Haldor Topsøe brought his knowledge of the nitrogen fertilizer industry to Prime Minister of India, Mrs. Indira Gandhi, and assisted her and India's technologists in crafting the strategies by which India might best use its newly discovered reserves of natural gas to meet its fertilizer needs. By the late 1980's, the strategy developed by Dr. Topsøe and his Indian colleagues had given India one of the world's largest national fertilizer manufacturing and marketing industries.

Haldor Topsøe's interests extend beyond fertilizer manufacture and the dissemination of knowledge of this technology throughout the world. In the environmental and energy area the company has created a series of technologies and catalysts for environmental protection and conservation of resources.

These technologies include:

The **WSA** process for recovery of concentrated sulphuric acid of commercial quality from sulphurous off-gases such as flue gas from utilities, off-gases from mineral roasters, coal and oil gasifiers, viscose plants or from spent acid.

The **DENOX** process for removal of nitrogen oxides from flue gases and other industrial off-gases.

The **SNOX** process – combining the WSA and DENOX processes for the efficient removal of sulphur oxides and nitrogen oxides from industrial off-gases and flue gases.

The **CATOX** process for removal of solvents and other combustibles (VOC's) in air and off-gases.

Recently, the company has developed a series of catalysts and processes aiming at **cleaner fuels,** i.e. improved diesel and reformulated gasoline.

Dr. Topsøe's deep conviction that technology, applied engineering, good scientific research and focused process and product development are the essential means for enhancing the opportunities for all the world's people to conquer hunger, malnutrition and disease as well as conservation of resources, is the driving force behind the accomplishment of the Topsøe company.

prises may be expected, and the next century could see significant environmental changes. At the same time, the human consumption of energy, water and non-renewable resources is increasing, on both a total and a per/capita basis, and shortages may ensue in many parts of the world even if environmental conditions were to remain unchanged. Social processes are subject to multiple variations across time and space, regions and culture. They both affect and are influenced by changing environmental conditions. Human factors are key driving forces in these intricate sets of relationships and exert their influence directly on global change. Therefore, study of the human dimensions of the causes and consequences of environmental change and of more sustainable development paths is essential.

Objectives One key objective is to improve and increase the fundamental understanding of the linkages between human and natural environmental systems and improve the analytical and predictive tools required to better understand the environmental impacts of development options by:

a Carrying out research programmes in order better to understand the carrying capacity of the Earth as conditioned by its natural systems, such as the biogeochemical cycles, the atmosphere/hydrosphere/lithosphere/cryosphere system, the biosphere and biodiversity, the agro-ecosystem and other terrestrial and aquatic ecosystems;

b Developing and applying new analytical and predictive tools in order to assess more accurately the ways in which the Earth's natural systems are being increasingly influenced by human actions, both deliberate and inadvertent, and demographic trends, and the impact and consequences of those actions and trends;

c Integrating physical, economic and social sciences in order better to understand the impacts of economic and social behaviour on the environment and of environmental degradation on local and global economies.

Activities

a Support development of an expanded monitoring network to describe cycles (for example, global, biogeochemical and hydrological cycles) and test hypotheses regarding their behaviour, and improve research into the interactions among the various global cycles and their consequences at national, subregional, regional and global levels as guides to tolerance and vulnerability;

b Support national, subregional, regional and international observation and research programmes in global atmospheric chemistry and the sources and sinks of greenhouse gases, and ensure that the results are presented in a publicly accessible and understandable form;

c Support national, subregional, regional and international research programmes on marine and terrestrial systems, strengthen global terrestrial databases of their components, expand corresponding systems for monitoring their changing states and enhance predictive modelling of the Earth system and its subsystems, including modelling of the functoning of these systems assuming different intensities of human impact. The research programmes should include the programmes mentioned in other Agenda 21 chapters which support mechanisms for cooperation and coherence of research programmes on global change;

d Encourage coordination of satellite missions, the networks, systems and procedures for processing and disseminating their data; and develop the interface with the research users of Earth observation data and with the United Nations EARTHWATCH system;

e Develop the capacity for predicting the responses of terrestrial, freshwater, coastal and marine ecosystems and biodiversity to short- and long-term perturbations of the environment, and develop further restoration ecology;

f Study the role of biodiversity and the loss of species in the functioning of ecosystems and the global life-support system;

g Initiate a global observing system of parameters needed for the rational management of coastal and mountain zones and significantly expand freshwater quantity/quality monitoring systems, particularly in developing countries;

h In order to understand the Earth as a system, develop Earth observation systems from space which will provide integrated, continuous and long-term measurements of the interactions of the atmosphere, hydrosphere and lithosphere, and develop a distribution system for data which will facilitate the utilization of data obtained through observation;

i Develop and apply systems and technology that automatically collect, record and transmit data and information to data and analysis centres, in order to monitor marine, terrestrial and atmospheric processes and provide advance warning of natural disasters;

j Enhance the contribution of the engineering sciences to multidisciplinary research programmes on the Earth system, in particular with regard to increasing emergency preparedness and reducing the negative effects of major natural disasters;

k Intensify research to integrate the physical, economic and social sciences to better understand the impacts of economic and social behaviour on the environment and of environmental degradation on local and global economies and, in particular:

i Develop research on human attitudes and behaviour as driving forces central to an understanding of the causes and consequences of environmental change and resource use;

ii Promote research on human, economic and social responses to global change;

l Support development of new user-friendly technologies and systems that facilitate the integration of multidisciplinary, physical, chemical, biological and social/human processes which, in turn, provide information and knowledge for decision makers and the general public.

Financing and cost evaluation $2 billion, including about $1.5 billion from the international community on grant or concessional terms.

C Improving long-term scientific assessment

Basis for action Meeting scientific research needs in the environment/development field is only the first step in the support that the sciences can provide for the sustainable development process. The knowledge acquired may then be used to provide scientific assessments (audits) of the current status and for a range of possible future conditions. This implies that the biosphere must be maintained in a healthy state and that losses in biodiversity must be slowed down. Although many of the long-term environmental changes that are likely to affect people and the biosphere are global in scale, key changes can often be made at the national and local levels. At the same time, human activities at the local and regional levels often contribute to global threats, e.g., stratospheric ozone depletion. Thus scientific assessments and projections are required at the global, regional and local levels. Many countries and organizations already prepare reports on the environment and development which review current conditions and indicate future trends. Regional and global assessments could make full use of such reports but should be broader in scope and include the results of detailed studies of future

Socio-economic development is accompanied by a justified anxiety brought about by the discrepancies existing in the world between the rich and the poor countries. It is a conflict between two systems with their own different laws and rhythms. Demographic growth, urban development, technological progress, accompanied by environmental degradation become ever growing problems. The global dimension of the issues leads to contradictory interests which confront both the developed countries and the poor countries. We consider the Earth Summit to be an example of the major responsibility of people in approaching joint problems and in reaching those solutions and recommendations that should allow everybody's lasting development, associated with the permanent responsibility for environment protection.
Ion Iliescu
President
Romania

conditions for a range of assumptions about possible future human responses, using the best available models. Such assessments should be designed to map out manageable development pathways within the environmental and socio-economic carrying capacity of each region. Full use should be made of traditional knowledge of the local environment.

Objectives The primary objective is to provide assessments of the current status and trends in major developmental and environmental issues at the national, subregional, regional and global levels on the basis of the best available scientific knowledge in order to develop alternative strategies, including indigenous approaches, for the different scales of time and space required for long-term policy formulation.

Activities

a Coordinate existing data- and statistics-gathering systems relevant to developmental and environmental issues so as to support preparation of long-term scientific assessments, e.g., data on resource depletion, import/export flows, energy use, health impacts, demographic trends, etc.; apply the data obtained through the activities identified in programme area B to environment/development assessments at the global, regional and local levels; and promote the wide distribution of the assessments in a form that is responsive to public needs and can be widely understood;

b Develop a methodology to carry out national and regional audits and a five-year global audit on an integrated basis. The standardized audits should help to refine the pattern and character of development, examining in particular the capacities of global and regional life-supporting systems to meet the needs of human and non-human life forms and identifying areas and resources vulnerable to further degradation. This task would involve the integration of all relevant sciences at the national, regional, and global levels, and would be organized by governmental agencies, non-governmental organizations, universities and research institutions, assisted by international governmental and non-governmental organizations and United Nations bodies, when necessary and as appropriate. These audits should then be made available to the general public.

Finance and cost evaluation $35 million, including about $18 million from the international community on grant or concessional terms.

D Building up scientific capacity and capability

Basis for action In view of the increasing role the sciences have to play in dealing with the issues of environment and development, it is necessary to build up scientific capacity and strengthen such capacity in all countries – particularly in developing countries – to enable them to participate fully in the generation and application of the results of scientific research and development concerning sustainable development. There are many ways to build up scientific and technological capacity. Some of the most important of them are the following: education and training in science and technology; assistance to developing countries to improve infrastructures for research and development which could enable scientists to work more productively; development of incentives to encourage research and development; and greater utilization of their results in the productive sectors of the economy. Such capacity-building would also form the basis for improving public awareness and understanding of the sciences. Special emphasis must be put on the need to assist developing countries to strengthen their capacities to study their own resource bases and ecological systems and manage them better in order to meet national, regional and global challenges. Furthermore, in view of the size and complexity of global environmental problems, a need for more specialists in several disciplines has become evident world wide.

Objectives The primary objective is to improve the scientific capacities of all countries – in particular, those of developing countries – with specific regard to:

a Education, training and facilities for local research and development and human resource development in basic scientific disciplines and in environment-related sciences, utilizing where appropriate traditional and local knowledge of sustainability;

b A substantial increase by the year 2000 in the number of scientists – particularly women scientists – in those developing countries where their number is at present insufficient;

c Reducing significantly the exodus of scientists from developing countries and encouraging those who have left to return;

d Improving access to relevant information for scientists and decision makers, with the aim of improving public awareness and participation in decision-making;

e Involvement of scientists in national, regional and global environmental and developmental research programmes, including multidisciplinary research;

f Periodic academic update of scientists from developing countries in their respective fields of knowledge.

Activities

a Promote the education and training of scientists, not only in their disciplines but also in their ability to identify, manage and incorporate environmental considerations into research and development projects; ensure that a sound base in natural systems, ecology and resource management is provided; and develop specialists capable of working in interdisciplinary programmes related to environment and development, including the field of applied social sciences;

b Strengthen the scientific infrastructure in schools, universities and research institutions – particularly those in developing countries – by the provision of adequate scientific equipment and access to current scientific literature, for the purpose of achieving and sustaining a critical mass of highly qualified scientists in these countries;

c Develop and expand national scientific and technological databases, processing data in unified formats and systems, and allowing full and open access to the depository libraries of regional scientific and technological information networks. Promote submission of scientific and technological information and databases to global or regional data centres and network systems;

d Develop and expand regional and global scientific and technological information networks which are based on and linked to national scientific and technological databases; collect, process and disseminate information from regional and global scientific programmes; expand activities to reduce information barriers due to language differences. Increase the applications – particularly in developing countries – of computer-based retrieval systems in order to cope with the growth of scientific literature;

e Develop, strengthen and forge new partnerships among national, regional and global capacities to promote the full and open exchange of scientific and technological data and information and to facilitate technical assistance related to environmentally sound and sustainable development. This should be done through the development of mechanisms for the sharing of basic research, data and information, and the improvement and development of international networks and centres, including regional linking with national scientific databases, for research, training and monitoring. Such mechanisms should be designed so as to enhance professional cooperation among scientists in all countries and to establish strong national and regional alliances between industry and research institutions;

f Improve and develop new links between existing networks of natural and social scientists and universities at the international level in order to strengthen national capacities in the formulation of policy options in the field of environment and development;

g Compile, analyse and publish information on indigenous environmental and developmental knowledge, and assist the communities that possess such knowledge to benefit from them.

Financing and cost evaluation $750 million, including about $470 million from the international community on grant or concessional terms.

Chapter 36 Promoting education, public awareness and training

Education, raising of public awareness and training are linked to virtually all areas in Agenda 21, and even more closely to the ones on meeting basic needs, capacity-building, data and information, science, and the role of major groups. This chapter sets out broad proposals, while specific suggestions related to sectoral issues are contained in other chapters. The Declaration and Recommendations of the Tbilisi Intergovernmental Conference on Environmental Education[1] organized by UNESCO and UNEP and held in 1977, have provided the fundamental principles for the proposals in this document.

A Reorienting education towards sustainable development

Basis for action Education, including formal education, public awareness and training should be recognized as a process by which human beings and societies can reach their fullest potential. Education is critical for promoting sustainable development and improving the capacity of the people to address environment and development issues. While basic education provides the underpinning for any environmental and development education, the latter needs to be incorporated as an essential part of learning. Both formal and non-formal education are indispensable to changing people's attitudes so that they have the capacity to assess and address their sustainable development concerns. It is also critical for achieving environmental and ethical awareness, values and attitudes, skills and behaviour consistent with sustainable development and for effective public participation in decision-making.

To be effective, environment and development education should deal with the dynamics of both the physical biological and socio-economic environment and human (which may include spiritual) development, should be integrated in all disciplines, and should employ formal and non-formal methods and effective means of communication.

In the developed countries a level of public awareness has been achieved with recycling basic products. A much wider understanding is necessary in both developed and developing countries.

Objectives Recognizing that countries, regional and international organizations will develop their own priorities and schedules for implementation in accordance with their needs, policies and programmes, the following objectives are proposed:

a To endorse the recommendations arising from the World Conference on Education for All: Meeting Basic Learning Needs[2] (Jomtien, Thailand, 5-9 March 1990) and to strive to ensure universal access to basic education, and to achieve primary education for at least 80 per cent of girls and 80 per cent of boys of primary school age through formal schooling or non-formal education and to reduce the adult illiteracy rate to at least half of its 1990 level. Efforts should focus on reducing the high illiteracy levels and redressing the lack of basic education among women and should bring their literacy levels into line with those of men;

b To achieve environmental and development awareness in all sectors of society on a world-wide scale as soon as possible;

c To strive to achieve the accessibility of environmental and development education, linked to social education, from primary school age through adulthood to all groups of people;

d To promote integration of environment and development concepts, including demography, in all educational programmes, in particular the analysis of the causes of major environment and development issues in a local context, drawing on the best available scientific evidence and other appropriate sources of knowledge, and giving special emphasis to the further training of decision makers at all levels.

Activities Recognizing that countries and regional and international organizations will develop their own priorities and schedules for implementation in accordance with their needs, policies and programmes, the following activities are proposed:

a All countries are encouraged to endorse the recommendations of the Jomtien Conference and strive to ensure its Framework for Action. This would encompass the preparation of national strategies and actions for meeting basic learning needs, universalizing access and promoting equity, broadening the means and scope of education, developing a supporting policy context, mobilizing resources and strengthening international cooperation to redress existing economic, social and gender disparities which interfere with these aims. Non-governmental organizations can make an important contribution in designing and implementing educational programmes and should be recognized;

b Governments should strive to update or prepare strategies aimed at integrating environment and development as a cross-cutting issue into education at all

SAUDI ARABIA

Saudi Arabia's commitment to the protection and enhancement of the natural environment is second to none. It is an integral part of the Kingdom's spiritual and cultural heritage.

Given Saudi Arabia's resolve to promote a clean and healthy environment, the entire process of industrialisation has adopted the latest environment-friendly technologies. Strict environmental legislation has been enacted from the very beginning. The greening of the desert and the cities, the protection of wildlife along with a careful nourishment of its coastal seas have given Saudi Arabia a high quality of environment.

The result has been that Saudi Arabia has received world-wide recognition for its role in the protection of the environment. Two new industrial cities, Jubail on the east coast and Yanbu on the west coast, have received many industrial safety and environmental protection awards, including the UN award. These two cities are among the leading producers of petrochemicals in the world today.

Saudi Aramco has always been a leading force in the protection of the waters of the Arabian Gulf. It has consistently maintained high standards of safety in the oil fields. It is no stranger to the hazards of oil spills and little wonder, therefore, that Saudi Aramco was in the forefront of the mammoth and successful effort to clean the intentional and potentially disastrous oil spill during the Gulf war. The Gulf waters are now as healthy as ever.

The Saudi Marketing and Refining Company (SAMAREC) is upgrading its refineries to produce cleaner and lighter fuels. Its refineries have gained international recognition for safety and environmental protection. It will soon become one of the largest MTBE producers in the world. This will enable SAMAREC to contribute to cleaner emissions from automobiles the world over.

It is possible to confront the environmental problems of desertification, pollution, scarcity of fresh water, extinction of species, and poverty if they are recognized and dealt with within the framework of planning for sustainable development on both national and international levels. It is unrealistic and impractical to view the environmental problem only within a narrow, national context. This necessitates cooperation among all nations, particularly in the transfer of environmentally sound technology recognising the requirements of each society and its particular phase of development. The Kingdom has recognised this concept in its ambitious programme of donation and assistance, during the last twenty years, for more than sixty developing nations and offers an example to industrial nations of what can be done to achieve sustainable development and a better habitat for all of us on this planet.
Sultan Bin Abdul Aziz Al-Saud
Second Deputy Premier
Saudi Arabia

levels within the next three years. This should be done in cooperation with all sectors of society. The strategies should set out policies and activities, and identifyneeds, cost, means and schedules for their implementation, evaluation and review. A thorough review of curricula should be undertaken to ensure a multidisciplinary approach, with environment and development issues and their socio-cultural and demographic aspects and linkages. Due respect should be given to community-defined needs and diverse knowledge systems, including science, cultural and social sensitivities;

c Countries are encouraged to set up national advisory environmental education coordinating bodies or round tables representative of various environmental, developmental, educational, gender and other interests, including non-governmental organizations, to encourage partnerships, help mobilize resources, and provide a source of information and focal point for international ties. These bodies would help mobilize and facilitate different population groups and communities to assess their own needs and to develop the necessary skills to create and implement their own environment and development initiatives;

d Educational authorities, with the appropriate assistance from community groups or non-governmental organizations, are recommended to assist or set up pre-service and in-service training programmes for all teachers, administrators, and educational planners, as well as non-formal educators in all sectors, addressing the nature and methods of environmental and development education and making use of relevant experience of non-governmental organizations;

e Relevant authorities should ensure that every school is assisted in designing environmental activity work plans, with the participation of students and staff. Schools should involve schoolchildren in local and regional studies on environmental health, including safe drinking water, sanitation and food and ecosystems and in relevant activities, linking these studies with services and research in national parks, wildlife reserves, ecological heritage sites etc.;

f Educational authorities should promote proven educational methods and the development of innovative teaching methods for educational settings. They should also recognize appropriate traditional education systems in local communities;

g Within two years the United Nations system should undertake a comprehensive review of its educational programmes, encompassing training and public awareness, to reassess priorities and reallocate resources. The UNESCO/UNEP International Environmental Education Programme should, in cooperation with the appropriate bodies of the United Nations system, Governments, non-governmental organizations and others, establish a programme within two years to integrate the decisions of the Conference into the existing United Nations framework adapted to the needs of educators at different levels and circumstances. Regional organizations and national authorities should be encouraged to elaborate similar parallel programmes and opportunities by conducting an analysis of how to mobilize different sectors of the population in order to assess and address their environmental and development education needs;

h There is a need to strengthen, within five years, information exchange by enhancing technologies and capacities necessary to promote environment and development education and public awareness. Countries should cooperate with each other and with the various social sectors and population groups to prepare educational tools that include regional environment and development issues and initiatives, using learning materials and resources suited to their own requirements;

i Countries could support university and other tertiary activities and networks for environmental and development education. Cross-disciplinary courses could be made available to all students. Existing regional networks and activities and national university actions which promote research and common teaching approaches on sustainable development should be built upon, and new partnerships and bridges created with the business and other independent sectors, as well as with all countries for technology, know-how, and knowledge exchange;

j Countries, assisted by international organizations, non-governmental organizations and other sectors, could strengthen or establish national or regional centres of excellence in interdisciplinary research and education in environmental and developmental sciences, law and the management of specific environmental problems. Such centres could be universities or existing networks in each country or region, promoting cooperative research and information sharing and dissemination. At the global level these functions should be performed by appropriate institutions;

k Countries should facilitate and promote non-formal education activities at the local, regional and national levels by cooperating with and supporting the efforts of non-formal educators and other community-based organizations. The appropriate bodies of the United Nations system in cooperation with non-governmental organizations should encourage the development of an international network for the achievement of global educational aims. At the national and local levels, public and scholastic forums should discuss environmental and development issues, and suggest sustainable alternatives to policy makers;

l Educational authorities, with appropriate assistance of non-governmental organizations, including women's and indigenous peoples' organizations, should promote all kinds of adult education programmes for continuing education in environment and development, basing activities around elementary secondary schools and local problems. These authorities and industry should encourage business, industrial and agricultural schools to include such topics in their curricula. The corporate sector could include sustainable development in their education and training programmes. Programmes at a post-graduate level should include specific courses aiming at the further training of decision makers;

m Governments and educational authorities should foster opportunities for women in non-traditional fields and eliminate gender stereotyping in curricula. This could be done by improving enrolment opportunities, including females in advanced programmes as students and instructors, reforming entrance and teacher staffing policies and providing incentives for establishing child-care facilities, as appropriate. Priority should be given to education of young females and to programmes promoting literacy among women;

n Governments should affirm the rights of indigenous peoples, by legislation if necessary, to use their experience and understanding of sustainable development to play a part in education and training;

o The United Nations could maintain a monitoring and evaluative role regarding decisions of the United Nations Conference on Environment and Development on education and awareness, through the relevant United Nations agencies. With Governments and non-governmental organizations, as appropriate, it should present and disseminate decisions in a variety of forms, and should ensure the continuous implementation and review of the educational implications of Conference decisions, in particular through relevant events and conferences.

Means of implementation \$8 – \$9 billion, including about \$3.5 – \$4.5 billion from the international community on grant or concessional terms.

The Gaia Boat arrives at the Rio Conference. This children's boat sailed from Denmark to illustrate the level at which children wished to be involved and the importance of their future role.

In the light of country specific situations, more support for education, training and public awareness activities related to environment and development could be provided, in appropriate cases, through measures such as the following:

a Giving higher priority to those sectors in budget allocations, protecting them from structural cutting requirements;

b Shifting allocations within existing education budgets in favour of primary education, with focus on environment and development;

c Promoting conditions where a larger share of the cost is borne by local communities, with rich communities assisting poorer ones;

d Obtaining additional funds from private donors concentrating on the poorest countries, and those with rates of literacy below 40 per cent;

e Encouraging debt for education swaps;

f Lifting restrictions on private schooling and increasing the flow of funds from and to non-governmental organizations, including small-scale grass-roots organizations;

g Promoting the effective use of existing facilities, for example, multiple school shifts, fuller development of open universities and other long-distance teaching;

h Facilitating low-cost or no-cost use of mass media for the purposes of education;

i Encouraging twinning of universities in developed and developing countries.

B Increasing public awareness

Basis for action There is still a considerable lack of awareness of the interrelated nature of all human activities and the environment, due to inaccurate or insufficient information. Developing countries in particular lack relevant technologies and expertise. There is a need to increase public sensitivity to environment and development problems and involvement in their solutions and foster a sense of personal environmental responsibility and greater motivation and commitment towards sustainable development.

Objective The objective is to promote broad public awareness as an essential part of a global education effort to strengthen attitudes, values and actions which are compatible with sustainable development. It is important to stress the principle of devolving authority, accountability and resources to the most appropriate level with preference given to local responsibility and control over awareness-building activities.

Activities Recognizing that countries, regional and international organizations will develop their own priorities and schedules for implementation in accordance with their needs, policies and programmes, the following activities are proposed:

a Countries should strengthen existing advisory bodies or establish new ones for public environment and development information, and should coordinate activities with, among others, the United Nations, non-governmental organizations and important media. They should encourage public participation in discussions of environmental policies and assessments. Governments should also facilitate and support national to local networking of information through existing networks;

b The United Nations system should improve its outreach in the course of a review of its education and public awareness activities to promote greater involvement and coordination of all parts of the system, especially its information bodies and regional and country operations. Systematic surveys of the impact of awareness programmes should be conducted, recognizing the needs and contributions of specific community groups;

c Countries and regional organizations should be encouraged, as appropriate, to provide public environmental and development information services for raising the awareness of all groups, the private sector and particularly decision makers;

d Countries should stimulate educational establishments in all sectors, especially the tertiary sector, to contribute more to awareness building. Educational materials of all kinds and for all audiences should be based on the best available scientific information, including the natural, behavioural and social sciences, and taking into account aesthetic and ethical dimensions;

e Countries and the United Nations system should promote a cooperative relationship with the media, popular theatre groups, and entertainment and advertising industries by initiating discussions to mobilize their experience in shaping public behaviour and consumption patterns and making wide use of their methods. Such cooperation would also increase the active public participation in the debate on the environment. UNICEF should make child-oriented material available to media as an educational tool, ensuring close cooperation between the out-of-school public information sector and the school curriculum, for the primary level. UNESCO, UNEP and universities should enrich pre-service curricula for journalists on environment and development topics;

f Countries, in cooperation with the scientific community, should establish ways of employing modern communication technologies for effective public outreach. National and local educational authorities and relevant United Nations agencies should expand, as appropriate, the use of audio-visual methods, especially in rural areas in mobile units, by producing television and radio programmes for developing countries, involving local participation, employing interactive multimedia methods and integrating advanced methods with folk media;

g Countries should promote, as appropriate, environmentally sound leisure and tourism activities, building on The Hague Declaration of Tourism (1989) and the current programmes of the World Tourism Organization and UNEP, making suitable use of museums, heritage sites, zoos, botanical gardens, national parks, and other protected areas;

h Countries should encourage non-governmental organizations to increase their involvement in environmental and development problems, through joint awareness initiatives and improved interchange with other constituencies in society;

i Countries and the United Nations system should increase their interaction with and include, as appropriate, indigenous people in the management,

For the first time in history nations of the world met to discuss the twin problems of environment and development. The link between them is vital. Furthermore, we do not have the option of first solving the problems of today and then those of tomorrow. We have to find ways to integrated solutions. UNCED 1992 gave the international community a necessary opportunity for reflection and action. My sincere wishes for the success of the ideals of the Conference are shared by the Swedish people.
King Carl XVI Gustaf
Sweden

planning and development of their local environment, and should promote dissemination of traditional and socially learned knowledge through means based on local customs, especially in rural areas, integrating these efforts with the electronic media, whenever appropriate;

j UNICEF, UNESCO, UNDP and non-governmental organizations should develop support programmes to involve young people and children in environment and development issues, such as children's and youth hearings, building on decisions of the World Summit for Children;

k Countries, the United Nations and non-governmental organizations should encourage mobilization of both men and women in awareness campaigns, stressing the role of the family in environmental activities, women's contribution to transmission of knowledge and social values and the development of human resources;

l Public awareness should be heightened regarding the impacts of violence in society.

Finance and cost evaluation $1.2 billion, including about $110 million from the international community on grant or concessional terms.

C Promoting training

Basis for action Training is one of the most important tools to develop human resources and facilitate the transition to a more sustainable world. It should have a job-specific focus, aimed at filling gaps in knowledge and skill that would help individuals find employment and be involved in environmental and development work. At the same time, training programmes should promote a greater awareness of environment and development issues as a two-way learning process.

Objectives

a To establish or strengthen vocational training programmes that meet the needs of environment and development with ensured access to training opportunities, regardless of social status, age, gender, race or religion;

b To promote a flexible and adaptable workforce of various ages equipped to meet growing environment and development problems and changes arising from the transition to a sustainable society;

c To strengthen national capacities, particularly in scientific education and training, to enable Governments, employers and workers to meet their environmental and development objectives and to facilitate the transfer and assimilation of new environmentally sound, socially acceptable and appropriate technology and know-how;

d To ensure that environmental and human ecological considerations are integrated at all managerial levels and in all functional management areas, such as marketing, production and finance.

Activities Countries with the support of the United Nations system should identify workforce training needs and assess measures to be taken to meet those needs. A review of progress in this area could be undertaken by the United Nations system in 1995.

National professional associations are encouraged to develop and review their codes of ethics and conduct to strengthen environmental connections and commitment. The training and personal development components of programmes sponsored by professional bodies should ensure incorporation of skills and information on the implementation of sustainable development at all points of policy- and decision-making.

Countries and educational institutions should integrate environmental and developmental issues into existing training curricula and promote the exchange of their methodologies and evaluations.

Countries should encourage all sectors of society, such as industry, universities, government officials and employees, non-governmental organizations and community organizations, to include an environmental management component in all relevant training activities, with emphasis on meeting immediate skill requirements through short-term formal and in-plant vocational and management training. Environmental management training capacities should be strengthened, and specialized "training of trainers" programmes should be established to support training at the national and enterprise levels. New training approaches for existing environmentally sound practices should be developed that create employment opportunities and make maximum use of local resource-based methods.

Countries should strengthen or establish practical training programmes for graduates from vocational schools, high schools and universities, in all countries, to enable them to meet labour market requirements and to achieve sustainable livelihoods. Training and retraining programmes should be established to meet structural adjustments which have an impact on employment and skill qualifications.

Governments are encouraged to consult with people in isolated situations, whether geographically, culturally or socially, to ascertain their needs for training to enable them to contribute more fully to developing sustainable work practices and lifestyles.

Governments, industry, trade unions, and consumers should promote an understanding of the interrelationship between good environment and good business practices.

Countries should develop a service of locally trained and recruited environmental technicians able to provide local people and communities, particularly in deprived urban and rural areas, with the services they require, starting from primary environmental care.

Countries should enhance the ability to gain access to, analyse and effectively use information and knowledge available on environment and development. Existing or established special training programmes should be strengthened to support information needs of special groups. The impact of these programmes on productivity, health, safety and employment should be evaluated. National and regional environmental labour-market information systems should be developed that would supply, on a continuing basis, data on environmental job and training opportunities. Environment and development training resource-guides should be prepared and updated, with information on training programmes, curricula, methodologies and evaluation results at the local, national, regional and international levels.

Aid agencies should strengthen the training component in all development projects, emphasizing a multidisciplinary approach, promoting awareness and providing the necessary skills for transition to a sustainable society. The environmental management guidelines of UNDP for operational activities of the United Nations system may contribute to this end.

Existing networks of employers' and workers' organizations, industry associations and non-governmental organizations should facilitate the exchange of experience concerning training and awareness programmes.

Governments, in cooperation with relevant international organizations, should develop and implement strategies to deal with national, regional and local environmental threats and emergencies, emphasizing urgent practical training and awareness programmes for increasing public preparedness.

The United Nations system, as appropriate, should

extend its training programmes, particularly its environmental training and support activities for employers' and workers' organizations.

Finance and cost evaluation $5 billion, including about $2 billion from the international community on grant or concessional terms.

1 Intergovernmental Conference on Environmental Education: Final Report (Paris, UNESCO, 1978), chap. III.
2 Final Report of the World Conference on Education for All: Meeting Basic Learning Needs, Jomtien, Thailand, 5-9 March 1990, Inter-Agency Commission (UNDP, UNESCO, UNICEF, World Bank) for the World Conference on Education for All, New York, 1990.

Chapter 37 National mechanisms and international cooperation for capacity-building

Basis for action The ability of a country to follow sustainable development paths is determined to a large extent by the capacity of its people and its institutions as well as by its ecological and geographical conditions. Specifically, capacity-building encompasses the country's human, scientific, technological, organizational, institutional and resource capabilities. A fundamental goal of capacity-building is to enhance the ability to evaluate and address the crucial questions related to policy choices and modes of implementation among development options, based on an understanding of environmental potentials and limits and of needs as perceived by the people of the country concerned. As a result, the need to strengthen national capacities is shared by all countries.

Building endogenous capacity to implement Agenda 21 will require the efforts of the countries themselves in partnership with relevant United Nations organizations, as well as with developed countries. The international community at the national, subregional and regional levels, municipalities, non-governmental organizations, universities and research centres, and business and other private institutions and organizations could also assist in these efforts. It is essential for individual countries to identify priorities and determine the means for building capacity and capability to implement Agenda 21, taking into account their environmental and economic needs. Skills, knowledge and technical know-how at the individual and institutional levels are necessary for institution-building, policy analysis and development management, including the assessment of alternative courses of action with a view to enhancing access to and transfer of technology and promoting economic development. Technical cooperation, including that related to technology transfer and know-how, encompasses the whole range of activities to develop or strengthen individual and group capacities and capabilities. It should serve the purpose of long-term capacity-building and needs to be managed and coordinated by the countries themselves. Technical cooperation, including that related to technology transfer and know-how, is effective only when it is derived from and related to a country's own strategies and priorities on environment and development and when development agencies and Governments define improved and consistent policies and procedures to support this process.

Objectives The overall objectives of endogenous capacity-building in this programme area are to develop and improve national and related subregional and regional capacities and capabilities for sustainable development, with the involvement of the non-governmental sectors. The programme should assist by:

a Promoting an ongoing participatory process to define country needs and priorities in promoting Agenda 21 and to give importance to technical and professional human resource development and development of institutional capacities and capabilities on the agenda of countries, with due recognition of the potential for optimal use of existing human resources as well as enhancement of the efficiency of existing institutions, and non-governmental organizations including scientific and technological institutions;
b Reorienting and reprioritizing technical cooperation including that related to technology transfer and know-how process with due attention to the specific conditions and individual needs of recipients, while improving coordination among providers of assistance to support countries' own programmes of action. This coordination should also include non-governmental organizations and scientific and technological institutions, as well as business and industry whenever appropriate;
c Shifting time horizons in programme planning and implementation addressing the developing and strengthening of institutional structures to enhance their ability to respond to new longer-term challenges rather than concentrate only on immediate problems;
d Improving and reorienting existing international multilateral institutions with responsibilities for environment and/or development matters to ensure that those institutions have the capability and capacity to integrate environment and development;
e Improving institutional capacity and capability, both public and private, in order to evaluate the environmental impact of all development projects.

Specific objectives include the following:
a Each country should aim to complete, as soon as practicable, if possible by 1994, a review of capacity- and capability-building requirements for devising national sustainable development strategies, including those for generating and implementing its own Agenda 21 action programme;
b By 1997, the Secretary-General of the United Nations should submit to the General Assembly a report on achievement of improved policies, coordination systems and procedures for strengthening the implementation of technical cooperation programmes for sustainable development, as well as on additional measures required to strengthen such cooperation. That report should be prepared on the basis of information provided by countries, international organizations, environment and development institutions, donor agencies and non-governmental partners.

Activities
A *Build a national consensus and formulate capacity-building strategies for implementing Agenda 21*
As an important aspect of overall planning, each country should seek internal consensus at all levels of society on policies and programmes needed for short- and long-term capacity-building to implement its Agenda 21 programme. This consensus should result from a participatory dialogue of relevant interest groups and lead to an identification of skill gaps, institutional capacities and capabilities, technological and scientific requirements and resource needs to enhance environmental knowledge and administration to integrate environment and development. The United Nations Development Programme in partnership with relevant specialized agencies and other international intergovernmental and non-governmental organizations could assist, upon request of Governments, in the identification of the requirements for technical cooperation including those related to technology transfer and know-how and development assistance for the implementation of Agenda 21. The

Section IV

Technological cooperation at work. A WHO/TDR project shows solar panels being used as an energy source for a health centre used by the Yanamami people in the Amazon.

national planning process together, where appropriate, with national sustainable development action plans or strategies should provide the framework for such cooperation and assistance. The United Nations Development Programme should use and further improve its network of field offices and its broad mandate to assist, using its experience in the field of technical cooperation for facilitating capacity-building at the country and regional levels and making full use of the expertise of other bodies, in particular the United Nations Environment Programme, the World Bank and regional commissions and development banks, as well as relevant international intergovernmental and non-governmental organizations.

B *Identify national sources and present requests for technical cooperation, including that related to technology transfer and know-how in the framework of sector strategies*

Countries desiring arrangements for technical cooperation, including that related to technology transfer and know-how, with international organizations and donor institutions should formulate requests in the framework of long-term sector or subsector capacity-building strategies. Strategies should, as appropriate, address policy adjustments to be implemented, budgetary issues, cooperation and coordination among institutions, human resource requirements, and technology and scientific equipment requirements. They should cover public and private sector needs and consider strengthening scientific training and educational and research programmes, including such training in the developed countries and the strengthening of centres of excellence in developing countries. Countries could designate and strengthen a central unit to organize and coordinate technical cooperation, linking it with the priority-setting and resource allocation process.

C *Establish a review mechanism of technical cooperation in and related to technology transfer and know-how*

Donors and recipients, the organizations and institutions of the United Nations system, and international public and private organizations should review the development of the cooperation process as it relates to technical cooperation, including that related to technology transfer and know-how activities linked to sustainable development. To facilitate this process, the Secretary-General could undertake, taking into account work carried out by the United Nations Development Programme and other organizations in preparation for the United Nations Conference on Environment and Development, consultations with developing countries, regional organizations, organizations and institutions of the United Nations system, including regional commissions, and multilateral and bilateral aid and environment agencies, with a view to further strengthening the endogenous capacities of countries and improving technical cooperation, including that related to the technology transfer and know-how process. The following aspects should be reviewed:

a Evaluation of existing capacity and capability for the integrated management of environment and development, including technical, technological and institutional capacities and capabilities, and facilities to assess the environmental impact of development projects; and evaluation of abilities to respond to and link up with needs for technical cooperation, including that related to technology transfer and know-how, of Agenda 21 and the global conventions on climate change and biological diversity;

b Assessment of the contribution of existing activities in technical cooperation, including that related to technology transfer and know-how, towards strengthening and building national capacity and capability for integrated environment and development management and assessment of the means of improving the quality of international technical cooperation, including that related to technology transfer and know-how;

c A strategy for shifting to a capacity- and capability-building thrust that recognizes the need for the operational integration of environment and development with longer-term commitments, having as a basis the set of national programmes established by each country, through a participatory process;

d Consideration of greater use of long-term cooperative arrangements between municipalities, non-governmental organizations, universities, training and research centres and business, public and private institutions with counterparts in other countries or within countries or regions. Programmes such as the Sustainable Development Networks of the United Nations Development Programme should be assessed in this regard;

e Strengthening of the sustainability of projects by including in the original project design consideration of environmental impacts, the costs of institution-building, human resource development and technology needs, as well as financial and organizational requirements for operation and maintenance;

f Improvement of technical cooperation, including that related to technology transfer and know-how and management processes, by giving greater attention to capacity- and capability-building as an integral part of sustainable development strategies for environment and development programmes both in country-related coordination processes, such as consultative groups and round tables, and in sectoral coordination mechanisms to enable developing countries to participate actively in obtaining assistance from different sources.

D *Enhance the expertise and collective contribution of the United Nations system for capacity- and capability-building initiatives*

Organizations, organs, bodies and institutions of the United Nations system, together with other international and regional organizations and the public and private sectors, could, as appropriate, strengthen their joint activities in technical cooperation, including that related to technology transfer and know-how, in order to address linked environment and development issues and to promote coherence and consistency of action. Organizations could assist and reinforce countries, particularly least developed countries, upon request, on matters relating to national environmental and developmental policies, human resource development and fielding of experts, legislation, natural resources and environmental data.

The United Nations Development Programme, the World Bank and regional multilateral development banks, as part of their participation in national and regional coordination mechanisms, should assist in facilitating capacity- and capability-building at the country level, drawing upon the special expertise and operational capacity of the United Nations Environment Programme in the environmental field as well as of the specialized agencies, organizations of the United Nations system and regional and subregional organizations in their respective areas of competence. For this purpose the United Nations Development Programme should mobilize funding for capacity and capability-building, utilizing its network of field offices and its broad mandate and experience in the field of technical cooperation, including that related to technology transfer and know-how. The United Nations Development Programme, together with these international organizations, should at the same time continue to develop consultative processes to enhance mobilization and coordination of funds from the international community for capacity and capability-building, including the establishment of an appropriate database. These responsibilities may need to be accompanied by strengthening of the United Nations Development Programme's own capacities.

The national entity in charge of technical cooperation, with the assistance of the United Nations Development Programme resident representatives and the United Nations Environment Programme representatives, should establish a small group of key actors to steer the process, giving priority to the country's own strategies and priorities. The experience gained through existing planning exercises such as the national reports for the United Nations Conference on Environment and Development, national conservation strategies and environment action plans should be fully used and incorporated into a country-driven, participatory and sustainable development strategy. This should be complemented with information networks and consultations with donor organizations in order to improve coordination, as well as access to the existing body of scientific and technical knowledge and information available in institutions elsewhere.

F *Harmonize the delivery of assistance at the regional level*

At the regional level, existing organizations should consider the desirability of improved regional and subregional consultative processes and round-table meetings to facilitate the exchange of data, information and experience in the implementation of Agenda 21. The United Nations Development Programme, building on the results of the regional surveys on capacity-building that those regional organizations carried out on the United Nations Conference on Environment and Development initiative, and in collaboration with existing regional, subregional or national organizations with potential for regional coordination, should provide a significant input for this purpose. The relevant national unit should establish a steering mechanism. A periodic review mechanism should be established among the countries of the region with the assistance of the appropriate relevant regional organizations and the participation of development banks, bilateral aid agencies and non-governmental organizations. Other possibilities are to develop national and regional research and training facilities building on existing regional and subregional institutions.

Financing and costs The cost of bilateral expenditures to developing countries for technical cooperation, including that related to technology transfer and know-how, is about $15 billion, or about 25 per cent of total official development assistance. The implementation of Agenda 21 will require a more effective use of these funds and additional funding in key areas.

Estimated average total anual cost between $300 million and $1 billion from the international community on grant or concessional terms.

Chapter 38 International institutional arrangements

Basis for action The mandate of UNCED emanates from General Assembly resolution 44/228 which, *inter alia*, affirmed that UNCED should elaborate strategies and measures to halt and reverse the effects of environmental degradation in the context of increased national and international efforts to promote sustainable and environmentally sound development in all countries and that the promotion of economic growth in developing countries is essential to address problems of environmental degradation. The intergovernmental follow-up to the Conference process shall be within the framework of the United Nations system, with the General Assembly being the supreme policy-making forum that would provide overall guidance to Governments, United Nations system and relevant treaty bodies. At the same time, Governments, as well as regional economic and technical cooperation organizations, have a responsibility to play an important role in the follow-up to UNCED. Their commitments and actions should be adequately supported by the United Nations system and multilateral financial institutions. Thus, national and international efforts would mutually benefit from one another.

In fulfilling the mandate of the Conference, there is a need for institutional arrangements within the United Nations system in conformity with, and providing input to the restructuring and revitalization of the United Nations in the economic, social and related fields, and the overall reform of the United Nations, including ongoing changes in the Secretariat. In the spirit of reform and revitalization of the United Nations system, implementation of Agenda 21 and other conclusions of UNCED shall be based on an action- and result-oriented approach and consistent with the principles of universality, democracy, transparency, cost-effectiveness and accountability.

The United Nations system, with its multisectoral capacity and the extensive experience of a number of specialized agencies in various spheres of international cooperation in the field of environment and development, is uniquely positioned to assist Governments establish more effective patterns of economic and social development with a view to achieving the objectives of Agenda 21 and sustainable development.

All agencies of the United Nations system have a key role to play in the implementation of Agenda 21 within their respective competence. To ensure proper coordination and avoid duplication in the implementation of Agenda 21, there should be an effective division of labour between various parts of the United Nations system based on their terms of reference and comparative advantages. Member States, through relevant governing bodies, are in a position to ensure that these tasks are carried out properly. In order to facilitate evaluation of agencies' performance and promote knowledge of their activities, all bodies of the United Nations system should be required to elaborate and publish reports of their activities on the implemen-

The Swiss authorities, deeply concerned about the urgency of all the problems of development and the environment, committed themselves unreservedly to the process leading to Rio. They are equally determined to ensure a follow-up to the Earth Summit and to take part in the construction of a new ethic governing relations between states, between the rich and the poor, between man and nature. Rio confirmed our conviction that there must be no development without protection of the environment and that this must be a pillar of our economic strategies. Rio was an undeniable success which must beget others.
Rene Felber
President
Swiss Federation

tation of Agenda 21 on a regular basis. Serious and continuous reviews of their policies, programmes, budgets and activities will also be required.

The continued active and effective participation of non-governmental organizations, the scientific community and the private sector as well as local groups and communities are important in the implementation of Agenda 21.

The institutional structure envisaged below will be based on agreement on financial resources and mechanisms, technology transfer, the Rio Declaration and Agenda 21. In addition, there has to be an effective link between substantive action and financial support, and this requires close and effective cooperation and exchange of information between the United Nations system and the multilateral financial institutions for the follow-up of Agenda 21 within the institutional arrangement.

Objectives The overall objective is the integration of environment and development issues at national, sub-regional, regional and international levels, including in the United Nations system institutional arrangements.

Specific objectives shall be:

a to ensure and review the implementation of Agenda 21 so as to achieve sustainable development in all countries;

b to enhance the role and functioning of the United Nations system in the field of environment and development. All relevant agencies, organizations and programmes of the United Nations system should adopt concrete programmes for the implementation of Agenda 21 and also provide policy-guidance for United Nations activities or advice to Governments upon request, within their respective areas of competence;

c to strengthen cooperation and coordination on environment and development in the United Nations system;

d to encourage interaction and cooperation between the United Nations system and other intergovernmental and non-governmental sub-regional, regional and global institutions and non-governmental organizations in the field of environment and development;

e to strengthen institutional capabilities and arrangements required for the effective implementation, follow-up and review of Agenda 21;

f to assist in the strengthening and coordination of national, sub-regional and regional capacities and actions in the areas of environment and development;

g to establish effective cooperation and exchange of information between the United Nations organs, organizations, programmes and the multilateral financial bodies, within the institutional arrangements for the follow-up of Agenda 21;

h to respond to continuing and emerging issues relating to environment and development;

i to ensure that any new institutional arrangements would support revitalization, clear division of responsibilities and the avoidance of duplication in the United Nations system and depend to the maximum extent possible upon existing resources.

Institutional structural

A *General Assembly*

The General Assembly, as the highest level intergovernmental mechanism, is the principal policy-making and appraisal organ on matters relating to the follow-up of UNCED. The General Assembly would organize a regular review of the implementation of Agenda 21. In fulfilling this task the General Assembly could consider the timing, format and organizational aspects of such a review. In particular, the General Assembly could consider holding a special session no later than 1997 for the purposes of overall review and appraisal of Agenda 21, with adequate preparations at a high level.

B *Economic and Social Council*

The Economic and Social Council, in the context of its Charter role *vis-à-vis* the General Assembly and the ongoing restructuring and revitalization of the United Nations in the economic, social and related fields, would assist the General Assembly through overseeing system-wide coordination, overview on the implementation of Agenda 21 and making recommendations in this regard. In addition, the Council would undertake the task of directing system-wide coordination and integration of environmental and developmental aspects in the United Nations' policies and programmes and make appropriate recommendations to the General Assembly, specialized agencies concerned and Member States. Appropriate steps should be taken to obtain regular reports from specialized agencies on their plans and programmes related to the implementation of Agenda 21, pursuant to Article 64 of the Charter of the United Nations. The Economic and Social Council should organize a periodic review of the work of the Commission on Sustainable Development envisaged in paragraph 38.11, as well as of system-wide activities to integrate environment and development, making full use of its high-level and coordination segments.

C *Commission on Sustainable Development*

In order to ensure the effective follow-up of the Conference, as well as to enhance international cooperation and rationalize the intergovernmental decision-making capacity for the integration of environment and development issues and to examine the progress of the implementation of Agenda21 at the national, regional and international levels, a high-level Commission on Sustainable Development should be established in accordance with Article 68 of the Charter of the United Nations. This Commission would report to the Economic and Social Council in the context of the Council's role under the Charter *vis-à-vis* the General Assembly. It would consist of representatives of States elected as members with due regard to equitable geographical distribution. Representatives of non-member States of the Commission would have observer status. The Commission should provide for active involvement of organs, programmes and organizations of the United Nations system, international financial institutions and other relevant intergovernmental organizations, and encourage the participation of non-governmental organizations, including industry and the business and scientific communities. The first meeting of the Commission should be convened no later than 1993. The Commission should be supported by the secretariat envisaged in Chapter 38. Meanwhile the Secretary-General of the United Nations is requested to ensure adequate interim administrative secretariat arrangements.

The General Assembly, at its forty-seventh session, should determine specific organizational modalities for the work of this Commission, such as its membership, its relationship with other intergovernmental United Nations bodies dealing with matters related to environment and development, and the frequency, duration and venue of its meetings. These modalities should take into account the ongoing process of revitalization and restructuring of the work of the United Nations in the economic, social and related fields, in particular measures recommended by the General Assembly in resolutions 45/264 of 13 May 1991 and 46/235 of 13 April 1992 and other relevant Assembly resolutions. In this respect, the Secretary-General of the United Nations, with the assistance of the Secretary-General of the United Nations Conference on Environment and Development, is requested to prepare for the Assembly a report with

We have to find a balance between the needs of people and the environment in which they live. We have to find a balance between the exploitation of that environment, which is vital for people's survival, and the conservation of that environment which is vital for its survival. We have to find a balance between the needs of the living and our obligations to future generations. Recall Voltaire's luckless hero, Candide, he decided to turn his back on the world and to stay at home "to cultivate his garden". We do not have that choice, the world is our garden and together we must cultivate it.
John Major
Prime Minister
United Kingdom

appropriate recommendations and proposals.

The Commission on Sustainable Development should have the following functions:

a To monitor progress in the implementation of Agenda 21 and activities related to the integration of environmental and developmental goals throughout the United Nations system through analysis and evaluation of reports from all relevant organs, organizations, programmes and institutions of the United Nations system dealing with various issues of environment and development, including those related to finance;

b To consider information provided by Governments, including, for example, in the form of periodic communications or national reports regarding the activities they undertake to implement Agenda 21, the problems they face, such as problems related to financial resources and technology transfer, and other environment and development issues they find relevant;

c To review the progress in the implementation of the commitments contained in Agenda 21, including those related to provision of financial resources and transfer of technology;

d To receive and analyse relevant imput from competent non-governmental organizations, including the scientific and the private sector, in the context of the overall implementation of Agenda 21;

e To enhance the dialogue within the framework of the United Nations with non-governmental organizations and the independent sector as well as other entities outside the United Nations system;

f To consider, where appropriate, information regarding the progress made in the implementation of environmental conventions which could be made available by the relevant Conferences of Parties;

g To provide appropriate recommendations to the General Assembly, through the Economic and Social Council, on the basis of an integrated consideration of the reports and issues related to the implementation of Agenda 21; and

h To consider, at an appropriate time, the results of the survey to be conducted expeditiously by the United Nations Secretary-General of all UNCED recommendations for capacity-building programmes, information networks, task forces and other mechanisms to support the integration of environment and development at regional and sub-regional levels.

Within the intergovernmental framework, consideration should be given to allow non-governmental organizations including those related to major groups, particularly women's groups, committed to the implementation of Agenda 21 to have relevant information available to them including information, reports and other data produced within the United Nations system.

D *The Secretary-General*

Strong and effective leadership on the part of the Secretary-General is crucial, since he/she would be the focal point of the institutional arrangements within the United Nations system for the successful follow-up to the Conference and for the implementation of Agenda 21.

E *High-level interagency coordination mechanism*

Agenda 21, as the basis for action by the international community to integrate environment and development, should provide the principal framework for coordination of relevant activities within the United Nations system. To ensure effective monitoring, coordination and supervision of the involvement of the United Nations system in the follow-up to the Conference, there is a need for a coordination mechanism under the direct leadership of the Secretary-General.

This task should be given to the Administrative Committee on Coordination (ACC) headed by the Secretary-General. ACC would thus provide a vital link and interface between the multilateral financial institutions and other United Nations bodies at the highest administrative level. The Secretary-General should continue to revitalize the functioning of the Committee. All heads of agencies and institutions of the United Nations system shall be expected to cooperate with the Secretary-General fully in order to make ACC work effectively in fulfilling its crucial role and ensure successful implementation of Agenda 21. The ACC should consider establishing a special task force, subcommittee or sustainable development board, taking into account the experience of the Designated Officials on Environmental Matters (DOEM) and the Committee of International Development Institutions on the Environment (CIDIE) as well as the respective roles of the UNEP and UNDP. Its report should be submitted to the relevant intergovernmental bodies.

F *High-level advisory body*

Intergovernmental bodies, the Secretary-General and the United Nations system as a whole may also benefit from the expertise of a high-level advisory board consisting of eminent persons knowledgeable about environment and development, including relevant sciences, appointed by the Secretary-General in their personal capacity. In this regard, the Secretary-General should make appropriate recommendations to the 47th session of the General Assembly.

G *Secretariat support structure*

A highly qualified and competent secretariat support structure within the United Nations Secretariat, drawing, *inter alia*, on the expertise gained in the UNCED preparatory process is essential for the follow-up to the Conference and the implementation of Agenda 21. This secretariat support structure should provide support to the work of both intergovernmental and interagency coordination mechanisms. Concrete organizational decisions fall within the competence of the Secretary-General as the chief administrative officer of the Organization, who is requested to report on the provisions to be made, covering staffing implications, as soon as practicable, taking into account gender balance as defined in Article 8 of the United Nations Charter, and the need for the optimum use of existing resources in the context of current and ongoing restructuring of the United Nations Secretariat.

H *Organs, programmes, organizations of the United Nations system*

In the follow-up to the Conference, in particular implementation of Agenda 21, all relevant organs, programmes and organizations of the United Nations system will have an important role within their respective areas of expertise and mandates in supporting and supplementing national efforts. Coordination and mutual complementarity of their efforts to promote integration of environment and development can be enhanced through countries encouraging to maintain consistent positions in the various governing bodies.

1. United Nations Environment Programme In the follow-up to the Conference, there will be a need for an enhanced and strengthened role of UNEP and its Governing Council. The Governing Council should within its mandate continue to play its role with regard to policy guidance and coordination in the field of the environment, taking into account the development perspective.

Priority areas on which UNEP should concentrate include the following:

a strengthening its catalytic role in stimulating and promoting environmental activities and considerations throughout the United Nations system;

b promoting international cooperation in the field of environment and recommending, as appropriate, policies to this end;

c developing and promoting the use of techniques such as natural resource accounting and environmental economics;

d environmental monitoring and assessment, both

through improved participation by the United Nations system agencies in the Earthwatch programme and expanded relations with private scientific and non-governmental research institutes; strengthening and making operational its early warning function;

e coordination and promotion of relevant scientific research with a view to providing a consolidated basis for decision-making;

f dissemination of environmental information and data to Governments and to organs, programmes and organizations of the United Nations system;

g raising general awareness and action in the area of environmental protection through collaboration with the general public, non-governmental entities and intergovernmental institutions;

h further development of international environmental law, in particular conventions and guidelines, promotion of its implementation, and coordinating functions arising from an increasing number of international legal agreements, *inter alia*, the functioning of the secretariats of the Conventions, taking into account the need for the most efficient use of resources, including possible co-location of secretariats established in the future;

i further development and promotion of the widest possible use of environmental impact assessments, including activities carried out under the auspices of United Nations specialized agencies, and in connection with every significant economic development project or activity;

j facilitation of information exchange on environmentally sound technologies, including legal aspects, and provision of training;

k promotion of sub-regional and regional cooperation and support to relevant initiatives and programmes for environmental protection including playing a major contributing and coordinating role in the regional mechanisms in the field of environment identified for the follow-up to UNCED;

l providing technical, legal and institutional advice to Governments, upon request in establishing and enhancing their national legal and institutional frameworks, in particular, in cooperation with UNDP capacity-building efforts;

m supporting Governments, upon request, and development agencies and organs in the integration of environmental aspects into their development policies and programmes, in particular through provision of environmental, technical and policy advice during programme formulation and implementation;

n further developing assessment and assistance in cases of environmental emergencies.

In order for UNEP to perform all of these functions, while retaining its role as the principal body within the United Nations system in the field of environment and taking into account the development aspects of environmental questions, it would require access to greater expertise and provision of adequate financial resources and it would require closer cooperation and collaboration with development and other relevant organs of the United Nations system. Furthermore, UNEP's regional offices should be strengthened without weakening its headquarters in Nairobi, and UNEP should take steps to reinforce and intensify its liaison and interaction with UNDP and the World Bank.

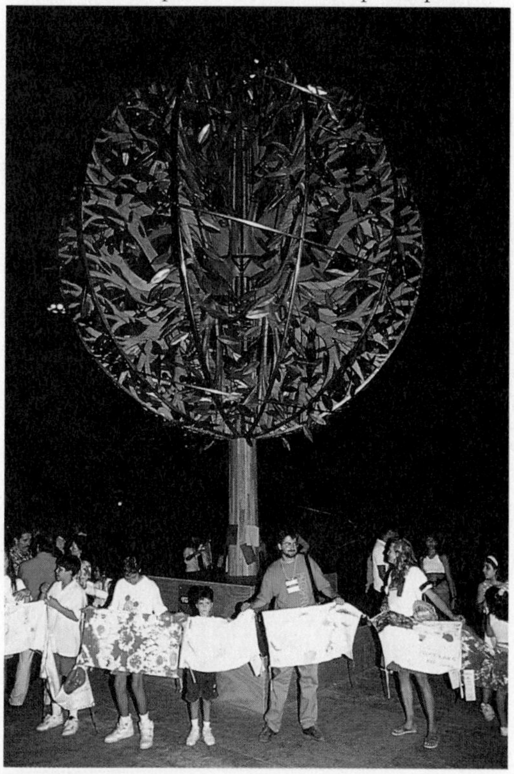

2. United Nations Development Programme UNDP, like UNEP, also has a crucial role in the follow-up to the UNCED. Through its network of field offices it would foster the United Nations system's collective thrust in support of the implementation of Agenda 21, at the country, regional, interregional and global levels, drawing on the expertise of the specialized agencies and other United Nations organizations and bodies involved in operational activities. The role of the Resident Representative/Resident Coordinator of UNDP needs to be strengthened in order to coordinate the field-level activities of the United Nations operational activities.

Its role would include the following:

a acting as the lead agency in organizing United Nations system efforts towards capacity-building at the local, national and regional levels;

b mobilizing donor resources on behalf of Governments for capacity-building in recipient countries and, where appropriate, through the use of UNDP round-table mechanisms;

c strengthening its own programmes in support of follow-up to UNCED without prejudice to the Fifth Programme Cycle;

d assisting recipient countries, upon request, in the establishment and strengthening of national coordination mechanisms and networks related to activities for the follow-up of the UNCED;

e assisting recipient countries, upon request, in coordinating the mobilization of domestic financial resources;

f promoting and strengthening the role and involvement of women, youth and other major groups, in recipient countries in the implementation of Agenda 21.

3. United Nations Conference on Trade and Development The United Nations Conference on Trade and Development should play an important role in the implementation of Agenda 21 as extended at the eighth session of the Conference, taking into account the importance of the interrelationships between development, international trade and the environment and in accordance with its mandate in the area of sustainable development.

4. United Nations Sudano-Sahelian Office The role of the United Nations Sudano-Sahelian Office, with added resources that may become available, operating under the umbrella of UNDP and with the support of UNEP, should be strengthened so that this body can assume an appropriate major advisory role and participate effectively in the implementation of Agenda 21 provisions related to combating drought, desertification as well as land resource management. In this context, the experience gained could be used by all other countries affected by drought and desertification, in particular those in Africa, with special attention to countries most affected or classified as least-developed countries.

The Tree of Life at the Global Forum in Rio featured pledges from people world-wide prepared to make a commitment to changing their lives to benefit the environment. Generating action and raising awareness in the area of environmental protection is an integral part of the UNEP programme.

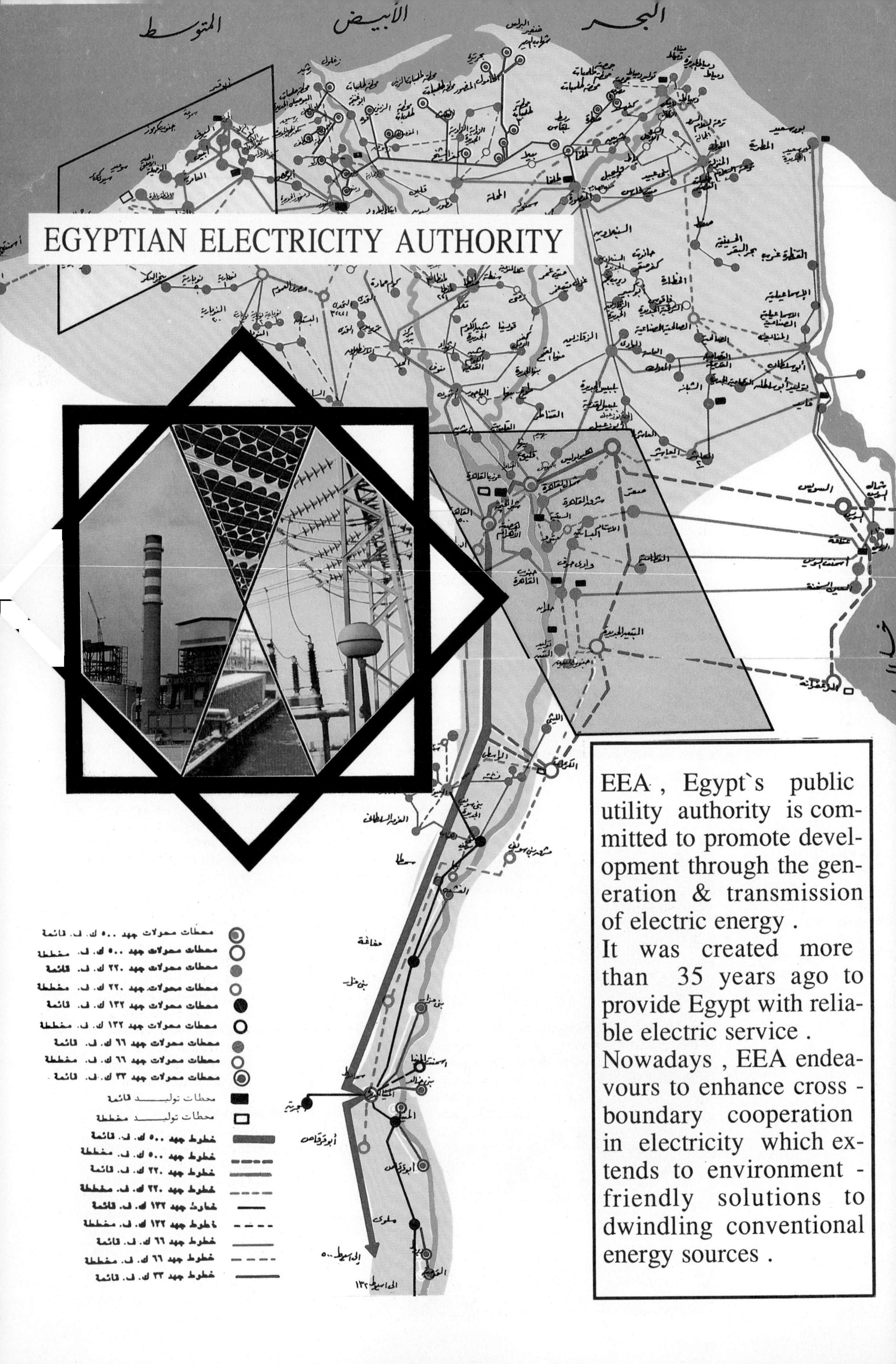
البحر الأبيض المتوسط
EGYPTIAN ELECTRICITY AUTHORITY
محطات محولات جهد ٥٠٠ ك. ف. قائمة
محطات محولات جهد ٥٠٠ ك. ف. مخططة
محطات محولات جهد ٢٢٠ ك. ف. قائمة
محطات محولات جهد ٢٢٠ ك. ف. مخططة
محطات محولات جهد ١٣٢ ك. ف. قائمة
محطات محولات جهد ١٣٢ ك. ف. مخططة
محطات محولات جهد ٦٦ ك. ف. قائمة
محطات محولات جهد ٦٦ ك. ف. مخططة
محطات محولات جهد ٣٣ ك. ف. قائمة
محطات توليد قائمة
محطات توليد مخططة
خطوط جهد ٥٠٠ ك. ف. قائمة
خطوط جهد ٥٠٠ ك. ف. مخططة
خطوط جهد ٢٢٠ ك. ف. قائمة
خطوط جهد ٢٢٠ ك. ف. مخططة
خطوط جهد ١٣٢ ك. ف. قائمة
خطوط جهد ١٣٢ ك. ف. مخططة
خطوط جهد ٦٦ ك. ف. قائمة
خطوط جهد ٦٦ ك. ف. مخططة
خطوط جهد ٣٣ ك. ف. قائمة
EEA , Egypt`s public utility authority is committed to promote development through the generation & transmission of electric energy .
It was created more than 35 years ago to provide Egypt with reliable electric service .
Nowadays , EEA endeavours to enhance cross - boundary cooperation in electricity which extends to environment - friendly solutions to dwindling conventional energy sources .

The presence of non-governmental organizations was very strong at Rio through the Global Forum. One proposal of Agenda 21 includes the setting up of an Earth Council as a representative body for NGOs.

5. United Nations specialized agencies and related organizations and other relevant intergovernmental organizations All United Nations specialized agencies, related organizations and other relevant intergovernmental organizations within their respective fields of competence have an important role to play in the implementation of relevant parts of Agenda 21 and other decisions of UNCED. Their governing bodies may consider ways of strengthening and adjusting activities and programmes in line with Agenda 21, in particular, regarding projects for promoting sustainable development. Furthermore, they may consider establishing special arrangements with donors and financial institutions for project implementation that may require additional resources.

I *Regional and sub-regional cooperation and implementation*

Regional and sub-regional cooperation will be an important part of the Conference outcome. The United Nations regional economic commissions, regional development banks and regional economic and technical cooperation organizations, within their respective agreed mandates, can contribute to this process by:

a promoting regional and sub-regional capacity-building;

b promoting the integration of environmental concerns in regional and sub-regional development policies;

c promoting regional and sub-regional cooperation, where appropriate, regarding transboundary issues related to sustainable development.

Regional economic commissions, as appropriate, should play a leading role in coordinating regional and sub-regional activities by sectoral and other United Nations bodies and shall assist countries in achieving sustainable development. These commissions, regional programmes within the United Nations system, as well as other regional organizations should review the need for modification of ongoing activities, as appropriate, in light of Agenda 21.

There must be active cooperation and collaboration among the regional commissions and other relevant organizations, regional development banks, non-governmental organizations and other institutions at the regional level. UNEP and UNDP, together with the regional commissions, would have a crucial role to play, especially in providing the necessary assistance, with particular emphasis on building and strengthening the national capacity of Member States.

There is a need for closer cooperation between UNEP and UNDP, together with other relevant institutions, in the implementation of projects to halt environmental degradation or its impact, and to support training programmes in environmental planning and management for sustainable development at the regional level.

Regional intergovernmental technical and economic organizations have an important role to play in helping Governments to take coordinated action in solving environment issues of regional significance.

Regional and subregional organizations should play a major role in the implementation of Agenda 21 provisions related to combating drought and desertification. UNEP, UNDP and UNSO should assist and cooperate with those relevant organizations.

Cooperation between regional and subregional organizations and relevant organizations of the United Nations system should be encouraged, where appropriate, in other sectoral areas.

J *National implementation*

States have an important role to play in the follow-up of UNCED and the implementation of Agenda 21. National level efforts should be undertaken by all countries in an integrated manner so that both environment and development concerns can be dealt with in a coherent manner.

Policy decisions and activities at the national level, tailored to support and implement Agenda 21 should be supported by the United Nations system upon request.

Furthermore, States could consider the preparation of national reports. In this context, the organs of the United Nations system should, upon request, assist countries, in particular developing countries. Countries could also consider the preparation of national action plans for the implementation of Agenda 21.

Existing assistance consortia, consultative groups and round tables should make greater efforts to integrate environmental considerations and related development objectives into their development assistance strategies, and consider reorienting and appropriately adjusting their membership and operations to facilitate this process and better support national efforts to integrate environment and development.

States may wish to consider setting up a national coordination structure responsible for the follow-up of Agenda 21. Within this structure, which would benefit from the expertise of non-governmental organizations, submissions and other relevant information could be made to the United Nations.

K *Cooperation between United Nations bodies and international financial organizations*

The success of the follow-up to the Conference is dependent upon an effective link between substantive action and financial support, and this requires close and effective cooperation between United Nations bodies and the multilateral financial organizations. The Secretary-General and heads of United Nations programmes, organizations and the multi-lateral financial organizations have a special responsibility in forging such a cooperation, not only through full participation in the United Nations high-level coordination mechanism (Administrative Committee on Coordination) but also at regional and national levels. In particular, representatives of multilateral financial institutions and mechanisms, as well as the International Fund for Agricultural Development, should be actively associated with deliberations of the intergovernmental structure responsible for the follow up to Agenda 21.

L *Non-governmental organizations*

Non-governmental organizations and major groups are important partners in the implementation of

Section IV

Agenda 21. Relevant non-governmental organizations, including scientific community, the private sector, women's groups, etc., should be given opportunities to make their contributions and establish appropriate relationships with the United Nations system. Support should be provided for developing countries' non-governmental organizations and their self-organized networks.

The United Nations system, including international finance and development agencies, and all intergovernmental organizations and forums should, in consultation with non-governmental organizations take measures to:

a design open and effective means to achieve the participation of non-governmental organizations, including those related to major groups, in the process established to review and evaluate the implementation of Agenda 21 at all levels and promote their contribution to it;

b take into account the findings of non-governmental organizations' review systems and evaluation processes in relevant reports of the Secretary-General to the General Assembly and all pertinent United Nations agencies and intergovernmental organizations and forums concerning implementation of Agenda 21 in accordance with its review process.

Procedures should be established for an expanded role for non-governmental organizations, including those related to major groups, with accreditation based on the procedures used in UNCED. Such organizations should have access to reports and other information produced by the United Nations system. The General Assembly, at an early stage, should examine ways of enhancing the involvement of non-governmental organizations within the United Nations system in relation to the UNCED follow-up process.

The Conference takes note of other institutional initiatives for the implementation of Agenda 21, such as the proposal to establish a non-governmental Earth Council and the proposal to appoint a guardian for future generations as well as other initiatives by local Governments and business sectors.

Chapter 39 International legal instruments and mechanisms

Basis for action The recognition that the following vital aspects of the universal, multilateral and bilateral treaty-making process should be taken into account:

a The further development of international law on sustainable development, giving special attention to the delicate balance between environmental and developmental concerns;

b The need to clarify and strengthen the relationship between existing international instruments or agreements in the field of environment and relevant social and economic agreements or instruments, taking into account the special needs of developing countries;

c At the global level, the essential importance of the participation in and the contribution of all countries, including the developing countries, to treaty-making in the field of international law on sustainable development. Many of the existing international legal instruments and agreements in the field of environment have been developed without adequate participation and contribution of developing countries, and thus may require review in order to reflect the concerns and interests of developing countries and to ensure a balanced governance of such instruments and agreements;

d Developing countries should also be provided with technical assistance in their attempts to enhance their national legislative capabilities in the field of sustainable development;

e Future codification projects for the progressive development and codification of international law on sustainable development should take into account the ongoing work of the International Law Commission; and

f Any negotiations for the progressive development and codification of international law concerning sustainable development should, in general, be conducted on a universal basis, taking into account special circumstances in the various regions.

Objectives The overall objective of the review and development of international environmental law should be to evaluate and to promote the efficacy of that law and to promote the integration of environment and development policies through effective international agreements or instruments, taking into account both universal principles and the particular and differentiated needs and concerns of all countries.

Specific objectives are:

a To identify and address difficulties which prevent some States, in particular developing countries, from participating in or duly implementing international agreements or instruments and, where appropriate, to review or revise them with the purposes of integrating environmental and developmental concerns and laying down a sound basis for the implementation of these agreements or instruments;

b To set priorities for future international law-making on sustainable development at the global, regional or sub-regional level, with a view to enhancing the efficacy of international law in this field through, in particular, the integration of environmental and developmental concerns;

c To promote and support the effective participation of all countries concerned, in particular developing countries in the negotiation, implementation, review and governance of international agreements or instruments, including appropriate provision of technical and financial assistance and other available mechanisms for this purpose, as well as the use of differential obligations where appropriate;

d To promote, through the gradual development of universally and multilaterally negotiated agreements or instruments, international standards for the protection of the environment that take into account the different situations and capabilities of countries. States recognize that environmental policies should deal with the root causes of environmental degradation, thus preventing environmental measures from resulting in unnecessary restrictions to trade. Trade policy measures for environmental purposes should not constitute a means of arbitrary or unjustifiable discrimination or a disguised restriction on international trade. Unilateral actions to deal with environmental challenges outside the jurisdiction of the importing country should be avoided. Environmental measures addressing international environmental problems should, as far as possible, be based on an international consensus. Domestic measures targeted to achieve certain environmental objectives may need trade measures to render them effective. Should trade policy measures be found necessary for the enforcement of environmental policies, certain principles and rules should apply. These could include, *inter alia*, the principle of non-discrimination; the principle that the trade measure chosen should be the least trade-restrictive necessary to achieve the objectives; an obligation to ensure transparency in the use of trade measures related to the environment and to provide adequate notification of national regulations; and the need to give consideration to the special conditions and development requirements of developing countries as they move towards

internationally agreed environmental objectives.
e To ensure the effective, full and prompt implementation of legally binding instruments, and to facilitate timely review and adjustment of agreements or instruments by the parties concerned, taking into account the special needs and concerns of all countries, in particular developing countries;
f To improve the effectiveness of institutions, mechanisms and procedures for the administration of agreements and instruments;
g To identify and prevent actual or potential conflicts, particularly between environmental and social/ economic agreements or instruments, with a view to ensuring that such agreements or instruments are consistent. Where conflicts arise, they should be appropriately resolved;
h To study and consider the broadening and strengthening of the capacity of mechanisms, *inter alia* in the United Nations system, to facilitate, where appropriate and agreed by the parties concerned, the identification, avoidance and settlement of international disputes in the field of sustainable development, duly taking into account existing bilateral and multilateral agreements for the settlement of such disputes.

Activities Activities and means of implementation should be considered in the light of the above Basis for Action and Objectives without prejudice to the right of every State to put forward suggestions in this regard in the General Assembly of the United Nations. These suggestions could be reproduced in a separate compilation on sustainable development.

A Review, assessment and fields of action in international law for sustainable development

While ensuring the effective participation of all countries concerned, Parties should at periodic intervals review and assess both the past performance and effectiveness of existing international agreements or instruments as well as the priorities for future law-making on sustainable development. This may include an examination of the feasibility of elaborating general rights and obligations of States, as appropriate, in the field of sustainable development, as provided by General Assembly resolution 44/228. In certain cases, attention should be given to the possibility of taking into account varying circumstances through differential obligations or gradual application. As an option for carrying out this task, earlier UNEP practice may be followed whereby legal experts designated by governments could meet at suitable intervals to be decided later with a broader environmental and developmental perspective.
a Measures in accordance with international law should be considered to address, in times of armed conflict, large-scale destruction of the environment that cannot be justified under international law. The General Assembly and the Sixth Committee are the appropriate fora to deal with this subject. The specific competence and role of the International Committee of the Red Cross should be taken into account.
b In view of the vital necessity to ensure safe and environmentally sound nuclear power, and in order to strengthen international cooperation in this field, efforts should be made to conclude the ongoing negotiations for a nuclear safety convention in the framework of the International Atomic Energy Agency.

B Implementation mechanisms

The parties to international agreements should consider procedures and mechanisms to promote and review their effective, full and prompt implementation. To that effect, States could, *inter alia*:
a Establish efficient and practical reporting systems on the effective, full and prompt implementation of international legal instruments;
b Consider appropriate ways in which relevant international bodies, such as UNEP, might contribute towards the further development of such mechanisms.

C Effective participation in international law-making

In all these activities and others that may be pursued in the future, based on the above Basis for Action and Objectives, the effective participation of all countries, in particular developing countries, should be ensured through appropriate provision of technical assistance and/or financial assistance. Developing countries should be given "headstart" support not only in their national efforts to implement international agreements or instruments, but also to participate effectively in the negotiation of new or revised agreements or instruments and in the actual international operation of such agreements or instruments. Support should include assistance in building up expertise in international law particularly in relation to sustainable development, and in assuring access to the necessary reference information and scientific/technical expertise.

D Disputes in the field of sustainable development

In the area of avoidance and settlement of disputes, States should further study and consider methods to broaden and make more effective the range of techniques available at present, taking into account, among others, relevant experience under existing international agreements, instruments or institutions and, where appropriate, their implementing mechanisms such as modalities for dispute avoidance and settlement. This may include mechanisms and procedures for the exchange of data and information, notification and consultation regarding situations that might lead to disputes with other States in the field of sustainable development and for effective peaceful means of dispute settlement in accordance with the Charter of the United Nations including, where appropriate, recourse to the International Court of Justice, and their inclusion in treaties relating to sustainable development.

Chapter 40 Information for decision making

In sustainable development, everyone is a user and provider of information considered in the broad sense. That includes data, information, appropriately packaged experience and knowledge. The need for information arises at all levels, from that of senior decision makers at the national and international levels to the grass-roots and individual levels. The following two programme areas need to be implemented to ensure that decisions are based increasingly on sound information.

A Bridging the data gap

Basis for action While considerable data already exist, as the various sectoral chapters of Agenda 21 indicate, more and different types of data need to be collected, at the local, provincial, national and international levels, indicating the status and trends of the planet's ecosystem, natural resource, pollution and socio-economic variables. The gap in the availability, quality, coherence, standardization and accessibility of data between the developed and the developing world has

The consequences of the Iraqi invasion have inflicted serious environmental damages in the air, on the ground and in the sea. The burning of about 700 oil wells and the spill of unlimited amounts of crude oil in addition to millions of land and sea mines, have exposed the Gulf region and especially Kuwait and Saudi Arabia to enormous dangers. Human and animal lives have really been threatened.

Kuwait has exerted every possible effort to eliminate or at least to minimize the damages imposed by this pollution and cooperated with many of the best fire fighting teams from all over the world. A Kuwaiti fire fighting team has made remarkable progress. There is also The Regional Organization for the Protection of Marine Environment in the Gulf area which began its activities in 1980.

This organization comprises the States of the Gulf Co-operation Council and Iran. It was established to coordinate and promote mutual cooperation among its members regarding the fighting of oil pollution in the sea. It carries out vital studies about pollution in cooperation with the universities and scientific institutes and liaises with competent firms and laboratories in the region in conducting training courses for its workers.

Kuwait has actively participated in Earth Summit 1992 and was represented by a delegation headed by His Highness The Emir, to underline its great interest in the protection of the environment.

Kuwait Airways Corporation is no less interested in environmental issues than the Kuwaiti Government. It is keen to purchase aircraft which are environmentally friendly and conform to world standards regarding noise dampening and abatement, as part of its contribution to protect the environment.

Maurice Strong, Secretary-General of UNCED and, below, Gro Harlem Brundtland, Prime Minister of Norway, two of the key personalities behind the Earth Summit.

been increasing, seriously impairing the capacities of countries to make informed decisions concerning environment and development.

There is a general lack of capacity, particularly in developing countries, and in many areas at the international level, for the collection and assessment of data, for their transformation into useful information and for their dissemination. There is also need for improved coordination among environmental, demographic, social and developmental data and information activities.

Commonly used indicators such as the gross national product (GNP) and measurements of individual resource or pollution flows do not provide adequate indications of sustainability. Methods for assessing interactions between different sectoral environmental, demographic, social and developmental parameters are not sufficiently developed or applied. Indicators of sustainable development need to be developed to provide solid bases for decision-making at all levels and to contribute to a self-regulating sustainability of integrated environment and development systems.

Objectives The following objectives are important:

a To achieve more cost-effective and relevant data collection and assessment by better identification of users, in both the public and private sectors, and of their information needs at the local, provincial, national and international levels;

b To strengthen local, provincial, national and international capacity to collect and use multisectoral information in decision-making processes and to enhance capacities to collect and analyse data and information for decision-making, particularly in developing countries;

c To develop or strengthen local, provincial, national and international means of ensuring that planning for sustainable development in all sectors is based on timely, reliable and usable information;

d To make relevant information accessible in the form and at the time required to facilitate its use.

Activities

A *Development of indicators of sustainable development*

Countries at the national level and international governmental and non-governmental organizations at the international level should develop the concept of indicators of sustainable development in order to identify such indicators. In order to promote the increasing use of some of those indicators in satellite accounts, and eventually in national accounts, the development of indicators needs to be pursued by the Statistical Office of the United Nations Secretariat, as it draws upon evolving experience in this regard.

B *Promotion of global use of indicators of sustainable development*

Relevant organs and organizations of the United Nations system, in cooperation with other international governmental, intergovernmental and non-governmental organizations, should use a suitable set of sustainable development indicators and indicators related to areas outside of national jurisdiction, such as the high seas, the upper atmosphere and outer space. The organs and organizations of the United Nations system, in coordination with other relevant international organizations, could provide recommendations for harmonized development of indicators at the national, regional and global levels, and for incorporation of a suitable set of these indicators in common, regularly updated, and widely accessible reports and databases, for use at the international level, subject to national sovereignty considerations.

C *Improvement of data collection and use*

Countries and, upon request, international organizations should carry out inventories of environmental, resource and developmental data, based on national/global priorities for the management of sustainable development. They should determine the gaps and organize activities to fill those gaps. Within the organs and organizations of the United Nations system and relevant international organizations, data-collection activities, including those of Earthwatch and World Weather Watch, need to be strengthened, especially in the areas of urban air, freshwater, land resources (including forests and rangelands), desertification, other habitats, soil degradation, biodiversity, the high seas and the upper atmosphere. Countries and international organizations should make use of new techniques of data collection, including satellite-based remote sensing. In addition to the strengthening of existing development-related data collection, special attention needs to be paid to such areas as demographic factors, urbanization, poverty, health and rights of access to resources, as well as special groups, including women, indigenous peoples, youth, children and the disabled, and their relationships with environment issues.

D *Improvement of methods of data assessment and analysis*

Relevant international organizations should develop practical recommendations for coordinated, harmonized collection and assessment of data at the national and international levels. National and international data and information centres should set up continuous and accurate data-collection systems and make use of geographic information systems, expert systems, models and a variety of other techniques for the assessment and analysis of data. These steps will be particularly relevant, as large quantities of data from satellite sources will need to be

UNCED was a gathering of the utmost importance. Not only did it draw the world's attention to the problems which most threaten the survival of our planet, but also the need to protect the environment and the urgency in finding solutions to the problems which affect two thirds of mankind – hunger, disease and ignorance. It is now the urgent task of all countries, especially those with greater financial and technological resources, to pursue and put into practice the agreements signed in order to face the environmental and developmental challenges upon which a better world may be built, a world with a healthier environment and with greater solidarity among all human beings.

Mario Soares
President
Portugal

processed in the future. Developed countries and international organizations, as well as the private sector, should cooperate, in particular with developing countries, upon request, to facilitate their acquiring these technologies and this know-how.

E *Establishment of a comprehensive information framework*
Governments should consider undertaking the necessary institutional changes at the national level to achieve the integration of environmental and developmental information. At the international level, environmental assessment activities need to be strengthened and coordinated with efforts to assess development trends.

F *Strengthening of the capacity for traditional information*
Countries, with the cooperation of international organizations, should establish supporting mechanisms to provide local communities and resource users with the information and know-how they need to manage their environment and resources sustainably, applying traditional and indigenous knowledge and approaches when appropriate. This is particularly relevant for rural and urban populations and indigenous, women's and youth groups.

Finance and cost evaluation $1.9 billion from the international community on grant or concessional terms.

B Improving availability of information

Basis for action There already exists a wealth of data and information that could be used for the management of sustainable development. Finding the appropriate information at the required time and at the relevant scale of aggregation is a difficult task.

Information within many countries is not adequately managed, because of shortages of financial resources and trained manpower, lack of awareness of the value and availability of such information and other immediate or pressing problems, especially in developing countries. Even where information is available, it may not be easily accessible, either because of the lack of technology for effective access or because of associated costs, especially for information held outside the country and available commercially.

Objectives Existing national and international mechanisms of information processing and exchange, and of related technical assistance, should be strengthened to ensure effective and equitable availability of information generated at the local, provincial, national and international levels, subject to national sovereignty and relevant intellectual property rights.

National capacities should be strengthened, as should capacities within Governments, non-governmental organizations and the private sector, in information handling and communication, particularly within developing countries.

Full participation of, in particular, developing countries should be ensured in any international scheme under the organs and organizations of the United Nations system for the collection, analysis and use of data and information.

Activities

A *Production of information usable for decision-making*
Countries and international organizations should review and strengthen information systems and services in sectors related to sustainable development, at the local, provincial, national and international levels. Special emphasis should be placed on the transformation of existing information into forms more useful for decision-making and on targeting information at different user groups. Mechanisms should be strengthened or established for transforming scientific and socio-economic assessments into information suitable for both planning and public information. Electronic and non-electronic formats should be used.

B *Establishment of standards and methods for handling information*
Governments should consider supporting the efforts of governmental as well as non-governmental organizations to develop mechanisms for efficient and harmonized exchange of information at the local, national, provincial and international levels, including revision and establishment of data, access and dissemination formats, and communication interfaces.

C *Development of documentation about information*
The organs and organizations of the United Nations system, as well as other governmental and non-governmental organizations, should document and share information about the sources of available information in their respective organizations. Existing programmes, such as those of the Advisory Committee for the Coordination of Information Systems (ACCIS) and the International Environmental Information System (INFOTERRA), should be reviewed and strengthened as required. Networking and coordinating mechanisms should be encouraged between the wide variety of other actors, including arrangements with non-governmental organizations for information sharing and donor activities for sharing information on sustainable development projects. The private sector should be encouraged to strengthen the mechanisms of sharing its experience and information on sustainable development.

D *Establishment and strengthening of electronic networking capabilities*
Countries, international organizations, including organs and organizations of the United Nations system, and non-governmental organizations should exploit various initiatives for electronic links to support information sharing, to provide access to databases and other information sources, to facilitate communication for meeting broader objectives, such as the implementation of Agenda 21, to facilitate intergovermental negotiations, to monitor conventions and efforts for sustainable development to transmit environmental alerts, and to transfer technical data. These organizations should also facilitate the linkage of different electronic networks and the use of appropriate standards and communication protocols for the transparent interchange of electronic communications. Where necessary, new technology should be developed and its use encouraged to permit participation of those not served at present by existing infrastructure and methods. Mechanisms should also be established to carry out the necessary transfer of information to and from non-electronic systems to ensure the involvement of those not able to participate in this way.

E *Making use of commercial information sources*
Countries and international organizations should consider undertaking surveys of information available in the private sector on sustainable development and of present dissemination arrangements to determine gaps and how those gaps could be filled by commercial or quasi-commercial activity, particularly activities in and/or involving developing countries where feasible. Whenever economic or other constraints on supplying and accessing information arise, particularly in developing countries, innovative schemes for subsidizing such information-related access or removing the non-economic constraints should be considered.

Finance and cost evaluation $165 million from the international community on grant or concessional terms.

Index to Agenda 21

This sub-section is provided to serve as a guide to the full United Nations text of Agenda 21. It contains all the chapter titles and sub-headings with their relevant paragraph numbers. It is supplied in order to provide a link between the abridged text in *Earth Summit '92* and the full UN documentation. The official United Nations text of Agenda 21 notates each paragraph according to its chapter heading number i.e. Chapter 1 paragraphs 1.1-1.7.

Background

Agenda 21 is a complex document which has been some two years in development and production. The chapter headings can suggest that subjects are dealt with specifically according to subject heading. However, most chapters overlap and many issues are reinforced by repetition and elaboration throughout the document. It bears stressing that chapters on specific issues are complemented by other chapters relating to the subjects.

It is worth looking at the process involved in creating and developing Agenda 21 to fully understand and appreciate the time and effort put in by the many people, organisations, bodies and governments involved in creating the document.

In December 1989 the United Nations formally resolved to convene a United Nations Conference on Environment and Development (UNCED) and agreed the terms and aims of UNCED in an enabling resolution, no 44/228. A Preparatory Committee (Prepcom) of States' members of the United Nations and the members of specialized agencies was set up, responsible for coordinating all of the work leading to the conference, particularly the input from the UN system, governments and Non-Governmental Organisations. A secretariat was set up in Geneva and Maurice Strong was appointed as Secretary-General to the Conference. Over the next two years four Prepcoms were held.

Prepcom I, August 1990, Nairobi

The Secretariat was requested to produce reports to help define the action programmes on the many UNCED issues. Two working groups were established: Working Group I covered protection of the atmosphere (climate change, ozone depletion, transboundary air pollution), land resources (deforestation, desertification and drought), biodiversity and biotechnology. Working Group II covered oceans, seas and coastal areas, freshwater and hazardous and toxic wastes. In addition every country was asked to produce a comprehensive national environment and development report.

It was at this Prepcom that Maurice Strong outlined the broad ideals of UNCED and emphasised the hope that Agenda 21 would prove to have a stronger influence than the normal UN Action Plans and that new mechanisms would result to encourage, if not force, governments into action.

Prepcom II, March 1991, Geneva

After reviewing the Secretariat's reports, discussions at this Prepcom began to focus on the actions needed to address the issues and problems. A third Working Group was established to focus on legal and institutional matters. It was decided that the Prepcom would examine the issues involved and the options available on a convention on forests, but any agreement on such a convention would have to be taken at the conference.

Maurice Strong's ideas for Agenda 21 were more clearly articulated at this Prepcom. He envisaged a programme of action for the implementation of the principles enunciated in the Earth Charter with clearly articulated objectives, goals, targets, strategies and action programmes, costing and allocation of institutional roles. He wanted a clear and simple mechanism of targets, schedules and money. This was not easy to achieve given the attempt to provide both a framework for the many issues together with a framework for action incorporating the various UN bodies, NGOs and governments involved.

Prepcom III, August 1991, Geneva

The composition of Agenda 21 began to emerge. It was to set global goals on the issues involved, define the direction which actions would take, determine priorities and evaluate progress. Targets to achieve the goals would be set. Draft texts were presented at this Prepcom indicating the final form of Agenda 21.

Prepcom IV, March 1992, New York

This was the final Prepcom and focused largely on negotiation of texts of which 90 per cent were agreed. This left some of the most contentious subjects of finance, technology transfer, climate and biodiversity, institutional questions, poverty, consumption, high seas fisheries, biotechnology and safety to be discussed and agreed at Rio. The draft Rio Declaration on Environment and Development was agreed at this Prepcom.

EARTH SUMMIT '92 is published by The Regency Press Corporation, a division of The Regency Press Corporation Limited whose Registered Office is at 10 Station Court, Station Approach, Wickford, Essex SS11 7AT, United Kingdom. Registration No. 2523823.